W9-CZU-467

STUDIO POTTER BOOK

1 4
2 5
3 6
4 7   Henry Abbots
5 B
6 2   Blazing star
7 3   Set cabbage slips
8 4   went to town
9 5
10 6   (receipts)
11 7   planted early
12 B   a light snow
13 2   a cold backward
14 3   fish had wood
15 4   a little rainy
16 5   burnt wood
17 6   rainy laid bare
18 7   storring yorth
19 B   frosty morn
20 2   frosty morn
21 3   helled Plumburn
22 4   fowl weather
23 5   do
24 6   planted my corn
25 7
26 B
27 2
28 3   harrowed in hay seed
29 4   split wood
30 5   do
31 6   a rainy day worked in the barn

rainy

Esqr. Rent 2 doll.
Walker
after 26th July
kinton, agreat
cellar inches
Henry Abbot wood
lading 2nd kiln

Saml Clark 21
kinton

Docr Davis
where we
settled with people in the
                        street

St Ballard hauld clay
sent wt to Ambrose
fish hauld clay
sold ware to putney warner

STUDIO POTTER BOOK

Edited by Gerry Williams, Peter Sabin and Sarah Bodine

VNR VAN NOSTRAND REINHOLD COMPANY
NEW YORK   CINCINNATI   TORONTO   LONDON   MELBOURNE

(Frontis)
The Diary of Daniel Clark. A country potter, Clark worked in
Concord, New Hampshire, during the 18th and early 19th centuries. The Diary is one of the few records existing on the life and
work of a colonial New England potter. Daniel Clark is believed to
have died of lead poisoning. Diary owned by the New Hampshire
Historical Society, Concord, New Hampshire.

Copyright © 1978 by Daniel Clark Books

Library of Congress Catalog Card Number 78-73702

ISBN 0-442-29461-1

Printed in the United States of America

Published in 1979 by Van Nostrand Reinhold Company
A division of Litton Educational Publishing, Inc.
135 West 50th Street, New York, NY 10020, U.S.A.

Van Nostrand Reinhold Limited
1410 Birchmount Road
Scarborough, Ontario M1P 2E7, Canada

Van Nostrand Reinhold Australia Pty. Ltd.
17 Queen Street
Mitcham, Victoria 3132, Australia

Van Nostrand Reinhold Company Limited
Molly Millars Lane
Wokingham, Berkshire, England

Designed by Jane Martell
Set in 9 point Century Old Style by Harold Black Inc.
Printed and bound by R. R. Donnelley & Sons Company

16 15 14 13 12 11 10 9 8 7 6 5 4 3 2 1

ACKNOWLEDGEMENTS

66381

Among the many who have worked on the book, the editors would especially like to thank the following for their kind assistance, encouragement and good humor: Armand Szainer, Julie Williams, Richard and Marby Blanchard, Scott Burton, Rudy Houk, Courtney Pitt, Neil Castaldo, Bill Finney, Gorg Niloak, Cynthia Bringle, John Glick, Michael Boylen, and Fred Olsen.

THE DIARY OF DANIEL CLARK

Fragile and faded, the diary of Daniel Clark is a link with our past. Written 150 years ago, its line-a-day entries bring to life a colonial potter of great character and strength, a man whose sweating industry built one of New Hampshire's most successful potteries. The diary, published here for the first time in facsimile, is an extraordinary document – a window into 40 full years of a country potter's life.

Daniel Clark's America was a place of expansion and development after the revolution. Washington, D.C. was the new capitol; Jefferson was president. The pottery tradition of New England, which had its roots in Europe and England, was developing vigorously along its own lines, dictated by a pioneer environment.

Daniel Clark, who had come north from Massachusetts to seek good clay, found it near Concord, New Hampshire in 1792: "Good clay @ Bradys." A man of great energy, Clark produced throughout his lifetime an increasing quantity of ware; while taking pleasure in the details of living – settling debts, raising animals, constructing houses, sowing crops, and haying his fields.

Throwing pots from spring to early winter, and firing all year, set the rhythm of his life. As with other Colonial potters, he produced mostly utilitarian ware: molasses jugs, milk pans, lard pots, cuspidors, pitchers, butter pots, and tobacco pipes.

He threw ware in kiln batches which were fired later with number identification: "May 1803 Burnt 11th kiln, made in 1802"; "October 1808 Finished making ware made 26 kiln ware this year."

There were the interminable chores of digging clay (only a mile away), and cutting wood: "April 1807 Finished cutting wood for the kiln about 30 chord." He notes: "Frogs peept."

Potshops in Colonial times were usually manned by three or four persons. Daniel Clark, as owner, probably did most of the throwing, but the apprentices and another man usually did the firing. The apprentice system was in vogue; Clark's first apprentice began at age 11; later, another left who had been with him 20 years. While sons and apprentices did not always continue in the trade, the Clark pottery functioned without interruption into the next generation.

Daniel Clark recorded his regular buying and selling trips about the state, shrewdly commenting on the value of goods for which he bartered: flour, sheepskins, paper bags, and sometimes real money. A bill of sale dated April 29, 1830 lists 85 pots (including 4 dozen milk pans), and sold for $10.00, less a 20% discount.

Matters of fate were approached with respectful resignation. Deaths and births were duly recorded: "June 1795

Brother Benjamin's wife got to bed with her second daughter after a number of fits and bewilderment." Other notations are less pregnant, more cryptic: "August 1815 B. Abt put in gaol"; "May 1817 Sam. Wilkins went off mad."

Daniel Clark became increasingly ill with lead poisoning and apparently finally succumbed to its lethal effects. Running through his diary are careful notations of lead purchases, with the counterpoint of mounting sickness: "November 1799 Bot ld for 4 kilns of Thorndike at 11. dolls"; "November 1820 Ground lead at the mill, taken sick with cholick"; "February 1823 Very lame in feet"; "November 1827 Myself unwell – Colic and palpitations – Dr. came 6 times." The final running down of the spidery handwriting came in May 1828, and he died in August of that year.

For whatever reason Daniel Clark felt the need to preserve his moment in history, we are fortunate it survived. If there is meaning to this ghostly resurrection across the years, it lies, perhaps, in the feeling of identity it evokes. In Daniel Clark we see ourselves. There is a kinship that exists between potters; not age, place, nor time itself can alter or diminish that kinship.

CONTENTS

New Hampshire
Potters Guild 1972

PREFACE

In 1972, a group of New Hampshire potters met to exchange ideas, relate experiences and enjoy the kinship of their fellow craftsmen. The outgrowth of this meeting was a new magazine written by potters, for potters, about the issues and ideas of greatest concern to potters.

Studio Potter, since its first appearance 12 issues ago, has attracted countless technical insights from working potters across the country: inspirational, instructive and honest information. The magazine has been met with enthusiastic response from our growing readership in its attempt to speak to their common needs. *Studio Potter* is rapidly becoming known as the forum for the free exchange of ideas for the community of potters everywhere.

Within these issues of the magazine, there have appeared a number of articles by master potters revealing their studio secrets. We would like to preserve these timeless contributions in the present anthology. We take pride in presenting this material to you and hope it will help you in your work.

THE WAY OF THE NA'WA'YA'THITSE

by Helen Cordero

We have our own clay. It comes from our own land up here in the hills.

Sometimes we go up in a truck and haul a big load to use through the whole year. We dig it with a shovel and pick. It comes in big lumps. I bring buckets full into my home. Then I bring a big canvas and spread it out. I have a grinding stone called "yacate." I start pounding with a hammer into little pieces. Then I soak it in water overnight. Next morning it will be ready.

I will mix a little pumice dirt with it, so as not to crack it. More of clay than pumice. Pumice comes from our own place on the hill. In Indian we call pumice "aiyanshin." We do it like we do with clay. But then we sift it to get the fine dirt.

The white slip is called "ayashpican." We used to buy white slip from another village, but now we can get it from a Spanish man. He charges ten dollars a pound. He knows we really need it. We just soak it in water and mix it up when ready. We put white slip over the whole piece several times, heating up the piece so the white slip will stick over the piece.

After the white slip, I paint it with the red and black slips.

We have our own place for the red slip. A long ways. We go walking and we bring it on our back. We soak it in water and make it ready. The red dirt is called "micuna."

The black slip comes from the bee weed [Cleome (genus) Serrulta]. We boil the whole leaves and stems till it cooks all the plant. Then we strain and cook over again and boil it a long time till it gets thick. Then we let it dry, and when we want to use it we just cut a little piece off and soak it in water. When it's like this it's brown. In the fire it turns black. The black painting slip is called "waque."

See, our old people – the Na'wa'ya'thitse – used [these traditional methods] when they were here. I'm pretty sure

they would like us to do what they did. People will treasure it more because it came from our old people.

ON FINDING AND USING LOCAL CLAYS

by Hal Riegger

Some years back, on one of my primitive pottery workshops, there were, among the adults, two young girls eight and eleven years old. While some of the adults were looking for hydrous aluminum silicate (a word on a page, and in black and white at that), the girls found clay. When quizzed by our adult potter as to how they knew, the reply was, "Well, you can see – a cow stepped in it. See the footprint."

Which, with youthful directness and perception, can close a discussion of the first part of the business of finding local clays. Facetiousness aside, what else does one need to know? Further than this, it is a matter of the potter being willing to learn what a particular clay will do, and this strikes at the core of my philosophy of working with ceramic materials. I maintain that no clay is bad, if one will discover how to use it – and that sometimes means as a glaze ingredient and not as a more or less plastic forming material.

Looking back in history we find that early potters did just this. Not knowing technology, not having a laboratory, they learned how to handle the material they had on hand. They had to if they wanted to make pots or figures; they couldn't send off to the east or west coast for a "good" clay. When I was a student at Alfred beginning ceramic engineering was required; I'm sure much of what was taught has been a great help in the years following, although I couldn't identify loess, or some of the other clay minerals we were taught about.

For our purposes there are two or three types of clay: the more pure primary and secondary clays that have varying degrees of plasticity and that are rarely white burning; the silt types of clays that can be largely organic or contain other nonclay material, and that generally are quite difficult but not impossible to work with; and, lastly, the highly alkaline clays that are thixotropic, presenting moderate challenges in handling. The matter of their purity or impurity is one of personal opinion, and it is my recommendation to test a clay without screening or purifying it in any manner.

Next step is to fire it. Just that simple. Run a series of tests using the normal testing procedures that show shrinkage, warpage, color, and refractoriness, or its lack, starting at a low firing temperature of about cone 06 and continuing on up at about 100° F increments until you can observe from the results that you've gone far enough. The only criterion here that I use is the more or less arbitrary practice of accepting a fired porosity of 7% or less as being a mature clay. It is well worth remembering that so very much can be done in ceramics when clays are not fired to maturity.

The clay's impurities may have caused cracking or spit-outs or some other phenomenon not present in refined clays. Are these actually physically harmful? How do you react aesthetically? Be sure you aren't caught in that old rut that all clays must be purified to be good, and remember that many times clays are "unpurified" with the addition of pigment, grog, or feldspar.

In writing this way I may, perhaps, leave you less than satisfied, because you see, clay is a most personal, subjective thing. In the context of the artist-potter many of the rules of industry do not apply. This is really all there is to the matter of using local clays. You make the adjustment yourself in the handling of the clay (because the clay isn't going to change for you). There are no secrets, no rules; you're on your own. The acceptance of this responsibility and the matter of standing by your choice is the hard thing because probably you will be stepping out of line in terms of the crowd. Remember Thoreau's wise phrase about the Drummer.

Pardon the pun, but on a more down-to-earth level, the state bureau of mines, or geology, will have published bulletins listing, locating, and describing the clay resources in your area. For me, this is always a first in finding out what my area offers me. But equally rewarding is going out into the fields, the hills, or the valleys and, with a bit of plain logic as to how clay could have gotten where it is, looking myself for clay. Road cuts, river and lake banks are examples of likely places. Earth that doesn't erode too easily indicates the possibility of its being clay. If it is wet it's easy enough to feel if it's plastic at all, and if not a bit of spit on it will help.

This is what we do, and I believe the early American Indian potters, as well as primitive potters the world around, would do the same; just as they would adjust their working methods to the quality of the clay. This accounted for the marvellous range of pottery types and styles we once had in this country: Pennsylvania Dutch slipware, the Ohio Salt-glazed stoneware, varieties of American Indian pottery, the Appalachian mountain wares, and others.

A revived interest in the materials of one's area and a sensitive use of them can help get us out of the boring, repetitive sameness of ceramics made from Jordan stoneware or California fireclay based bodies. Clay exists as one of the most plentiful minerals on the face of the earth, and in such a fantastic variety as to be almost unimaginable; we are depriving ourselves if we fail to take advantage of this fact.

TOWARD SELF-SUFFICIENCY IN CLAY

by Brian Van Nostrand

For the past seven years I have blended my clay body from a variety of local clays dug by hand and processed with simple homemade or salvaged equipment. I use four or more tons of ready-to-throw clay each year, and have found using local clays in that amount both economically feasible and efficient in terms of time and labor. This is true despite the lack of large or commercial-grade deposits in my area. My clays do not appear as discrete, pure seams: it was a surprise to discover that what often looked like common earth along roadsides and in gardens, when cleaned and washed, yielded high-quality pottery clay. I was relieved to dispense with the high cost of commercial clays and freight charges and the annoyance of unreliable deliveries to our rural area. The cost of self-sufficiency in this respect is 12 to 14 days (nonconsecutive) each year for digging and processing.

Weathering

I depend upon as many natural aids as possible in the preparation of clay, and the weathering of crude clay is a very important one. A season of weathering, by repeated freezing and thawing, wetting and drying, helps immeasurably to break down shaly, tightly compacted clays which might otherwise require power crushing equipment. The brick industries often rely upon weathering to diminish crushing needs. I place 6 or 8'' of crude clay on plastic spread on the ground and leave it for a season or two. With all weathering, however, particular care must be taken to avoid excessive loss or segregation of the fine particles. I avoid the problem simply by placing the clay on level ground within a board frame. In this way rain water may seep through but will not run off and carry clay with it.

I also depend upon the weather to dry out the crude clay before further processing. After a spell of warm, dry weather, several inches from the top of the piles in the weathering frames are bone dry and can be taken up for storage in bins inside. If the clay comes from the pile in chunks too large for thorough drying, I sometimes use the slip-dryers (Figures 1 and 2) or crush it somewhat with a homemade lawn roller on the concrete floor and leave it for a short while before shoveling into the bins. Because I slip-process all my clay, this thorough drying is very important. Most potters are very familiar with the phenomenon of slaking, which causes bone-dry clay to form a lump-free slip while damp clay remains in chunks almost impossible to mix or soak away.

Slip Preparation

Because clays here are so impure, filled with rocks, roots, sand, and other undesirable matter, I have found a washing stage necessary. The clay is reduced to thin slip and screened. Besides just cleaning the clay, a significant gain

in plasticity results. A local porcelain insulator plant is able to develop a highly plastic body which contains less than 50% clay, and most of that kaolin, by blunging slip with hot water. A slip so thin is produced that a flocculent is necessary to prevent particle loss through the filter-press cloth. When industries use air-floated clays, which have usually been partially calcined during the milling and air-floating, slip preparation may become mandatory to obtain plasticity in low-clay bodies. In my case, however, I am simply improving an already plastic clay.

Settling and Evaporation

The natural action of settling and evaporation does for me what a filter press does for the industry. After screening the slip, it is stored in settling drums for at least a week and preferably a month or more. At the end of a month, about a third of the volume can be siphoned off as clear water to be reused in the next batch. Care must be taken to remix the thick slip left in the drums, for the clay has settled in layers of fine and coarse particles and would be much more difficult to mix later in a dryer form.

After experimenting with different types of dryers, I settled upon wooden frames with hardware cloth bottoms lined with muslin, which can be used for both crude clay and slip drying indoors or out. They are light and easy to store away when not in use (Figures 1 and 2) and can be stacked with spacers for the crude clay or spread out singly for slip. I have built them so that a standard sheet of metal roofing makes a cover, and the filled dryers can stay out in any kind of weather with evaporation continuing from the top and bottom.

Freeze-drying

In the winter, slip may be dried more quickly by allowing it to freeze and thaw once or twice. After being frozen the water seems to run off very quickly as the clay thaws, and I find that slip-drying time is cut by as much as 80%. Here in West Virginia the temperature often drops below freezing at night and rises to thaw the clay the next day, which is ideal. In colder weather, dryers on wheels which can be rolled outdoors to freeze and indoors to thaw are good. It is tricky to catch the clay at just the right time, because one freeze and thaw too many can easily remove more water than desirable; so I keep a fairly close watch. Freezing seems to bring about a further breakdown of the clay and consequently, a slight gain in plasticity often results. A good hard freeze (below 25° F) works best.

Rhythm

My year falls into a pattern: clay digging in the late summer or early fall when the ground is dry and warm, and slip-drying in midwinter or midsummer. Clay dug in the fall

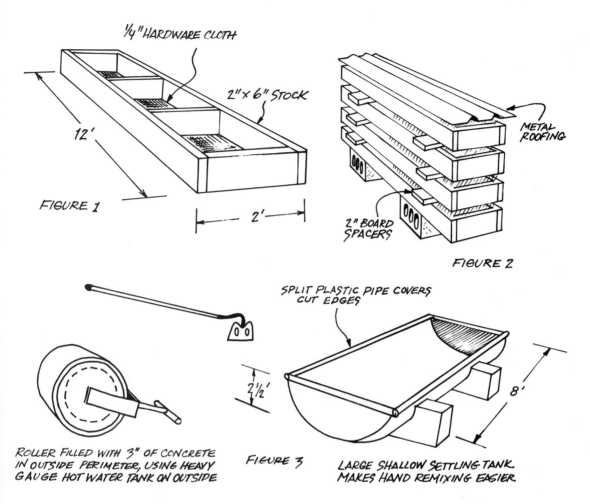

¼" HARDWARE CLOTH

2" x 6" STOCK

12'

2'

FIGURE 1

METAL ROOFING

2" BOARD SPACERS

FIGURE 2

SPLIT PLASTIC PIPE COVERS CUT EDGES

2½'

8'

ROLLER FILLED WITH 3" OF CONCRETE IN OUTSIDE PERIMETER, USING HEAVY GAUGE HOT WATER TANK ON OUTSIDE

FIGURE 3

LARGE SHALLOW SETTLING TANK MAKES HAND REMIXING EASIER

is put away to weather until next year. Slip is screened in the fall and spring when the weather is warm and placed in settling drums until the siphoning and drying. I try to keep at least a year ahead so that my throwing clay has a chance to age and mature. Thus at any given time I have clay weathering, dry crude clay in bins, slip settling in the drums, and ready-to-throw clay in storage. In this way I never run out, and the lack of urgency allows me to pick the most convenient times to work up more.

Equipment

There are innumerable types of clay-processing setups from one extreme to the other in terms of quantity of equipment. One of the advantages of the process I have outlined is the small amount and inexpensive nature of the necessary tools. For years my major requirements have been:
1. Ten 55 gallon drums for settling tanks
2. Four wooden slip dryers (Figures 1 and 2)
3. Three used wringer washing machines for blungers
4. One homemade lawn roller for crushing
5. Extra drums to collect rain water from the roof (my sole water supply for clay preparation)

6. Plenty of indoor and outdoor work and storage space
For convenience I have recently consolidated a little by adding one homemade blunger (Figure 4) to replace the washers and I plan to have one slip tank to replace the many drums. I am satisfied with the four dryers, which yield about 2400 pounds of ready-to-throw clay each turn. In summer by evaporation, 6'' of slip will dry in them in 10 to 14 days. In a dryer climate the time would perhaps be much shorter. Under proper conditions, slip will freeze-dry in them to throwing consistency in about 72 hours.

Working Alone

This is a long, slow method, but once set in motion it yields a continuous supply without much time and effort on my part. This is particularly important to me because I work alone without apprentices to share the labor. I find it satisfying, also, to be able to carry the whole process through from beginning to end. Other potters, however, would have to judge in terms of their own situations and requirements whether the extra trouble to prepare clay in this way would be justifiable.

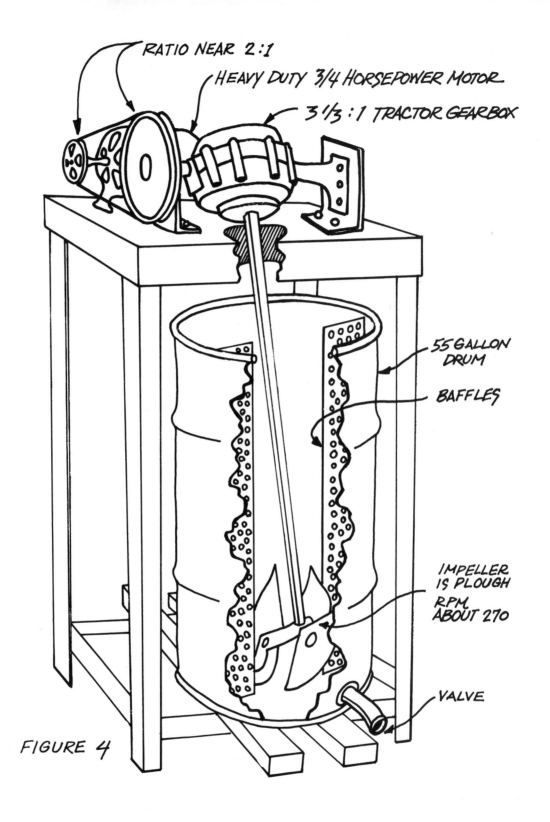

RATIO NEAR 2:1

HEAVY DUTY 3/4 HORSEPOWER MOTOR

3 1/3 : 1 TRACTOR GEARBOX

55 GALLON DRUM

BAFFLES

IMPELLER IS PLOUGH

R.P.M. ABOUT 270

VALVE

FIGURE 4

Crude Clay Digging
- Remove overburden to expose clay deposit
- Eliminate, by hand picking, any large impurities, e.g., roots, large rocks, etc.
Equipment: mattock, round-point shovel, vehicle, wheelbarrow

This flow sheet would vary depending upon the climate and the particular nature of the potter's clays.

Weathering
- Crude clay is spread out in about a 6″ layer on ground on plastic sheet or boards, with board frame on perimeter
- Freezing action breaks up shaley clays
- Rain can wash out undesirable soluble impurities
- Weathering improves both slaking and dry-crushing qualities later on
- Care should be taken that no clay is washed or carried away by rain

Blunging
- Various crushed clays are added to blunger in proper clay body proportion and allowed to slake in blunger tank before starting motor
- Slaking allows the larger pieces of clay to break down and thus eases the starting load on motor and shortens blunging time

Screening
- Blunged slip is screened into settling tank or drums – 30-mesh screen is the size best suited to my clays

Crude Clay Drying
- Weathered clay put in dryers (Fig. 2) or in any well-ventilated enclosure

Remixing
- Water is siphoned off and stored for next batch after one month of settling
- The thick slip is remixed by hand with mortar hoe

Roll Crushing
- Weathered clay is roll crushed by hand on concrete floor
- This is primarily to break up large pieces of crude clay, resulting in a size reduction to nothing larger than ¾″

Drying
- Slip is poured in wooden dryers until ready for removal to storage

Storage
- Crushed clay is stored indefinitely in bins after crushing

Storage
- Clay is stored and aging begins

CLAY: WHY IT ACTS THE WAY IT DOES

by Frederick H. Norton

In this article an attempt is made to describe, in terms understandable to the average potter, the structure of clay and the reasons why it acts in such a unique way when used in a pottery body.

Types of Pottery Clay

The purest type of clay is kaolin, found in great quantities in our southern states. There are several kinds of kaolin. The most plentiful are the sedimentary kaolins which may be used as mined or put through a washing process to remove unwanted minerals such as quartz, feldspar, or iron oxide. Then there are residual kaolins which must always be washed as they contain large amounts of nonclay minerals. When properly treated, however, they become our whitest kind of clay. One other kaolin of interest, found in northern Florida, has high plastic properties.

Kaolins are almost never used as the complete pottery body because of low plasticity, high drying shrinkage and very high firing temperatures to vitrify. They are white burning, however, and serve as the basis for white earthenware and porcelain after an additive of quartz and feldspar.

Another class of clays is the ball clays found in Kentucky and Tennessee. These are fine-grained clays containing organic matter. They are not used as the complete body, but rather in additions of 10% to 20% to give added plasticity, better green strength, and improved casting properties. These clays are not as white burning as the kaolins, but when used in small amounts have little adverse effect on the fired color.

Another class of clays used by the potter is stoneware clays. These clays burn buff or gray and usually contain enough nonplastic material to give good working and firing properties. In some cases, however, these clays are washed and some additions made to give enhanced properties.

The early pottery used in this country was made from red-burning glacial clays found in nearly all villages in the eastern United States – the same clay that was used for making bricks. These clays are quite plastic and are still used for some types of pottery, but it is difficult to fire them into a water-tight body.

Another clay similar to the last one, known as slip clay, is used as a glaze for stoneware and electric insulators. The traditional source is Albany, New York.

Lastly, there is an extremely fine-grained clay called bentonite that is used as very small additions to bodies for enhancing their plasticity.

Nature of Clay

If one takes any finely grained nonclay mineral and mixes it with water, a crumbly mass will be produced with almost zero formability. If the same is done with clay, however, there is produced a mass that is readily formed into any desired shape and, most interesting of all, it will retain that shape under the force of gravity. In other words, the clay mass has three unique properties: first, it may be deformed without cracking; second, when the deforming force ceases, the shape will remain fixed; and third, when the clay mass is dried, it has considerable strength.

It should be of interest to the potter to learn the reasons why the clay mass behaves in this way. This can be done by examining the individual clay particles as to shape and size and their reaction with the associated water.

The Clay Particle

The optical and electron microscopes have made it possible to examine the clay particles of all sizes. It is found that each particle is a crystalline plate with an hexagonal outline as shown in Fig. 1. The average diameter of this plate is one micron (one millionth of a meter), a size so small it can only be observed by a high-power microscope. Other particles in the clay are as large as 50 microns and as small as one-tenth micron in diameter. The thickness of the clay particle is about one-tenth the diameter with the faces flat and smooth.

In the clay mass most of the particles are stacked together somewhat as shown in Fig. 2. In most clays the clay material is kaolinite with the formula $(OH)_4Al_2Si_2O_5$, but other clay minerals occur in small amounts.

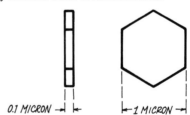

0.1 MICRON   1 MICRON

FIG.1 TYPICAL CLAY CRYSTAL

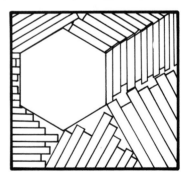

FIG.2 PACKING OF CLAY CRYSTALS

The Clay Particle and Water

In a batch of moist clay, the water forms thin films between the faces of the clay plates. These films are very thin, averaging six-thousandths of a micron in thickness. Of course, the more water added to the class mass, the thicker these films will be. A sort of equilibrium exists in the clay mass with the particles pulled together by attractive forces and at the same time held apart by the water films. Therefore the wetter the clay mass, the thicker the water films will be and the more easily the clay particles can be forced to move in relation to each other. This explains why a wet clay may be molded with less force than a dryer one.

It is interesting to note that when dry clay is mixed with a nonpolar liquid, such as kerosene, a workable mass cannot be produced. This is due to lack of attractive forces which occur with water.

Plasticity

This term may be defined as the ease with which the clay may be formed. If the amount of extension of a clay-water specimen is plotted against the force to move it, curves such as those in Fig. 3 are obtained. It will be seen that the specimen elongates elastically as the force is increased until point (a) (the yield point), then flows plastically, and point (b) (the breaking point) is reached. The most highly plastic masses have both a high yield point and a long extension range before fracture.

Much work has been carried out by ceramists to develop a quantitative measure of plasticity, but nothing has really taken the place of the hands of the experienced potter.

Drying, Shrinkage, and Warpage

When a plastic clay dries, the following steps occur: (1) the water in the layers between clay particles gradually diffuses to the surface where it evaporates until finally the particles touch each other and the shrinkage stops; (2) the remaining water in the pores then dries out with no further shrinkage; and (3) absorbed water on the particle surface disappears. This explains why a formed clay article must be dried slowly during stage 1 to prevent cracking, whereas stages 2 and 3 may safely take place quite rapidly. This is shown diagrammatically in Fig. 4 where the black areas represent the water.

Warpage in drying thin ware is due to uneven shrinkage. This can be prevented by slow overall drying or by retarding the drying of certain parts by covering. The question often comes up as to why warpage occurs when a newly formed piece has a uniform water content and the dry piece has a low but also even content. This can be explained by a drying tile resting on a smooth surface. The upper face will dry first and the tile will curl up because the upper face is smaller than the lower face. Later when the tile is completely dry the curl remains as the body is too rigid to completely straighten out. This warpage is shown in Fig. 5.

Casting Slips

While casting slips may be made of nearly any inorganic powder, slips containing a major portion of clay are used by

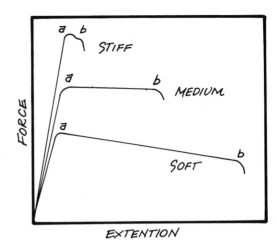

FIG. 3 FLOW OF CLAY PASTES

FIG. 4 STEPS IN DRYING A CLAY MASS

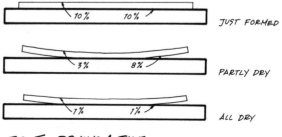

FIG. 5 DRYING A TILE

19

Crystals of washed kaolin (32,000x).

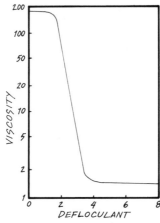

FIG. 6 DEFLOCULATION OF CASTING SLIP

FIG. 7   NON-PLASTIC IN CLAY

the potter. To produce a good casting slip, it is necessary to add more than water. The clay particles must be completely dispersed so each one is free to move about. This requires that the normal attractive forces between the particles be changed to repulsive forces, which can be done by adding a very small amount of chemicals with an alkaline reaction, such as a combination of silicate of soda and soda ash. Thus normal clay paste with 20% to 30% water would be in the plastic condition, whereas with the proper amount of alkalinity (deflocculation) the mix is fluid enough to be easily poured. In Fig. 6 is shown the viscosity of a clay slip with varying amounts of deflocculant. This shows the great decrease in viscosity by the proper use of deflocculating agents.

Green Strength

A nonplastic powder, for example potter's flint, has practically no green strength. On the other hand, clays have relatively high strengths running from 20 psi to 1,000 psi. The reason for this is not entirely clear but is probably due to the ionic attractive forces between the flat clay plates.

The clay must have sufficient green strength to be handled safely, but the great strength required for heavy pieces, like glass pots, is usually unnecessary.

The Influence of Nonplastics on Clay

Of course, most pottery clays contain natural nonplastics such as finely divided quartz or feldspar, but most pottery bodies have nonplastics added to the clay for various purposes, such as to reduce drying shrinkage or enhance firing properties.

As shown diagrammatically in Fig. 7, the nonplastic particles simply displace an equal volume of the clay-water mixture. As the nonplastic particles are stable in size, the overall drying shrinkage is reduced. For example, if the pure clay has a drying shrinkage of 5%, then 10% of added nonplastic should reduce the shrinkage to 4.5%. Actually the picture is more complicated than this due to the size and shape variations of the nonplastic.

The nonplastic has another effect in that it often makes a sticky clay more workable in the plastic state.

Conclusion

Moist clay is a material of many moods. The better we understand the underlying structure the more closely it can be adapted to our needs. The right clay used in the right way can be a faithful servant, but the wrong clay and the wrong use turns it into an exacting tyrant.

FLAMEWARE
by Ron Propst

FLAMEWARE

by Ron Propst

My interest in flameware first began when the stoneware body I was then using showed a disappointing inability to remain ovenproof. No matter how I changed the formula, casseroles continued to break. This caused both me and my customers great grief. I became determined to produce a type of pottery that would adapt to temperature changes gracefully.

Today my feelings remain the same. Considering the amount of technology presently available, studio potters should be able to produce a ware sufficiently stable to be capable of standing up under severe conditions of direct-flame thermal shock.

My first experiments in flameware were involved with the use of petalite. My work with this body was very brief, due to the Rhodesian embargo which halted shipments of petalite. The following are some comments on my general findings on the use of petalite in flameware bodies.

Most flameware bodies consisting of approximately half-clay and half-petalite work well. A higher percentage of fireclay and less of ball clay seems to be the most durable. If a flux is needed to seal the clay body, talc seems to be the best. I cannot include a list of such workable formulas, due on my part to lack of testing and general use of petalite bodies. There is, however, a little-known current American supplier of petalite, who will, I understand, also send samples for testing:

> Charles B. Chrystal Co., Inc.
> 53 Park Place
> New York, NY 10007

As soon as petalite became generally unavailable, I began work with a local mineral called spodumene. Spodumene is quite different from petalite. It is higher in lithium and iron oxide and lower in silica. Moreover, it has a strange talent: at 1700° F., the crystaline form of spodumene expands instead of shrinking.

In my first test with spodumene this trait became evident. The early tests involved using 50% spodumene and 50% clay. The clay body expanded about 2'' and sealed the ware to the kiln shelf above. While chipping at the kiln shelves, I decided that something needed to be changed. Not only did the body expand a great deal, but it was left very porous. It was like high-fire bisque ware.

The next series of tests was involved with using pyrophyllite and spodumene. Pyrophyllite is a low-grade mineral (an aluminum silicate) mined in North Carolina. It is used primarily in wall tile bodies where it decreases thermal expansion. I felt that the clay body needed an increase in alumina content and pyrophyllite would give the increase needed. This helped a great deal with the expansion problem, but the body was still quite porous.

Since that time I have revised the body at least 20 times. The following formula is the clay body I have used for the past five years. It is successful with different types of ball clay and fireclay. I am not sure how the body would measure up on a dilatometer (a machine which measures thermal expansion), but it has been very successful for me and a number of other potters around the country. Pottery made of this body has successfully been used on top of gas and electric stoves.

Flameware Formula

Spodumene, 200 (mesh)	30
Pyrophyllite, 200 (mesh)	10
Feldspar, 200 (mesh)	10
Ball clay, OM#4	20
A.P. Green fireclay	30
Western bentonite	2
Macaloid	1

It is very important to use the right type of spodumene. The best spodumene is mined by Foote Mineral at Kings Mt., North Carolina. For information on its chemical analysis and cost write:

> Foote Mineral Company
> Route 100
> Exton, PA 19341
> (215) 363-6500

It is the lowest in iron and highest in alumina content that I have tested. Lithium Corporation of America, Box 795, Bessemer City, NC 28016, also produces spodumene, but it is very high in iron content, which I found unacceptable. The problem of iron content is very hard to overcome due to the fact that the iron is chemically combined in the crystal. This makes useless the removal of iron by the magnetic process.

Foote Mineral is now producing a low-iron spodumene for the glass industry, but it is not ground in mesh sizes for use in a clay body. This low-iron spodumene would enable one to produce a light gray-to-white clay body. (The fired color of my flameware body is orange to deep red-brown.) They are also producing a calcined spodumene which I feel has great potential in lower temperature flameware bodies.

The pyrophyllite used is called Pyrotrol 200 (mesh), and comes from:

> Piedmont Minerals Company
> P.O. Box 7247
> Greensboro, NC 27407
> (919) 292-0947

I used Kona A3 feldspar in the flameware body up until it was discontinued. Since that time we have been using K 200, a feldspar mined by the following company:

> Feldspar Corporation of America
> Kings Mt., NC 28086

I have found it to be an excellent substitute. The body seals

up a little more, but I have found no adverse conditions in the flameproof qualities.

My reason for using Old Mine #4 ball clay is for its color. It is very light-burning and is as plastic as any ball clay I have ever used. I feel sure any ball clay would work as well.

The fireclay is dry-milled A.P. Green fireclay. It seems to be plastic enough, and I am interested in its large particle size, which I feel is important in this flameware body. We have used other plastic fireclays, but I found them unacceptable in the fired results. The clay body seals up more than necessary and lacks the terracotta appearance which it normally has.

No matter what clay formula you might come up with, the word *Macaloid* is an essential. Macaloid is a chemically combined Hector clay, used in industry as a suspension agent in lotions. In a clay body it is the greatest plasticizer I have ever used. Because the flameware body has too little clay, some type of superplastic material is essential to make it workable. Macaloid is the answer.

Macaloid is produced by National Lead Company. For information write:

TAM Division
Box C, Bridge Station
Niagara Falls, NY 14305

It is also being sold by some major ceramic suppliers. It is a very expensive material, but worth every penny.

You must remember that the information in this article is only a starting point for anyone becoming interested in flameware. I use this formula because it has been most serviceable for me. I feel sure that innumerable clay bodies can be developed from this basic formula. For instance, if the clays used are more refractory, use more flux; if the opposite, decrease the flux.

The glaze used on flameware is as important as the body. My experience shows that glazes with 15 to 25% spodumene or lepidolite will generally work well on flameware. Many other glazes, especially high-alumina glazes, will also work. Here are some basic formulas:

1. Flameware Glaze c/9-10

(White with red flecks)

Lepidolite	32	grams
Dolomite	25	
Whiting	3	
Talc	3	
Gerstley borate	2.5	
Kaolin	25	
Flint	9.5	

2. Flameware Glaze c/9-10

(Orange to white)

Potash feldspar	6	lbs
Spodumene	4	
Dolomite	4.5	
Kaolin	5	
Whiting	.75	
Tin oxide	1	

Addition of 2% cobalt carbonate gives a nice blue.

3. Flameware Glaze c/9-10

(Brown to green)

Dolomite	12.4	lbs
Whiting	1.6	
Potash feldspar	10	
Kaolin	12.8	
Flint	2.8	
Cobalt carbonate	.2	
Red iron oxide	.4	

Any glaze you use will change its image on flameware due to the large amount of flux in the body. This will make most glazes more fluid and tone out most colors. I enjoy color in my glazes, which leads me to fire flameware at just about cone 9 or 9½. This allows the glazes to be less fluid and does not burn the color away. My glaze firings, moreover, are reduced very little, due to the fact that we found the carbon deposits under the glaze to be damaging. They will cause the glaze to begin popping off the surface of the ware after several months of use.

During firing any protruding parts, such as skillet handles, must be supported. The body becomes so fluid during the end of the firing that it is capable of distorting itself. Those handles which are lightweight, however, will need no support.

I hope these remarks will enable you to make a start with flameware. They come from my own experience and, while I am not a trained technician, flameware has been an interest of mine for a number of years. A great deal of help was given by Foote Mineral Company and the Lithium Corporation of America. If you have an interest in lithium compounds, these people are more than willing to help and supply samples.

Ceramic Plaque
by Jenny Lind

CERAMIC CRYSTALLOGRAPHY
by Pat Malone

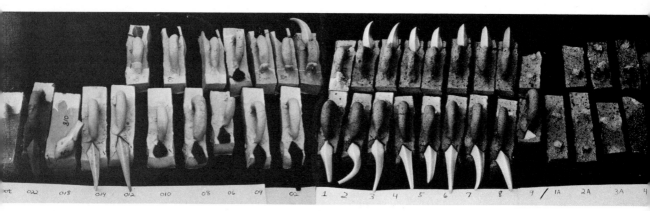

The following is a summary of my master's report completed at the University of Oregon, Fine Arts Department, in the spring of 1975. My main objective in doing the project was to achieve a better understanding of what fire is and how it affects ceramic materials.

Introduction

The clay was formed into draw trials with cones embedded, and then glazed on one end. The fire was a c/9 reduction fire (reduction atmosphere at c/06 and c/9). When the different cones melted, the draw trials were pulled from the kiln (quick-cooled), and later made into microscopic thin-sections. Thin-sectioning is a process used in geology, where a cross section of the sample is cut, mounted on glass, and then ground down until the original material is thin enough to pass light. The sample can then be studied with a microscope. In this experiment samples were taken at room temperature – to c/9 – to room temperature to try to determine what and when changes were occuring.

Identification of crystals was done with the help of Dr. Holser of the Geology Department. Due to the lack of published material about firing products produced under studio conditions, most identifications are tentative. Crystal identification is an interesting challenge, and I hope that I receive ideas from people who read this report.

Materials used Claybody	Source	Parts
Clayburn	Br. Columbia	1
Columbia	California	1
Lincoln	California	1
Kaiser Missouri	Missouri	1
(Kaiser) Denver	Colorado	1
OM 4 ball clay	Kentucky	1
Custer feldspar	S. Dakota	½
Red iron oxide		1/200

Glaze

Cornish stone	45%
Talc	23%
Whiting	12%
Silica	12%
Ajax P kaolin	9%

The Effects of Heat

The first material affected by heat is kaolinite (clay). The best image of the process is generated by Differential Thermal Analysis (DTA) which shows when endothermic (heat-consuming) and exothermic (heat-releasing) reactions are taking place. (See firing reactions chart.) In this process the material, i.e., kaolinite, is compared to the reference material alumina as the two materials are heated, and kaolinite's reactions are noted against the inert alumina.

Loss of Physically Combined Water. The last of the water which made the clay plastic must be evaporated. The finer the clay, the more water held and the more water to be driven off. This loss of water held by the surface of the clay takes place between 15° and 275° C. Enough time must be taken at this stage of the firing for the steam to escape; otherwise steam pressure will build up and the pot or a portion of it will blow up.

Loss of Hydroxyls (structural "water"). The theoretical formula for kaolinite, $2(Al_2O_3 \cdot 2SiO_2 \cdot 2H_2O)$, becomes $2Al_2O_3 \cdot 4SiO_2 + 4H_2O$ with a weight loss and a fairly sharp endothermic dip. This takes place about the time there is a visible red color in the kiln, 525° to 650° C. The product of this reaction is called metakaolin, which can regain its plastic properties only by extended contact with water; in a practical sense it has become rock.

Quartz. In our case the quartz wasn't added to the clay, as it came in with the Denver and Columbia fireclays. At 573° C the atomic arrangement of quartz shifts,

	low	high	
the	A	B	conversion point.
	alpha	beta	

There is a sudden increase in volume of 1% which is reversed upon cooling. This is one of the reasons why caution is exercised especially during the cooling when red heat is reached. If the shift proceeds too rapidly, it can cause cracking problems both of the clay body and the glaze.

Carbon Oxidation. The oxidation of organic matter ($C + O_2 = CO_2 + heat$) can take place from around 400° to 1150°C (c/1). If the clay body is fairly open and there is an excess of air this can be completed by 600° C. But the latest it can take place is c/1 when the glaze will be melting and the clay is getting more dense, making it more difficult for O_2 to penetrate. If not oxidized completely, the carbon can cause bloating problems. In the fire this oxidation began around c/018 (720° C) and was completed by c/06 (1020° C).

Spinel Phase of Kaolin. (See photo 1.) At 980° C metakaolin, $2Al_2O_3 - 4SiO_2$: Spinel plus free silica. This reaction will show up as a sharp exothermic peak with pure kaolinite, and is a precursor of the mullite formation stage which will be discussed later. (The above discussion of the fire has been composed from my own experience, Lawrence's *Ceramic Science for the Potter,* and Cardew's *Pioneer Pottery.* The upcoming discussion will rely more on my own experience with ceramics and my microceramic studies.)

With the exception of the oxidizing of carbon and some color changes due to the iron, there are no visible changes in

the clay or glaze until c/010 (900° C) is reached. By c/08 (950° C), the late-melting talc glaze is sintered; it no longer rubs off. This sintering, a melting of edges which establishes some contact between the particles, is on such a small scale that it is not visible with the microscope, but it is obvious to the touch.

Around c/06 (1000° C) the initial reduction was performed. From this time on it is possible to observe the movement, the diffusion of iron. The sources of this iron are the Fe_2O_3 (red iron) added to the clay body and the magnetite, Fe_3O_4 (black iron) and hematite, Fe_2O_3, which are present in the clays we use. (Under the microscope, Fe_3O_4 and FeO appear opaque black and Fe_2O_3 appears reddish brown. (See photo 2.)

The other observation at this temperature is the clouding over of some of the larger aggregate clay particles. An explanation for this cloudy appearance is the first formation of mullite ($3 Al_2O_3 \cdot 2SiO_2$) crystals plus gas and cracks which might be connected with this development (Insley,

Microscopy of Ceramics and Cements, page 79). At this point they are so small that they can't be resolved individually for more positive identification.

Both the iron dispersion and the haze become increasingly evident from c/02 (1125° C) on. (See photo 3.) Both types of iron are increasing in size by outward diffusion. Part of this diffusion mechanism is a gas generated by the iron reacting with oxygen, building up pressure until the iron is forced outwards into the surrounding clay. (Another part of

1

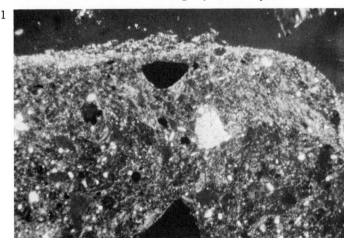

the explanation could be that the increasing density of the clay body squeezes the iron outwards – more true when the iron is in the glassy state after c/1.) The gas often penetrates into the clay body and leaves a gas pocket in the middle of the iron. These gas vacuoles (M) are present as early as c/06 and are very common by c/02. In the upper temperatures of the fire those areas develop crystals of mullite (more details later at c/9).

There is a striking difference between c/02 and c/1. In these two hours and 30° C the clay body has gotten darker, has lost much of its distinctiveness between the clay particle aggregates, and the mullite haze is no longer confined to the larger clay particles, but has become generally present throughout the clay body. (See photo 4.) The iron outline (O) is the only distinguishing feature of the large clay aggregates. This is the homogenizing of the clay body: the blurring of old distinctions on the way toward forming new ones. There has also been a marked decrease in porosity – from 35% to 8.5% and the linear shrinkage has jumped from 9% to 13%.

By c/4 the haze has developed generally over the clay. This continued development supports the idea that it is a microcrystalline development, probably mullite.

At c/4 the area shows the general clay becoming homogeneous, further development of iron-rich glass/gas areas (M), and an area of very active melting. With increasing magnification it is easy to see this is a melting feldspar crystal, the striations showing its twinned structure. (See photo 5.) The edges of this crystal were once □ but melting has rounded the edges. Melting has produced a glass around the perimeter of the crystal. In fact upon close examination

29

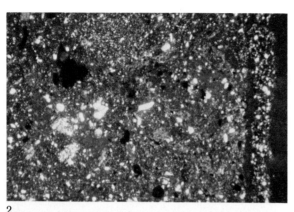

2

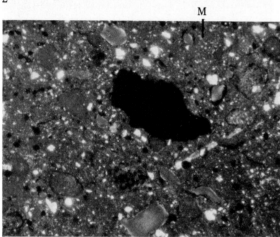

M

3

with the microscope, two distinct types of glassy material are evident. This indicates that the feldspar may have melted first, then fluxed the surrounding clay and started a melt there. The quick cool of the draw trial prevented these glasses from forming a single mixture.

I think this example, which happens to be of unusually large size, can be used as a general image for what happens to feldspar and other melting materials in the clay body.

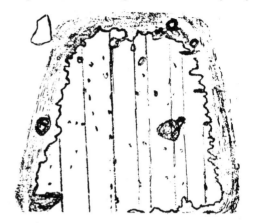

Feldspar melting is similar in appearance to an ice cube melting in water: first the edges go and then gradually the crystal is reduced in size because material is leaving from the outer edges.

The glaze, by c/6, has much more melted material than at c/4, but still has quite a ways to go before being mostly glass. The areas of the glaze which appear dark gray are the melted, glassy areas. The white areas are crystalline materials, mainly feldspars. (See photo 6.)

This particular thin-section has an unusually twinned crystal (just right of center – cc). This pattern was generated by the simultaneous growth of two types of feldspar. Each mineral which by itself would develop a straight-line pattern, was forced to accommodate the development of the other mineral – a compromise crystal.

At c/6 there is an example of a common mullite-forming area (M). There are no visible crystals yet, but much glass is present. The glassy content of the glaze at c/8 has increased markedly, although it is still not completely melted. (See photo 7.) The kaolin in the glaze is the bulk of the unmelted material with feldspar contributing a smaller amount. In the clay body (right of center) there is another unusual crystalline area (c) developing from a glassy matrix. The crystals are spiky, similar in shape to mullite, and have radical tendencies, possible cristabolite.

While c/9 was melting, the final glaze reduction was performed. A good image was developed of just how active a process the reduction of iron is. (See photo 8.) There was a large chunk of Fe_2O_3 (much of which was removed in the thin-sectioning). Fe_2O_3 was converted to FeO, a strong flux, by the reduction (fuel-rich) atmosphere. The FeO reacted with the surrounding clay and formed a glass. This glass was encouraged to flow outwards by a combination of the increasing density of the clay body squeezing the glass and by a gas produced in the reactions. The glaze was also fluxed by this intrusion of molten glass with the iron floating

to the surface, spreading out into a very large sphere – the iron volcano. Finding this example was really exciting to me because a few days earlier while speculating on the mechanism by which iron in the clay reaches the surface, I had thought of volcanos and the two seemed like similar processes. Finding this large-scale example was a nice meshing of speculation and results.

In the smaller, more usual type of iron-rich areas, large mullite needle crystals are developing. These are the same iron-rich areas that I spoke of developing as early as c/106. The iron $\begin{matrix} Fe_2O_3 \\ Fe_3O_4 \end{matrix}$ is reduced to FeO and diffuses outwards, beginning to melt around c/2, reacting first with feldspar (which ordinarily wouldn't melt before c/6) and then working on the surrounding clay. As was mentioned earlier, by 600° C the clay (kaolin) is in the metakaolin phase which at 980° C becomes spinel ($2\,Al_2O_3 \cdot 3SiO_2$) + free silica (SiO_2). Above 1050° C (c/02), the spinel phase of kaolin is transformed to mullite crystals ($3\,Al_2O_3 \cdot 2SiO_2$) and more free silica in the form of cristobalite. (Cracking problems can occur upon cooling if large amounts of cristobalite have been formed. It has a very sharp high-low phase conversion point – 200° C. This is mainly a concern of those working with high-silica clay bodies.)

By c/8 (1240°C), the mullite has developed to the point of being needle-shaped crystals, visible with a microscope, and will develop up to .5 mm in length. (See photo 9) (Mullite is rare in nature and the name comes from Mull, a location on the west coast of Scotland where this mineral occurs naturally. Kerr, *Optical Mineralogy,* p. 370.) By c/9 (1260°C), these "mullite nests" are very common in iron-rich areas, and contribute to the vitrification strength of stoneware clays, the glass and mullite acting as a binder in the clay body. These particular examples were quick-cooled, but if the melted material has more time in the liquid phase, these needle crystals will become rectilinear in shape. (See photo 10)

The glaze is very well melted with everything in a liquid-glassy state except clay particles and a few half-melted feldspar crystals. There are also crystals developing at the clay/glaze interface. Possibilities for their composition are cristobalite, SiO_2, or wollastonite, $CaSiO_3$.

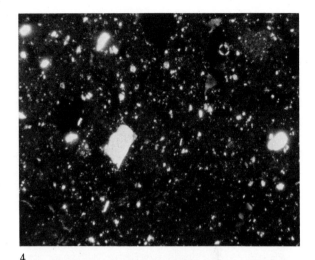

4

M

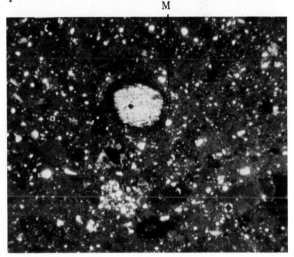

5

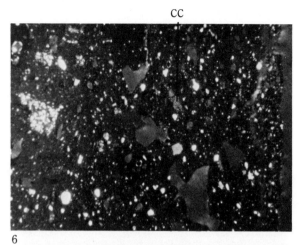

CC

6

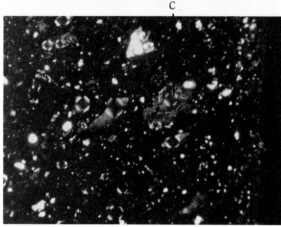

C

7

In this picture of the draw trial (first after gas shut-off, 1-A 1125° C), taken out five minutes after the kiln was turned off, these same clay/glaze interface crystals (I) are visible upon close examination. In the rest of the glaze and clay body there were no visible changes from c/9.

The draw trials removed from the kiln 15 minutes after it was shut off (1100° C) has larger clay/glaze crystals at the interface. By 35 minutes after (3A, 1080° C) these clay/glaze crystals have grown even larger. (See photo 11) But the most noticeable development is the glaze crystals that are using the unmelted clay particles for nucleation and developing radically from there. Photo 12 is a 560x close-up of the same area of 3A with parallel polars (only one polarizer in place). Notice the melty feldspar (F) in the clay just touching the glaze area – far right. These crystals are likely some kind of magnesium silicate, something within the pyroxene group of chain silicates. They could be enstitite, $MgSiO_3$, which fits most nearly the limited number of optical tests performable.

At this point I will try to summarize what I know about the way iron reacts in a stoneware reduction fire. Some of iron's properties have already been discussed, dispersion starting around c/06, and its role in glass formation (mullite areas).

We start with most of the iron in its most oxidized form, Fe_2O_3, ferric iron, red iron oxide. In this phase each iron atom shares three electrons with the neighboring oxygen atoms, each of which

accepts two electrons to fill its outer shell. Each oxygen thus becomes -2 and each iron $+3$ valence since each electron has 1 negative charge.

In a reduction (fuel-rich) atmosphere, both hydrogen and carbon monoxide gases can penetrate the clay and glaze in search of oxygen. They (H_2 and CO) stabilize themselves by sharing their outer electrons with the ever-receptive oxygen which needs two electrons to be satisfied (balanced).

It seems probable that hydrogen, H_2, is the chief reducing agent in gas-fired kilns, since it is lighter and can penetrate solids more easily than can CO gas. In any case reduction can not be accomplished by elemental carbon – soot – which is a solid (see Koenig, *Effect of Atmospheres in Firing Ceramics*, page 2). Hydrogen as the main reducing agent could explain the difference in reduction effects between

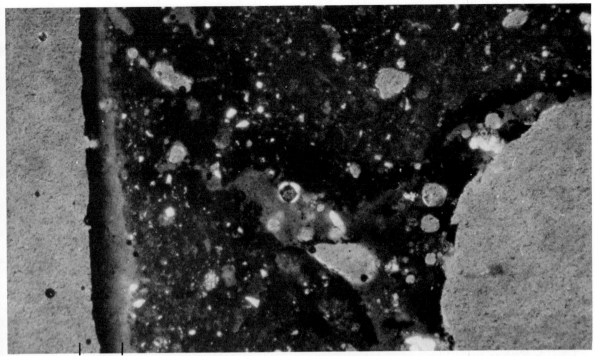

8 | GLAZE |

9

propane and natural gas-fired kilns. Natural gas has the highest hydrogen to carbon ratio (CH_4) of any naturally occurring fuel. Propane, C_3H_8, has proportionally less hydrogen. So if H_2 is the reducing agent, the following reaction is possible: $2(Fe_2O_3)+H_2 \rightarrow 4FeO+2OH$. This reduced iron (ferrous) would look like this:

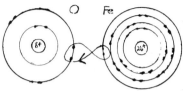

FeO is as reduced as iron can be, in the conditions we are dealing with. Using carbon monoxide (CO) as the reducing agent, the reaction would look like:

$2(Fe_2O_3+CO) \rightarrow 4FeO+2CO_2$.

The most reasonable approach to the theory of reduction would be to assume that both H_2 and CO react with the iron oxides present, but H_2 is probably the most important agent.

A reduction atmosphere during the fire produces gases which help iron concentrates to become diffused throughout the clay body. Some of this diffused iron ends up at the surface of the clay (and glaze). During cooling this surface iron

reoxidizes, resulting in brown or reddish brown oxidation colors. If the clay body is not too dense, too vitrified, and the cooling is slow enough, this complete reoxidation of iron can take place through part of or all of the interior of the clay body. (See the picture of the draw trials.)

The same clay body in a c/9 electric fire will be a very pale yellowish tan color, with the larger iron spots still very dense, and with little or no diffusion evident.

So with this particular clay body there isn't enough iron present to give reddish oxidation tones without the diffusing effects of a reduction atmosphere. With a clay body of higher iron content, reduction and diffusion isn't necessary or even desirable, since FeO is a strong flux and can produce so much melted material that the clay body becomes brittle.

The reversal of the reduction reaction was well under way by three hours after shutting off the kiln (draw trial 4A, 875° C). The black interior clay body color in the fire means that not all the FeO was completely reoxidized, possibly because of the high amount of glass formed during firing. Reoxidation occurs in the cooling of any kiln in which room air is allowed to circulate.

$FeO+O \rightarrow Fe_3O_4 \rightarrow Fe_2O_3$ black—fully

reduced $\rightarrow$ black-inbetween $\rightarrow$ red—fully oxidized

It is possible to maintain a reduction atmosphere during cooling even with the burners off by introducing a hydrocarbon material such as a methonal solution, CH_3OH, into the kiln. This was done in one case to get a blue-gray colored brick without having to fire the kiln down in a reduction atmo-

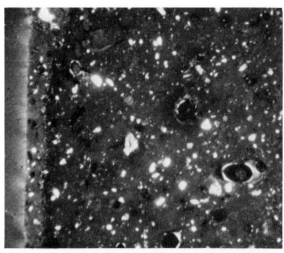

10

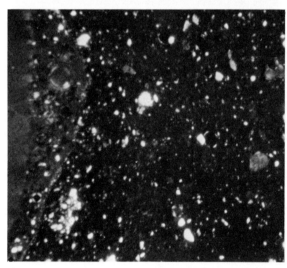

11

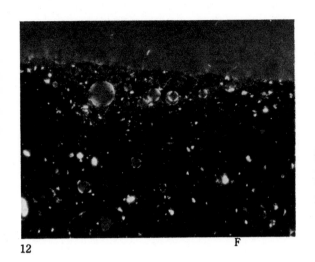

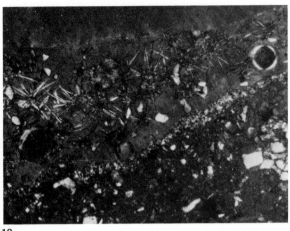

12   F   13

FIRING REACTIONS AND TEMPERATURES

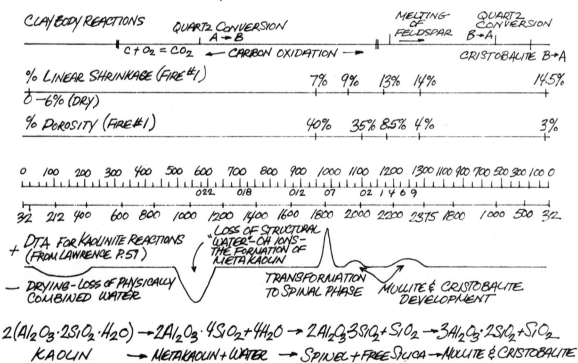

CLAY BODY REACTIONS   QUARTZ CONVERSION A→B   MELTING OF FELDSPAR   QUARTZ CONVERSION B→A

$C + O_2 = CO_2$ ← CARBON OXIDATION →   CRISTOBALITE B→A

% LINEAR SHRINKAGE (FIRE #1)   7% 9% 13% 14%   14.5%

0 –6% (DRY)

% POROSITY (FIRE #1)   40% 35% 8.5% 4%   3%

0 100 200 300 400 500 600 700 800 900 1000 1100 1200 1300 1100 900 700 500 300 100 0

022 018 012 07 02 1 4 6 9

32 212 400 600 800 1000 1200 1400 1600 1800 2000 2200 2375 1800 1000 500 32

+ DTA FOR KAOLINITE REACTIONS (FROM LAWRENCE P.57)

LOSS OF STRUCTURAL "WATER"- OH IONS - THE FORMATION OF METAKAOLIN

– DRYING- LOSS OF PHYSICALLY COMBINED WATER

TRANSFORMATION TO SPINAL PHASE

MULLITE & CRISTOBALITE DEVELOPMENT

$$2(Al_2O_3 \cdot 2SiO_2 \cdot H_2O) \rightarrow 2Al_2O_3 \cdot 4SiO_2 + 4H_2O \rightarrow 2Al_2O_3 3SiO_2 + SiO_2 \rightarrow 3Al_2O_3 \cdot 2SiO_2 + SiO_2$$

KAOLIN → METAKAOLIN + WATER → SPINEL + FREE SILICA → MULLITE & CRISTOBALITE

sphere (Berg, Vol. II, Page 205).

Twelve hours after turning off the kiln (5A, 650° C), it has cooled to red heat. There has been some increase in the number of glaze crystals but their size is similar to 3A. (See photo 13) Here is a picture of a highly crystalline area of 5A. The gas bubbles (the spheres) have developed probably as a reduction product and are increasingly noticeable after c/1. In some glazes they are present in sufficient numbers to cause an uneven surface – pinholing. The clay/glaze interface area has developed markedly during cooling – increasing depth of clay/glaze crystals from the clay body into the melted glaze.

The draw trial which was left in the kiln to cool in the normal manner was very little changed from 5A, so visible changes have occurred before cooling to red heat. But it is not possible to say absolutely that the fire is over – glazes continue to try to adjust themselves to the clay body; so we hear the pinging sound of glazes crazing. Acids in foods and soils can react with the alkalis of the glaze, thus ceaselessly changing its composition. So in some sense the fire never really goes out. The main difference between in and out of the kiln is the rate of change. Outside the kiln most changes are slow enough to be out of the human time scale.

References

Berg, P. "The Use of Controlled Atmospheres," *Science of Ceramics,* Vol. II, edited by G. H. Steward. Academic Press, New York, 1965.

Cardew, Michael. *Pioneer Pottery.* St. Martin's Press, New York, 1969.

Grimshaw, Rex. *The Chemistry and Physics of Clay,* 4th ed. Wiley-Interscience, New York, 1971.

Insley, H. and Frenchette. *Microscopy of Ceramics and Cements.* Academic Press, New York, 1955.

Kerr, Paul. *Optical Mineralogy,* 3rd ed. McGraw-Hill, New York, 1959. (This is a basic mineral identification textbook.)

Koenig, C. J. *Effect of Atmospheres in Firing Ceramics.* Southern California Gas Co., Los Angeles.

Lawrence, W. G. *Ceramic Science for the Potter.* Chilton Book Co., New York, 1972.

COMMENTARY ON THE MALONE REPORT

by James McKinnell

The reduction stoneware potter urgently needs to understand the crystallography of clay body compositions and the resultant interfacial reactions between those bodies and glazes when fired. Almost all research in the ceramic industry is done under oxidation rather than reduction conditions. Reduction firing, however, produces some highly unique (and potentially dangerous) structural phenomena. Pat Malone's firing project, "The Art and Science of Firing," is a milestone on the path to a much needed wider technological understanding on the part of the studio potter.

One of the most perplexing stoneware problems is the phenomenon of shivering and shattering under seemingly inexplicable conditions involving certain clay bodies and glazes, both of which are likely to be fairly high in iron contaminants or additives. The most perfect spiral crackling (the severest form of glaze compression) that I've seen was on an "as mined" red-burning stoneware-type mug (without spar) from clay mined in the periphery of greater London. The whole mug was marvelously cracked and physically separated like a huge spring.

Mr. Malone's long formula:

$$\text{kaolin} \xrightarrow[450°\,C]{} \text{metakaolin} \xrightarrow[950°\,C]{} \text{spinel mullite and cristobalite}$$

is the clue, in my opinion, to solving this problem. It is well buttressed by data from Cardew's excellent book, *Pioneer Pottery.* One should look up and study all the references in Cardew to cristobalite.

Cristobalite, a crystalline form of silica (SiO_2), is the basic problem. Whereas the ordinary quartz SiO_2 crystal expands and contracts at 1050° F or 573° C (first redness with lights out or last redness on cooling), with only 1% linear change, cristobalite has a sudden sharp contraction on cooling of 3%, at oven temperature (approximately 450° F). Both the glaze and the body are rigid below very dull redness, and this sudden severe contraction of the rigid body, 536° F - 428° F [Cardew on p. 304 shows 437° F; Ryan on p. 73 shows 280° C (536° to 428° F)], on cooling, causes glaze to shiver off the edges when certain specific glazes like temmoku are used. If severe enough, it can even shatter the pot by suddenly shrinking the body and placing the glaze into strong, crushing compression, as diagrammatically indicated by Dr. Ryan's drawing, in his Fig. 25, p. 74, entitled "Glaze put into compression by 'cristobalite squeeze.' " The phenomenon is even more severe and shattering when a lot of the cristobalite crystal is present, and if only one side of the pot is glazed, such as with hanging planters.

I will illustrate the chemical aspect of the problem by using the following two formulas:

When clay is fired for the first time, the kaolinite, also a crystal, is changed thusly:

$$Al_2O_3 \cdot 2\,SiO_2 \cdot 2H_2O \text{ heat } 3Al_2O_3 \cdot 2\,SiO_2$$
Clay (mullite)

forming the very desirable strength-giving crystals called mullite. The H_2O goes off as steam. All equations must balance, so one needs three clay molecules on the left side to get three Al_2O_3 on the right: that is,

$$3(Al_2O_3 \cdot 2\,SiO_2 \cdot 2\,H_2O) \text{ heat } 3\,Al_2O_3 \cdot 2\,SiO_2 + 4\,SiO_2$$
(mullite) (silica)

But in so doing we have four free SiO_2 left over on the right side at the end of the reaction. It's these four left-over free SiO_2, which are of extremely fine size, that can crystallize out as cristobalite, if all conditions are favorable to its growth. Here are the main conditions, in my opinion:

1. too little feldspar (less than 10%) (feldspar dissolves the cristobalite into a glass)

2. too little ball clay (less than 20%) (there are natural fluxes in ball clay)

3. too much Fe_2O_3 or red clay or brick clay (iron oxide in red-burning clays, and iron minerals act as a "catalyst" or "mineralizer")

4. too slow cooling (which permits sluggist SiO_2 crystals to grow)

5. very long firing cycle, producing longer periods of heavy reduction

6. very high percentage of pseudo-fireclays (like Lincoln and Sutter from Ione, CA) which are known to promote cristobalite more than the standard type fireclays, like Milled Missouri, Kaiser, or Grefco.

The quickest way to prevent cristobalite from growing is to use 10 to 12% spar in the body, which dissolves the SiO_2 into a glass. Glass has a much lower coefficient of expansion. My wife Nan and I generally avoid, where possible, using red clays or brick clays for color, relying more on commercial red iron oxide, at about an average of 2 to 3% total, to give body color. If red clays are used, the spar should be increased by 1 to 3% at least. Red-burning clays definitely accelerate growth of cristobalite in reduction. Also about ½ of all red clays can cause bloating, another problem.

In his book *Geology of Today* Professor J. W. Gregory (University of Glasgow) states: "the law of decreasing basicity asserts that the most basic elements in a molten rock solidify first, then those which are the next richest in basic materials follow, and the most acid solidify last." Pure SiO_2 is acid, and thus all mixtures will be less so.

Dr. Hewitt Wilson in "Mat Glazes and the Lime-Alumina-Silica System" (*The Bulletin of the American Ceramic Society,* Vol. 18, No. 12, Dec. 1939) states on page 447 that "mullite crystals form with great rapidity." Dr. Ryan points out that SiO_2 is the opposite, and is sluggish in

forming crystals, so that slow cooling will promote, aid, and abet the growth of cristobalite. When I was a ceramic engineering student, a national study was made in the 1930s, the general conclusion of which was that almost every plant in the whole ceramic industry was cooling too slowly. Britons now have available 76 ft.^{3} to 100ft.^{3} reduction kilns in England that are fired and cooled in 24 hours so they can be used every day in small production plants. They are cooled in 6 to 10 hours under forced, blower air, with no shivering or shattering problems when a properly designed stoneware body is used.

For a stoneware body, Nan and I like to use about 60% fireclay comprised of roughly equal parts of almost any 4 different fireclays, plus 30% ball clay, plus ± 10 to 12% spar, and not more than .75% red iron oxide. This normally will produce a modest, successful casserole (brownish tannish) body and will be shock-resistant, if the forms are less than 12′′ in diameter. For larger casseroles, 10% talc can be added but the spar must be reduced to about 5% of the body to prevent slumping or warping (or instead of talc, 15% petalite, or 22% zircon and 10% spar). All body formations must be in-service, destruction-tested, before safe commercial promotion. Freezer to hot oven, recycled over several weeks household usage is a fairly good test. If you get breakage, reduce clay content and increase low-expansion nonclay materials. After considerable research, Professor Robert Turner of Alfred once stated to a potting friend: "Clay is the real problem in casseroles."

I'm very impressed with what Mr. Malone has done. A possible future step could be to examine the microscopic thin sections of samples that have been allowed to cool slowly rather than quickly, withdrawing samples at various temperatures. Normal cooling will give a more accurate picture of the true crystal growth on cooling of slowly or more rapidly cooled stoneware.

Dr. Wilson also points out that the anorthite calcium feldspar crystals ($CaO \cdot Al_2O_3 \cdot 2\,SiO_2$) will grow and crystallize in high temperature mat glazes. The same is true of the wollastonite crystal ($CaO \cdot SiO_2$).

We all put whiting into almost every stoneware glaze, which helps to permit and stimulate these two crystals to grow and produce some degree of matness in the glaze as it cools.

Wilson also says, "Quartz, tridymite and cristobalite (all SiO_2), on the other hand, are slow to crystallize, although they have been identified in small quantities in matte glazes, and in one rare case they were reported to be the cause of matte texture."

In the reduction stoneware body beware of all cristobalite growth – nip it in the "formulation" bud. Don't set up conditions that promote its growth or your customers will crack their teapots, coffee mugs, platters, and casseroles sooner or later.

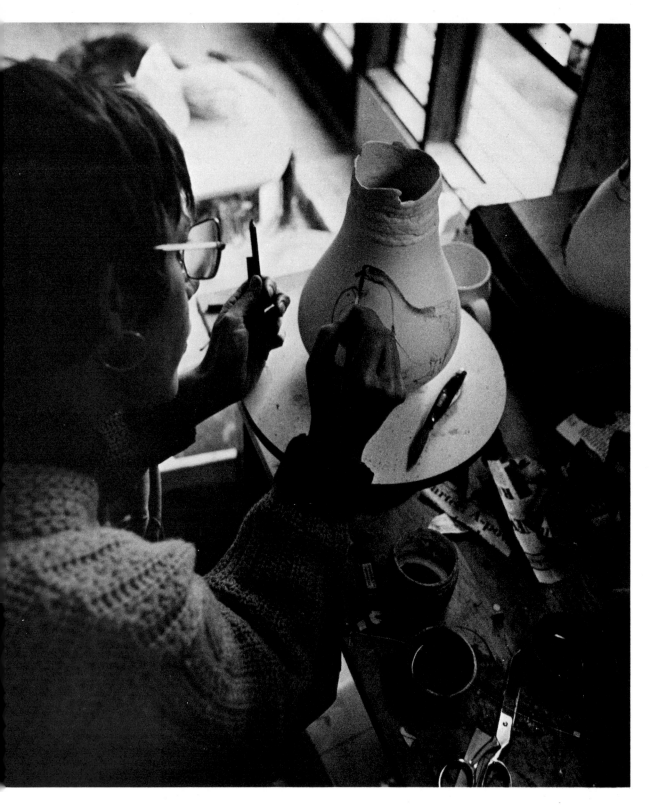

GLAZE PAINTING

by Jenny Lind

In the nine years that I have been working with clay, I have explored several processes, some of which have become stepping stones for my present work. I feel that these are worth sharing in that they may also serve another potter.

In the beginning, my ex-husband, Dick Masterson, had been throwing for about a year. At that time I offered my help in decorating his pots. I had been a painter, and the switch from canvas interested me. The pots sold well, but it wasn't until three years later that we were able to maintain ourselves solely from these sales. At first neither of us had any intention of becoming potters, but Dick just began to make more and more pots and he slowly eased into it. It took me longer than Dick as I wasn't as attracted by the process. Gradually, however, my involvement grew the more I was exposed to it.

In those days we got our clay by digging and processing local earthenware. We fired in an electric kiln to c/05. After a short while we started digging a stoneware clay and firing to c/5 and 6. I would paint on the freshly glazed surface with oxides, primarily cobalt, iron, rutile, and copper. The paintings, or drawings, were very simple and naive. I did not have enough control; sometimes they ran and sometimes not.

About one and a half years later we built a catenary arch updraft and began to fire to c/9 and 10. It was fired with oil and was patterned after a kiln built the previous year by our friend Priscilla. At that time there wasn't any material available to us on kiln construction. We simply jumped into it with some vague notion about how a kiln should work. Our first firing was memorable. The cones wouldn't bend and we kept pouring more oil and more air. The kiln belched and roared and smoked. It looked to be quite hot, but of course our eyes were being deceived; the cones weren't down. As we continued feeding this monster our concern grew. It really seemed hot. As I peeked in for another look at the cones I noticed a pot shifting. Not having witnessed such a thing before, and not knowing what to do with this new information, I took a second look in an effort to discredit what I had seen. This time I saw a second pot actually settle about a half-inch. After a seemingly interminable time I realized that the pots were melting, so I quickly said, "The pots are melting." We then turned the kiln off.

The following year Dick built a sprung arch with four gas burners. By this time we were earning our living by potting, and were thoroughly involved in being self-supporting crafts people.

One of our first discoveries while working in the c/9 to 10 range was that casting slip (60% ball clay and 40% talc) was an ideal slip glaze. For several years I carved animals and figures through this slipped surface. I haven't used or seen any slip work as well as this slip for carving. The slip should be the consistency of thick paint and applied to a dampish leatherhard pot. Then while the pot is still leatherhard but

dry to the touch, it can be carved. For best results it should be applied to a brown or red-brown stoneware and fired in moderate to heavy reduction. The result is a pot with dark carved areas and a creamy white surface. If fired in oxidation the slipped surface will appear dry and chalky. An addition of 2% cobalt to Albany clay makes a nice dark slip. Overlapping layers of the dark and the light slip produces a lovely gray blue or black image depending on the choice of the first coat. Porcelain slip is also a good basis for carving or line drawing. The slip should be applied to a freshly thrown piece and then carved when leatherhard. The pot is then glazed with a celadon or salt fired. Celadon is particularly nice to use, as it enhances the richness of a dark image against a white background.

The white porcelain slip may also be colored with stains and glazed with a celadon or transparent glaze.

After two and a half years of working on Dick's pots, I started to make my own coiled pots. I hadn't been working long when a friend sent a pound of porcelain from France. I loved it. The following month porcelain was available for the first time through our supplier. Immediately I ordered a ton and went to work coiling large containers. Another potter was sharing our studio at this time and she gave me a few instructions on the wheel.

I wanted to throw large pots for decorating, but my desire was ahead of my facility. So I began to throw and assemble sections in order to get larger-size pots. Putting the sections together neatly was another problem for me, but I soon remedied that by placing coils between each section. These sections were then slipped with a cobalt porcelain slip, carved, and glazed with clear.

Then I tried drawing on leatherhard porcelain using a sharp stick or pen. I bisqued the pots and then filled these incised lines with either iron or cobalt. Rutile, chrome, copper, iron, and cobalt were painted in afterwards. At that time I had an unsatisfactory clear glaze. I began using the H T51 formula, found it satisfactory, and still use it. It neither runs nor settles, and works in either reduction or oxidation.

During the tedium of filling lines I discovered that oxides could be erased with a common eraser. At that moment the eraser became one of my main tools. I still use one today. When using an eraser, be careful to remove all crumbs; otherwise they will resist the glaze. If there is some resist, the glaze can be gently rubbed with a finger to fill any pinholes. As I continued to work my pots grew larger and the forms began to approach those of my intentions. I was able to increase my color range by mixing different oxides together.

One day while sitting in my studio my eye caught sight of some old glaze stains we had used while firing to c/5. I mixed them directly with water and painted a test pot. Turquoise blue was the only color to survive, but I became so excited I immediately ordered from Westwood more stains. I found a pink, yellow, light blue, turquoise, and black. These all worked at c/10. For two years I continued incising, filling and coloring. Sometimes I used celadon that pooled in the lines or celadon over an iron-rutile mix that gave a kind of diffused, magical quality to the drawing.

Three years ago I bought some glaze pencils, and I found that black, brown, blue, and green would work at c/10. Two brands I know of that are good are Stewart and Chem-Clay Corp., England. These and the stains can be purchased from most ceramic supply houses. They can be used in addition to the oxides already mentioned. Be reminded that under reduction iron can go metallic and break through. Also cobalt, if not handled carefully, will show up after the firing in the most unfortunate places. Pink and yellow stains when

reduced come out green. In oxidation yellow, pink, and purple will be bright, and copper will be a lovely soft green. Reduction tends to tone the brightness down, but on the other hand it enhances the quality of the glaze. The trade-off becomes a personal choice. At first I preferred the bright colors, but now I seem to prefer the softer quality of reduction firing.

To apply, the stains and oxides are mixed with water and brushed on. This should be done after stirring, as they all seem to settle quickly. If the colorants are applied too thickly they may cause crawling. Sometimes the glaze crawls if the stain is freshly mixed. A bit of glaze added seems to help, and it is always better to keep the old batch going rather than starting a new one.

There are many new products available, such as pastel crayons and oxide markers. I use these occasionally, but basically I stick to drawing with pencils and painting with brushes. If one needs a preliminary sketch, it can be done with a regular graphite pencil, for the lines burn out at high temperatures. All the high-temperature stains work well at low temperatures in either reduction or oxidation.

Many of the colorants work in salt firings also. They must be applied to a white background, either a white slip or white body. They can be applied to a dark body and glazed with a salt clear. I usually work straight on greenware with brushes and oxides. The precise definition I get in my other work is lost, but the imprecision is a nice change for me.

Stencils can be utilized by those who wish not to draw, or perhaps feel intimidated by it. The stencils can be cut from paper, magazines, or photographs. Oxides can be brushed or blown over the stencil for a positive background, or the stencil can be waxed over for a negative background, or simply traced around. Details can always be added afterwards if desired.

I have been asked which I like to do more, draw or throw. I enjoy both, and understand the importance of their relationship. A weak drawing on a strong pot or a strong draw-

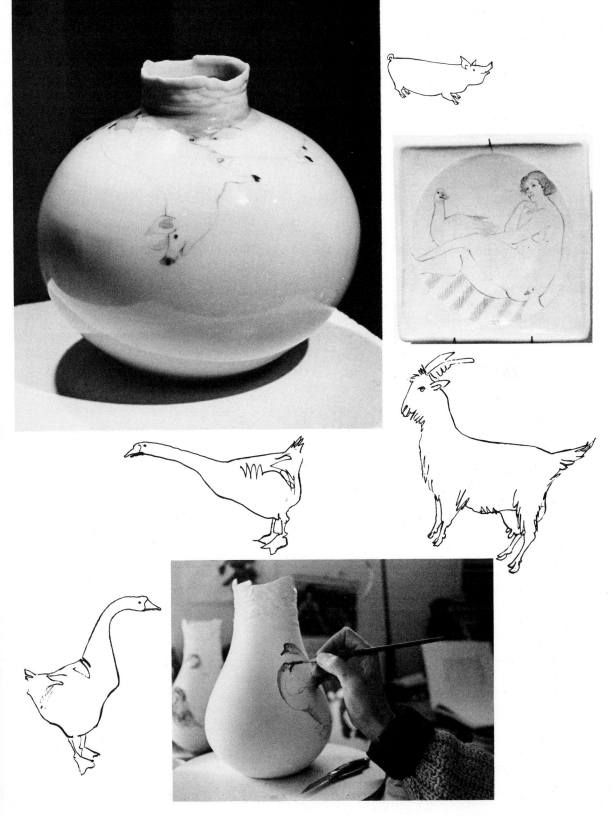

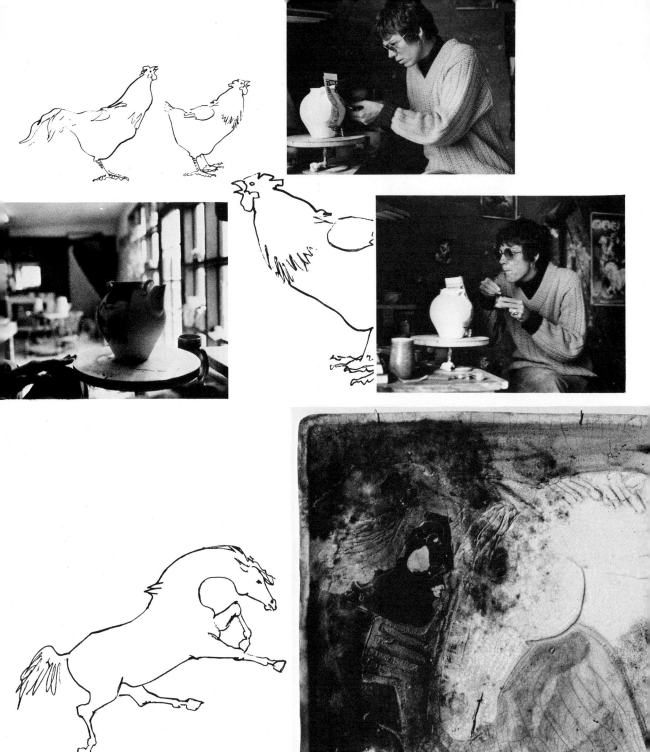

ing on a weak is equally unsatisfactory. Ideally a beautiful form should be complemented by a beautiful drawing.

The drawing and the throwing have both taken on new meaning for me over the last nine years. I see that there is another element in making either a pot or a drawing that works along with the craftsmanship. I'll call it "aesthetic regard." Unlike craftsmanship, it can't be learned or taught, certainly not by traditional means, anyway, because it doesn't have to do with taking in information. This quality or "aesthetic regard" comes out of us in much the same way it comes out of a child.

When I watch my children drawing, I see an openness which allows them to put out what's inside. Their drawings are beautiful, every one of them. They don't conform to any preconceived idea about what they should be doing, or how it should work, they simply let whatever is in there out. The honesty and the freshness, the originality, it's all there. Everything that we adults labor for is at their fingertips. Yet as I watch them grow, as they become more educated, as they learn about our world, I see that freshness fade. They are taught a new view of the world, but at the expense of the old, singular, inner view. So we grown-up artists, having shut the gate behind us, spend the rest of our lives trying to recapture our innocence.

Like the rest of us, I don't know how to get back there any more. I have come too far. So I draw the things that make me feel good. My drawings are somewhat naive, but it doesn't matter to me. The images I use are those that I see around me, that feed me. They are those that bring me joy as I observe them, and as I imagine them.

At the time of this writing I am living in La Cienega, New Mexico, with my three children, Anna Marie, Jessica, and Joshua; my husband, Allan Walter; and a variety of chickens, geese, guineas, gobblers, cats, dogs, horses, and other friendly creatures. We have an apprentice, or rather, as she prefers to be called, "a friendly helper," Blythe. There are two 30 cubic foot kilns, one of which is salt, one small raku kiln, two studios and a retail shop. Our shop is open six days a week and closed on Sunday. I work five to seven days a week, and like most potters my life isn't separate from my work.

Allan, who is also a potter, and I sometimes work on pots together, and generally always together glazing, loading and firing. I usually throw five to six days, bisque, and then start glazing. Glazing, which includes the drawing, takes another five to seven days.

After a firing, in the evening and the morning of the next day we clean, and in the morning of the second day we unload the kiln. That afternoon is spent grinding bottoms and pricing. Were the third day not cutting into our work week too much, we would probably take the day off. But being self-employed, it's back to work throwing and the start of a new cycle.

In the summer we place a greater emphasis on nonpottery sorts of things. We raise alfalfa, and usually have one or two building projects going on. Naturally our production slows down. By late summer, early fall, when our store is empty and has been empty for too long, when we've re-ceived one too many phone calls from our shops, we, in a panic, rev up production; usually this means spinning our wheels. After an awkward start we settle down to another year of potting.

I do not have a regular production line. The cups, bowls, plates, etc., are done on an irregular basis, mostly for relief from my normal work. I enjoy adding to thrown pieces; consequently I make a lot of teapots, sectioned vases, and goblets. Most things I make are done in a series, several vases, several teapots, etc. I find that by working in a series there is more room for expansion and exploration of ideas.

An unfortunate consequence of my work is that I must charge more for each piece because of the time involved in decorating. The increased price often forces the customer to have a different regard for the work than I wish. There becomes an element of preciousness about the work, and rather than being used as I had intended, it usually ends up tucked away on a shelf. For me, function is as important a consideration as the form and drawing are. I feel that by our not using the pot, by our not experiencing the function or the purpose of its existence, the pot is incomplete. Not that expensive pottery has to be exposed to everyday use, but surely there are appropriate occasions for the use of special pottery to underscore the significance of the event.

It makes no difference whether a potter produces singly or in quantity. What's important, though, is how we feel about our work. There are never enough beautiful things in our world.

Formula: H T51 Clear c/9-10

Feldspar (kingman)	27
Ball clay	19.5
Whiting	19.5
Silica	34

Formula: Light Celadon c/9-10
(can be used over colorants)

Feldspar (kingman)	33.68
Silica	21.76
Kaolin	8.
Whiting	14.
Iron	1.31

Formula for salt clear: c/9-10

Feldspar	2
Dolomite	1
Ball clay	1

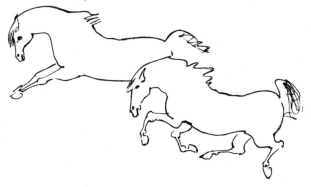

PHOTORESIST

by Gerry Williams

Images have long looked out from pots. Drawn, scratched, or painted, they speak of myths and nature and woman and gods.

The first stick to trace an image in soft clay began a communication of ideas and concepts continuing on through today. While technology may change, the need of the potter to express himself on the surface of his pots remains a strong motivating force.

Photography is the image maker of our time. We need not look far to see its impact on the arts. McLuhanites, we evoke a hot, real world on a mirror of ourselves. If pots are ourselves, and if the space and time we inhabit reflects in truth the mystery of our origin, then Sung and T'ang are not alone our roots, but also, Nixon.

On first looking into the ceramic work of Howard Kottler, Robert Engel, and others, I was intrigued by the use of photography on pottery. These potters were making use of Victorian techniques to produce witty contemporary statements. It appeared to me, however, that steps required for decal making and photosilkscreening were complicated and might preclude wider use. I wondered if one could go directly to the pot with a light-sensitive emulsion.

The thought was the key: through the suggestion of a photographer friend, I obtained information from Kodak on the use of emulsions developed for the microcircuitry industry.

Two of these emulsions, or resists, seemed useful to the potter: KPR (Kodak Photo Resist) and KOR (Kodak Ortho Resist). Basically resin solutions in an organic solvent (and not a silver bromide film), these emulsions "cross-link" or polymerize in areas struck with radiation through a transparency. The exposed areas are rendered soluble and the unexposed insoluble in the developer, leaving a tough, chemically resistant image in minute relief on the surface. Embedded in that image at the moment of development is the ceramic pigment, which remains behind after the resin has been fired off.

For the past several years I have been helped by friends and apprentices with the problems of adapting the photoresist process to pottery. It has essentially been the effort to translate a sophisticated industrial technique into one that is workable for the studio potter.

Staring with KPR and then going on to KOR, we have worked on both one-of-a-kind and limited-production pots. We have only begun to explore the wide range of possibilities. While its effectiveness is closely linked to a knowledge of photography, or at least to a friend who is a photographer, photoresist is well within the reach of most studio potters.

The KPR system requires a positive transparency to produce a contact print with an ultraviolet light source. It is as follows:

1. The pot or form to be photoresisted must be made beforehand and vitrified by firing to the proper glaze temperature. The surface to receive the photograph can be flat or slightly curved. It should be fired with white slip or white matt glaze as a neutral background. The surface must be clean.

2. For contact printing, the positive transparency must have maximum density in black areas and maximum transparency in white, and be as sharp as possible. The transparency, as large as the planned print, can be made with an enlarger under standard darkroom procedures (see photographic information following). An alternative method is by duplicating machine. I have used a studio-sized 3M Dry Photo Contact Duplicator Model 70, taking prints from casual sources, and doubling transparencies for greater density. Actually, any opaque object or graphic will do the trick. It is not necessary to use halftone as with photosilkscreening.

3. Work in safelight conditions from here on. Use a yellow 75-watt bug bulb, or wrap the bulb with orange Kodagraph paper. Work in a darkroom or in the studio at night. Brush on two medium coats of KPR, baking dry between each coat in a heating oven for 20 minutes at 80°C. (An electric heater with a sheetmetal box is easily constructed.) After cooling, the pot can be wrapped in black plastic (mulch plastic) to preserve the hardened emulsion until ready for exposure.

4. Under safelight conditions place the transparency in contact with the dry KPR surface. (Close contact is essential.) Tape down edges or place small weights on the darkest areas. Over an irregular surface improvise a vacuum table by placing the pot with transparency into a thin plastic bag, and suck air out with a vacuum cleaner.

5. Expose with ultraviolet light. Use a 275-watt sun lamp obtainable in drug stores or Sears for about $10.00. Other sources of ultraviolet light may be used, including the sun. Exposure for 275-watt bulb is 8 to 10 minutes at 12'' distance. Density of film requires experimentation to determine correct exposure. Underexposure causes the background to absorb more pigment, thereby reducing contrast, while overexposure undercuts the line and makes pigment release. (I built a wooden frame with graded scale allowing the bulb to be clipped on and moved for varying height of the pot.)

It is essential to protect eyes from ultraviolet light by wearing dark glasses.

6. Preparation of the ceramic pigments is done in advance. Some possibilities are:

(a) overglazes, with final firing about c/018.

Stoneware bowl 6 in. diam. KOR photo resist.

(b) underglazes combined with frit, in ratio of one to two, final firing near c/04;

(c) raw oxides such as copper or iron, final firing to c/6 to 10.

I prefer overglazes; they are finely ground, already fluxed, come in many colors, and require only a low final firing. Raw oxides are great but require high firing. Some strong overglazes can be high-fired with good results.

7. The developer fluid is n-butyl acetate, an industrial cleaning fluid obtainable in its "normal" state. Mix a small quantity of the butyl acetate with the pigment to form a creamlike mixture. Brush over the exposed emulsion. Development is instant. For single color treatment, brush all over. For various colors, brush on small separate portions of pigments at random or in areas prespecified by light pencil marks on the surface before emulsion is applied. A kind of multiple-color picture can be achieved by exposing and developing two separate sets of sympathetic pigments. (Butyl acetate is vile stuff and proper ventilation is advised while using it. This applies also to the resist emulsions.)

8. Dry the developed surface completely in air or over heat.

9. Wash the surface off with a sponge under running water until all excess pigment is removed and the photograph is completely revealed. (The emulsion is tough and can stand fairly hard scrubbing.)

10. Clean the edges or areas that need to be lightened with acetone. If necessary, completely remove all emulsion and start again. None of us is perfect.

11. Fire the pot to the temperature required by the ceramic pigment. The emulsion burns off, leaving the pigment as a vitrified ceramic photograph. Be sure all trapped water is removed in advance of firing.

The **KOR system** differs somewhat from that of KPR. KOR is said to be faster than KPR by factors of 8 to 16 times for ultraviolet light, and 20 to 40 times for tungsten. Its sensitivity to tungsten light, therefore, makes it particularly useful for projecting images through glass lenses onto round surfaces. KOR, however, is much trickier to use, appearing more unstable and temperamental than KPR. Care should be exercised in its use. Vapors of the resist emulsions are combustible and should be kept away from open flame. The emulsions have a long shelf life but viability will be increased by storage in a cool, dark place.

The use of KOR is as follows:

1. Prepare ceramic form as per instructions with KPR. Round forms may be used here, preferably integrating pot and photograph from the beginning.

2. Under safelight conditions (25-watt red bug bulb), brush on one thin-to-medium coat of KOR. A thinnish coat seems to give a higher photographic resolution than a thick one, due to complete absorption of radiant energy by the emulsion. Take care to avoid running and pooling by the emulsion, which causes cracks later on. Lay on just enough to cover the surface. Since KOR is oxygen-sensitive, pour out only enough from the bottle, into a small glass jar, to cover one pot at a time, and use immediately.

Bake dry in a heating oven for 20 minutes at 80°C.

3. Preparation of the 35 mm or 2x2 black-and-white positive transparency can be made with an enlarger in standard dark-room procedures (see photographic information following). Free compositions of patterns worked directly on a slide are effective. Project with a regular tungsten light system. (I use a Sawyer projector with 500-watt bulb and modified 3'' lens. Kodak Carousel is O.K. too.) Exposure with 500-watt bulb is approximately 4 minutes at 12''. The surface can be masked and exposed consecutively, or more than one projector used at the same time. Other sources of greater tungsten or ultraviolet light (a mercury-vapor lamp) may be used. The greater the light, the farther the projection; theoretically, one could photoresist a building or a mountain.

4. Develop with n-butyl acetate mixed with ceramic pigment, as per KPR instructions. Care must be taken in developing KOR so as not to disturb the softened emulsion; lay on the developer with a brush so as to cover each area only once. A better method with KOR is to use a small aerosol spray gun in applying butyl acetate and pigment. An even coating will give a completely undisturbed image.

5. Dry over heat, then scrub under running water to bring out the image. Clean with acetone if necessary.

6. Fire to required final temperature.

Having absorbed some of these instructions, the determined studio potter can perhaps develop photoresist into a practical technique geared to limited production. Indeed, the expense and time involved in learning suggests use on a continuing basis. Even though photoresisting almost equals the time spent in making the actual pot, multiples can be produced to sell at moderate retail prices.

A word of caution: sensitizing surfaces may lead in strange directions. Forces not fully understood can be at work, and may make the potter-photographer suspect that this is more an occult art than a science. The peculiarities of photoresist must be experienced to be appreciated: three-dimensional image distortion, light refraction on concave surfaces, seductions of graphics, laws of plagiarism (including the dangers of tampering with the sex life of Snow White), and other psychic matters.

Photography on pots should be approached for what it is: an experiment in a new direction. Easily misused, it is tasteless at worst. At best, it is fresh and intriguing.

Having decided to work in this direction, the potter will, therefore, find photoresist extremely useful. The imagery of photographic patterns, gracefully integrated with rich clay forms, can bring new vitality to one's work, and lead to laser paths.

Notes

Photographic Data

A positive film (transparency) is prepared for photoresist from a black-and-white negative as follows:

Set an enlarger for the area you require for the 135 mm or 2x2 slide; stop the lens down to its smallest diameter and expose for one-third the length of time normally given an 8x10 print. On Contrast Process Film, process in DK-50 for four minutes; fix, dry, and mount. (Dust and dirt are serious problems with contrast film, so be extremely careful about cleanliness.) A contact positive can also be made by the same procedure, using a printing frame under the enlarger light source. Variation can be obtained in a desired contrast by use of other developers and films.

A contact transparency is used with KPR; a projected transparency with KOR.

White Slip c/6-11

China clay	25
Ball clay	25
Buckingham feldspar	20
Flint	20
Superpax	5
Borax	5

White Matt Glaze c/10

Buckingham feldspar	48.9
China clay	27.6
Dolomite	22.4
Whiting	3.5

KPR – Available from any Kodak commercial outlet.

KOR – Ditto. Or from:
Treck Photographic Inc.
21 Needham Street
Newton Highlands, MA 02161

N-butyl acetate – Available from drug supply house. Or from:
Howe and French Inc.
45 Williams Street
Everett, MA 02149

Overglazes –
Mason Color and Chemical Works Inc.
206 Broadway
East Liverpool, OH 43920

Stoneware vase 23 in. high. KPR photo resist.

FIRING IN OXIDATION TO C/4,5,6

by Val Cushing

The firing range and atmosphere of c/4,5,6 oxidation does not get the attention it deserves by American potters. There are potters who use it and understand its advantages, but more often this range is used when other alternatives are denied. And the alternative most desired seems to be c/9,10, high-fire reduction firing. The seductive charms of high-fire reduction have continued to lure us into smoke-filled kiln rooms for the past 30 years. This dominance of high-fire reduction became epidemic during the middle 1940s and was given special prominence by Bernard Leach in his widely read and important book, *A Potter's Book*. Earlier work in high-fire reduction had been done by Binns and Charles Harder at Alfred University, at Ohio State University, and by a few other individuals around the country. But the Leach book was a turning point and focused attention on the generally quiet and subtle beauty of early Chinese, Korean, and more importantly, Japanese pottery. The romance became feverish. Reduction firing swept the country. Every exhibition, every craft store was flooded with subdued browns, muted grays, gray greens, and brown blacks which were the glaze colors resulting from this rather mysterious way of firing. It was new and challenging, with little information available about how to get results.

Formulas from a few soot-smudged notebooks began leaking out. A mystique developed. In the early 1950s eager students, like myself, were captivated. Studio production potters were working in reduction and those who went into teaching, as I did, perpetuated this whole system of firing. High-fire reduction is still dominant today, 30 years later, although many other ways of working and firing are prevalent in various parts of the country. The most influential change from the reduction system came through those potters who began working more with sculpture and less with the functional pot. Many potters in England and elsewhere in Europe have always fired in oxidation and continue to do so today. My point is that work in high-fire reduction, particularly among functional potters, has seemed to be almost mandatory; a sign of real professionalism and the only way for significant expression in pottery. Isn't it time we reexamined these assumptions? A growing number of potters think it is. I will try to present some reasons for and advantages of firing in oxidation at the range of c/4,5,6. At the end of this article I will list some formulas for clay bodies, slips, and glazes for this range which have proved interesting and may help others get started.

The most obvious benefit is economics. Not only is this range about 100°C lower than c/9,10, but oxidation is a faster fire than the long, slow soaking fires of reduction, as practiced by most high-fire reduction potters. The soot and smoke of reduction wastes fuel and is pollution in the atmosphere, no matter how slight in comparison to industrial violators. Oxidation firings do not require gas, oil, wood, or coal fuels and can actually be done most successfully in electric kilns. Surely this is an ecological gain, not to mention the prediction by some scientists that electricity will soon be the only available source of energy for most individuals. All the fossil fuels will be needed by generating plants to make this electricity.

Let's talk about the electric kiln. It is certainly easier and safer to fire, cheaper to build, more economical of floor space, and easier to locate in the kinds of studios many potters must use. There is a vast selection of electric kilns available commercially for those who cannot build their own—a far greater choice of size, shape, and price range than is possible for any other type of commercial kiln. Building one's own electric kiln may be a little more expensive than building a gas kiln, but the process lends itself to some of the technological innovations in materials that are flooding the market. I'm thinking here of various lightweight insulating materials like hardboards, blankets, castables, and systems of easy prefabrication. It should be emphasized at this point that there is a truly vast body of technical information available on kilns, firing, bodies, glazes, slips, engobes, and all other aspects of oxidation firing in the engineering and scientific literature. There is little on reduction from these particular sources because reduction firing is generally considered the enemy by the ceramic industry. Potters will find it easier to approach engineers, ceramic technologists, and scientists with questions and problems concerning oxidation firing since nearly all phases of the ceramic industry are exclusively concerned with oxidation. The reason for that is, as all potters know, that reduction firings are less reliable, less predictable, less controllable and filled with constant hazards. Oxidation firing does have advantages when it comes to those last points, if you are looking at practicality. It is certainly easier for potters to find a studio location near the urban centers, the real market place for pottery, when they are firing with an electric kiln. The electric kiln decision may have to be made on this point alone.

Our next consideration should be clays and clay bodies. If for some reason a potter had to be limited to one firing range, I believe the greatest versatility would be found at c/4,5,6. It is a perfect range in which to combine all the advantages of stoneware with all the advantages of earthenware. You can combine these two or do either separately. C/4,5,6 is the beginning of the stoneware range which is properly designated as c/4 to c/10. It is also just a little above the normal range of what we call earthenware which is ordinarily considered to be about c/06 to c/1 or 2. The c/4,5,6 middle range is the point at which real density and hardness begin to develop in stoneware clays, ball clays, most fireclays, and the plastic kaolins. Clay body formulation is easier and more logical when you can base the body on clays which are in their normal maturing ranges. A little more body flux, or the selection of a stronger body flux, is all you need to transform c/4,5,6 bodies into the rockhard, tough, durable, and non-absorbing bodies we associate with the c/9,10 range. The primary clay-body fluxes are feldspars, talcs, frits of various kinds, and iron oxide in various forms. Nepheline syenite, our lowest melting feldspar, is ideal for c/4,5,6 bodies. Any c/9,10 body can be dropped to c/4,5,6 with an increase in flux or by switching to nepheline syenite without losing any of the properties or characteristics it has at c/9,10. (Specific formulas will be given later.)

In this discussion I am making assumptions about clay bodies that I should explain in more detail. By clay bodies I mean plastic clay bodies, suited for normal wheel throwing and handbuilding uses. These bodies should have total shrinkage, from the plastic stage to the fired stage, of about 12 to 14%. They should also have an absorbency of under about 6%, which means they will not leak or absorb foods. They will be resistant to warping and cracking under normal drying and firing conditions. If properly designed there is no way you could tell a c/4,5,6 body from a c/9,10 body without putting it under a microscope or through some other scientific testing device. Up to this point I have been speaking of bringing c/9,10 bodies to the c/4,5,6 range. Now let's start with earthenware bodies and clays.

Natural earthenware clays are those clays which contain fairly high amounts of iron oxide in combination with fluxing agents like calcium oxide and sodium oxide. These clays are plastic and fire to the warm earthy colors of tan, orange, red, brown, etc., although their unfired colors may range from red to gray to green to blue to black. Their normal firing range is approximately c/06 to c/1,2. Some clays of this type can withstand firings of up to c/4,5,6 without bloating or melting or showing other signs of being overfired. We use three clays of this type at Alfred and they are easily available throughout the East. They are Redart, Ocmulgee, and Calvert. These clays make ideal body ingredients for c/4,5,6 bodies. They are fine grained, plastic, richly colored, and very dense when fired to c/4,5,6. One can find these "common" red iron bearing clays all over the U.S.A. Deposits of these clays are often found along stream beds, the edges of lakes, ponds, rivers, or in thick layers just below the surface sod and top soils. These earthenware clays can be the basis of c/4,5,6 bodies in the same way that stoneware clays can be used. In some earthenware clays you may need to use less body flux or to add some higher-firing clays in order to be certain that they will not overfire. One very simple body for c/4,5,6 is as follows:

Any stoneware clay	50%
Any earthenware clay	50%
	100%

This body has much to recommend it, although it could be improved. It is quite acceptable in plasticity and absorbency. I hope you will see that it is a logical bringing-together of the high fire and the low fire to the middle range. Naturally this body may need adjusting to the particular stoneware and earthenware clays you are using. If you have a very low maturing earthenware clay, you may need to use only 25 to 40% earthenware to 75 or 60% stoneware clay. In many c/4,5,6 bodies the iron oxide and other fluxes in the earth-

enware will take the place of an added body flux and give you the rich and warm colors of earthenware in combination with stoneware and other high-fire clays. C/4,5,6 oxidation allows you to take advantage of all the rich and full earthy color and plasticity of earthenware as well as the tougher, more durable and "toothy" qualities of stonewares. It is an ideal range for expressive clay bodies. One last point on body colors: high-firing reduction potters know that reduction firing at any temperature "cools" and grays down the fired color of their bodies. Iron oxide (Fe_2O_3) becomes FeO in reduction, which is dark gray to black in color and stays that color except for the very surface layer of exposed clay which reoxidizes (partially) back to Fe_2O_3 during the cooling cycle. I think many reduction potters would admit that they would very much like to retain the warm orange brown body colors that are so simple to get and all so characteristic in oxidation—the earthy colors in oxidation have more zest and brightness. Before going on to a discussion of c/4,5,6 glazes we should consider the question of white firing bodies. Here again we find c/4,5,6 oxidation an ideal range. We can capitalize on the plasticity and chalky whiteness of white earthenware in combination with the density, hardness, and translucency (if desired) of higher-fire china and porcelain. True porcelain is of course, by technical definition, reduction fired and cannot be authentically duplicated in oxidation. It should be said that c/4,5,6 reduction firing can exactly duplicate c/9,10 reduction fired porcelain, but that is another discussion. In my view there is no point whatever in firing to c/9,10 oxidation for white clay bodies (or stoneware either, for that matter). Everything you can possibly achieve at c/9,10 is possible at c/4,5,6. In fact, you can do all high-fire effects and much more at c/4,5,6 for less money and time.

As was the case with stoneware bodies, discussed earlier, making white bodies at c/4,5,6 is essentially a matter of increasing the amount of the primary body flux or changing to a stronger flux in order to get the equivalent density, hardness, and fired strength of c/9,10 china. If you are making a truly white body you will be restricted to the use of kaolins and ball clays—no other clays are white-firing. In many cases you need only add more flux or change to a stronger flux like nepheline syenite to transform the very same c/9,10 body to make it have the exact same properties as it had at c/9,10. If translucency is wanted, you may need to add some additional flux, as you would need to do at c/9,10. Actual whiteness will be improved at c/4,5,6 because the kaolins and ball clays have a natural tendency to darken or become off-white at higher temperatures.

You can also use higher percentages of the plastic kaolins and ball clays at c/4,5,6 because their fired shrinkage is lowered when they are fired at the beginning of their maturing range. For this reason c/4,5,6 white can be made more plastic and workable without risk of excessive warping and cracking. The main body fluxes for c/4,5,6 white bodies are nepheline syenite and talc. Where translucency is wanted it may be necessary to make additions of whiting ($CaCO_3$), or Gerstley borate (colemanite), or commercial frits to cause more glass to be formed in the body and therefore more translucency.

The basic fired effects of clay slips and engobes is essentially unaffected by different firing temperatures and atmospheres. All slips and engobes give specific effects which can all be duplicated at all temperatures and in oxidation or in reduction. The main and decided advantage of clay slips and engobes in oxidation is the expanded possibilities for color development. We all know that color is very much limited by reduction fire. This applies to clay bodies as well as to slips, engobes, and of course to glazes. The formulation of slips for c/4,5,6 follows the lines previously described for making white clay bodies. White base slips for c/4,5,6 are the same general composition as c/9,10 slips except that fluxes are either increased in amount or switched to smaller amounts of more powerful fluxes. Frits are commonly used for this purpose along with Gerstley borate and soluble materials like soda ash and borax. Color effects will be discussed in the next section in conjunction with glazes.

Glazes designed for this temperature and atmosphere have the decided advantage of a greatly increased color range. And as we have seen with clay bodies it is possible to utilize both high-fire stoneware effects and the nearly complete range of earthenware glazes. The material of prime importance for c/9,10 glazes is feldspar. Feldspars are natural materials that are nearly perfect glazes by themselves. They are mixtures high in silica, which is the main glass-forming oxide, along with alumina and small amounts of the important fluxing oxides of sodium, potassium, and calcium. Feldspars form the basis of all c/9,10 glazes. In the earthenware range the primary glaze ingredients are either frits, which are commercially blended low-fire glasses, or silicates formed with lead, or glasses formed by using B_2O_3 (boric oxide), another glass-forming oxide.

At c/4,5,6 most feldspars are slightly underfired and have not quite reached a complete glassy state. The exception here would be nepheline syenite which, as already mentioned, is quite fluid at this temperature. Most of the frits, the lead silicates, and borosilicates are overfired at c/4,5,6. But you need only combine the high-fire feldspars with the lower fired ingredients just mentioned to make excellent c/4,5,6 glazes. Of course, small additions of clay and flint may be needed to complete these glazes but that is true for high- and low-fire glazes as well. I don't want to seem to be oversimplifying, but I hope you can see the logic and the parallels between glaze making at c/4,5,6 with the approach already suggested for clay bodies. A simple example given here may illustrate my point. You have already seen that an acceptable body can be made by adding 50% stoneware clay to 50% earthenware clay. The following glaze is a c/4,5,6 glossy transparent:

Any feldspar	50%	(high-fire ingredient)
Gerstley borate (colemanite)	50%	(low-fire ingredient)
	100%	

You could work out a series of similar glazes using approximately 50% feldspar combined with approximately 50% frit. A simple line blend would be run between 100% spar and 100% frit, going 80/20, 70/30, 60/40, 50/50, 40/60, 30/70, 20/80 to 100%. The ideal melt would be found somewhere

in that blend. (Remember that small amounts of clay and flint may also be needed.) There are literally hundreds of different frits that could give an infinite variety of glazes, along with any one of several different feldspars. The particular choice of a feldspar and the particular choice of a frit are crucial to the development of specific colors. For example, copper blues require alkaline mixtures, uranium oxide reds require lead mixtures, and so on. What I am trying to illustrate is that c/4,5,6 glazes can result from fairly simple blending of the essential high-fire glaze-making ingredients with the essential ingredients of low-fire glazes. It is obviously not possible to go into extensive glaze theory and lectures in this article. My only aim is to give some insight into the question.

As I stated earlier the wide color range is the main advantage of c/4,5,6 oxidation over high fire. As for general glaze characteristics there is no difference between c/4,5,6 and c/9,10. You can make glazes with any degree of light transmission. From transparent, to translucent, to semiopaque, to opaque. You can make matt glazes, satin glazes, glossy glazes, and glazes of any other desired surface texture. You can make wood ash glazes at c/4,5,6 as well as Albany slip glazes, crystalline glazes, adventurine glazes, fired in lusters, salt glazing, soda glazing, residual firings, majolica glazes, and nearly any other effect that I can think of.

One reason that more color is possible at c/4,5,6 is that lead glazes can be used and they are the type of glazes that open up a whole range of color. More on this in a moment. In general, more color is possible because high-fire greatly limits the color range and reduction firing limits the color still more. Lead glazes should not be reduced and can not be used higher than c/6, where they volatilize away. C/4,5,6 is the safest temperature range for lead glazes, from the point of view of lead release. I am speaking of safe lead glazes. Lead glazes can be perfectly safe from causing lead poisoning, if the potter understands the theory. You may be surprised to know that most of the very finest translucent china dinnerware is glazed with lead-bearing glazes. Lead glaze colors have a special warmth. The soft honey amber colors from iron, lustrous yellow greens from copper, brilliant reds and oranges from uranium and selenium oxides, the sparkling crystals of adventurines, strong yellows from vanadium, burnt orange colors from antimony, rutile and iron oxide combinations, and many, many more. In fact, oxidation firing opens up the whole range of color from red to orange, to yellow, which except for copper reds is unobtainable in reduction firing. The most brilliant red and orange colors are low-fire oxidized colors, but many exotic and unusual colors can be developed at c/4,5,6 oxidation. You can get delicate pinks, crimsons, red violets, chartreuse, and many blended shades of reds to oranges to browns to yellows. I can't describe every color, but if a real color field is your desire, then oxidation is the way to fire.

If I have expressed my thoughts clearly then we can now all agree that c/4,5,6 oxidation firings will save us money. We will be able to use both high-fire stoneware and low-fire earthenware glazes and bodies. We will be able to use a much fuller range of colors than is possible at high fire. We will also be able to develop the tough and durable feldspathic glazes of c/9,10 at c/4,5,6. Our firings will be more reliable, more dependable, more predictable. We will be able to get more technical help from industry. We will have an easier time in locating a studio, because electric kilns are less trouble in this regard than fuel kilns. We will be safer, less polluting, and more ecological. Will that help convince you?

I wish I could end this paper by telling you that I have also made the conversion to c/4,5,6 oxidation. Maybe some day!

C/4,5,6 Oxidation Plasic Clay Bodies
(Throwing or Handbuilding)
All have approximately 12-14% shrinkage and 6% or less absorption

1. C/4,5,6, White Body

EPK (kaolin)	30
Tennessee #9 ball clay	30
Kingsley kaolin	10
Nepheline syenite	10
Talc	8
Flint	12
	100
+ Bentonite	2%

2. C/4,5,6, Off-White Stoneware

Goldart stoneware clay	20
Pine Lake fireclay	15
EPK (kaolin)	20
Tennessee #9 ball clay	20
Nepheline syenite	20
Flint	5
	100

3. C/4,5,6, Light Sandy-Tan Stoneware

Goldart stoneware clay	30
Pine Lake fireclay	15
Kentucky OM #4 ball clay	20
Ocmulgee red clay	25
Talc	10
	100

4. C/4,5,6 Medium Dark Red, Brown Cinnamon Stoneware

Goldart stoneware clay	20
Pine Lake fireclay	20
Ocmulgee red clay	35
PBX fireclay	20
Nepheline syenite	5
	100
Grog (20/30 mesh) if desired	6%

5. C/4,5,6 Sculpture Body

Low shrinkage. Not very plastic.
Good for large heavy pieces.

AP Green fireclay	30
Pine Lake fireclay	25
Ocmulgee red clay	15
PBX fireclay	15
Wollastonite	15
	100
+ Grog (20/30 mesh)	30%
Sand	15%

6. C/4,5,6 White China Translucent

(Not too plastic) C/6 for translucency

EPK (kaolin)	20
Grolleg china clay	20
Kentucky ball clay	5
Nepheline syenite	30
Gerstley borate	5
Flint	20
	100
+ Bentonite	3%

7. C/4,5,6 Dark Brown (Very Dark) Stoneware

Ocmulgee red clay	50
Pine Lake fireclay	15
Goldart stoneware clay	15
Kentucky OM #4 ball clay	10
Barnard clay	10
	100
+ Iron oxide	4%
Grog (20/30 mesh)	6%

66381

C/4,5,6 Oxidation White Base Slips (Engobes) for c/4,5,6

1. C/4,5,6, White Base Slip

EPK (kaolin)	30
Kentucky OM #4 ball clay	30
Nepheline syenite	10
Ferro frit #3124	10
Flint	10
Zircopax	5
Kingsley kaolin	10
	105

For wet-to-leatherhard application.
Color tests can be run to any white slip.

2. C/4,5,6 White Base Slip

Kingsley kaolin	10
Calcined kaolin	10
Kentucky OM #4 ball clay	10
Nepheline syenite	15
Ferro frit #3124	10
Flint	25
Borax	5
Zircopax	15
	100

For dry-to-bisque application.

3. C/4,5,6 Wood Ash Glaze

Wood ash (sifted)	40
Nepheline syenite	30
Talc	15
PBX fireclay (Valentine)	15
	100

Should be strong fluxing type ash, like elm, etc.

4. C/4,5,6 Dark Slip

Albany slip clay	50
Barnard clay	35
Gerstley borate	15
	100

Use under glazes.
Will work nicely coming up through glazes
for dark iron texture.

Some Glazes for C/4,5,6, Oxidation

Not all have the full range of 4,5,6. All should work at c/5, some may be best at c/4,5, some at c/5,6.

1. C/5,6 Stone Matt, Whitish Base

Nepheline syenite	50
Barium carbonate	10
Ferro frit #3124	5
Whiting	5
Lithium carbonate	5
EPK (kaolin)	10
Flint	15
	100

Good matt glaze for color, run tests with copper, iron, chrome, etc.
3% iron oxide gives yellow green.

2. C/5,6 Albany Slip Glaze

Albany slip clay	72
Barium carbonate	10
Cryolite	6
Gerstley borate	12
	100

Smooth matt, yellow, orange brown.

3. C/5,6 Alkaline Matt

Base glaze is a whitish, stony point matt.

Nepheline syenite	30
Ferro frit #3110	25
Barium carbonate	10
Whiting	15
EPK (kaolin)	10
Flint	10
	100

1. 1% copper carb—light blue
2. 5% iron oxide—yellow with orange greenish streaks.
3. 1% manganese dioxide—pinkish purple.

4. C/5,6 "Weird" Matt, Speckled

Gerstley borate	50.00
Talc	35.00
Rutile	15.00
Granular ilmenite	.25%
	100.25

Yellow, orange, tannish, use thick and thin

5. C/5,6 "Safe" Raw Lead

Glossy, transparent, bright, good glaze.

White lead	26
Custer feldspar	23
Whiting	10
Zinc oxide	6
Flint	29
Talc	1
EPK (kaolin)	5
	100

Add 10% Zircopax for whitish opaque.

6. C/4,5,6 Leadless, Glossy Transparent

Base glaze.

Kona F/4 feldspar	35
Gerstley borate	23
Barium carbonate	8
Whiting	8
EPK (kaolin)	8
Flint	18
	100

1% copper carb.—blue/green.

7. C/5,6 Barium Stone Matt

Very good for intense color, particularly over a white body.

Nepheline syenite	60
Barium carbonate	24
Lithium carbonate	5
EPK (kaolin)	6
Flint	5
	100

1. 3% copper carb—very strong blue.
2. 2% iron oxide—brownish, yellow w/green.
3. 1% chrome oxide—yellow green.
4. 6% Mason's vanadium stain—yellow (bright).
5. ½% manganese dioxide—pinkish violet.

8. C/5,6 Satin Matt, Smooth Whitish

Nepheline syenite	25
Ferro frit #3124	25
Whiting	20
EPK (kaolin)	15
Flint	15
	100

Interesting glaze for color. Run tests.

9. C/5,6 Smooth Satin Matt Glaze

Nepheline syenite	45
Whiting	18
EPK (kaolin)	20
Zinc oxide	12
Flint	5
	100

Color may be added to this base.

TRIAXIAL BLEND

by Nan McKinnell

Do you need a lift out of the rut of your tired old glaze? "But," you say, "I don't know enough about glaze calculation to attack the problem." Then you are just the one to try triaxial blends. You will certainly gain some new glazes as well as some knowledge about glaze materials and reactions at the same time. You may wish to call it a scientific method (it's used in industry) or a calculated risk or just a good way to gamble. No matter, you'll have some winnings that will make it worth the time and trouble. This brief article will give only a simplified introduction to the vast possibilities of the triaxial. (See end of chapter for other references.)

The three sides of the triaxial are each simple line blends. The results inside the triangle are blends (or proportions) of all three corners (see diagram). Of course you may use the triaxial in blending for clay bodies and engobes as well as glazes. You may add color or change the colors of your favorite glazes, or make changes in your glazes by adding other materials.

For finer blending increase number of divisions of your triaxial. The 21 points we will use here are generally adequate.

The wet blend method is probably the fastest and easiest and the one we will use here. You may also wish to try the dry blend or the weighed blend for extremely accurate results in certain instances, but it takes much more time.

Follow the directions and diagram carefully.

1. Shards: Unless you are testing for once-fired ware you must have 21 bisque fired shards for each kind of clay (better make extras—some always get broken). Remember that different clay bodies affect the glaze results, sometimes drastically, due to interfacial reaction between the glaze and the clay body. For high temperatures try your regular stoneware body (either dark and spotty or light) and perhaps a porcelain body. For earthenware firings use a dark, red brown, coarse body and a light finer body. To make thrown shards, use plaster or other bats, throw several pie-shaped pieces, 5'' or 6'' in diameter, with turned-up edges and good rims. Put some sgraffito lines and some texture on both horizontal and vertical surfaces. When firm, slice each pie into eight wedges. On the underside scratch the name or number of the clay body. For additional information, put some brush lines of your favorite colored engobes on the back vertical side. Or you may wish to make some slabs and cut them into strips about 1''x3''; press or sgraffito some textures, blend one-third of the slab up into a vertical position, smooth the edges, and continue as above.

2. On a large square of wrapping paper (18'' or 20'' at least) lay out your triaxial diagram (just as in the original diagram only on a much larger scale). Number medium-sized paper cups or plastic cocktail cups from 1 to 21 and place them on the diagram.

3. Choose a glaze or a fusible clay, a frit or other special ceramic concoction for each of the three corners (A, B, C)

or numbers 1, 16, and 21. "But," you say, "How do I know what to choose?" One way to choose is to use glazes that are already mixed up. "Here is a bad one—runs too much and is a terribly strong blue. I'll try that for glaze A and perhaps by blending with the others I'll have something better. Here is one that's off-white, matt in texture and a little too dry: glaze B. Now for C—what about this lower temperature glaze or ingredient or chemical? Would I dare? (Great idea really.) Or, here's that stuff I dug in the mountains. It's almost a glaze—a little too bubbly and dark—(another good idea)—or, how about a frit?" (Now make up your mind, they are all good ideas—gamble a little.) You do not have to have good glazes on the corners. Use some bad ones. Also, at least one of your corners can have a much lower temperature glaze, such as a c/4 or c/6 in a c/10 triaxial.

4. Number the bottoms of the fired shards from 1 to 21 as shown in the diagram. Use a ceramic pencil and press hard or, better still, use a good slip or engobe base plus several oxides for strong marking color. Here is a formula if you don't have one.

Kaolin	20 grams
OM Kentucky #4 ball clay	20
Nepheline syenite	25
Flint	30
Borax	5
	100
	(base engobe)
Plus	
Iron oxide	75 grams
Cobalt carbonate	5
Manganese dioxide	5

Wet to a medium cream consistency, screen, and apply with a small brush. (Store in closed jar for future use.) Wax bottom after marking, place in correct order on your wrapping-paper chart.

5. If you are choosing unmixed glazes from your notebook or other references, weigh about 500 grams for each of the corner glazes, stir, wet to a thick cream consistency, screen through a 60- or 80-mesh screen. If you are careful, as you wash the glaze from the screen and container you'll add just enough water to thin the glaze to a good dipping and pouring consistency. Don't get it too thin. Each of the three glazes should be approximately the same consistency. For your measuring device you might use a small lotion bottle cap or a quart bottle soft drink cap (holding about 1½ to 2 teaspoons when full). Measure each of your prepared glazes into your numbered cups according to the amounts on your diagram. Put in all the A quantities first, then the Bs and Cs to save confusion or errors and to save washing your measuring device so often. Stir each wet mixture well.

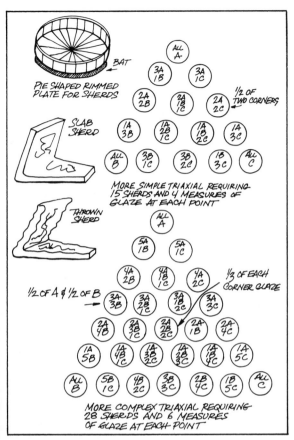

PIE SHAPED RIMMED PLATE FOR SHERDS

SLAB SHERD

THROWN SHERD

BAT

ALL A

3A 1B   3A 1C

2A 2B   2A 1B 1C   2A 2C   ½ OF TWO CORNERS

1A 3B   1A 2B 1C   1A 1B 2C   1A 3C

ALL B   3B 1C   3B 2C   1B 3C   ALL C

MORE SIMPLE TRIAXIAL REQUIRING 15 SHERDS AND 4 MEASURES OF GLAZE AT EACH POINT

ALL A

5A 1B   5A 1C

4A 2B   4A 1B 1C   4A 2C   ⅓ OF EACH CORNER GLAZE

½ OF A & ½ OF B →

3A 3B   3A 2B 1C   3A 1B 2C   3A 3C

2A 4B   2A 3B 1C   2A 2B 2C   2A 1B   2A 4C

1A 5B   1A 4B 1C   1A 3B 2C   1A 2B 3C   1A 1B 4C   1A 5C

ALL B   5B 1C   4B 2C   3B 3C   2B 4C   1B 5C   ALL C

MORE COMPLEX TRIAXIAL REQUIRING 28 SHERDS AND 6 MEASURES OF GLAZE AT EACH POINT

or as close as possible within a percent or so. Example: if your formula totals 252 parts as glaze B does, divide each ingredient by the total number of parts (252 in this case) and multiply by 100 to get correct percentage so that the total equals 100% or near that, as follows:

Cornwall stone
$$187.5 \div 252 = .744 \times 100 = 74.4$$
Kaolin
$$32.5 \div 252 = .128 \times 100 = 12.9$$
Whiting
$$23.5 \div 252 = .0932 \times 100 = 9.32$$
Dolomite
$$7.25 \div 252 = .0287 \times 100 = 2.87$$
Cobalt carbonate
$$1.25 \div 252 = .0049 \times 100 = \underline{.49}$$
$$99.98$$

Step 2. Suppose glaze 9 is the best on your triaxial. It says on the diagram it has 2 parts of A, 2 parts of C, and 1 part of B. So multiply each ingredient in A and C by 2 and add to the ingredients in B, lumping together the like materials. Your total should be close to 500. Now divide each material by 5 and you should get a 100% (or very close) formula for your chosen glaze. Weigh it up and try it on a small pot, and see how close it compares with the original glaze 9 test.

10. Here are examples of other possible experiments with triaxial blends:

A. For adding more color to your favorite white or clear glaze: mix glaze A—your formula; glaze B—your formula + 1% cobalt carbonate; and glaze C—your formula + 4% tin oxide and 4% copper carbonate. Your B corner will probably be a strong blue. Your C corner could be red in reduction firing and blue green in oxidizing firing. Results from your triaxial blend could range from some purples and pinks and soft blues in reduction to a variety of blues, blue greens, and greens in oxidation. This is just one example. Now you try some others such as iron, rutile, chrome, nickel, opacifiers, commercial stains, powdered granite, a red burning clay, and so on.

B. A fine way to learn about various glaze materials is to add them to any glaze (it can be scrap glaze if you have accumulated some extra). Use the chosen glaze straight on corner A, and add a different material to each of the other corners, after you have done some reference reading about those materials (see below). Some suggestions might be an addition of 10% to 30% of one of the following: talc, feldspar, Cornwall stone, Gerstley borate, whiting, barium carbonate, or others. It doesn't hurt to have extremes at the corners. You'll have an interesting picture to study after firing.

Doing the first triaxial is the most time consuming. After that, ideas for others begin to pop into your mind and once you know all of the steps, the next triaxials will become easier. Just think, if you use half a day each month for a new triaxial blend, you will soon be the envy of all your potting friends with your beautiful new glazes. And more importantly, if you carefully study the picture from each test you will begin to gain necessary knowledge about your materials.

6. Dip the shards in once—to cover vertical back, front, and horizontal surfaces. Let dry a moment, then dip about a third of each shard again (both horizontal and vertical surfaces) for a partial, double thickness area. (Some glazes are better thicker and some thinner—and you won't know until firing tests are made comparing side-by-side on both the shards and later on test bowls.) Wipe bottoms with wet natural sponge to remove droplets of glaze on the waxed surface. Place on board ready for eventual loading into one particular kiln area between your pots (not all over the kiln unless your kiln fires very evenly). Keep your variables to a minimum.

7. Save the left-over mixtures in their cups. You may wish to do additional blending or use some of the best results on small test pots later. If you throw them away, it's much more difficult to make confirmation check tests subsequent to the initial firing. All reduction firings vary.

8. Place your glaze fired test shards on a white painted plywood board or heavy white cardboard following your triaxial diagram as a guide. Glue into place for future reference. Compare and choose the best glazes. Work out your formulas for each of them. Weigh up and do first testing on less desirable small pots, or small test pots made for that purpose—out of each type of clay.

9. To obtain a formula for any glaze of your choice:
Step 1. Have each corner glaze formula converted to 100%

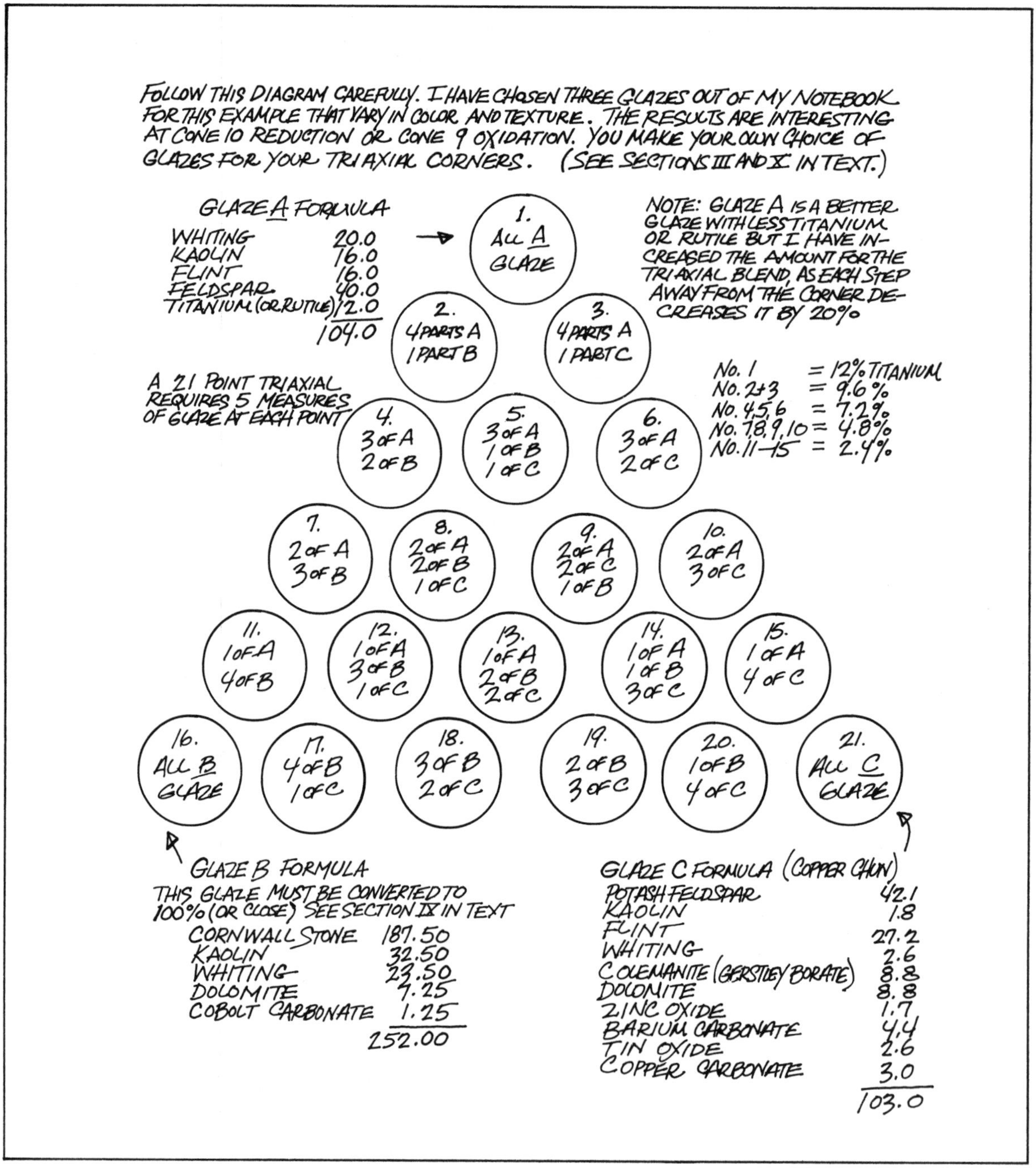

FOLLOW THIS DIAGRAM CAREFULLY. I HAVE CHOSEN THREE GLAZES OUT OF MY NOTEBOOK FOR THIS EXAMPLE THAT VARY IN COLOR AND TEXTURE. THE RESULTS ARE INTERESTING AT CONE 10 REDUCTION OR CONE 9 OXIDATION. YOU MAKE YOUR OWN CHOICE OF GLAZES FOR YOUR TRIAXIAL CORNERS. (SEE SECTIONS III AND X IN TEXT.)

GLAZE A FORMULA

WHITING	20.0
KAOLIN	16.0
FLINT	16.0
FELDSPAR	40.0
TITANIUM (OR RUTILE)	12.0
	104.0

NOTE: GLAZE A IS A BETTER GLAZE WITH LESS TITANIUM OR RUTILE BUT I HAVE INCREASED THE AMOUNT FOR THE TRIAXIAL BLEND, AS EACH STEP AWAY FROM THE CORNER DECREASES IT BY 20%

1. ALL A GLAZE

2. 4 PARTS A 1 PART B

3. 4 PARTS A 1 PART C

A 21 POINT TRIAXIAL REQUIRES 5 MEASURES OF GLAZE AT EACH POINT

4. 3 OF A 2 OF B

5. 3 OF A 1 OF B 1 OF C

6. 3 OF A 2 OF C

No. 1 = 12% TITANIUM
No. 2+3 = 9.6%
No. 4,5,6 = 7.2%
No. 7,8,9,10 = 4.8%
No. 11–15 = 2.4%

7. 2 OF A 3 OF B

8. 2 OF A 2 OF B 1 OF C

9. 2 OF A 2 OF C 1 OF B

10. 2 OF A 3 OF C

11. 1 OF A 4 OF B

12. 1 OF A 3 OF B 1 OF C

13. 1 OF A 2 OF B 2 OF C

14. 1 OF A 1 OF B 3 OF C

15. 1 OF A 4 OF C

16. ALL B GLAZE

17. 4 OF B 1 OF C

18. 3 OF B 2 OF C

19. 2 OF B 3 OF C

20. 1 OF B 4 OF C

21. ALL C GLAZE

GLAZE B FORMULA
THIS GLAZE MUST BE CONVERTED TO 100% (OR CLOSE) SEE SECTION IX IN TEXT

CORNWALL STONE	187.50
KAOLIN	32.50
WHITING	23.50
DOLOMITE	7.25
COBOLT CARBONATE	1.25
	252.00

GLAZE C FORMULA (COPPER CHUN)

POTASH FELDSPAR	42.1
KAOLIN	1.8
FLINT	27.2
WHITING	2.6
COLEMANITE (GERSTLEY BORATE)	8.8
DOLOMITE	8.8
ZINC OXIDE	1.7
BARIUM CARBONATE	4.4
TIN OXIDE	2.6
COPPER CARBONATE	3.0
	103.0

References

Ceramics Industry Magazine. January issue. 1976 Order from Ceramics Industry, 270 St. Paul St., Denver, CO 80206, about $3.00.

Hamer, Frank. The Potter's Dictionary of Materials & Techniques. Watson-Guptill Publications, New York; Pitman Publishing, London.

Cardew, Michael. Pioneer Pottery. St. Martin's Press, New York, 1969.

Reeve, John. A Potter's Way to Understand Glazes, Book One.

ONE-FIRE GLAZING

by Dennis Parks

I hate bisque firings. Always have. A real pain-in-the-ass. Carrying pots, loading, firing, unloading, carrying pots. And what have you got? Again your studio is full of unglazed pottery. When I used to get around to applying glaze to the bisque I would forget how I had planned to decorate them; when they were finally out of the kiln, I couldn't recall what I was thinking about when I made them. I was more interested in what had just come off the wheel. To fit one bisque load of pots back in the kiln would take me at least two more labor cycles of carrying, stacking, loading, and firing.

My first exposure to one-fire glazing came in 1965. I was back in school, studying with Paul Soldner. We built a salt kiln, and at that time no one around Southern California was salting. We had to follow the few how-to hints we could find in history books. From reading, it appeared that the oldtimers all once-fired their saltware, so we did too, using for inside glazes the regular bisque glazes that happened to be around the studio. One worked fairly well, and the others all crawled.

What I learned was: First, one-firing worked! All the pieces didn't crack when I wet them with glaze. In the kiln they matured and after firing looked as good as twice-fired pots with half the work, or almost. Second, the formula of the glaze that adhered had a larger proportion of clay than did the glazes that crawled. Third, I liked the process. The immediacy. The intimacy of raw clay and glaze bond. The challenge of fragility. The finality of application with no erasures.

For the next two years I did nothing but salt glazing. I was obsessed with this "new" technique. When hired to set up a studio and teach ceramics at Knox College, I taught only what I was excited about. Those students learned only one-fire salt glazing for those two years. In retrospect I have been embarrassed at having given them such a specialized view of ceramics, though a few did go on to graduate school and apparently quickly picked up the other ways of firing.

About the time I left Illinois, for California and Nevada, my hell-bent faith in the salt processes was being eroded by having observed the relentless destructiveness of the vapor on a kiln. What with the short kiln life span and the expense of replacing shelves, the price looked too high if I had to reach into my own pocket instead of dipping into a departmental budget.

I decided to return to the higher contrasts: the rough textures, the definitions, the crisp outlines, the solid colors of regular, plain, unsalted stoneware. But at the same time, rekindling old interests, I did not want to be obliged to again pick up the burden of bisque firing.

For the last decade my own work has been almost exclusively one-fire c/10 stoneware. As with other technical/aesthetic tools, you never seem to know all the answers, but with practice, fits, and starts, you learn most of the questions.

The Process and Principles

When my shelves are filled with bone-dry pieces, I get ready to glaze. Dust or fingerprints have never caused the glazes to crawl. Half the time I blow the dust off, but if I happen to have a cigar stuck in my mouth, I don't bother.

Mix your glazes slightly thinner than for those you apply to bisque ware. If the glaze needs a thicker skin, develop the technique of the quick double dip. A syrupy mixture wants to destroy your work, dissolving lips and cracking bottoms.

In one-fire glazing you must remain aware that the piece you are applying glaze to has not been preshrunk and petrified in a bisque firing. The piece of clay that you are holding in your hand, contemplating glazing, is alive, delicate and fragile. Raw clay expands in glazing.

When you pour the liquid glaze into your piece, slosh it around and empty it out. The inside wall has absorbed all of the moisture. The clay quite naturally begins to expand in all directions exerting pressure against the dry outer wall. If, without haste or delay, you apply a wet glaze to the outside, this surface will soften slightly and begin an equalizing expansion. Even only partially glazing the outside serves the purpose.

If the pot is to be glazed only on the inside, the outside should be sponged with water or dipped briefly into a bucket of water. This can be done immediately before or after pouring the interior glaze.

Do not glaze on the assembly line. A potter/friend who was unaccustomed to one-firing set out six pitchers that he wished to glaze similarly. He stirred up the glaze for the inside, and in sequence poured all six. Then he located the glaze in which he planned to dip the outside. By the time he got the lumps out and reached for the first pitcher, he saw that he now had 12 half-pitchers on the ware board. Glaze only one piece at a time.

After you have applied a one-fire glaze, you have committed that piece. There is the devil to pay if you try removing a glaze once applied. Water, steelwool, sandpaper, anything you use sadly deteriorates the surface of the clay and threatens the life of the piece. There is no erasing. Think, do it, and fire it. This builds character in potters. The absence of a second chance at best gives an immediacy and dignity to one-fire ware.

I have found the technique of one-firing does not force any change in the shapes I make, or in wall thickness, or size of feet. Though as a matter of personal aesthetics (read: habit) I usually throw healthy lips and trim generous feet. Probably a good strong lip does cut down on the chance of rims cracking and a foot that you can grip facilitates glazing, even with bisque ware.

Until the pieces are unloaded from the kiln they are green and fragile. They are particularly vulnerable immediately after glazing when they still retain this added moisture. Lips, handles, and spouts should not be touched. I usually delay loading the kiln for a day after glazing, not only for safety in handling, but also to cut down the danger of steam forming in the clay and exploding.

Dusting is another application technique that is natural to one-fire pottery. This adds no water to the clay. A 50- or 75-mesh screen is your tool. If there is much granular refractory material in your "dust," the smaller mesh is advisable.

Some dust glazes I use include sagebrush ash, aspen ash, eucalyptus ash, mixed citrus wood ash, and Portland cement. Sagebrush ash is the only one that melts into a serviceable, bright, utilitarian glaze. The others display varying degrees of mattness. Of course you can always use any standard, one-fire glaze in powder form.

Flat objects such as plates are best suited to dust glazes. The major limitation is that the particles rain straight down, lodging only on relatively flat or gently sloping surfaces, these being the lips, shoulders, and interior bases of traditional shapes. You may want to dust, for example, an ash on top of a normally applied glaze as an enrichment. If you do this while the original glaze is still moist, you can overcome the gravitational problem.

Medieval potters dusted powdered galena through a cloth sack onto their wet pots straight off the wheel. These potters often died young. Just don't dust poisonous powders. Sift glazes only in a well-ventilated area or wear a mask, or do both.

Loading the one-fire kiln is about the same as loading a glaze kiln with bisque ware. One exception is large plates. Because the total fired shrinkage takes place in one setting, the pots must retract further than in the accustomed bisque or glaze firings. Plates, being mostly all bottom, are the likeliest to get hooked on a rough kiln shelf. I facilitate their movement in shrinkage by sprinkling a thin layer of alumina on the shelf, being careful not to rain any on the pots below. These refractory particles act as hundreds of ball bearings moving with the pot. For the same reason you may also wish to use alumina under any heavy piece with a large circumference. I use alumina oxide (calcined), 200 mesh, from Westwood Ceramics, City of Industry, CA 91744.

In firing your kiln treat the warm-up and the early stages the same as you would in bisque; once it reaches red heat, treat as a glaze kiln. Our main kiln here is 125 cubic feet, oil-fired, sprung arch, downdraft, with soft brick inside and earthen bricks outside. The average cycle takes 20 hours and uses about 15 gallons of #2 diesel and 60 gallons of drain oil.

This kiln was constructed in 1973 with Joe Soldate, Barbara Chestnutt, and Cecilia Lanahan. To keep expenses down we bought firebrick only for the inside wall. Hard brick (Kaiser Morex 2800) were laid up to one course about the burner ports, and also in the sub floor and stacking floor. The rest of the interior wall, the arch and the door were constructed with insulation bricks (Babcock & Wilcox K-28). The decision to use soft brick was made solely to cut

down on the exorbitant freight costs of hard brick. (My prejudice has always been towards the heat-retentive qualities of hard brick.)

We pressed out earthen bricks for the exterior courses with a Cinva-Ram Block Press. This had been purchased from Bellows-Valvair, 200 W. Exchange Street, Akron, OH 44309, for $175, cheap when you figure we saved close to $400 just on this one kiln. These machines have been used extensively throughout the world by the Peace Corps.

Our kiln required about 460 earthen bricks (3¾'' x 5½'' x 11½''), which we made by combining one part cement to twelve parts dirt. The walls have withstood a hard winter of rain, sleet, snow, -0°F temperatures, and 50 mph winds on the outside and repeated c/10 firings in the inside with no visible deterioration. I cannot see why I would ever build a kiln any other way.

The Materials

For one-fire glazing I have used several different clay bodies, changing details in the formulas as dictated by: casseroles, sculpture, color, proximity to supply, and so on. But I have never had any difficulty in relating the glaze to the changing clay materials. Here are four common clay mixes I presently use:

All-purpose Buff Stoneware

Lincoln fireclay	100 lbs.
Kentucky OM #4 ball clay	50
Feldspar	15
Silica	10
Grog (30/60)	25

plus a volume of Mica equal to the grog.

White Stoneware

Lincoln fireclay	50 lbs.
Kentucky OM #4 ball clay	50
Feldspar	50
Silica	50
Grog (30/60)	10

plus Mica

Porcelain

Kaolin	50 lbs.
Kentucky ball clay	50
Feldspar	50
Silica	50
Grog (30/60)	10

plus Mica

Salt Clay

Lincoln fireclay	100 lbs.
Kentucky OM #4 ball clay	50
Feldspar	25
Silica	20
Magnesium carbonate	5
Sand (30/60)	20

plus Mica

The glaze recipes listed here should be regarded as takeoff points. With a few experiments, similar simple glazes can be found everywhere.

I throw in at least a handful of dextrine per gallon of glaze. This helps to counter the tendency of high clay glazes to lift when you decorate with oxides on their surface. Use more in ash glazes, for here the dextrine keeps the heavy particles in solution, and drys to form a skin that keeps the ash glued to the pot.

The colors referred to can be expected on a buff stoneware. They are lighter and brighter on white bodies, with the B.P.W. appearing clear.

B.P.W. Gloss Best Possible (Parks) Oatmeal White c/10

EPK (kaolin)	1 lb.
Kentucky ball clay	1
Nepheline syenite	5
Silica	1
Gerstley borate	1
Talc	1
Zinc	0.15

This glaze evolved after using the porcelain body as an engobe in salt firing.

B.P.W. Semimatt

Kaolin	1 lb.
Ball clay	1
Nepheline syenite	5
Silica	1
Gerstley borate	1
Whiting	1

B.P.W. Matt
Double whiting in semimatt recipe

Phillips Sand Glaze

A western Albany slip c/10
Outside of town here, on the slope of Mt. Blitzen, about a mile west of Hill '76 is the abandoned Phillips Gold Mine. When their crushers were active, tons of earth and rock were reduced to sand in the process of extracting the gold. This sand I use as a raw material.

Phillips sand	10 parts by measure
Dolomite	1 part

add water and mill from four to ten hours until smooth.

Sagebrush Ash Glaze

Dark Honey c/10
At the south end of Main Street, below the pilings of the old Dexter Mill is a mound of sagebrush ash dating from just after the turn of the century. This was the only fuel to smelt

the ore. Up-wind on the pile, I sift a quantity of ash through a window screen into a box.

Sagebrush ash	1 part by measure

Add water and mill from four to ten hours. Before using, it is essential to dump in enough dextrine to keep the mixture in solution.

Cement Glaze

A broken surface, matt green c/10
Over by the Navajo Mine there is a heap of low-fire, bluish white clay, full of quartz, that looks like a beached Moby Dick when you drive up to it. I slake some of this down, run it through a 30-mesh screen, then dry and powder the resultant slurry.

Moby Dick clay	2 parts by measure
Sagebrush ash	1 part
Portland cement	1 part

Add water and freeze solid to prevent the glaze from setting up. Thaw and mill for four to ten hours.

Recently I have had very good luck converting favorite biscuit glaze recipes that students bring with them by simply adding between 3 and 5% bentonite. For a potter trying to glaze for the first time this one-fire seems to be a logical starting point.

ASH GLAZES

by Jack O'Leary

I started working with wood ash glazes about 12 years ago because I had an abundant supply from our three wood burning stoves. The use of wood ash in glazes is not a new method as all potters know, but its preparation is often misunderstood and its compatibility with one-firing not widely known. The glaze formulas included in this article are the ones with which I have had the most success for the past 10 years. In most of these glazes I have used only elm, birch, or hickory as we have a sufficient quantity available to reproduce similar effects. Our best source for hickory ash comes from a small commercial cheese factory where they smoke cheese with hickory sawdust.

1. Tariki Glaze

Wood ash	50%	16 Mesh
Kaolin	50%	

2. Tariki Glaze

Wood ash	20%	
Feldspar	45%	48 Mesh
Dolomite	15%	
Kaolin	20%	

3. Tariki Glaze

Wood ash	20%	
Albany slip	45%	
Whiting	10%	16 Mesh
Feldspar	15%	
Red iron oxide	10%	

4. Tariki Glaze

Wood ash	20%	
Feldspar	35%	
Kaolin	15%	48 Mesh
Flint	25%	
Dolomite	5%	
Tin oxide	3%	
Red iron oxide	1-3%	

Tariki Stoneware Clay—for throwing one-fired ash glazed pots

Missouri fireclay	35%
Jordan clay	40%
Ball clay	25%
Grog added up to	10%

1. Tariki Glaze

This glaze is really a slip glaze. It should always be applied shortly after trimming while the pots are still in the green state. I enjoy using a broad brush with which to apply the glaze. The slip glaze should be thick, not too thin. It works best on pots and slab forms to be used outdoors. The finished color is sand-toned, warm like the earth. It gives me a feeling of antiquity.

2. Tariki Glaze

This one has a range of c/8-10, and is best in reduction firings. The pots should all be bone dry, and dipping or pouring the glaze works best. With large platters or bowls, I have always screened the glaze on dry without adding water; this avoids cracking. It gives the effect of spraying but is far more economical, as there is little waste. After firing, the glaze is a warm matt with a yellowish tone. Good for production pots. Engobes may be used underneath this glaze with excellent results. Oxides may be added, but I generally use no more than 2 to 3% of any oxide as it will tend to lose its matt quality. Tariki Glaze 3 works well with glaze, giving slight contrasts for framing effects, particularly on lips of pots.

3. Tariki Glaze

This glaze is typical of many iron glazes that potters use today. It usually gives a matt finish at c/8 to 9, with normal slow cooling of the kiln. With fast cooling, I find the glaze will tend to be glossy and more like an oil-spot glaze.
It should be applied on bone-dry pots for best results. I use 16-mesh screen on the ash, as this gives a better textural break in the glaze.
Michigan slip or Barnard clay can be substituted for Albany, giving a much duller surface.
Tariki glaze 3 works well under glaze 4 as it tends to pick up color and depth. Also excellent with wax resist.

4. Tariki Glaze

This is a good, working glaze at c/8 to 10. Development of celadon is excellent in our kiln. I like to use this glaze over 3, in a combination of overlapping and wax resist.

Notes On Using Ash Glazes For Single Firing: Wood ash glazes and single firing are a natural combination. The process is uncomplicated, time saving and inexpensive, and the results satisfying. There are, however, some variables which I think should be mentioned.
• In preparing wood ash for glazes, I feel it is not necessary to wash the ash or even to remove the charcoal. All we do is sift the ash dry through regular 16-mesh window screening. For certain matt glazes, I like to sift through a 48-mesh screen, which helps to give a smoother surface to the glaze. Retaining the charcoal in the glaze is important, I think, as it aids in the reduction. The slight pockets left in the glaze as the charcoal burns out will just smooth over later as the glaze begins to melt.
• As all ashes have soluble salts, I try to avoid stirring the mess with my hands. Use a wooden stick. (We lost a good

apprentice once this way—but it made a good glaze anyway.)
• There is a natural tendency for some of these glazes to flake. We use Irish moss to help get around this problem.
• I find that I have to be more aware of my glaze technique with raw pots than with bisque pots. For instance, in glazing large pots for single firing, there are many limitations. For large bowls and platters it is easier to dry screen the glaze on without introducing water. Dusting the dry glaze on through a screen is really an excellent technique for the studio potter. On large coil or slab pots I enjoy using a slip glaze such as Tariki 1, as it allows the glaze to be painted on while I am still building the pot.
• Time and cost are obviously important factors for the studio potter. Large pots are particularly costly to make through the bisque process. By single firing, however, the potter can save considerable hassle and the end result can be wholly satisfactory.

RAKU REDUCTION

by Robert Piepenburg

Reduction as associated with raku pottery is usually thought of as a post-firing treatment; the glazed or unglazed pottery is put into an oxygen-poor atmosphere after it has been fired and removed, while still glowing hot, from the kiln. Frequently, however, such reduction procedures are too weak or too late for many glazes, especially those bearing copper, to properly respond.

If glaze reduction after the firing is to be effective the pottery should be fired first in a partially reduced atmosphere within the kiln.

In theory and practice the reduction firing of raku varies little from stoneware glaze reduction and the reduction firing of high-temperature kilns. Time and temperatures are the differences.

Raku pottery fired in electric kilns spends no time in reduction save for the 10 or 15 minutes of reduction spent in an enclosed container after the firing. The reduction results, nevertheless, can be quite handsome, especially if the ware is fired to temperatures higher than required and if it is placed in a strong reducing atmosphere formed by a dense combustible such as dry sawdust upon immediate removal from the kiln. The risk, however, is that the glazed surface may be badly pitted or full of unwanted impressions formed when the combustibles came into contact with the still molten glaze.

Glaze ware fired in gas kilns, on the other hand, can be made to undergo a partial or a heavy reduction while being fired in the kiln. When removed, noticeable chemical changes will already be apparent in some glazes. The post-firing reduction in an enclosed container is still employed for the sake of body reduction and additional glaze effects, but the ware need not be tightly buried in sawdust. A looser combustible such as dry straw or hay can be used.

Many rakuists refer to any reduction in the kiln as primary reduction and to post-firing reduction in an air-tight chamber containing dry combustibles as secondary reduction. Post firing or secondary reduction is an American technique that only goes back in time 13 or 14 years and has no precedent in the traditional raku of Japan.

Because electric kilns utilize electrical resistance instead of oxygen to produce heat, primary reduction can only occur in fuel-burning kilns where combustion requires oxygen. Where there is a sufficient supply of oxygen available during combustion to combine with free carbon, the kiln atmosphere is in a state of oxidation and the flame coming from the burner will appear very strong and blue, burning very clean and hot. Fuel-burning raku kilns are most effectively fired under oxidation until the maturing temperature of the glaze is approached. As the glaze firing temperature is reached the kiln's atmosphere may be changed to a full or partial state of reduction by cutting back the supply of oxygen.

Perhaps the best way to reduce a raku kiln is through the

operation of a damper, which can simply be a piece of broken kiln shelf or brick placed over the flue opening to interrupt the updraft circulation responsible for the brisk draw of oxygen through the kiln. As the flue opening is restricted, back pressure builds up within the kiln, causing flame to appear at the burner port, at the spy hole or from chinks in the kiln wall. The flame coming from the burner will now be very lazy and yellow, burning dirty and cold. The accompanying smoke is from hot, unburned carbon existing within the kiln. If the reduction results appear inadequate with the damper the primary air supply for the burner can also be cut back. The secondary air supply may also be cut back by diminishing the open area of the burner port. Small dry twigs may periodically be injected at the burner port for additional reduction. The result should be a reducing atmosphere within the kiln where oxygen is in such short supply that it is robbed from the metallic oxides in glazes that contain it as an element, reducing them to their metallic base colors.

The firing and reducing of raku kilns is ultimately a process of intuitive responses to ourselves, our experiences, our rhythms, our super-senses. When and how much to reduce has to be a matter of personal reaction and timing. The beauty and joy of the raku firing is that it demands total involvement with and attention to the moment—the now. If the rakuist were not in an extended state of harmony with the forces at hand he might, for example, find the pots covered with a black carbon soot when the kiln was opened. Fortunately, this would not be an irrecoverable mistake as the soot on the overreduced ware can simply be burned off in a minute or two by reoxidizing the kiln's interior.

Good primary reduction results are often obtained by partially reducing the glaze after the surface bubbling has ceased and then allowing one or two minutes of heavy reduction after the glaze has fully matured. The heavy reduction at the end of the firing also gives the glaze a slight but beneficial soaking by slowing the kiln down.

The results of primary reduction can only be maintained by transferring the pot, while the glaze is still molten, immediately to a chamber with a strong reducing atmosphere for cooling. The secondary reduction chamber should be located close to the kiln, as no time should be lost in making the exchange after the kiln has been opened.

A good reduction chamber would be a hole larger than the pot dug in the ground and covered with a metal garbage can lid. The lid can readily be stood upon and its rim forced into the soft ground to form an air-tight seal. The hole itself is lined with a dry combustible, such as excelsior or straw, and should not be covered until the heat from the pot causes it to ignite. After combustion takes place and the hole is sealed an extremely strong reducing environment is created by a lack of oxygen and an excess of hot carbon.

The glaze, because it is still molten, continues to undergo further chemical changes resulting from a shortage of oxygen in its locality. Any exposed or unglazed clay surfaces undergo color changes ranging from smoky grays to jet blacks as they absorb excess carbon. If the reduction effects are to be retained the pot must remain in the secondary reduction chamber until it is relatively cool and unreceptive to atmospheric circumstances. A period of 10 to 15 minutes would be a normal minimum although a longer time period might be required if the pot has been fired to a relatively high temperature, if its walls are exceedingly thick, or if the combustible material is not suitable in density, quality, and dryness.

Quenching a pot in water after secondary reduction is seldom necessary and is often dangerous as it becomes an additional thermal-shock for the pot to survive. Some rakuists, however, employ quenching strictly as a decorative technique, while the pot is still warm, to accentuate glaze crackles, by submergence in water containing stains or soluble coloring matter. The only time post-reduction quenching might become inescapable is when one notices a change taking place in the color characteristics of a reduced glaze as it begins to reoxidize through exposure to air. Quenching would then be required to fix the outcome of reduction by rendering the glaze immobile to the effects of reoxidation. As long as a raku glaze is warm enough to be chemically contingent upon atmospheric conditions it must be allowed to cool in a reduction atmosphere or have the reduction results made permanent through immediate quenching and cooling.

When you understand the nature of reduction you can do a tremendous amount for your pottery on your own. When your senses are ready you'll know that reduction as associated with raku cannot be conceptualized or squeezed into a system of techniques. The ultimate joy of raku is not realized through manipulation of predictable controls but rather through a free and open response to experience. A responsive spirit creates responsive raku.

SOURCES OF SODIUM AS VAPOR GLAZE

by Jack Troy

Salt, by virtue of its wide distribution and relative cheapness, is the traditional source of sodium in vapor glazing. Until comparatively recently it was the only feasible material available for such purposes. A brief look at the material itself may be of interest.

Common salt (NaCl) is often known as halite, or rock salt, to distinguish it from a class of chemical compounds known as "salts." It is essential to the health of humans and animals. Table salt is finely granulated, and, being hygroscopic (moisture-attracting), contains additives to keep it free-flowing. Small quantities of sodium aluminosilicate, tricalcium phosphate, or magnesium silicate are added for this purpose. Pure rock salt usually contains none of these additives.

Salt is used in the manufacture of sodium bicarbonate (baking soda), sodium hydroxide (caustic soda), hydrochloric acid, chlorine, and many other chemicals, as well as in the food-processing and meat-packing industries. It is widely used in cold climates to melt ice, and it is employed in water softeners to remove magnesium and calcium compounds.

The Greeks and Romans often used salt as an offering in religious rituals, where its characteristics as preservative led to its symbolic representation of enduring qualities. Arabs used the expression, "There is salt [fidelity] between us," and, in English, an individual is respected for being the "salt of the earth." Cakes of salt have been used as money in Africa and as stipend in the Roman armies. The word "salary" derives from the Roman "salarium"—an allowance of money for salt.

Most salt comes from mining rock-salt deposits, such as those occurring along the United States Gulf Coast, by evaporating sea water—which contains salt in a ratio of 3.5 to every 100 parts—or by processing natural brines, which occur in Great Britain and the eastern United States.

Salt as a Source of Sodium Vapor

It should interest any ceramist to know that salt melts at 1472°F.—far lower than the temperature at which most salt glazing is accomplished—and can be used in vapor glazing at raku or earthenware temperatures. As long as the clay body is mature, glaze will form as a surface coating and will influence slips and glazes by fluxing them.

To observe the process described above during a salt firing, one should wear glasses designed to protect the eyes from ultraviolet rays. Toss a tablespoon or two of salt into the firebox of the kiln when the maturing point of the clay is being reached. Individual grains hitting the hot bricks will be seen to liquify instantaneously, forming a vapor which will follow the paths of convection and draft in the kiln. Small quantities of salt may be tossed or blown directly onto the objects being fired, if care is taken to avoid creating un-

necessarily runny effects, which can adhere the piece to a shelf or the floor of the kiln.

In passing from a solid to a gas, salt liquifies. In this state it is highly corrosive to refractories, especially those containing silica, which it attacks, causing spalling. Small amounts of salt introduced rather frequently—at 10 to 20 minute intervals—will cut down on refractory wear. By comparison, larger quantities of salt thrown in at one time may be less effective, since the charges volatilize more slowly, producing greater quantities of liquid salt. In older kilns, especially, large salt charges may cause a molten flow to leak from the kiln, which will solidify on contact with air. From 1 to 2 cups of salt per charge may be considered average. Much more than this may choke off the rate of heat increase by lowering the temperature of the fireboxes.

Granulated salt, being of a fine texture, vaporizes readily as it enters the kiln, in some cases being sprinkled directly on the ware, as in groundhog kilns. The fine crystals are well suited to being blown into the chamber through a pipe attached to a vacuum cleaner motor, as well. Dendritic salt is the finest type manufactured, volatilizes extremely rapidly, and may be ordered through firms purchasing salt in large quantities.

Rock salt has a tendency to snap and pop when introduced into a hot kiln, at times creating dangerous projectiles, which may fly from the firebox with some force as far as 6 feet. For this reason, the use of goggles during salting is urged, especially when using rock salt. The larger crystals present more surface area to the hot atmosphere, and, containing more moisture than smaller granules, disperse with greater force.

Block salt, used to feed livestock, can be used if broken into manageable chunks for insertion into the kiln; but large pieces, especially if damp, could explode from the release of steam within a chunk, possibly endangering the ware, bagwalls, and individuals nearby.

State of the Salt upon Introduction. The question of whether to use dry, damp, or wet salt seems to provoke much discussion. Those who favor dry salt point to the ease of handling the material, the lack of corrosive liquids near metal burners and gas pipes, and the simplicity of eliminating yet another step in the process. The damp salt proponents point to the notion that more vapors in the kiln assist in the dispersion of sodium, itself in vapor form, promoting better results. This variable is simply one more that must be explored and tested individually to determine its applicability. Wet salt certainly increases pollution from the kiln.

Before leaving the matter entirely, however, it can be said for certain that the introduction of water into any heat-containing structure is potentially dangerous. Water can volatilize, forming steam with explosive force, damaging a kiln, and creating an extremely dangerous situation for all

Salt-glazed Crock
by Jack Troy

concerned. If salt is to be dampened, it is best contained in paper packets when introduced into the kiln.

Trace Minerals in the Salt. The presence or absence of trace minerals in any form of salt used in glazing is largely a matter of personal preference. The purity of the material is generally sought after, even though trace minerals such as magnesium and calcium do occur and are bound to have slight but noticeable effects on the quality of the glaze. They may either flux or inhibit the melting of the sodium-alumina-silicate glaze, depending on their concentration in the salt and the degree to which they are already present in the clay. So many types of clay are in use, and so many varieties of salt available, that experimentation can be conducted quite easily. While personal preference for one kind of salt or another may develop, the differences among them will probably not be radical.

Drawbacks of Using Salt. The chief drawback to using salt is the liberation of chlorine gas, which accompanies the breakdown of sodium chloride at high temperatures. Water vapor, in the form of highly visible fog, is another drawback, especially where it may be mistaken for smoke from any uncontrolled fire.

Sodium Compounds Other than Salt
Several sodium-bearing compounds other than salt are: sodium bicarbonate ($NaHCO_3$) Sal soda (Na_2CO_3), known also as sodium carbonate, washing soda, or soda ash, and monosodium glutamate ($NaOOCCH_2 CH_2CHNH_2$), used in the food industry. At the present writing all have been used with varying degrees of success, either as substitutes for salt or in combination with it. Of the many sodium compounds these are among the cheapest and most available.

Sodium bicarbonate is perhaps the least expensive and most readily available salt substitute. It can be purchased in bulk and is commonly referred to as baking soda.

The tendency of sodium bicarbonate to dissipate slowly in comparison to salt has been a problem, but the process can be hastened by spraying or blowing it into the kilns. The glaze produced with sodium bicarbonate, while not identical to that made from salt, can be handsome, though the surface tends to be somewhat more "dry." The addition of 3 to 10% borax to the baking soda may brighten the surface considerably, and if wood is used as a primary or secondary fuel, effects virtually indistinguishable from those obtained from salt vapors may be obtained.

The attractiveness of sodium bicarbonate as a salt substitute in glazing stems from the elimination of chlorine gas as a byproduct in the process. With sodium bicarbonate, carbon dioxide, a relatively harmless gas, is produced, along with some water vapor.

Salt and sodium bicarbonate may be combined, which helps cut back on the less desirable effects of each. Sodium carbonate (soda ash) may also be combined with sodium bicarbonate, since in combination they disperse well, especially if blown into the kiln.

Experiments with various sodium compounds should be conducted in a new kiln where salt has not been used, or at least new bricks should be installed in the firebox-bagwall areas, which retain most residual sodium from previous salt firings. Residual sodium from salt may cause corrosive buildups when sodium carbonate or soda bicarbonate are used. Generally speaking, similar amounts of these compounds could be used, but smaller quantities may be efficient if the damper is shut for a few minutes after the introduction of the material.

In using any salt substitute, the tendency is to want to reproduce the effects of "salt glazing," at the risk of bypassing visual and tactile qualities which might be best exploited for their own unique characteristics. One of the most inhibiting factors in the glazing of any type of ceramics is preconceiving desired effects. Comparatively few individuals seem willing to try such materials as sodium bicarbonate and soda ash because the surfaces are different from those they had anticipated, whereas the effects might well be used to aesthetic benefit. This is an area where much more experimentation is needed and may be demanded as air-quality standards become more stringent.

Amounts of Sodium Compound
Several factors influence this decision, and can be posed as questions:

What Type of Surface Is Desired? Assuming the kiln is fired to a temperature sufficient to mature the body, glaze accumulation will be directly proportional to the amount of glazing material introduced. In a small kiln—30 cubic feet—coated with alumina, or composed of high-alumina bricks, as little as 1 to 3 pounds of salt may be necessary to produce well-glazed objects. However, the same kiln made of unprotected brick may require much more salt, especially for first firings, since a comparatively small proportion of vapors ends up on the objects intended to be glazed.

What Type of Clay Will Be Used? Some clays are much more receptive to vapor glaze than others and require less sodium agent to be added to the kiln. However, a typical high-alumina clay with little free silica may take as much as three to four times the amount of agent to produce the same effect. The temperature at which glazing takes place is a further variable. Some clays may require much more sodium to produce a glaze at, say, c/7 to 8, than they do at c/10, when the silica may combine more readily with a smaller amount of vaporous sodium. Naturally, clay body experimentation will help determine this factor.

What Firing Methods Will Be Employed? Many variations in firing are practiced among contemporary ceramists. Some work with extremely tight kilns, using close damper control, and, in effect, are conservative in the way they retain sodium vapors in the kiln. Others use comparatively large amounts of glazing agents and give little heed to the obvious escape of great quantities of potential glaze-producing vapors. To a large degree, much of the "bad press" about salt glazing is due to such individuals. Simply stated, glazing operations frequently do not have to be as obvious as they often appear.

How Can Glaze Accumulation Be Measured? The best way

during a firing is to use from three to five draw trials— rings of clay which are removed in sequence after specific amounts of glazing agent have been introduced. Since the draw trials are removed and cooled readily (they may be dunked in water immediately), they are invariably poor indicators of clay color but do show quite accurately the depth of glaze buildup.

What Is an Average Amount of Glaze Agent to Consider Introducing? About 10 to 20 ounces per cubic foot of kiln space.

Methods of Introduction

As with the decision of how much sodium compound to use, this is an area open to a wide range of possibilities.

1. The simplest method is to toss the glazing agent into the firebox area through the port made for the same purpose (although the traditional German and groundhog kilns are salted through ports in the roof of the kiln, directly onto the wares). The compound can be loose, in which case it may scatter around outside the kiln with corrosive effects on most metals, or it may be made up into packets of newspaper or paper cups to be thrown or dropped into the firebox area. Plastic bags should *never* be used since they liberate extremely dangerous hydrocarbons when they burn.

2. A simple metal pipe and plunger arrangement can be made by fitting a wooden handle onto a plug which slides piston-fashion in the pipe, pushing a charge of glazing agent out the end and into the firebox. A piece of angle iron about 3 by 3'' also works well, inserted in the port and tipped to one side to spill the charge into the firebox.

3. The material can be blown into the kiln through a pipe inserted into the ports and connected to a compressed-air source or a vacuum-cleaner type of blower.

4. Sodium brine solution may be dripped into the kiln if care is taken to regulate the flow evenly. Too much water vapor entering the kiln has explosive potential and must be guarded against. A gentle dripping of brine may be an effective means of producing a foggy vapor in the kiln, but would mean devising a noncorrosive holding container and flow regulator, along with a feeding pipe or tube directed into a firebox or other area. I personally would never use such a system due to the complications and potential safety hazard.

5. Brine-soaked wood thrown into the kiln is yet another means of introducing the glazing agent. Salt and other compounds can be dissolved in a crock or bucket of hot water, stirring the liquid until saturated. Sticks of dry wood or wood shavings can then be soaked and introduced after they are dried (wet wood ignites slowly and may cause the kiln to lose heat). Dry wood ignites rapidly, dispersing sodium vapors along flame paths, often flashing objects to advantage. Long slivers and sticks of such wood may be painted with soluble colorants and pushed into the kiln to flash nearby pieces when they ignite. Porcelain clay is especially receptive to such random effects. A few sticks of wood about 1 by 1 by 12'', stoked sparingly during the salting, should show their effects on the ware.

The glaze produced in this manner may exhibit characteristics normally attributed to fortuitous "accidents" in firing and warrants exploration. Seaweed, salt-saturated sawdust, and most soft, porous woods will be found to work best. Such combustible agents can be made up some time in advance of the firing and dried to be used as needed. While large amounts of such supplementary fuel might be needed to add all the sodium in this manner, it should be tried by anyone willing to depart from a regular firing schedule, since it is an alternative with considerable potential for certain effects unobtainable by other means.

6. Another method, long in use in central France, is that of placing salt in small— ¼ to ½ cup— clay containers throughout the kiln among the ware. As the temperature increases, sodium vapors permeate the kiln, flashing the pieces. Pottery made in the vicinity of LaBorne, near Henrichemont, south of Bourges, is an example of the effectiveness of this technique. Here the kiln reaches approximately c/12; the ware is vitreous, and sodium vapors do not produce an orange-peel effect, but show up as subtle highlights, often with pleasing shifts in clay tonality. No additional salt is thrown into the kiln during the firing.

7. An experimental technique in recent use consists of placing one or more objects to be vapor glazed in a sagger, together with a cup containing salt and/or various combinations of borax, sodium carbonate, and sodium bicarbonate. As the soda compound volatizes, the objects in the container become glazed, and, since they are in a confined space, very little glazing agent is required. The inside of the sagger may be coated with alumina hydrate or other sodium-resistant wash if desired. Small cups may be thrown, bisqued, and used to hold 1 or 2 tablespoons of say, 90% salt and 10% borax, or 50% sodium carbonate and 50% sodium bicarbonate. Pots in such saggers should be placed on wads in case the glaze-producing material flows out of the cup. Although this method needs more investigation, it remains a tantalizing alternative to conventional salt glazing because of the possibility of producing sodium-glazed objects without the need for a special kiln. Since vapors would be contained in the sagger, virtually no atmospheric effluents would come from the process. Several promising trials along these lines were done at the NCECA Conference at Louisiana State University and at the Penland School of Crafts in the summer of 1976. A surprisingly small amount of vapor agent was sufficient to produce obvious results, although some substances such as borax, which assists vaporization, left undesirable residual deposits in the saggers.

Article and photographs reproduced from *Salt-Glazed Ceramics* (May 1977) by Jack Troy with permission of the publisher, Watson-Guptill Publications, 1515 Broadway, New York, N.Y. 10036.

Beverly Pottery (MA)
Fire – May 14, 1883

PART THREE
KILNS

BROOKFIELD KILN

The Brookfield kiln is a 30 cubic foot downdraft gas-fired kiln. It was built at the Brookfield Craft Center, Brookfield, CT in June 1972. Designed by Harry Dedell, from a kiln by Marion Hubbell, it was constructed during a kiln workshop conducted by Gerry Williams and Marion Hubbell. These plans are published by permission of the Brookfield Craft Center, and are taken from drawings by Frank d'Autilia. The Brookfield Craft Center is a nonprofit organization with summer instructional programs in the crafts, including pottery. Jean d'Autilia is the director.

By definition a sprung arch is any arch supported by abutments at the sides and ends only. Derived in part from the 19th-century German Cassel and English Newcastle kilns, the sprung arch kiln in its present form is widely used by potters in this country. It is, along with the catenary kiln, the workhorse of the American studio potter. The sprung arch is favored for the efficient use it makes of interior space, and for the ease with which it can be built, altered, or repaired.

KILN PERSPECTIVE

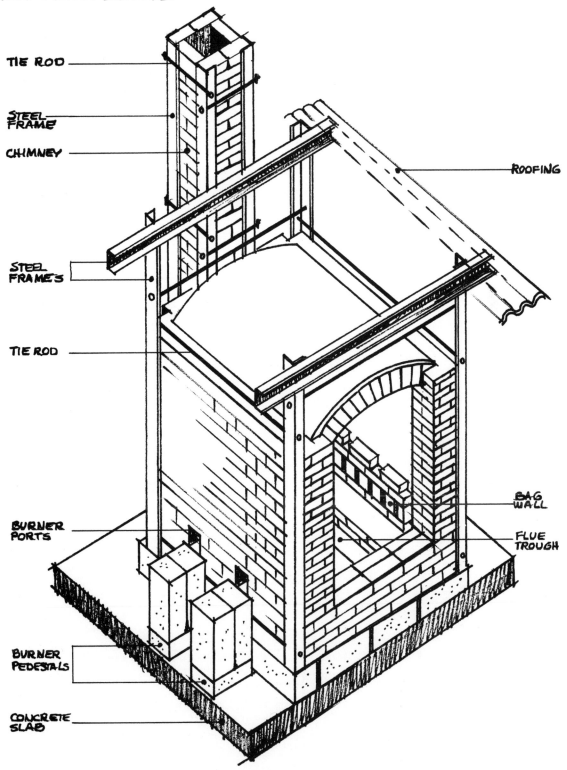

TIE ROD

STEEL FRAME

CHIMNEY

STEEL FRAMES

TIE ROD

ROOFING

BURNER PORTS

BAG WALL

FLUE TROUGH

BURNER PEDESTALS

CONCRETE SLAB

Foundations

The Brookfield kiln is built in an uncovered courtyard. Climate requires 30″ of concrete subfoundation, and adequate drainage. A 6″ concrete slab rests upon foundations. In starting to build the kiln, slight variations in slab level can be compensated for by sprinkling fine sand as cement blocks are laid. Place cement blocks, dry, with openings horizontal—airflow cools underside of kiln and provides for pipe lines if necessary.

Floor and Walls

Begin base of kiln with hard firebrick. Use low-duty straights here on any course one brick away from fireface; high-duty on fireface of trough and floor. Square the base of kiln by measuring opposite corners exactly. Brick laying should be as level and true as possible, using carpenters level and straightedge—small discrepancies can be magnified higher up. Crosshatch bricks on floor base wherever possible. Note placement of small firebrick straights (s) on perimeter of first and second courses—they are the key to later rod placement.

Flue-trough down floor center designed to assist exit of flame and allow more even heating of floor. After constructing fireports (high-duty firebrick), use insulating firebrick straights for walls: K 26 on inside for heat resistance; K 20 on outside for high insulating value. Use K 26 as header course every three layers after fireport.

Spyholes cut two-thirds way up left and right wall, towards rear. Additional spyholes top and bottom in door. Thermocouple in protective porcelain sleeve in middle of back wall.

Place corner angle irons in position and thread rods. Put standard side-skews in place, with 4 x 3″ skew support angle iron indented into brick so as to be flush with outside wall. Temporarily place two broom handles cut to 3′ across walls and tighten top rods. With walls level and exactly measured, prepare for arch.

CEMENT BLOCK BASE PLAN

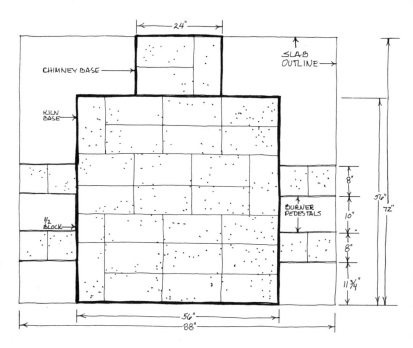

PLAN VIEW SECTION

SCALE: 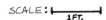 1 FT.

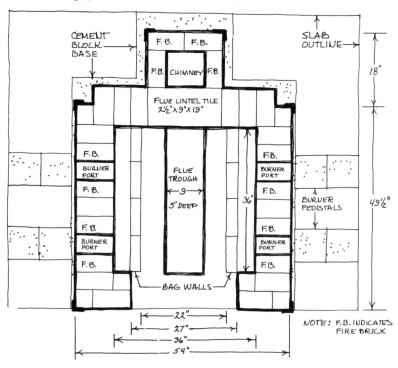

NOTE: F.B. INDICATES FIRE BRICK

72

Front View

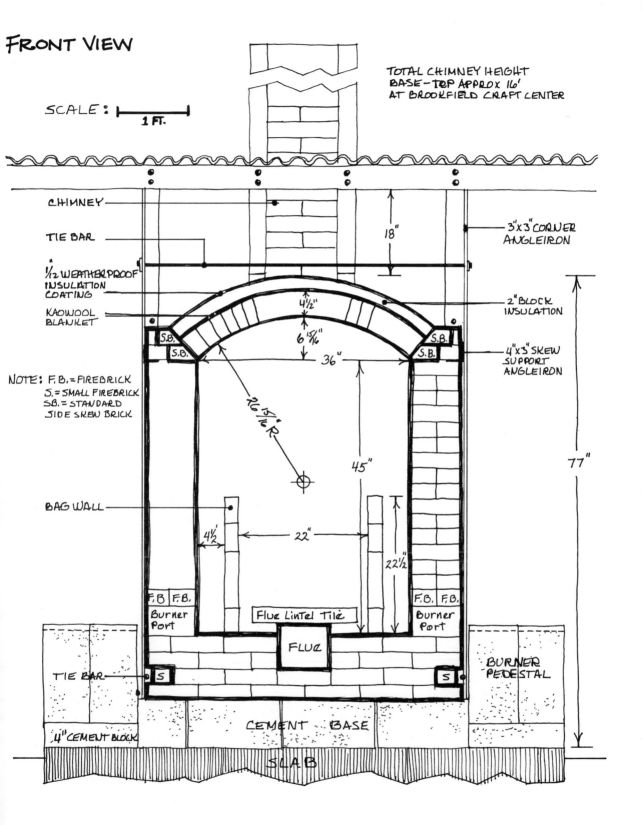

SCALE: |———| 1 FT.

TOTAL CHIMNEY HEIGHT BASE—TOP APPROX 16' AT BROOKFIELD CRAFT CENTER

CHIMNEY

TIE BAR

½" WEATHERPROOF INSULATION COATING

KAOWOOL BLANKET

NOTE: F.B.=FIREBRICK
S.=SMALL FIREBRICK
S.B.=STANDARD SIDE SKEW BRICK

BAG WALL

TIE BAR

4" CEMENT BLOCK

18"

3"x3" CORNER ANGLEIRON

2" BLOCK INSULATION

4"x3" SKEW SUPPORT ANGLEIRON

77"

S.B.
S.B.
S.B.
S.B.

4½"
6 15/16"
36"
26 15/16" R
45"
22"
4½"
22½"

F.B | F.B.
Burner Port

F.B. | F.B.
Burner Port

Flue Lintel Tile

FLUE

S

S

BURNER PEDESTAL

CEMENT BASE

SLAB

73

CROSS SECTION BAG WALLS NOT SHOWN

SCALE: |⎯⎯| 1FT.

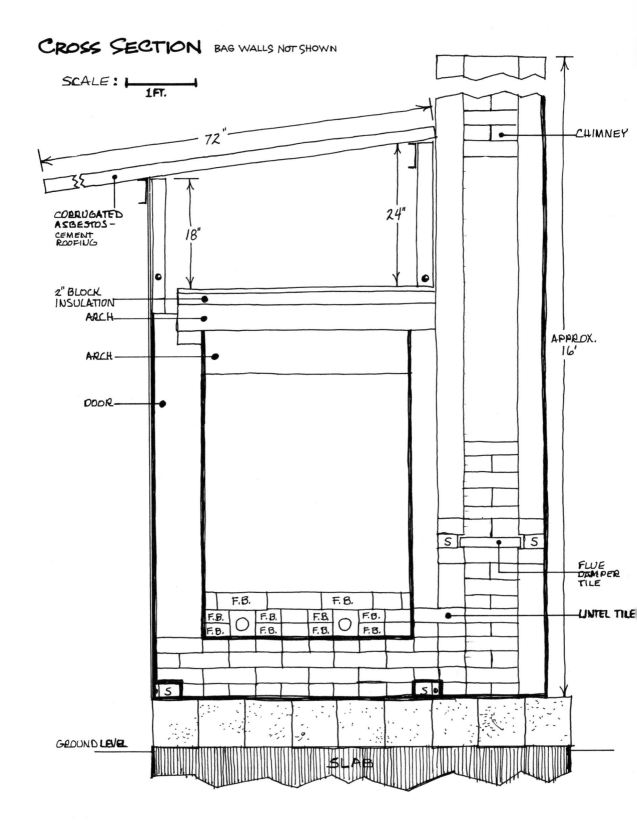

72"

24"

18"

CORRUGATED
ASBESTOS-
CEMENT
ROOFING

CHIMNEY

2" BLOCK
INSULATION

ARCH

ARCH

DOOR

APPROX.
16'

S S

FLUE
DAMPER
TILE

F.B.   F.B.

F.B. ◯ F.B.   F.B. ◯ F.B.

F.B.   F.B.   F.B.   F.B.

LINTEL TILE

S   S

GROUND LEVEL

SLAB

Arch

Low rise arch (2 to 2½'' per rising foot) most satisfactory. For arch and brick computation, consult *Handbook of Firebrick Combinations,* available from AP Green or North American Refractories. Sprung arch tables indicating span, rise, and inside radius will give number and type of brick required. For 36'' span with rise of 6 15/16'', and inside radius of 26 15/16'', use 18 K 26 No. 1 arch insulating bricks and 1 K 26 insulating straight for each course. Build arch support: Cut three 1'' boards inscribed with exact arch radius, less ¼'' to compensate for plywood. Be sure outside edge of plywood is nailed firmly in a straight line. Form is installed with removable legs wedged in place by shingles.

Arch bricks now laid. Hammer gently into place with short 2x4. Remove arch support.

Blanket Kaowool ½'' thick insulates and seals arch from air leaks. Place 2'' block insulation (1900°F. only) in place, split in center to conform to arch. If kiln is outside use finishing cement with chicken wire reinforcement (avoid carcinogenic asbestos). Where no kiln roofing required, corner angle irons need be only high enough to clear top tie rod.

BAG WALL CONSTRUCTION
no cutting required
SIDE VIEW

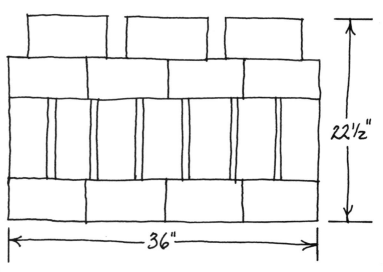

22½"

36"

CHIMNEY FLUE DAMPER
SIDE VIEW

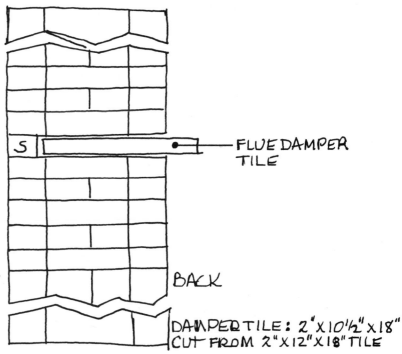

FLUE DAMPER TILE

FRONT

BACK

DAMPER TILE: 2"x10½"x18"
CUT FROM 2"x12"x18" TILE

PLAN VIEW

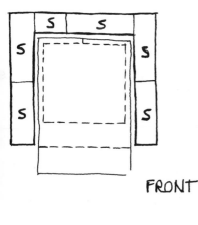

Door

Use K 26 inside, K 20 outside. Headers of K 26 every third course will prevent door being sucked in. Air lock recommended by making outside layer one-half brick wider on each side, with wall conforming.

Inside wall cut to arch radius. Outside wall uncut.

Burners

Four Sina-12 atmospheric gas burners, from Flynn Burner Co., 425 Fifth Ave., New Rochelle, NY 10802. Each is equipped with low-pressure gauge, needle valve, and Baso safety valve. BTU ratings usually determined by gas pressure, orifice size, and efficiency of combustion. At medium pressure of 1-10 PSI (1 PSI equals 27.2'' water column), BTU/HR normally released per cubic foot of chamber space is 40,000 to 50,000. This figure times cubic footage of chamber gives BTU requirements. Divide this by number of burners, giving BTU rating for each burner. Tables issued by burner manufacturers give relationship between gas pressure and orifice size. Low pressure with larger orifice desirable for potters. For more detailed information write for data sheet No. 1A-5d from Pyronics Inc., 7700 Miles Ave., Cleveland, OH 44105.

Arch Support Plan

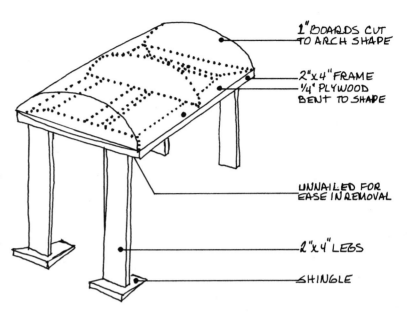

1" BOARDS CUT TO ARCH SHAPE

2"x4" FRAME ¼" PLYWOOD BENT TO SHAPE

UNNAILED FOR EASE IN REMOVAL

2"x4" LEGS

SHINGLE

Piers & Door Bricking

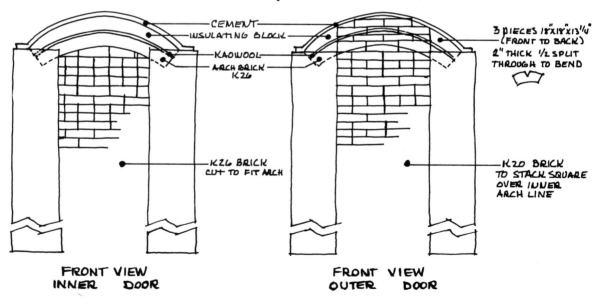

CEMENT
INSULATING BLOCK
KAOWOOL
ARCH BRICK K26

K26 BRICK CUT TO FIT ARCH

3 PIECES 18"x18"x13¼" (FRONT TO BACK)
2" THICK ½ SPLIT THROUGH TO BEND

K20 BRICK TO STACK SQUARE OVER INNER ARCH LINE

FRONT VIEW INNER DOOR

FRONT VIEW OUTER DOOR

Gas Hookup

Brookfield kiln uses LP bottled gas. 1000 gallon tank helps prevent line freeze-up during severely cold weather. Meter allows quantity reading on each firing. Manifold is 3'' threaded black pipe to sustain pressure head for the two ¾'' branches to kiln, plus future pull-offs. Advisable to have additional regulators on each side of burner lines, set at 50'' water column to prevent damage to low-pressure gauges on burners.

Chimney

Exit flue 9x9'', or approximately 1/15th floor space. Flue should be somewhat larger than combined fireport space to allow for expansion of hot gases. Height of Brookfield kiln 16' due to bank surrounding kiln area; 12' considered normal. Usual formula for chimney height 3' up for every 1' down; 1' up for every 3½' horizontal. Clay damper tile in plans should be replaced with silicon carbide shelf.

Metal Framework Plan

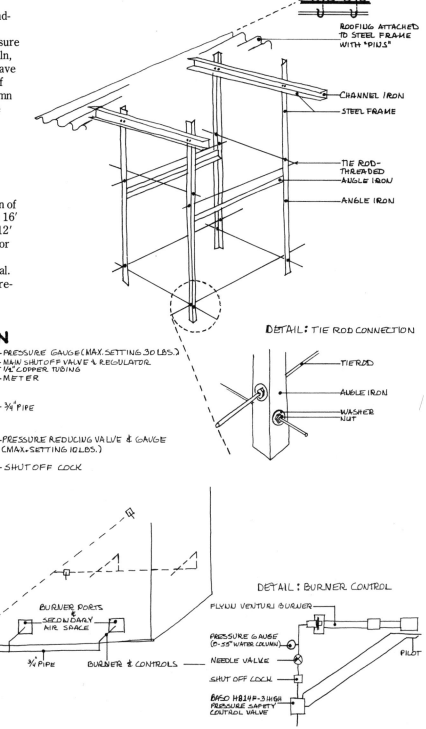

ROOFING ATTACHED TO STEEL FRAME WITH "PINS"

CHANNEL IRON

STEEL FRAME

TIE ROD- THREADED ANGLE IRON

ANGLE IRON

DETAIL: TIE ROD CONNECTION

TIE ROD

ANGLE IRON

WASHER NUT

Gas System Plan

1000 GALLON PROPANE GAS TANK

PRESSURE GAUGE (MAX. SETTING 30 LBS.)
MAIN SHUTOFF VALVE & REGULATOR
½" COPPER TUBING
METER

¾" PIPE

PRESSURE REDUCING VALVE & GAUGE (MAX. SETTING 10 LBS.)

SHUT OFF COCK

BURNER PORTS & SECONDARY AIR SPACE

4" MANIFOLD

BRANCH SHUT-OFF

¾" PIPE

BURNER & CONTROLS

TO OTHER OUTLETS

DETAIL: BURNER CONTROL

FLYNN VENTURI BURNER

PRESSURE GAUGE (0-55 WATER COLUMN)

NEEDLE VALVE

SHUT OFF COCK

BASO H814F-3 HIGH PRESSURE SAFETY CONTROL VALVE

PILOT

77

First Firing

PLACE: Brookfield   DATE: July 5-6

TYPE KILN: Gas   GAUGE: 4703-4871

INITIAL STAGES: A) SOAK   6:30-7:00 - Soak burner (л.л.)

B) PRE-500°   TURN ON   UP 400°-6:00 AM 2 burner (л.л.) 600°f.-7:00 #3 & 4 burners on

(handle on on left shut-off broke)

WEATHER:

COLOR

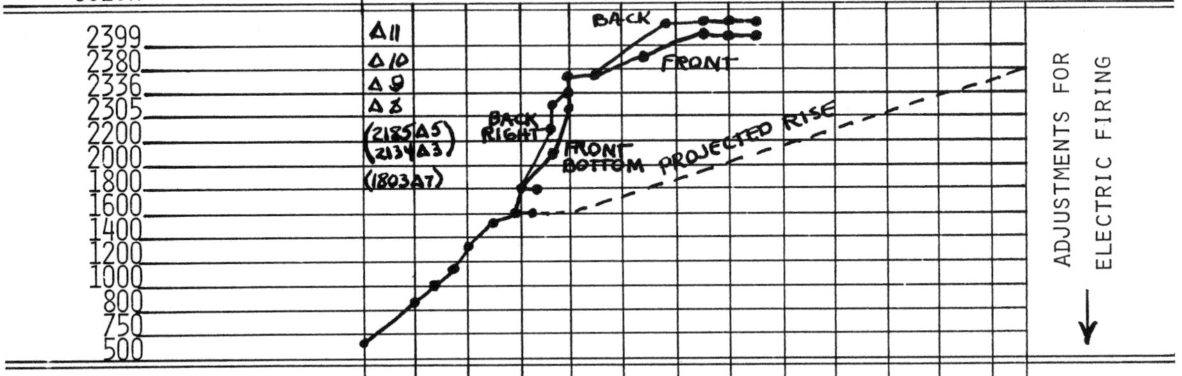

TIME:	7	8	9	10	11	12	1	2	3	4	5	6	7	SAME
DAMPER:	open a little		closed to reduce	open 1½"		adjusted			↑					OPEN OR CLOSED
BURNER AIR: PRIMARY	open	"	open a little	closed a little					turned off					SWITCH #1
SECONDARY	open	"												#2
BURNER GAS: (PRESSURE)	½ lb	4 lb	3	1½	¼	¼	¼	Seems to be						#3
CONES:				Δ5 Δ8 Δ11		evening out good Δ throughout								SAME
COMMENTS:														

1. Shut-off handle broken

too fast turned down gas - pressure damper

why so fast:
① new kiln - tight
② Bright day
③ Excess gas pressure
④ Psychic high of students

next time: Careful!!

NEXT DAY!
GOOD REDUCTION
GLAZES OK!

(right side, rotated) ADJUSTMENTS FOR ELECTRIC FIRING ↓

CONE PLACEMENT ON BACK

Material Cost Estimate Table for Brookfield Kiln

DESCRIPTION	QUANTITY		UNIT PRICE	AMOUNT
Silicon carbide kiln shelves 18½x16½x⅝	15		$26.45 ea.	$396.75
Empire D.P. 9″ straights	280			
Empire D.P. small 9″ straights	30	330	.70 ea.	231.00
Empire D.P. side skews	20			
Mizzou 60% Alumina 9″ straights	30		1.30 ea.	39.00
Strasburg low-duty 9″ straights	220		.40 ea.	88.00
Empire 2½x9x18″	1		4.42 ea.	4.42
G-26 9″ straights	775		.87 ea.	674.25
K-20 9″ straights	175		.62 ea.	108.50
G-25 #1 arch	100		.95 ea.	95.00
Block insulation 2x12x36	18 sq.ft. (ctn.)		29.90 ctn.	29.90
Kaowool blanket ½″	24 sq.ft.		1.30 sq.ft.	31.20
AP Green insulating cement (nonasbestos)	50 lb. bag		14.20 bag	14.20
Empire posts 9x2½x2¼″	12		.75 ea.	9.00
Empire posts 6x2½x2¼″	12		.45 ea.	5.40
Empire posts 4½x2½x2¼″	12		.45 ea.	5.40
Empire posts 3x2½x2¼″	12		.45 ea.	5.40
Angle irons 2½x2½x¼x91″	2			
Angle irons 2½x2½x¼x97″	2			
Angle irons 3½x2½x¼x49″	2		230.00 lot	230.00
Channel irons 3″x4.1 lb./ft.x108″	2		all precut	
Angle irons 2x2x¼x144	2		to length	
Angle irons 2x2x¼x79″	2			
Threaded rods and necessary nuts and washers 72x½″	13		4.50 ea.	58.50
Cement blocks 8x8x16	35		.75 ea.	26.25
Cement blocks 4x8x16	4		.50 ea.	2.00
Ransome B-4 gas burners with control valves	4		52.00 ea.	208.00
Ransome combination warm-up and pilot burners	4		22.00 ea.	88.00
Baso HiPressure ¾″ safety shut-off valves with fittings	4		38.00 ea.	152.00
Baso heavy-duty thermocouples	4		6.00 ea.	24.00
Copper tubing ¼″O.D.x30″ lengths	4		1.15 ea.	4.60
Water column (32 oz.) pressure gauges with fittings 55″	4		26.00 ea.	104.00
Rockwell second-stage gas pressure regulator 0-6psi range	1		40.00	40.00
Roofing materials	highly variable			
Steel frame fabrication			75.00 lot	75.00
Damper blade cutting charge (to cut one 18½x16½x⅝ kiln shelf to 18½x10½x⅝)			9.25	9.25
Total cost FOB Danbury, CT and Waltham, MA.				$2,759.02

Prices quoted by Harry Dedell, pottery sales manager, New England Ceramic & Kiln Supply Div., Cor. Lee Mac Ave. and Shelter Rock Rd., Danbury, CT 06810 and Cutter Fire Brick Co., 54 Emerson Rd., Waltham, MA 02154, August 1977.

FASTFIRE WOOD

by Fred Olsen

Over a year ago Bruce Dedmon and I began to experiment with an extremely fast firing and cooling cycle, using a 300 cubic foot insulation blanket hood envelope gas updraft kiln. The normal firing/cooling cycle was 24 hours. We decreased the firing cycle and started to fire 2,000 slip-cast greenware planters to c/10 in 8 hours and cooled in 8 hours. This cycle worked fine but we still needed more production. The only way was to fire the kiln twice a day. We went to an 8 hour firing/cooling cycle—4 to 5 hours to c/10, 3 hours for cooling. Then we pop the hood and move to the second pad. Thus we fire 4,000 greenware planters to c/10 in two 8 hour cycles with one hood and two pads.

Through Ray Grimm (of Portland, Oregon) I met George Wright, a clay and material supplier for Portland area potters. George, an old-time wood kiln fireman in the brick and tile kilns, built himself and his wife a small 8 to 10 cubic foot stacking wood-fired kiln which fires beautifully and fast. This lead me to thinking about a small wood kiln kit that I could put together. It could fit in my pick-up truck; could be built in 2 or 3 hours; fired to c/10 in 4 to 6 hours with no fuel cost involved; cooled in 4 to 6 hours; and taken down in an hour and moved to a new area. So I built myself a 20 cubic foot downdraft wood-fired prototype. I call this knockdown portable kiln kit "fastfire wood."

A lot has been written lately about our impending fuel crisis, and we are all aware of the coming problems. Solutions are harder to come by. Perhaps an intermediate solution is to have kilns capable of extremely fast firings and efficient fuel consumption. Four hours to c/10 in the hood kiln with an even firing is one solution. The illustrated fastfire wood kiln proves that it is also possible with wood as a fuel.

The last few kiln building workshops I have done have concentrated on the fastfire wood kilns that are extremely efficient and time saving. At the Casa Del Sol workshop in Ashland, Oregon (John Connors), a number of workshoppers took off for the swimming hole after the kiln had been built, stacked, and ignited. They returned three hours later only to find that the firing was almost done. I have received a letter recently (October 1975) from Chuck Hindes concerning the fastfire wood kilns built during a workshop I did at the University of Iowa: "We have put sprung arches on both kilns. Both of them fire very well. Bunny's class (head ceramic professor Bunny McBride) fired the downdraft to c/10 in 4 hours. Can you believe that?"

Fastfire Wood

Three important design principles which set the minimum standard for wood are:

1. The firebox area should be 10 times the horizontal cross-section of the chimney. For fastfire increase firebox

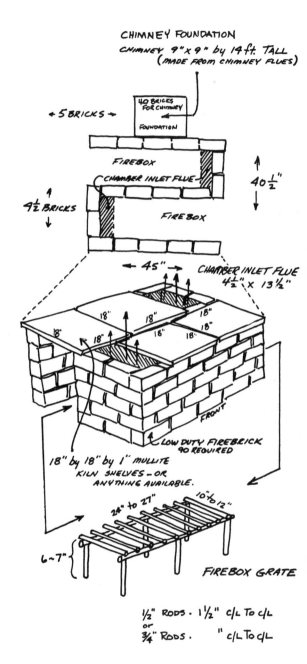

CHIMNEY FOUNDATION
CHIMNEY 9" x 9" by 14 ft. TALL
(MADE FROM CHIMNEY FLUES)

40 BRICKS FOR CHIMNEY FOUNDATION

← 5 BRICKS →

FIREBOX

CHAMBER INLET FLUE

40 1/2"

9 1/2 BRICKS

FIREBOX

← 45" →

CHAMBER INLET FLUE
4 1/2" x 13 1/2"

18"   18"   18"
18" 18"   18"   18"

FRONT

LOW DUTY FIREBRICK
90 REQUIRED

18" by 18" by 1" MULLITE
KILN SHELVES - OR
ANYTHING AVAILABLE.

24" to 27"   10" to 12"

6~7"

FIREBOX GRATE

1/2" RODS. 1 1/2" c/L TO c/L
or
3/4" RODS.   " c/L TO c/L

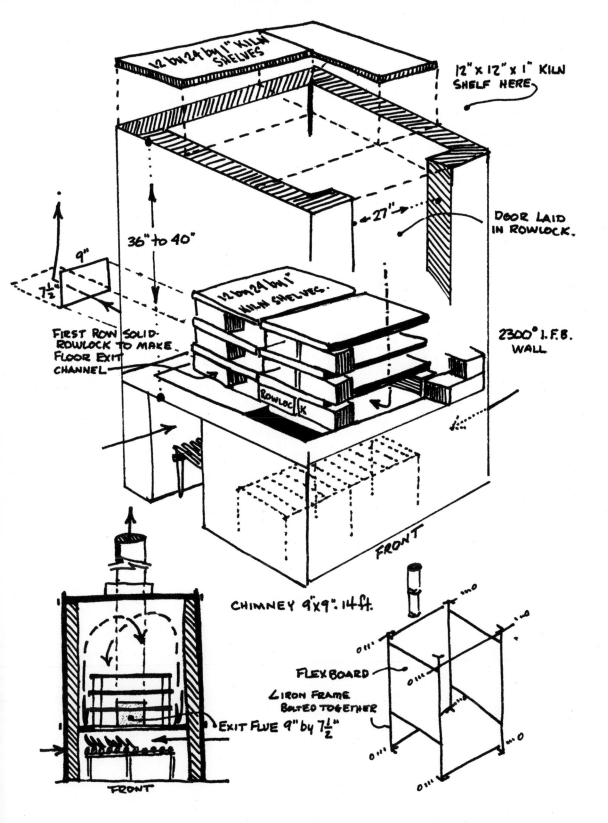

12 by 24 by 1" KILN SHELVES

12" X 12" X 1" KILN SHELF HERE.

DOOR LAID IN ROWLOCK.

36" to 40"

27"

9"

7½

FIRST ROW SOLID ROWLOCK TO MAKE FLOOR EXIT CHANNEL

12 by 24 by 1" KILN SHELVES.

ROWLOCK

2300° I.F.B. WALL

FRONT

CHIMNEY 9"x9". 14 ft.

FLEXBOARD

L IRON FRAME BOLTED TOGETHER

EXIT FLUE 9" by 7½"

FRONT

area by 20%.

2. More than ½ the firebox volume should be below the grate bars—thus basically ½ plus for the ash pit and ½ minus for the combustion area.

3. Chimney height—three times the height of the kiln's chamber plus the height of the firebox and then add 1 foot of chimney for every 3 feet of horizontal travel of the flue gases. For altitudes over 4,000 feet an additional 3 feet of chimney or more may be needed and increase chimney diameter by 50% and exit flue size (square inches) by 40%.

Firing

Start one firebox and fire until a bed of coals is accumulated. Then start the other side (which will be around 1000 to 1100°F.) firebox and begin an alternating stoking pattern—never full stoke both sides at once. Fill grate to half-capacity and let burn down—eventually, in one hour or so, the firebox will take only four to six kindling-size pieces each stoking, every 3 minutes or so. When one firebox is stoked with its four to six pieces, the other side may need one or two to carry it through until its turn. Have a spyhole in the door open, preferably at the top, at all times. Watch the flame out of this spyhole and the chimney smoke. When the flame sucks back into the kiln and the chimney has cleared, it is time to stoke. Critical temperatures are around 1100° and 2000°F. where care must be taken not to choke the kiln. I use a pyrometer when firing and as long as it shows an increase, the stoking quantity and rate is perfect. If it loses temperature, rake and clear some of the coals out of the firebox and beat down the wood on top of the grate so more oxygen is made available. When c/9 is down on top, I insert a metal rod through the hole in the side wall and push the trick brick back to open up the exit flue that is above the first kiln shelf, thus sucking the majority of the draft directly to the back and bottom wall and evening out the temperature in the whole kiln. The kiln will use less than a quarter of a cord of wood for a 3½ to 4 hour firing.

THE MARK OF THIS FIRE: CATENARY ARCH, DOWNDRAFT, WOOD-FIRED KILN

by Ruth Gowdy McKinley

A WOOD-FIRED KILN

by Ruth Gowdy McKinley

For me the involvement with and commitment to forming and firing have always been of equal importance. In recognizing this and seeing some Bizen ware the choice of a wood-fired kiln was, and still is, in complete harmony with that commitment. The physical effort of throwing a pot is equaled, possibly exceeded, in the physical effort of firing with wood. The same amount of thought and consideration given to the form of a piece is also required to form the fire. The thrown pot speaks of its forming—the wood-fired pot gives evidence of its firing. As the potter directly forms the clay, so that same potter directly forms the fire.

A wood-burning kiln is not automatic. The fuel does not inject itself. You put the fuel where it needs to be and that placement changes as the wood is consumed; the rate of input increases as the temperature climbs. Just as gas and oil kilns should have good power reserves in their burners to overcome heat losses and still raise temperatures at a desired rate, so the stoker of a wood burning kiln must have reserves. At least two are required: strength, both physical and mental—you are the power source; stockpiles of dry wood, both ample and handy—it is your fuel.

The cost of wood as fuel may still be lower than gas (natural or propane), oil, or electricity. From 1959 to 1968 it was $15.00 a load, delivered. Through 1972 it was $20.00 for the same load, delivered. This spring a $5.00 delivery charge was added. (The delivery charge is not unreasonable; the saw mill is 25 miles away: a 50-mile round trip.) Just now a load was delivered and the wood is $30.00 plus the $5.00 delivery charge.

A truck load of mill slab, as I get it from the saw mill, is just under two cords. (One cord is 4' wide and 4' high by 8' long or 128 cubic feet.) One load does approximately three firings—or 76 cubic feet of wood (a bit less than two-thirds of one cord) will take my 14 cubic foot ware chamber to c/10 in 21 to 24 hours. Fuel costs are between $10.00 and $12.00 a firing.

There is a minimal equipment investment with a wood-burning kiln: grate bars, an ax, a sledge hammer, some wedges, a chopping block, and possibly a chain saw or scoop shovel. Because you are handling the fuel, a sturdy but flexible pair of gloves is needed, and also because you are looking at more fire for more of the firing time, a pair of furnace glasses is necessary. In 1960 I bought a pair of #3 furnace glasses from E. E. Bosch in Rochester, New York. Then they were $12.50, with frames. The lack of eye strain and fatigue was happily noticed before I finished the next firing.

Sources of Wood

For many years my main source of wood has been various saw mills. The wood fuel has been, and continues to be, their by-product—mill slab. Slab wood when delivered can range from yule log proportions to slivers. The pieces between these extremes are slabs roughly 8 to 14'' long and 6 to 12'' wide with the thickest sections from 1 to 4''. Most of the slab wood has bark on one side.

As the size is assorted so is the wood; hard and soft woods are to be found in any load. The hard woods I have fired with are hickory, oak, maple, birch, walnut, ash, elm, basswood, and applewood; soft woods have been pine, hemlock, spruce, and fir. Because of this mix in the load there never has been a firing with only one kind of wood. There have been a few firings with mostly ash, hickory, spruce, or pine. There did not seem to be any difference in the results, either in the amount of ash deposit or color and textural difference in fusion with clay, engobe, or glaze.

Possibly a factory manufacturing furniture, hockey sticks, or baseball bats would be a good source; they may, however, have their own methods of scrap re-cycling. At one time, while living in western New York state, my wood source was a garden tool handle factory. The wood was ash and hickory and it had all been kiln dried then turned. The diameter was 2'' and lengths ranged from 12'' to less than the diameter. It was for these "chips" I used a scoop shovel. Another source during this time period was a ladder factory; the wood from it was spruce and ash.

Sometimes my husband Don and I would go to the saw mill, tool handle or ladder factory and pick up the wood. We could then avoid the yule logs and slivers at the saw mill; with the small "chips" from the factories it was less time consuming to shovel them into fruit and vegetable crates than to sort them.

The advantages of fruit and vegetable crates are that the crates are open enough to permit drying, are small enough to handle, and can be stacked firmly enough to serve as end supports for rows of unboxed wood. Occasionally we were charged a modest amount, $1.00 or $2.00, for a VW pick-up truck load—often there was no charge. However, the time away from the shop and the effort expended in loading and then unloading the wood makes the "free for the taking" another aspect to be weighed in the time versus money dilemma.

Lands being cleared by developers may be another source. Here a chain saw would be indispensible, then sledge and wedges after the sawn tree sections have dried. If you are fortunate enough to own land densely treed you could clear the inevitable slash or log the woods for your fuel; this wood could be cut to the appropriate length for your firebox.

A few other sources might be telephone poles that have been replaced, snow fences that have seen too many snows, nurserymen who could tell you what is being cut and where, salvage yards after old and very dry buildings have been razed. It seems to me a kiln firing would provide an honorable and useful end to this wood.

Wood Delivered. Salvage Skid Wood. Stacked Wood Kiln. End Wall

Wood Stacking, Storing, Drying

Proper stacking and storing are important regardless of wood condition. If you have a source of dried wood, such as industrial scrap, its low moisture content should be maintained by keeping it off the ground and under cover. On the other hand, wet or green wood must be stacked to allow air circulation and "roofed" to keep off rain and snow to achieve drying. With slab wood, stacked in the open, the top of each stack can be covered with the largest slabs – bark side out. A ridge down the center of each stack, before laying the "roofing" slabs, would give a pitch for drainage. As firing time approached a tarpaulin or plastic sheet should be handy as cover for this dry wood. I figure it takes two weeks of summer sun and wind to drive off two days of rain or wet snow; even then some in the middle of the stack might still be damp.

If the mill slab is green, newly felled, you should allow at least a year of drying before using it. From 25 to 45% of the weight of green wood is water and this extra moisture reduces heat value by about one-sixth. Frequently trees cut in early or late fall remain where felled till the following spring when they are hauled to the saw mill. Some drying has taken place in this instance but I still allow one year from the time I stack it before I fire with it. There is no such thing as wood that is too dry. If it "sizzles" when it is in the firebox you know some of its potential heat is being wasted in removing moisture. This results in a longer firing time and more wood will be needlessly consumed than if it were dry.

Stack the wood well ahead of building your kiln. Wood sheds can be built of course; here finances and space are key factors. If you plan a kiln shed, possibly the roof structure might be extended to cover the wood supply, or part of

it. Allow no less than 4' of space between stoke holes, primaries, and wood piled near the kiln. This is for fire prevention as well as for safety and ease of movement when stoking, adjusting primaries, shaking ashes, and changing damper settings during the firing.

You might want to consult *The Woodburners Handbook* by David Havens, Media House, Portland, ME for more information.

When we built this kiln in the fall of 1968, we knew it would have to be moved before its life cycle had ended. The channels between the foundation blocks were to give room under the slab for jacks to raise the kiln in preparation for a fork lift to move it.

This kiln was originally built in the Ceramic Department's clay storage building on the campus of Sheridan College, School of Design, where we continued to live and work. As the school expanded the heretofore unused areas I was occupying were needed.

In September 1971 we rented a four ton fork lift and moved the kiln 123 yards to my new shop. The floor area where the kiln and stack would be had been poured 14'' thick and the cement was strengthened with alternate layers of reinforcing rod and 6'' square wire mesh.

The kiln traveled well and Don built a new flue run and stack.

The Kiln

In the initial planning of this catenary arch, downdraft kiln, the size and proportion of the ware chamber and firebox were considered in relation to the following:
• the amount of ware to be fired
• frequency of firing with relation to production
• available brick sizes
• existing or obtainable kiln shelf sizes
• size of stack
• space kiln will occupy
• financing for a kiln of some permanence.

Planning the Arch. After the mental juggling act with all of the above factors the planning of the arch was begun. A thin chain was hung in front of a large sheet of paper fastened to the wall and its catenary curve transferred by using a can of spray paint. The chain was taken down and the paper removed from the wall. Cardboard templates of the end views of the refractories required for the arch were made. We decided on the standard 9'' and 13½'' series. The 13½'' series was chosen so that fewer bricks need be cut in meeting the requirements of masonry construction. (Some did have to be cut in the areas of stoke holes and ash pit.)

The templates were accurately cut from illustration board and were end views of straights, #1, #2, and #3 arch brick. These templates moved about along the catenary curve till the best arrangement of bricks, conforming closest to the curve, was determined. Then I traced around each template allowing ⅛'' between each brick for mortar. Then the same procedure was followed in planning the insulating brick layer. Here we used only the 9'' series as insulating bricks are easily and accurately cut. No allowance was made for mortar as these were to be laid dry. The arch then consists of 4½'' of heavy duty refractory brick and 4½'' of 2300°F insulating brick.

By considering the door thickness, depth of ware chamber, thickness of bag wall, width of the firebox and end wall section we established the overall length of the kiln. Having completed plotting the catenary curve with the necessary straight and arch brick we then determined how many of each shape were needed by counting the number in a course and multiplying by the number of courses.

Foundation and Slab. One layer of new cement foundation block was positioned in spaced rows on the floor with voids vertical and covered with a sheet of ¼'' masonite. Then Don made a wood frame and placed it around the outside top edge of the cement block. The frame extended 4½'' above the surface of the blocks and was held in position by strapping around and supporting below. It was checked for square and level. At the front and back edges of both sides the wooden frame is angled to a slope of 1'' in 10''.

After placing 6'' square reinforcing mesh in the form, ½'' diameter reinforcing rods were put along each side, 3'' in from the perimeter of the foundation; three more were star-crossed in the center with their ends overlapping the side rods. All seven metal rods were securely fastened together with wire. This reinforcing structure was positioned and held about 2'' above the bottom of the slab form so that when the cement filled the frame the rods would become the structural filling for the cement sandwich. While the cement was wet we used a long straight board to shape the outer 10'' (on both sides of the slab) to the slope cut in the frame. The slab was poured October 15, 1968 and dried for about a week.

Form and Arch. A wooden and masonite form was made. Don cut four wood pieces to the same but slightly smaller curve than the catenary shape drawn. This was to allow for the sheet of ¼'' masonite which was nailed over these four equally spaced upright curves, the thickness of the stretchers bracing the bottom of the form and the small wedges placed under each corner of the form when it was positioned on the slab. To have a strong and rigid form we used the ¼'' masonite; because it would not bend tightly enough to the top of the arch, without splitting, a parallel series of partial saw cuts was made. To insure maximum strength for this kiln we used masonry construction; the bricks are overlapped and the joints are staggered. By using both the 9'' and the 13½'' refractory series we avoided quite a bit of brick cutting in achieving this structural result.

As arch building progressed, refractories were laid to frame the openings in the stoke holes, ash pit, and flue exit. These refractory faces will take the inevitable abrasion of metal tools when shaking and removing ashes while firing as well as the rasping when removing and replacing the grate bars after firing. Removable grate bars are an advantage because they permit easier clean-out of the ash pit and laying of the first wood charge for the next firing.

When the refractories were all in place the four wedges under the form were pushed out. The form dropped to the slab and was slid out from under the arch. This, for me, has always been the most splendid and spectacular moment in the kiln construction—a new, clean, clear form—truly the birth of a kiln.

Kiln Floor. There are six courses of brick from the slab to the floor of the kiln within the arch. This additional height raises the stoke holes, for me, to something other than back-breaking level when stoking and, short of excavating the floor (a possibility in another location), it allows space for the ash pit below the grates and for the flue channel across the ware chamber. These six courses are not all refractory brick, there is insulating brick (salvaged from a former wood kiln) in the center. The refractories were mortared in place.

Bag Wall and Door. The refractory bag wall rises from the kiln floor to within 2 or 3'' of the top of the arch. It is rather tightly checkered with openings of ½'' to ⅝'' in width and 2½'' high. The first five or six courses should be mortared so wood pressing against or hitting into the bag wall does not rearrange it. After two or three firings all bricks have accumulated and fused enough ash to hold them in place. Every third course braces against the sides of the arch.

The door bricks are all separate—both refractories and insulating. In the inner refractory section of the door the top and bottom spyholes are fireclay and alumina-hydrate bricks I have made with openings that widen toward the cone packs in the chamber. The outer insulating brick section has 6½'' long spyhole bricks which are removed when checking cones.

As firings deposit ash on the ware and kiln shelves it also accumulates on the kiln, especially on the walls of the firebox. When the bag wall needs replacing the refractory door bricks are recycled into the bag wall. New refractories are cut and fitted for the door. Since the bricks must be carefully cut and fitted for the door of a catenary arch, it is important to keep them in order when not in the kiln. I have

numbered them in sequence to avoid confusion and store them, inverted, in a wheeled rack the shape of the arch. (See photograph.)

End Wall and Primaries. In the end wall, facing the firebox, the bottom of the first row of primary air openings is at the same level with the floor of the kiln and in alignment with the base of the bag wall. There are seven openings in the bottom row and six in the top. These two courses and the next one above are heavy duty refractories which frame the primaries. They are mortared. From here up there is a 4½'' wall of refractories inside and 4½'' of insulating brick outside. They all are cut, fitted, and mortared to fill the arch opening and be flush with its end.

Flue Damper and Stack. The flue channel runs across the center of the ware chamber and parallel with the firebox. It is all heavy duty refractory firebox mortared in place.

The damper, a horizontal one, is a 10'' wide kiln shelf that is supported in a slot of heavy duty refractory firebrick—all mortared.

The bottom of the stack consists of heavy duty refractory firebrick cased with insulating brick. The stack is completed with refractory flue liners (12'' x 12'' x 2'') cased with cinder block (4''x8''x16'') mortared with sakrete and strapped around. Between the flue liners and the cinder block, vermiculite is poured as back-up insulation. This stack is 14'' high but may be varied to fit your situation.

Kiln Drying. After the refractory arch was completed in wood kiln #3, small portable electric heaters were placed in the chamber overnight, every night. As it was late October

this was probably more for our benefit than to dry the kiln, but it helped do that too. When the kiln and stack were completed a small fire was built and it slowly burned most all of the day before a biscuit was stacked. This first firing was taken very slowly, even for a biscuit, and 20 hours after it was lit stoking ceased when c/04 fell on top, c/08 was over on the bottom with 06 at 3 o'clock. Wood kiln #3 had very successfully completed its baptism of fire.

Grates. The grates in the first wood kiln were cast iron window sash weights built into the firebox spanning its width. In the second wood-burning kiln bars of scrap iron were built into the firebox, again spanning its width. When, after two or three years, these had all but disappeared, sections of ornamental iron fencing (grape clusters, ivy leaves, and cherubs) were torch-cut to rest on the "spurs" remaining from the iron bars. Each of these lasted about two firings. Then in a scrap metal yard we located stainless steel bar stock. A local auto mechanic cut and welded these into a grate which hung between the stoke holes. By c/9 the grate always sagged enough to be visible through the primary air openings. Each firing I would turn it over—between c/4 and 8 it would always level out. The stainless proved to be very satisfactory—long lived—and until we moved away from that particular source two or three more grates were made.

The present wood kiln has two grates made from #310 stainless steel stock 1''x¼''. These have been used for about 25 firings and there is no deterioration evident. They were costly but so far the cost seems to be justified.

Stacking. There are three 8''x20''x1'' silicon carbide shelves, which are supported at each corner, 2½'' above the floor of the ware chamber. They are spaced 2'' from the sides of the arch with approximately 2'' between each shelf. Under the centers of the two side shelves there is a post set into the floor of the flue. This becomes the base support for the third post in the three-point setting for the two tiers of shelves stacked on up into the arch from above the first three shelves. A channel of ½ to 2'' is maintained between these two tiers and is at right angles to the flue. Some full

pots extend into this space but I try to stagger the channel spaces these pots occupy.

In general a wood-fired kiln is stacked as evenly but not as tightly as I have stacked other fuel kilns. (A tight stacking, to me, is one where the pieces are separated only by a hair and are of compatible shape with not more than ¼'' between the tops of pots and shelf above.) Any kiln should be stacked evenly; with even stacking the chances are better for even firing. If, when standing back and seeing the final stacking, you are aware of an even distribution of pots and kiln furniture, in balance with the open spaces, the kiln is evenly stacked.

To use the catenary curve more efficiently and easily when stacking I ordered shelves of varying widths. They are all 20'' long and are 12'', 10'', 9'', 8'', and 7'' wide. Thickness for the 12''x20'' is 1⅛''; all the others are 1'' thick.

The kiln posts are heavy duty refractories cut at the brick yard to useful heights and proportionally supportive thicknesses.

Cone Packs. These are made in groups well ahead of stacking so they can dry. Also, because several are made at one time, if one is broken during stacking there is a dry replacement. The top cone pack starts with c/04, followed by c/4, 8, 9, 10, and 11. The bottom cone pack (on the opposite side of the ware chamber) starts with c/08, then c/04, 4, 8, 9, 10, and 11. In front of each cone pack I put a small biscuit pinch bowl to catch the lower cones as they melt.

Cone 4 is an important and useful cone in a c/9 to 11 firing. Its falling gives a timely warning and corrections can be made for time/temperature differences top to bottom, if they exist, before c/8 and 9 begin falling. It is also a morale booster during the firing—from c/04 to c/8 is a long and hot way when you are alone splitting and stoking.

Kiln Wash. This is equal parts of alumina hydrate, flint, and kaolin (EPK). This mix is usually screened through a 35-mesh sieve. After the kiln shelves have been wire brushed, possibly glaze chipped and patched back to level, I spray them with the kiln wash. By doing this necessary (however unpleasant) job immediately after unstacking, the shelves are still warm, and two thin, even coats of wash can be sprayed on, drying very quickly. As the kiln is unstacked the ends of the kiln posts are checked for flatness, chipped and ground if necessary, then dipped into the kiln wash. This helps keep them from sticking to the shelves. After the wash has dried, which it does quickly as they are still warm, I lightly grind the washed ends flat. It is a rather good feeling to come to stack again and not be faced with the chore of grinding, chipping, and washing shelves.

Alumina Hydrate. Pots stacked rim to rim, foot to foot, or inside each other are naturally unglazed in those contact areas; but because ash could glaze them together I brush on a thin coating of alumina hydrate in a gum solution. For all casseroles, teapots, and storage jars this is done.

If the foot of a pot is in uninterrupted alignment with a

bag-wall opening, a bit of this alumina hydrate is brushed on the foot. During the 16 years that I have been wood firing, countless pots have been successfully opened or removed from kiln shelves because of this cautious procedure.

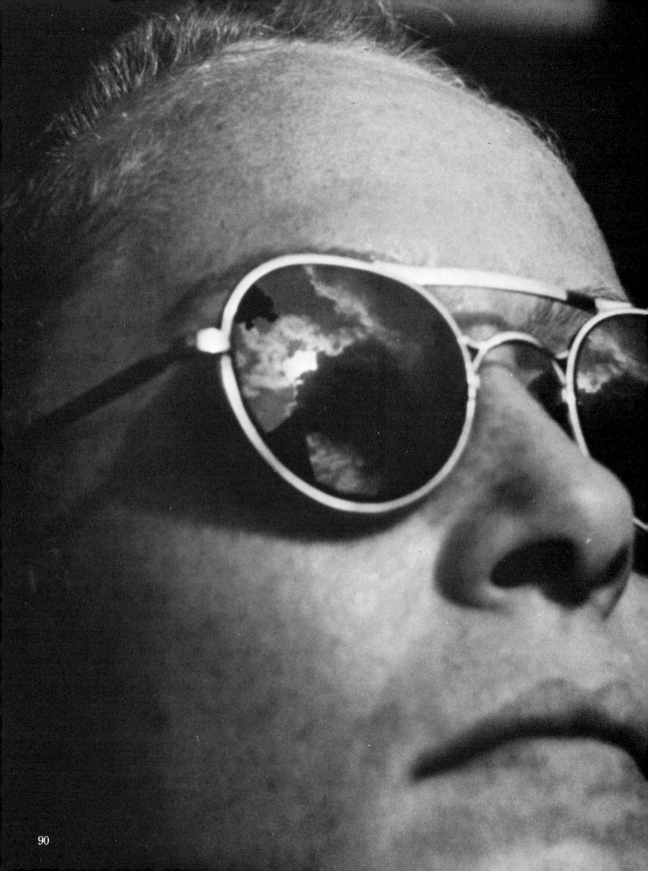

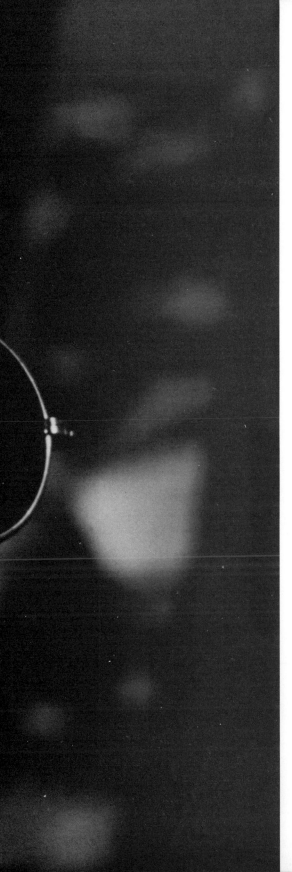

The Mark of This Fire

I am not interested in how fast I can reach temperature. If rapid firing were my goal, wood surely would not be my choice of fuel. It is the oneness with the kiln—the exhilaration—the awe of firing. Both of these emotions are heightened by the physical effort involved.

From dull red to bright yellow a quiet strength is gathering in the kiln. During the glaze reduction there is a "voice" in the stack—I usually reply.

All firing alters the ware, but my pots, fired unsaggered in this wood-burning kiln, have an additional alteration. During the firing, wood ash is deposited on the ware throughout the pot chamber; when high temperatures are reached the ash melts and fuses with the glaze, engobe, or with the clay of the pot.

Over the years that I have fired with wood these variable effects of the wood ash have become more and more predictable and thus planned for. It is this variable and unique quality—the mark inherent to this fire—that continues to hold my interest, is often my delight, and that always demands my respect.

Kiln Cycle

Following is my usual procedure for firing the kiln.

Firing: Stoking. Overnight, both grates are filled with dry, large, knotty, and unsplittable wood. This is replenished two or three times during the night. As the firing progresses the next day less and less wood is stoked into the lower grate as coals falling from the top grate accumulate, are more consumed, and fall into the ash pit. It was for this more efficient burning that the top grate was designed with five bars while the lower grate has seven. As temperature increases stoking occurs more and more frequently. After red heat four to five pieces are added every three to four minutes; now I am splitting the slabs into sections of 1 x 2'' and 2 x 3''. It really does not need to be any smaller— smaller sections only mean more splitting and more rapid stoking. Rapid stoking is not the way to obtain an even and steady temperature rise throughout the kiln; keep the wood coming at an even and steady rate and in balance with the action of the primaries and stack. If your kiln is evenly stacked, it all, usually, works out.

The question of hard and soft woods in firing is often raised. The facts are these: hard woods burn longer with a steady flame while soft woods are consumed at a faster rate because they contain considerable amounts of resins and oils (refer to the *Woodburner's Handbook* mentioned previously). In each stoke I have found it best to throw the heavy hard wood in first, then "float" the lighter soft wood on top. The hard wood tends to break up—and to hasten the burning of—wood mostly consumed from the previous stoke. The lighter soft wood can be aimed to fall where it is needed while maintaining ample air flow from the primaries through the wood.

As much as possible the wood should be crisscrossed on the grate and covering it evenly. If it is all side-by-side the air is decreased—burning is slowed—then, as failure to climb is noticed, more wood is invariably added, compounding the situation. Too much wood is almost as bad as not enough. Put the wood when and where you see the grate burning clear; you are the fuel injector, keep it coming evenly in rhythm and timing with the kiln. The fire and coals should be lively and bright. If areas of dead coals or ashes build up and begin to clog primaries or grate areas, shake and rake these cinders out.

The stoke holes might be half-opened if more secondary air is required. Then an insulating brick is placed in the stoke hole toward the bag wall; by putting it there the cooler outside air is not pulled directly in and through the bag wall. During body and glaze reductions, or if it is windy, the stoke holes remain closed between stokings. Usually I keep them closed between stokings for the main part of the firing. (Stoke holes and ash pit are closed with 2300°F insulating brick.) The stokes are opened at the end of the firing for the last 10 to 15 minutes and the damper is pulled out while stoking continues. This clearing and oxidizing fire has a brightening effect on the ware which I quite like.

Although the ash pit could be regarded as a dead fuel basin, if I see any life there the insulating bricks closing the ash pit are opened one-quarter to one-third of the way.

When the stoke holes above are closed and the ash pit is partially opened this secondary air is well heated before joining forces with the primary air coming in under the top grate and across the lower one. Possibly this could be regarded as primary air for the coals filling the lower grate. It certainly gives more life to the fuel on the lower grate and the flames pull through the openings in the bottom of the bag wall more steadily.

Closing, Cooling, Opening. After temperature has been reached and oxidation concluded, the stoke holes and ash pit are closed and the top grate is allowed to burn clear. While this is happening the damper is pushed in a bit and the top primaries are closed with insulating bricks. As the top grate burns clear I close the bottom primaries and keep easing in the damper till no back pressure is noted at the spyholes. Then a sheet of transite is put up against the end wall covering the primaries and the expanded space between the arch and end wall. The stoke holes and ash pit are also covered.

Unlike gas or oil you cannot "turn off" the fuel in a wood fired kiln—there is still quite a charge of heat in the coals of the firebox long after that last stoke. There is also quite a bit of fly ash as these coals dissipate. If air circulates now through the firebox this ash will be deposited on the cooling ware. Depending on what is in the ware chamber this may or may not be disastrous—thus the rather elaborate closing.

The kiln cools 36 to 40 hours. Twenty-four hours after the firing I remove the transite from the door and end wall; the damper is opened an inch or so. Three or four hours later the damper is pulled out 2'' more. Seven to eight hours from then I take down the insulating layer of the door, plug the spyholes, and open the damper. After four hours (approximately) I push the damper back in and start taking down the refractory door bricks.

It is a slow process, for me, throughout the making, bisquing, glazing, stacking, firing, and cooling. It would be stupid and wasteful to drop a pot (or kiln shelf) now because it was too hot to handle so I wait till I can.

WOOD KILN LOG

Orton Cones: 9-10   **Atmosphere:** Reduction   **Date:** June 19 & 20 '74   **Weather:** Foggy in PM Clearing in AM

Time	Temperature	Top			Primary Air							Bottom		Damper Open	Remarks
		1	2	3	4	5	6	7	8	9	10	11	12	13		
4:30 PM		●	●	●	●	●	●	●	●	●	●	●	●	●	1″	small fire in ashpit. spy holes open: stoke holes closed.
8:30		●	●	●	●	●	●	●	●	●	●	●	●	●	1½″	fire laid both grates, started.
1:15 AM		●	●	●	●	●	●	●	●	●	●	●	●		1½″	both grates stoked.
3:30		●	●	●	●	●	●	●	●	●	▼	●	●		2½″	close bottom spy hole. stoked.
5:00	dull red color on top flames pulling in bottom	●	●	●	●	●	●	●	▼	●	▼	●	▼	●	3½″	close top spy hole. transite on door. open ashpit ¼.
6:00	color evening out	●	●	▼	●	▼	▼	▼		▼		▼		▼	4½″	shake ashpit. start splitting.
7:00	good color top & bottom	▼	▼	▼											6″	stokes closed between stokings.
8:00	red heat — even color														7″	all primaries open full.
9:30	c/08 softening bottom														8″	
10:00	c/04 softening top															
10:20	c/08 down bottom c/04 3 o'clock top															
10:30	c/04 down top c/04 1 o'clock bottom		●		●	●									5″	45 min. body reduction. close ash pit.
11:15	c/04 down bottom														8″	clear kiln 10 min. open stokes and ash pit.
11:25															6½″	close stokes, open ashpit ⅓.
2:00 PM	c/4 2 o'clock top c/4 3 o'clock bottom															shake & rake ashpit, shake & rake primary openings.
2:40	c/4 down top & bottom															
3:30	c/8 down top c/8 3 o'clock bottom															
4:10	c/9 3 o'clock top c/8 down bottom															
4:45	c/9 down top c/9 3 o'clock bottom															shake & rake ashpit and primary air openings.
5:15	c/10 1 o'clock top c/9 4 o'clock bottom	●		●		●	●								5″	45 min. glaze reduction. stokes closed. ashpit open ⅓.
6:00	c/10 3 o'clock top c/9 down bottom														8″	15 min. oxidation. open ash pit and stoke holes.
6:15	c/10 1 o'clock bottom c/10 down top with c/11 softening top. c/10 3 o'clock bottom.	●	●	●	●	●	●	●	●	●	●	●	●	●		last stoke. close stokes & ashpit. grate burns clear. close primaries. ease in damper.

all primaries closed

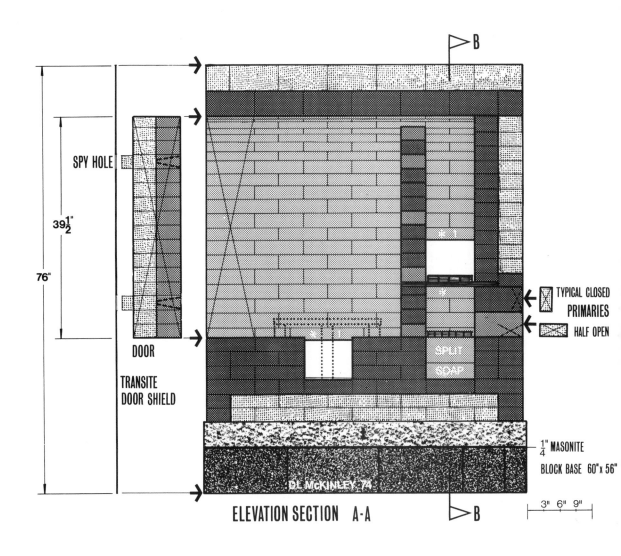

SPY HOLE

$39\frac{1}{2}"$

76"

DOOR

TRANSITE
DOOR SHIELD

B

#1

SPLIT

SOAP

TYPICAL CLOSED
PRIMARIES

HALF OPEN

$\frac{1}{4}"$ MASONITE

BLOCK BASE 60"x 56"

DL McKINLEY 74

ELEVATION SECTION A-A

B

3" 6" 9"

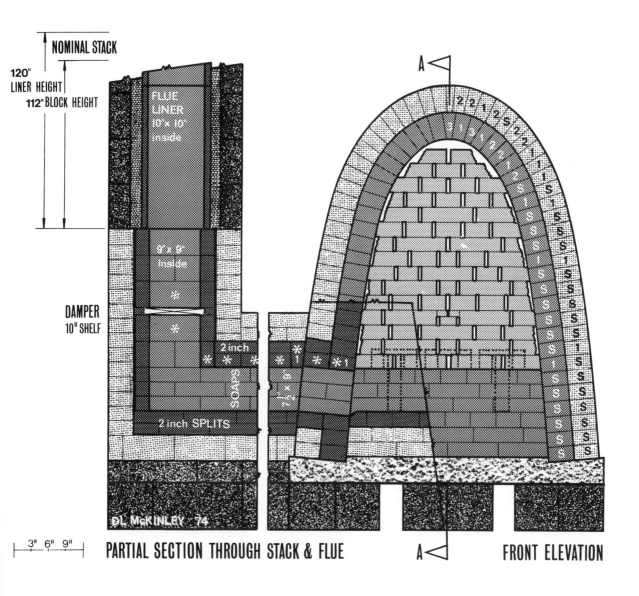

NOMINAL STACK

120" LINER HEIGHT

112" BLOCK HEIGHT

FLUE LINER 10" x 10" inside

9" x 9" inside

DAMPER 10" SHELF

2 inch

SOAPS

2 inch SPLITS

7½" x 9"

DL. McKINLEY '74

3" 6" 9"

PARTIAL SECTION THROUGH STACK & FLUE

A

A

FRONT ELEVATION

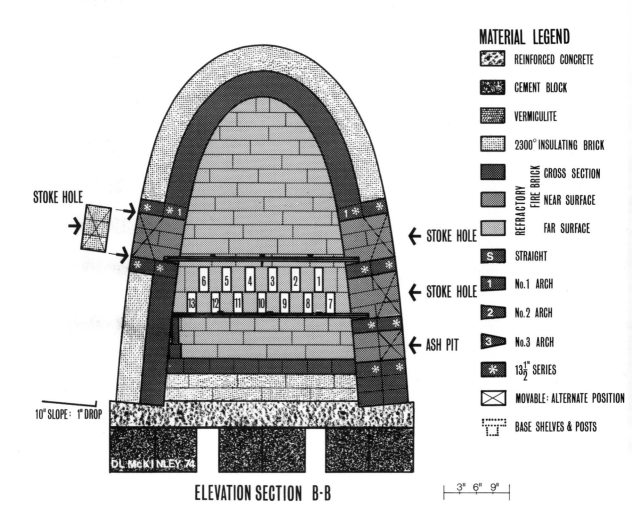

MATERIAL LEGEND

REINFORCED CONCRETE

CEMENT BLOCK

VERMICULITE

2300° INSULATING BRICK

REFRACTORY FIRE BRICK
- CROSS SECTION
- NEAR SURFACE
- FAR SURFACE

S STRAIGHT

1 No.1 ARCH

2 No.2 ARCH

3 No.3 ARCH

✳ $13\frac{1}{2}"$ SERIES

☒ MOVABLE: ALTERNATE POSITION

BASE SHELVES & POSTS

STOKE HOLE

← STOKE HOLE

← STOKE HOLE

← ASH PIT

10" SLOPE: 1" DROP

DL McKINLEY 74

ELEVATION SECTION B-B

3" 6" 9"

Double-lidded porcelain tobacco jar: 8'' high brushed red iron slip and ash-flashed outside C/10-11. Reduction: wood-fired. Medal Award: Ceramic International 1973.

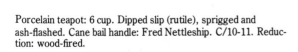

Porcelain teapot: 6 cup. Dipped slip (rutile), sprigged and ash-flashed. Cane bail handle: Fred Nettleship. C/10-11. Reduction: wood-fired.

Two Teapots: Left, stoneware. Right, porcelain. 5 Cup ea. Both glazed with same semi matt glaze w/2% iron. Not much evidence of wood firing as these were toward the center and under a shelf. C/9-11 reduction: wood fired.

Stoppered & Sprigged Stoneware Jugs: 10'' high Ash-Flashed Outside C/9-10 Reduction: wood fired

Stoneware Casserole: 5 Quart. Hand built handles with spriggs. Ash path across center of lid. c/ 10-11 reduction: wood fired

Great American Kilns: Warren McKenzies' Kiln 1975

THE MINNESOTA FLAT TOP KILN

by Nils Lou

The potter's ultimate tool is the flame-filled box of roaring madness. Building a kiln is a duel with the dragon of ancient secrets.

Presented here is the Minnesota Flat Top (MFT), a periodic car kiln which is the result of an evolutionary process having its origins in the sprung arch kiln made of brick. None of the features of this kiln is unique in itself; it is the combination of parts that makes it work. And each part has been worked out previously in an earlier kiln. The MFT design is efficient. Twelve have been built to date in Minnesota, and there are nine similar kilns that are not car kilns.

Features

Construction is of loose brick lay-up; the roof is a floating flat slab made of brick; the trolley seals like a cork; the flue is a tuned, double-venturi chamber; and the size is flexible.

It uses two liquid-withdrawal propane burners that develop one million BTU/hr. and work at temperatures below zero. Very efficient, they fire this kiln in seven and one-half hours, typically using less than $12 worth of propane (@$.35/gal.). Reduction is controlled by a ceramic fiber damper (M-Board). And without changing the firing characteristics the loading capacity can be altered from 30 to 60 cubic feet. If built initially to at least 30 cubic feet, additional space costs about $11 per cubic foot. Described here is the 45 cubic foot design which costs $1500 complete (prices as of April 1976).

Design Description

Brick construction was planned after determing that K-23 insulating firebrick (IFB) was the material of choice.

K-23 IFB has no problem working to c/10 temperatures. It is superior to K-26 IFB in insulation ability and costs significantly less. Don't be tempted to use K-26 IFB unless you are firing to c/12 and higher. All bricks in the MFT are laid with no mortar (except for the roof). No bricks need to be cut. The kiln can be dismantled as easily as it is built and all parts used again. The flat roof eliminates the need for arch or wedge brick as well as the need for curved templates. The geometry of the roof's 9'' thickness creates an internal dome that is held all around with a double tie rod system. It can't collapse if it can't spread out. Mortar slip is used on the roof bricks to prevent them from sliding out. It isn't used to hold the roof up.

The floor and door combine to make a trolley, which certainly helps to alleviate chronic back problems. Sealing the floor to the kiln when closed is accomplished by shaping the middle layer of IFB in the floor in a wedge or cork form. It's simple and it works! "Kiln experts" may say that the flue port in the MFT is too small. It is, in fact, an essential part of the tuned double-venturi flue chamber. With the slightest flame, an immediate draft is created and the damper effects exacting control on the kiln atmosphere.

Burners and Firing

The burners that I use with the MFT are liquid burners that vaporize the fuel at the burner head allowing for extreme cold weather firing. The complete burner system for this kiln cost approximately $185.00. If desired automatic safety shut-off valves (not requiring electrical connections) are available at a cost of about $285.00.

Firing the MFT is simple and straightforward. Each burner has its own needle valve which controls the flame size. The damper controls back pressure, hence reduction. No blower is required, so the kiln can be built practically anywhere. The downdraft design functions so well that cone packs placed in the extreme corners melt simultaneously if the load is of even density and stacked to allow good vertical circulation of heated air.

Construction Details

The kiln car (trolley) is the first thing to fabricate. Two lengths of channel steel form the main structure with 2'' angle welded between them producing a ladder shape. It is important to cut accurately and weld strongly. When welding the trolley, take pains to keep the top flat as this will be supporting the floor bricks. When orienting the castors, place them so the grease fitting is on the outside for easier access. (Once a year lubrication is sufficient.) When the trolley is assembled, place on the inverted 1¼'' angle which becomes the track. Be sure to allow enough room between the trolley and the kiln when open to walk. With the position determined and the track parallel, it should be anchored to the floor. Tabs welded to each end of the track can be drilled and anchor bolts will hold it fast.

The first layer (hard firebrick) is placed on the trolley with the bricks spanning the open spaces. This layer will be 36'' wide and 54'' long. It is the foundation for the door as well as the floor. K-23 IFB is used for the second layer and this is laid carefully in a wedge shape in order to provide the seal. To accomplish this the IFB layer must extend over the edges of the hard brick layer. Use the same number of bricks for this layer as the first. A wedge-shaped opening down the middle expands the size to provide the overlap. Fill this open space with IFB cut to fit (this is the only exception to the "no-cut" design). At the narrow end the opening will be about ½'' to 1½'' at the door end. This "cork" effect allows the seal to be broken instantly when the door is pulled open.

Be sure to have about ½'' overhand at the flue end of the floor, and check that the overhang is equal down the two sides so the trolley rolls out evenly. The third layer matches the first except that it does not include a row on the door foundation.

For the foundation of the walls around the trolley, standard cement blocks are used. Five on each side are spaced evenly with four blocks stretched end to end across the

Burner and burner port detail

Trolley fabricated and ready to begin construction

back. The space at each corner can be filled with either three hard firebricks or cement blocks turned 90°. Cement blocks will be used to support the flue chamber and the burners. The blocks on the sides are oriented with openings up. They will be supporting the flame trenches as well as the side walls. The drawing shows details of foundation brick placement, burner ports, and flue opening. Build the foundation with the trolley in place so the seal will have integrity. Move the trolley in and out to observe the spacing on the sides.

At this point the foundation is complete and the walls can be laid. This kiln will have 19 courses with each course consuming 40 bricks. Each course alternates in design so the bricks will overlap and the corners are locked. Note that every sixth row has two bricks turned 90° on each wall to tie the "inside" to the "outside."

The Roof

The roof is begun by cutting the ¾'' plywood to fit inside of and flush with the top of the three walls. It is propped in place with six 2x4s cut so they support at an angle for easy removal. The roof will require 336 bricks (12 rows of 28).

Start by mixing the mortar to a watery slip consistency; bricks are dipped to cover all faces that touch another brick. Slide the bricks together to ensure good contact.

For mortar we have used commercial refractory cement such as Trowleze or HiLoSet made by Babcock & Wilcox. The first row of 28 bricks is set across the front with attention given to straightness. It must be flat in order for the door to seal. The second row is begun by offsetting them slightly in order to keep the joints from lining up. Each row is alternated about ½'' to maintain the offset. In setting each brick keep it straight up and down as it is slid into place, and a good seal should be felt.

When all the bricks are in place the corner angles are set in place and the tie rods which have been threaded on the ends are attached and tightened. The rods in front are higher than the ones on the other three sides; this is to provide clearance for the door so it can overlap across the top 2½''. Before installing the upper tie rod on the front remember to slip on the two eyebolts which will be used to secure the door. Now the tie rods should be tightened gradually, working around the four sides. Try to snug up the pairs with equal tension and keep tightening until there is a slight "doming" of the roof. Now the roof should be slurried with thin mortar slip to fill in and seal any remaining cracks. High drama: remove the 2x4s and plywood—the roof stands!

The next step is to construct the door. Run the trolley in and check that the seal is good. Wedge the wheels and begin to lay up the door bricks overlapping just the way the walls were built. I build in two peepholes in the door by building around a full brick that is tapered slightly. The door itself should overlap the sides about 3'' and the top at least 2½''. With the bricks laid up tight against the kiln, the T-bar assembly (which is made with two angles bolted together with washer spacers separating them) is set on top of the door. The cable is attached to an eyebolt which is set in either extension on the trolley. The cable goes over the T-bar between the angles and down the other side to a turnbuckle set in the opposite extension. Snug the cable to the point where the top bricks are secure.

Door braces are now welded to the T-bar and bent down to meet the main channel extensions where they are either welded or bolted in place. I prefer bolts so it can be easily removed. Notches are cut in the T-bar to accept the eye bolts which hang on the upper front tie rod. These secure the door during firing. Wing nuts are convenient in conjunction with washers and need only finger tightening.

The Flue Chamber and Chimney Stack

What remains is to construct the flue chamber and erect the chimney. Begin by entering two cement blocks below the flue opening, forming a square foundation. The top layer of four bricks is positioned to form a square 5¾'' by 5¾''. This opening closely matches the lower kiln flue opening in area creating a double-venturi effect on the draft. The chimney liner sleeves will exactly fit around this opening. It may be necessary to scrape the M-Board damper a little so it will slide easily in its slot.

The stack is constructed by putting the three stovepipe sections together and erecting them so each upper section slides down inside of the lower one. It is the opposite of the normal orientation. This is done so the M-Board sleeves will slide down the pipe when dropped in from above. It is easier to slide them in place on the ground and then erect them; the pipe can of course be set "right side up." Roof flashing and storm collar are attached and the flashing holds the stack in place. If there is no roof then guy wires are required. The stack simply rests on top of the flue chamber and should not be mortared to it, as this will hold in the heat and corrode the metal. No hood or cover is needed as the sleeves are not adversely effected by the elements.

Ignition Procedure

For a biscuit firing I use a pressure of 8 lbs. on the regulator which allows a nice, soft flame initially and is quite enough pressure to finish with, firing to approximately 850°C. For a glaze firing I set the regulator at 18 lbs. and leave it there for the entire firing. The burners will ignite instantly but will begin to burn more efficiently after 10 minutes or so as the coil heats up and begins to actively vaporize the liquid propane.

There are four settings of flame that can be usefully described and they are: 1. A soft, yellow flame that is just sucked into the kiln chamber. 2. A stronger flame that has some blue color. 3. A forceful flame that is mostly blue but has some yellow. 4. A roaring flame that is blue having little or no yellow, and increasing the valve opening produces no visible difference in the flame structure. This last setting is used when the temperature has reached 700°C and no further increase is needed to reach final heat. After reaching maturity the kiln can be cooled very slowly by shutting the damper and blocking the burner ports. The M-Board damper holds the heat in well as it is a good insulator. M-Board shapes cut to fit are good to close the burner ports with as well.

Safety Trip Valve

It is recommended that a trip valve (REGO-7553S) be installed in the line between the regulator and the supply tank. A wire can be attached to the trip lever and extended into the kiln room. By fastening this wire to another that is attached to the wall around the kiln the valve can be tripped easily from anywhere near the kiln. It is a safety feature that offers peace of mind in case of difficulty.

Reduction Firing

Firing this kiln is an extremely simple matter. The burner valves are periodically turned up to increase the amount of heat in a controlled fashion. An oxidation firing is accomplished by leaving the damper in the open position. For reduction the damper is closed to the point where there is enough back pressure to reduce the amount of secondary air coming in at the burner ports. This is usually begun at early red heat (700°C) and continued throughout the firing. Just before vitrification (900°C) it may be wise to open the damper, producing an oxidation atmosphere, in case there is any carbon yet unburned in the clay. With clay mined near a coal vein, this is a common cause of bloating. By oxidizing at this time the unburned carbon is vaporized, which won't happen under reduction conditions.

Other factors which can effect the kiln atmosphere:

1. Fuel pressure. It is usually not necessary to set the regulator at more than 20 lbs. Weather conditions can affect firing, but there is no need to have a flame coming out of the stack.

2. Burner placement. The burner head should be about 2'' from the burner port. More or less distance will affect the amount of secondary air allowed in.

3. Tightness of kiln. Removing a peephole brick reduces pressure. The flame may be prominent at first and then reduce in size, even disappear. This occurs because the peephole opening is large enough to allow a reduction in pressure, letting more secondary air in at the burner ports. More complete combustion reduces the amount of unburnt fuel, hence no flame at the peep. Personally I adjust for this condition as an indication of slight to medium reduction.

Those of you who build this kiln will find it easy to fire, a joy to load, and efficient in its use of fuel.

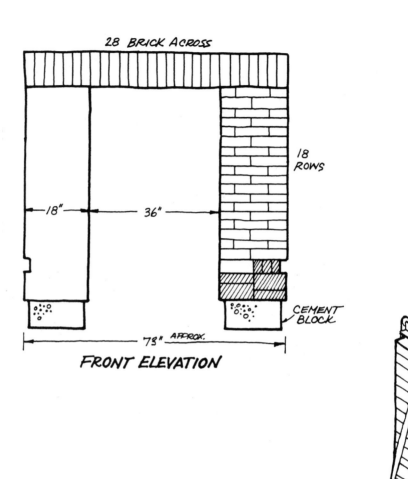

28 BRICK ACROSS

18 ROWS

18"   36"

CEMENT BLOCK

78" APPROX.

FRONT ELEVATION

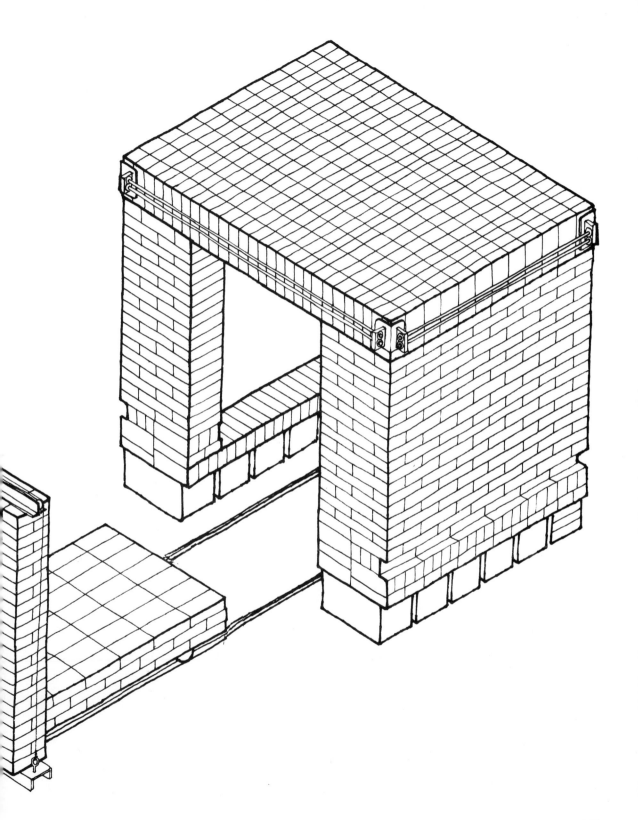

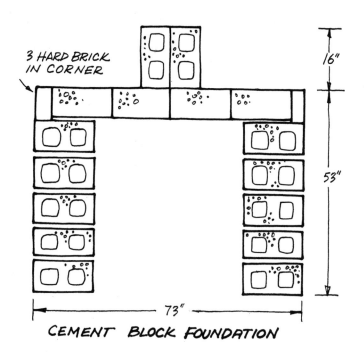

3 HARD BRICK
IN CORNER

16"

53"

73"

CEMENT BLOCK FOUNDATION

SIDE ELEVATION

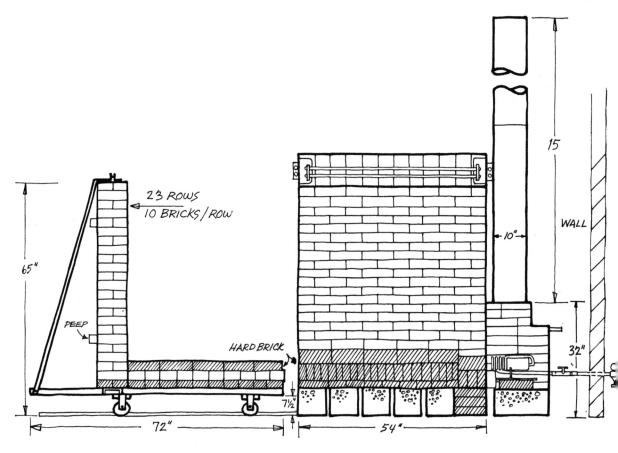

15

WALL

10"

23 ROWS
10 BRICKS / ROW

65"

PEEP

HARD BRICK

32"

7½"

72"

54"

FLUE CHAMBER   LAYER BY LAYER   BUILD-UP

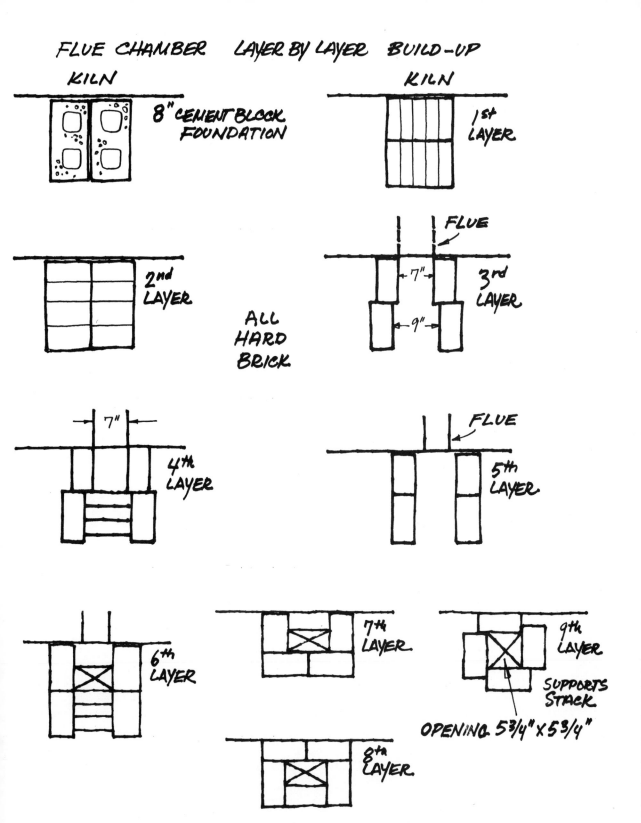

KILN — 8" CEMENT BLOCK FOUNDATION

KILN — 1st LAYER

2nd LAYER

ALL HARD BRICK

FLUE — 3rd LAYER — 7" — 9"

7" — 4th LAYER

FLUE — 5th LAYER

6th LAYER

7th LAYER

8th LAYER

9th LAYER — SUPPORTS STACK

OPENING 5¾" X 5¾"

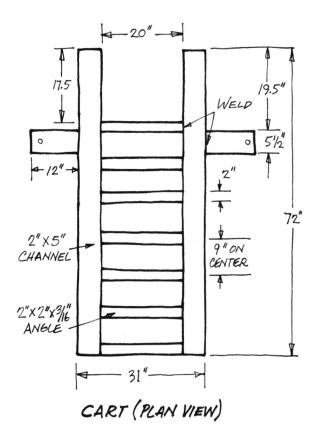

CART (PLAN VIEW)

20"

17.5

19.5"

WELD

5½"

12"

2"

2"X5"
CHANNEL

9" ON
CENTER

72"

2"X2"X3/16"
ANGLE

31"

Bill of Materials

1300 K-23 IFB straights (9''x4½''x2½'') (B & W)
300 medium-duty hard refractory bricks, straights
(9''x4½''x2½'') (B & W)
20 standard cement blocks (7½''x7½''x15'') (local)
4 V-groove steel castors (Bassick H-4981-2cw)
Steel: (local)
14' channel (2''x5'') for trolley
30' angle (2''x2''x3/16'') for door braces, door T-bar hold-
down, trolley
24' angle (1¼''x1¼''⅛'') for track
3' angle (3''x3''x¼'') for roof corners
40' rod (½'' hot rolled) for roof ties

Chimney:

3 sections 24 gauge stovepipe (5'x10'') galvanized (local)
1 roof flashing and storm collar assembly for 10'' stack
(local)
15 M-Board sleeves (8½'' I.D.) (B & W)

Burners:

2 FL-1 liquid propane burners, valves and regulator
(Nils Lou)
Assorted high pressure hoses, connectors and tees
(Nils Lou)
1 Trip valve (REGO 7553S) (Nils Lou)

Miscellaneous:

1 M-Board slab (9''x20''x1'') (B & W)
100 lbs. refractory mortar (Trowleze or fireclay slip)
(B & W)
1 pyrometer and thermocouple assembly (0 to 1300°C scale
(Skutt)
1 sheet of plywood (4'x8'x¾'') (local)
6 2''x4''x6' dimensional lumber (local)
16' wire cable (3/16'') (local)
Assorted nuts, bolts, washers, eye bolts, turnbuckle, and
cable clamps (local)
Approximate cost of above materials as of April 1976 was
$1500.

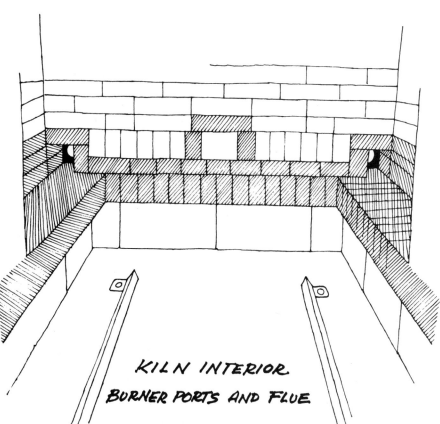

KILN INTERIOR
BURNER PORTS AND FLUE

THE CRANEY HILL OXIDATION KILN

by Dave Robinson

An electric kiln has a distinct advantage in that it produces little or no pollution at the kiln site, and poses less of a fire danger than a fuel-fired kiln because it has no flame, chimney, or back-pressure. In comparing an electric oxidation kiln, however, with any fuel-fired kiln it should be realized that ultimately there is a significant loss of energy in the production and transmission of electricity.

I have developed an inexpensive loosebrick electric kiln which is easy to build, durable, expandable, and recyclable. As needs change all materials except the elements can be rearranged. The switchboard and some of the bricks in the kiln pictured have been used in about 1,000 firings in various kilns including a 4 cubic foot low-fire version, and 30 cubic foot high-fire (c/8) version.

Foundation and Floor

Many kilns are built with two floor courses (2½'' direction)

of insulating firebrick (IFB) on a concrete slab. The concrete could crack; however, if it is properly reinforced and/or supported this shouldn't be a problem. If more insulating is desired a third course of insulating firebrick may be used on top of 8'' concrete blocks laid to permit horizontal circulation of air. On wooden floors concrete blocks should be mounted on a steel platform set on brick supports. Enough space should be left beneath the platform to be able to reach under to check that the wood does not become too hot to touch during the firing and for the duration of the cooling cycle.

Figures 5, 6, and 7 show the three course floor used in this presentation of a c/8 kiln.

Walls

The walls are built from 2½''x4½''x9'' IFB laid up in a pattern indicated in figure 8.

To groove the bricks for the elements make two cuts and break out the scrap (see figures 9 and 10). Use a worn out rip or cross-cut hand saw (after cutting bricks it will never work on wood again) or a table saw with a silicon carbide disc blade (motor and bearings must be protected from the abrasive brick dust; low RPM is preferable).

Courses 11 and 12 are laid up above the frame so that they can be partly taken down to facilitate loading. Additional courses may be added for bisque firings.

Peepholes

The kiln tends to fire evenly horizontally, but usually needs to have one or more elements turned off briefly towards the end of the firing to balance it vertically. By making six peepholes (see figures 11, 12, and 1), I'm sure to have several that aren't blocked by shelves in almost any stacking arrangement. Peepholes are needed on only one side of the kiln.

Roof

The lids shown in the photograph are built with the 2½''x9'' brickface towards the heat. They have been fired 500 times to bisque and earthenware temperatures with virtually no maintenance. For high-fire kilns, however, the type of lids shown in figure 3 are recommended. If desired, five lids spanning the length of the kiln may be used rather than nine lids spanning the width. As a general rule, the longer the span of the lid, the shorter its life. No mortar is used in any of these lids.

Frame

Wall courses 1 thru 6 are laid up tightly and checked with a carpenter's level. Course 7 should be notched to receive frame part D before placement in the wall (figures 2 and 4), using a worn out wood rasp or other tool. Place and weld

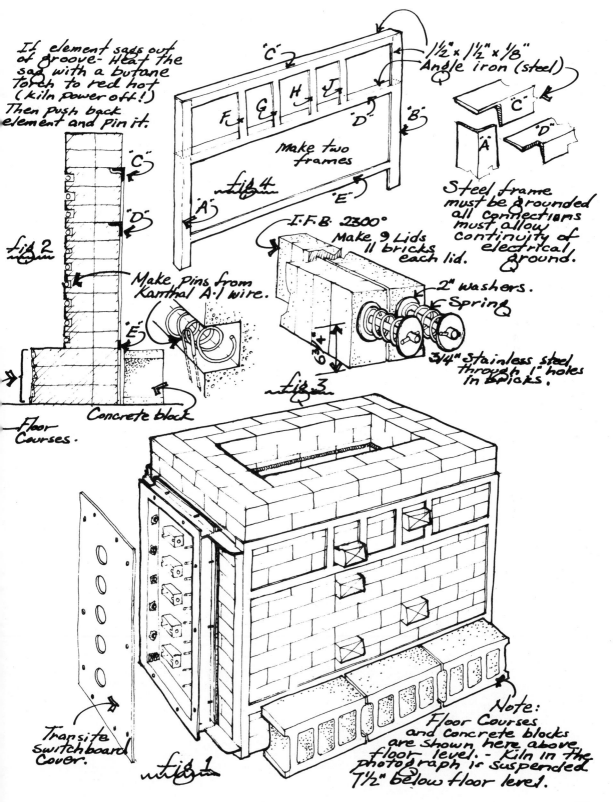

If element sags out of groove- Heat the sag with a butane torch to red hot (kiln power off!) Then push back element and pin it.

"C"
"D"

fig 2

Make pins from Kanthal A·1 wire.

"E"

Concrete block

Floor Courses.

"C"
"F" "G" "H" "J"
"D"
"B"

make two frames

fig 4
"A"
"E"

1½" x 1½" x ⅛" Angle iron (steel)

"C"
"A"
"D"

Steel frame must be grounded all connections must allow continuity of electrical ground.

I.F.B. 2300°
Make 9 Lids 11 bricks each lid.

2" washers.
Spring

3/4" Stainless steel through 1" holes in bricks.

6½"

fig 3

Note:
Floor Courses and Concrete blocks are shown here above floor level. - Kiln in the photograph is suspended 7½" below floor level.

Transite Switchboard Cover.

fig 1

111

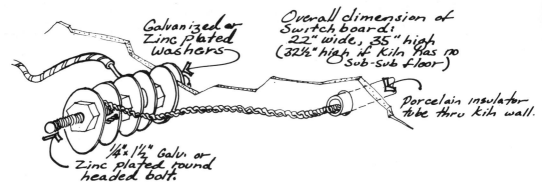

Galvanized or Zinc plated Washers

Overall dimension of Switchboard: 22" wide, 35" high (32½" high if Kiln has no Sub-sub floor)

¼"x 1½" Galv. or Zinc plated round headed bolt.

Porcelain insulator tube thru kiln wall.

~WIRE KEY~
Black...
White...
Ground.
Asbestos.

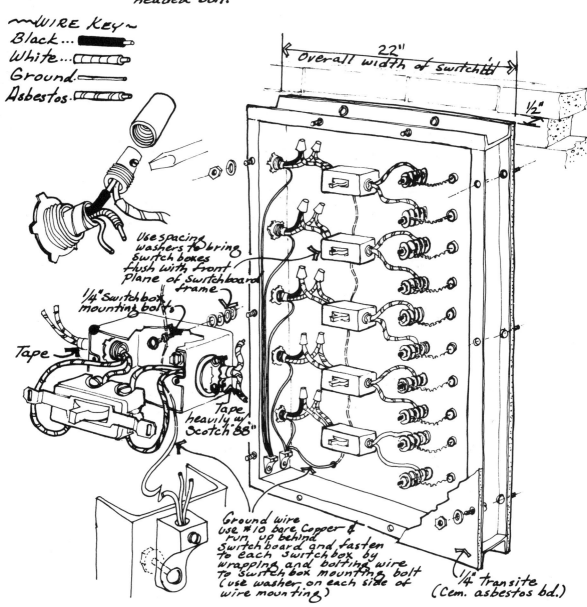

22"
Overall width of switchbd.

½"

Use spacing washers to bring switch boxes flush with front plane of switchboard frame

¼" Switchbox mounting bolts

Tape

Tape heavily w/ Scotch "88"

Ground wire use #10 bare Copper & run up behind Switchboard and fasten to each switchbox by wrapping and bolting wire to switchbox mounting bolt (use washer on each side of wire mounting)

¼" transite (Cem. asbestos bd.)

parts A and B to D leaving approximately ⅛'' for brick expansion in the 54'' direction. Lay up courses 8 and 9. Notch course 10 for part C before placement, then install C over course 10 and weld to A and B (figure 4). Knee rests F, G, H, J (figure 4), and toe guard E are made from ⅛''x1½'' steel strap welded flush to the outer face of the frame. Weld four short angle irons from A to the sides of the switchboard (figure 1) to hold front of frames together, leaving about 1/16'' for expansion and at the same time holding the back of the switchboard ½'' out from the brickface. (The kiln in the photo varies from this because re-use of a previously designed switchboard required a more complex connection.) The backs of the frames are held together by two bars or straps of steel, again welded to leave 1/16'' for expansion.

If a welder is not available a bolted frame can be designed. In either case the following guidelines apply:
• LEAVE EXPANSION ROOM
• ARRANGE FOR PEEPHOLE LOCATIONS
• ALLOW FOR EASE OF LOADING KILN
• AVOID SHARP CORNERS AND EDGES
• PROVIDE ½'' AIR SPACE BETWEEN BACK OF SWITCHBOARD AND BRICKFACE

Elements

Some people find the calculation and coiling of elements to be the major stumbling block in building an electric kiln. Rather than go through a lot of calculations for each kiln I build, I always use the same two elements. Both are made of 13-guage Kanthal A-1 wire. The element shown in figure 14 uses 560 grams of wire and draws 3000 watts at 240 volts. The other element uses one-sixth more wire (653 grams) and draws one-sixth less power (2500 watts). In a 4 cubic foot low-fire kiln I used two 2500 watt elements, each going around the kiln four times, and in a 30 cubic foot high-fire kiln I used ten 3000 watt elements, each going around the kiln one time. The kiln presented here uses five 3000 watt elements, each going around two times. While these may not be the ideal elements for each kiln, I have found their life to be very satisfactory. The winding set-up shown in figure 14 is crude but with a little practice elements can be produced that are hard to distinguish from those professionally wound. If the first element comes out a little light or heavy, the next one can be wound slightly longer or shorter. The hotter elements (the shorter, lighter ones) can be used at the bottom of the kiln. A set of 3000 watt elements ranging from, say, 540 to 580 grams is perfectly acceptable.

Power and Switchboard

The power comes to the kiln from the five circuit breakers via five cables. At 240 volts the kiln will draw 52 or 62.5 amps depending on which size elements are used. In either case a 60 amp main circuit breaker will *not* be sufficient since circuit breakers are good for only 80% of their rated capacity under continuous load.

The switchboard (figure 13) uses five parallel 20 amp double-pole switches. An electrician should be consulted during the planning stage to check for compliance with local codes.

Bill of Materials

This list covers the basic kiln: it does not include circuit breakers and cables leading to kiln, foundation, kiln furniture, tools, etc.
11¼ cubic foot c/8 kiln with three-course floor, nine 11-brick lids, and 3000 watt elements.

283 Babcock & Wilcox 2300° IFB	$202
344 Babcock & Wilcox 2000° IFB	$224
100# Steel	$ 30
*41# Stainless steel rod	$115
**6¼# Kanthal A-1 Wire	$ 40
Cement asbestos board	$ 10
Other	$ 75
	$696

*I have seen the lids in figure 3 on several kilns but have not built any myself. I am reasonably sure that ⅜'' rod rather than ¾'' rod could be used, especially on the 11-brick version, thus reducing the cost of stainless steel to about $35.
**Available from Kanthal Corp., Bethel, CT. $200 minimum order. Prewound elements are available from Newton Potter's Supply, 93 Rumford Avenue, W. Newton, MA:
  3000 watt element, Cat. #92100 $15
  2500 watt element, Cat. #92101 $17
  (For low-fire version)

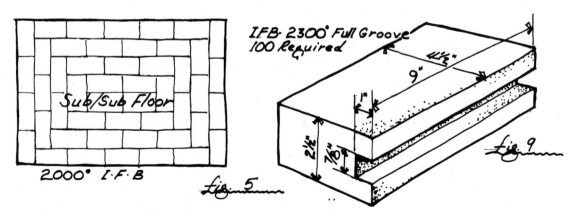

Sub/Sub Floor

2,000° I.F.B

fig. 5

IFB-2300° Full Groove
100 Required

9"

4½"

1"

2½"

¾"

fig. 9

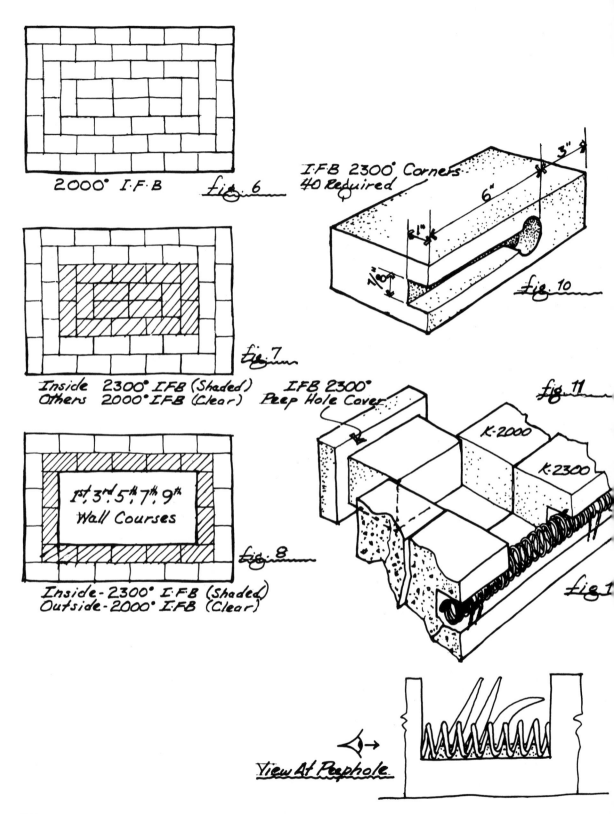

2000° I.F.B — fig. 6

Inside 2300° IFB (Shaded)
Others 2000° IFB (Clear) — fig. 7

1st, 3rd, 5th, 7th, 9th
Wall Courses

Inside - 2300° I.F.B (Shaded)
Outside - 2000° I.F.B (Clear) — fig. 8

I.F.B 2300° Corners
40 Required — fig. 10

3"
6"
1"
7/16"

IFB 2300°
Peep Hole Cover — fig. 11

K-2000
K-2300

fig. 1

View At Peephole

114

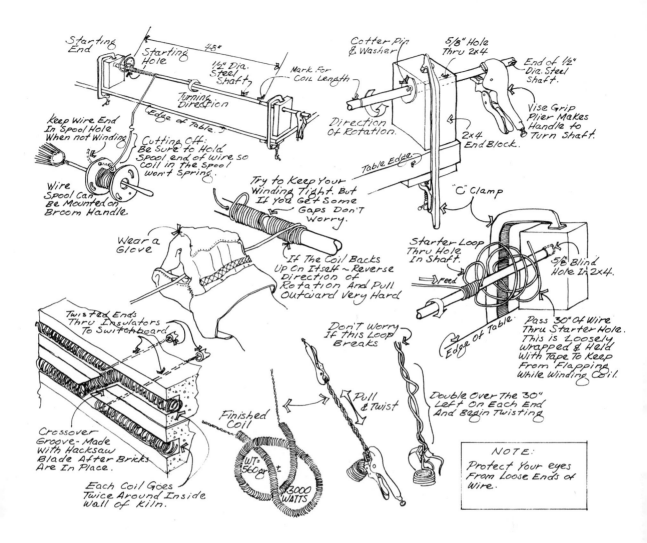

Starting End

Starting Hole

45"

½" Dia. Steel Shaft

Mark For Coil Length

Turning Direction

Edge of Table

Keep Wire End In Spool Hole When not Winding

Cutting Off: Be Sure to Hold Spool end of wire so Coil in the Spool won't spring.

Wire Spool Can Be Mounted on Broom Handle.

Cotter Pin & Washer

5/8" Hole Thru 2x4

End of ½" Dia. Steel Shaft.

Direction Of Rotation.

2x4 End Block.

Vise Grip Plier Makes Handle to Turn Shaft.

Table Edge

"C" Clamp

Try to Keep Your Winding Tight. But If you Get Some Gaps Don'T Worry.

Wear a Glove

If The Coil Backs Up On Itself ~ Reverse Direction of Rotation And Pull Outward Very Hard

Starter Loop Thru Hole In Shaft.

Feed

5/8 Blind Hole In 2x4.

Edge of Table

Pass 30" Of Wire Thru Starter Hole. This is Loosely wrapped & Held With Tape To Keep From Flapping While Winding Coil.

Twisted Ends Thru Insulators To Switchboard

Don'T Worry If This Loop Breaks

Pull & Twist

Double Over The 30" Left On Each End And Begin Twisting

Crossover Groove- Made With Hacksaw Blade After Bricks Are In Place.

Each Coil Goes Twice Around Inside Wall of Kiln.

Finished Coil

WT= 560 gr

3000 WATTS

NOTE: Protect Your eyes From Loose Ends of Wire.

Safety

Electrical Shock:
DON'T TOUCH ELEMENTS or take off switchboard cover unless all circuit breakers are off.
DON'T HAVE DAMP FLOORS– danger of electrocution.
DON'T FIRE new kiln without checking out with an electrician.

Fire:
LEAVE PLENTY OF ROOM between kiln and all flammable surfaces.
DON'T OPEN KILN until it is cool.
CONSULT your local fire marshall during planning stage and before new kiln is fired.
DON'T LEAVE KILN UNATTENDED during firing and cooling.
PROVIDE PROPER VENTILATION for dissipation of fumes and heat.

115

Great American Kilns: Pete Voulkos' Kiln circa 1955

ON BURNERS

by Norman Schulman

The safest and in the long run most economical solution to burners is to purchase them from a reputable commercial firm. Most burner manufacturers have field representatives or sales agencies with engineering staffs who willingly evaluate needs and recommend burner and pipe layouts to accommodate kiln requirements in terms of individual fuel resources. These people may be located in the Yellow Pages, through your gas company, or in the Ceramic Data Book, published by Cahners Publications, 221 Columbus Avenue, Boston, MA 02116.

Should this assistance not be conveniently available, the various gas-controls manufacturers publish handbooks. My "bible" is by the Fisher Governor Company, Marshalltown, IO: *LP-Gas Handbook of Technical Data*, 1960 edition— 50 cents. A sampling of information covered is: what size and where to locate tanks, size of pipe or tubing, testing for leaks, kinds of regulators to use, factual information about LP-Gas, and orifice capacities.

Considering primarily stoneware-porcelain firing ranges in downdraft periodic gas-fired kilns and the possibility of some raku firings, the compulsion by economic need, or the desire to "make your own," I offer for trial a series of burners that I have used successfully over the past decade-and-a-half.

I urge the use of new pipe and fittings and careful checking of joints for leaks. The pipe should be black iron and the fittings black malleable iron (double check where local codes are applicable). Also preferred are good quality needle, ball, or globe valves designed for use with the particular fuel installed. I have found in many instances that gas shut-off clocks do not work well as regulators. They don't "fine-tune" and they tend to leak.

It is preferable to install the pipes out of your working path and mount the burners as close to the kiln as possible. It is also a good idea to have a master shut-off valve upstream and handy to the kiln, which can be turned off easily in an emergency and which can be locked shut when the kiln is not firing. For additional safety information consult the following chapter by Dudley Giberson on Safety Systems.

The drawings are self-explanatory and allow for careful experimentation. Each application will have peculiar demands that require variation. The notes on the drawings suggest limits and alternatives.

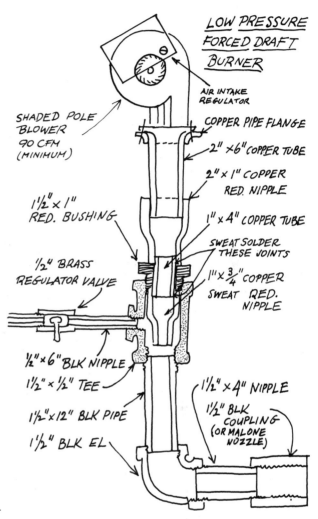

LOW PRESSURE FORCED DRAFT BURNER

AIR INTAKE REGULATOR

SHADED POLE BLOWER 90 CFM (MINIMUM)

COPPER PIPE FLANGE

2" × 6" COPPER TUBE

2" × 1" COPPER RED. NIPPLE

1" × 4" COPPER TUBE

SWEAT SOLDER THESE JOINTS

1" × ¾" COPPER SWEAT RED. NIPPLE

1½" × 1" RED. BUSHING

½" BRASS REGULATOR VALVE

½" × 6" BLK NIPPLE

1½" × ½" TEE

1½" × 12" BLK PIPE

1½" BLK EL

1½" × 4" NIPPLE

1½" BLK COUPLING (OR MALONE NOZZLE)

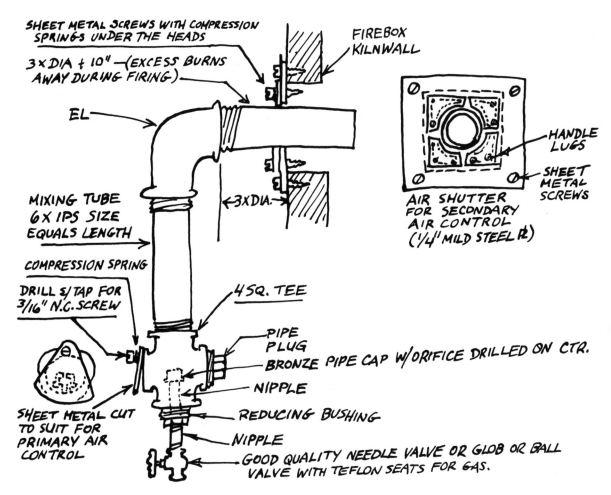

SHEET METAL SCREWS WITH COMPRESSION SPRINGS UNDER THE HEADS

3 × DIA ± 10" — (EXCESS BURNS AWAY DURING FIRING)

EL

MIXING TUBE 6 × IPS SIZE EQUALS LENGTH

COMPRESSION SPRING

DRILL & TAP FOR 3/16" N.C. SCREW

SHEET METAL CUT TO SUIT FOR PRIMARY AIR CONTROL

FIREBOX KILNWALL

←3×DIA.

4 SQ. TEE

PIPE PLUG

BRONZE PIPE CAP W/ORIFICE DRILLED ON CTR.

NIPPLE

REDUCING BUSHING

NIPPLE

GOOD QUALITY NEEDLE VALVE OR GLOB OR BALL VALVE WITH TEFLON SEATS FOR GAS.

HANDLE LUGS

SHEET METAL SCREWS

AIR SHUTTER FOR SECONDARY AIR CONTROL (1/4" MILD STEEL ℔)

USE BLACK IRON PIPE ONLY APPROXIMATE PIPE SIZES FOR 250M BTU BURNER ON 2 L♯. PRESSURE, NATURAL GAS. – –

NOZZLE, TUBE, EL, & SQ. TEE — 2 IN. IPS.
NIPPLES & VALVE 1/2 IN. IPS.
ORIFICES (SERIES) 1/16", 1/8", 3/16", 1/4" (CHANGE DURING FIRING AS NEEDED BEGIN WITH SMALLEST)

NATURAL DRAFT GAS BURNER

SIMILAR TO OLD ALFRED TYPE USED WITH NATURAL GAS AT 2# PRESSURE, BUT ADAPTABLE TO OTHER CONDITIONS BY USING APPROPRIATE ORIFICES.

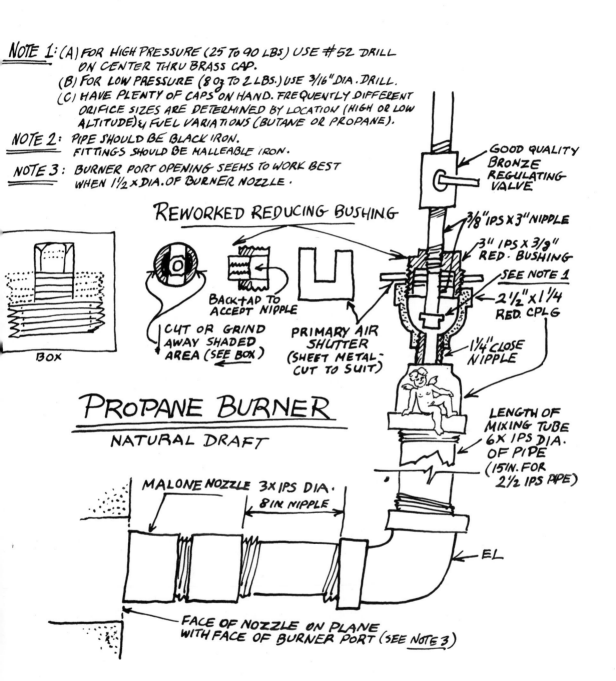

NOTE 1: (A) FOR HIGH PRESSURE (25 TO 90 LBS) USE #52 DRILL ON CENTER THRU BRASS CAP.
(B) FOR LOW PRESSURE (8 OZ TO 2 LBS.) USE 3/16" DIA. DRILL.
(C) HAVE PLENTY OF CAPS ON HAND. FREQUENTLY DIFFERENT ORIFICE SIZES ARE DETERMINED BY LOCATION (HIGH OR LOW ALTITUDE) & FUEL VARIATIONS (BUTANE OR PROPANE).

NOTE 2: PIPE SHOULD BE BLACK IRON. FITTINGS SHOULD BE MALLEABLE IRON.

NOTE 3: BURNER PORT OPENING SEEMS TO WORK BEST WHEN 1½ X DIA. OF BURNER NOZZLE.

REWORKED REDUCING BUSHING

BOX

BACK-TAP TO ACCEPT NIPPLE

CUT OR GRIND AWAY SHADED AREA (SEE BOX)

PRIMARY AIR SHUTTER (SHEET METAL - CUT TO SUIT)

GOOD QUALITY BRONZE REGULATING VALVE

3/8" IPS X 3" NIPPLE

3" IPS X 3/8" RED. BUSHING

SEE NOTE 1

2½" X 1¼ RED. CPLG

1¼" CLOSE NIPPLE

LENGTH OF MIXING TUBE 6X IPS DIA. OF PIPE (15 IN. FOR 2½ IPS PIPE)

PROPANE BURNER

NATURAL DRAFT

MALONE NOZZLE 3X IPS DIA.

8 IN NIPPLE

FACE OF NOZZLE ON PLANE WITH FACE OF BURNER PORT (SEE NOTE 3)

E.L.

FOR NATURAL DRAFT BURNERS —
SIMPLE INSPIRATOR WITH AIR SHUTTER

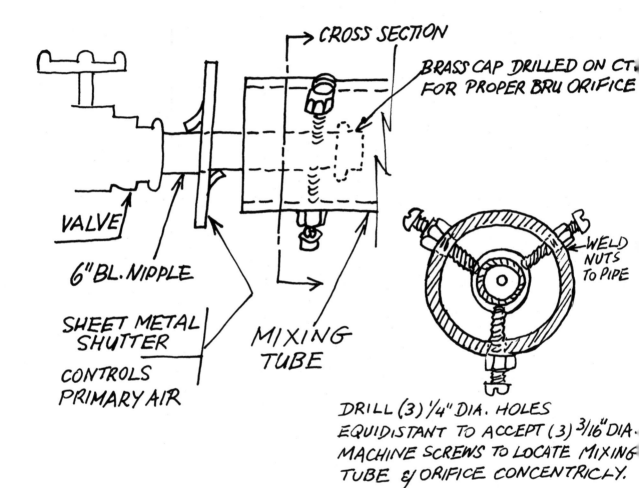

CROSS SECTION

BRASS CAP DRILLED ON CT. FOR PROPER BRU ORIFICE

VALVE

6" BL. NIPPLE

SHEET METAL SHUTTER

CONTROLS PRIMARY AIR

MIXING TUBE

WELD NUTS TO PIPE

DRILL (3) 1/4" DIA. HOLES EQUIDISTANT TO ACCEPT (3) 3/16" DIA. MACHINE SCREWS TO LOCATE MIXING TUBE & ORIFICE CONCENTRICLY.

COUPLING

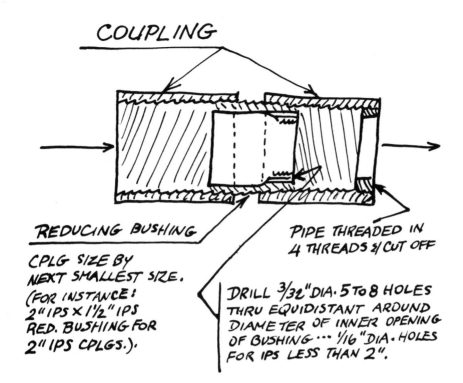

REDUCING BUSHING

CPLG SIZE BY NEXT SMALLEST SIZE. (FOR INSTANCE: 2" IPS × 1½" IPS RED. BUSHING FOR 2" IPS CPLGS.).

PIPE THREADED IN 4 THREADS & CUT OFF

DRILL 3/32" DIA. 5 TO 8 HOLES THRU EQUIDISTANT AROUND DIAMETER OF INNER OPENING OF BUSHING ··· 1/16" DIA. HOLES FOR IPS LESS THAN 2".

MALONE-IRVING BURNER NOZZLE:

FOR LOW TURNDOWN FLAME-RETENTION AND LONG FLAME AT HIGH TEMP. DEVELOPED BY TOM MALONE AND HIS STUDENT IN THE CERAMIC TECHNOLOGY COURSE AT STATE UNIVERSITY OF ILLINOIS NORMAL, ILL.

Materials Suppliers

Charles A. Hones, "Buzzer" Burners, 130 Grand Ave., Baldwin, NY 11510

Pyronics, Inc., 17700 Miles Ave., Cleveland, OH 44128

Surface Combustion Corp., Div. Midland Ross Corp., 2389 Dorr St., Toledo, OH 43601

North American Mfg. Co., 4455 E. 71st St., Cleveland, OH 44105

Flynn Burner Corp., 432 Fifth Ave., New Rochelle, NY 10802

Eclipse Engineering, 1105 Buchanan, Rockford, IL 61101

Johnson Gas & Appliance Co., 1940 O'Donnell St., Cedar Rapids, IO 52400

Weldit Div., Turner Co., 821 Park Ave., Sycamore, IL 60178

L.B. White Co., 1825 Thomas Rd., Onalaska, WI 54650

Ransome Torch & Burner Co., Inc., 2050 Farallon Dr., San Leandro, CA 94577

Useful Terminology

The primary parts of the burner, starting upstream, are: regulating valve, primary air control, orifice, mixing tube, nozzle.

Pipe is identified in terms of the inner diameter, IPS (internal pipe size), and by the length, threaded at both ends. Short lengths are termed nipples. The shortest possible for any IPS is termed "close" nipple.

Tubing is identified by its pressure use and its outer diameter size (O.D.).

GAS BURNERS AND THEIR SAFETY SYSTEMS

by Dudley Giberson

I got interested in gas safety equipment the morning I almost blew my studio up because my propane regulator froze, the furnace went cold, the sun came up and thawed the regulator, and the gas came on. Lucky for me the furnace did not lose too much heat so it lit itself. The room did not fill with gas— but it could have and BOOM!

So I had to find a simple safety system with a pilot that would work. When I mentioned what I was looking for to a few of my potter friends one said he knew of someone who had used Baso valves with a little success. The problem was that the thermocouples would burn out sometimes right in the middle of a firing. What a drag to have your kiln die on you in the middle of the firing! That person did not use a pilot, but simply stuck the thermocouple in the burner port. Well, it occurs to me that most any metallic thing will burn out at temperatures at near 3000°F. With this in mind I designed a great little pilot that does not burn out thermocouples.

How To Make Your NTBO Pilot Burner

1. Write to Ransome Torch and Burner Co., 2050 Farallon Drive, San Leandro, CA and purchase a P7S pilot burner (approximate cost with postage: $12) with one of the following orifices:
#72, for high-pressure Propane (0-25 psi)
#69, for medium-pressure Natural or Propane (0-5 psi)
#66, for low-pressure Natural or Propane (min. 6'' water col.)

II. Make these alterations to the face of the P7S

1. With standard hacksaw cut slits in face of the burner like this.

2. Cut out a 1''x1½'' piece of 16 gauge CRS, or hot-rolled, but not galvanized.

3. Braze steel tab onto the face of the burner at Xs.

4. Bend tab to make a cool pocket for the thermocouple to sit in. Wrap thermocouple wire around the body of the pilot. If further thermocouple stability is required wrap mechanic's wire around thermocouple and pilot body.

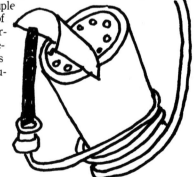

III. Back up your NTBO pilot burner with a high-quality needle valve (approximately $5). I use an "N-20-B" manufactured by Auto-Ponents, Grant & 30th Aves., Bellwood, IL. With this needle valve you can put perfect adjustment on the pilot so as not to waste fuel.

Schematic of Baso valve, Pilot Light, and Thermocouple with Venturi-Type Burner (or Alfred-Type Mixer)

If you have several burners on one side of your kiln, head them with a Baso monitored burner.

Only trouble with a forced-air burner is you have to install a more complex safety system. The schematic:

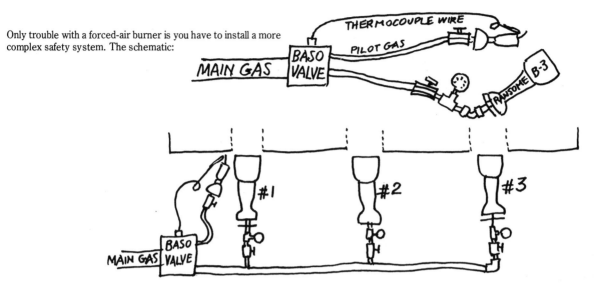

In drawing above the idea is to light the pilot and its burner, #1, for the overnight drying of the kiln. The next morning, manually light burners #2 and #3. Since all the gas to all the burners goes through the Baso valve, the whole trip shuts down if there is a problem.

Safety System For Forced-Air Burners

For starters, I highly recommend you make your own Dayton-powered Alfred mixer. For glass I recommend you head it with a ceramic head (send 25¢ for the Glassworks catalog #3-73, Box 202, Warner, NH 03278). For ceramic kilns there are many kinds of heads to choose from. Most of the heads fit National Pipe Thread Size 1½'', and their general configuration is a main hole of approximately 1¼'' in diameter surrounded with maybe eight ¼'' holes. The only exception is the Ransome "B" type burner heads which have lots of small holes. Write to Denver Fire Clay, Maximum, Buzzer, or Eclipse for information on their heads. Addresses at end of this chapter. (Cost from $5 to $35.)

Look up in Rhodes books *Kilns* or the Glassworks catalog #3-73 for information on how to make the Alfred Mixer, or just ask around.

I have used a variety of Dayton blowers (cheap, stay with a $12 to $15 job). Get these at your industrial materials suppliers.

Generally speaking for a forced-air burner with a capacity of 250,000 BTUs it will cost you:

Head (Alfred)	$ 5.00
Mixer	8.00 new parts or $3.50 used parts
Blower	12.00
	$25.00

How to Procure Things

First of all, the world out there makes just billions of gadgets, valves, switches, etc., for your use. I started by going from one wholesaler to another collecting catalogs. Wholesalers love problems. If something is bugging you, or you need something to work but don't know what to call it, go to the appropriate dealer. I get most of my engineering solved by going to one of five places. Two electrical dealers, one general plumbing and heating supplier, one specialist in heating (i.e., a heating equipment wholesaler), and a general machinery and die tool company.

These few places usually can get anything I want, since I deal with them frequently; if I have a special problem, they will tell me where to go to get it if they don't sell it.

Now, that's the easy way. But everything is not so easy to find out. For example, the first time I went looking for a Baso valve for high-pressure propane it took me nearly four months to locate the Penn-Baso Company. Many people spoke with much authority stating they did not make a high-pressure valve, but when I finally talked with one of the engineers at Ransome Torch and Burner Co., they told me to call Penn-Baso to find out the nearest distributor. As it turned out, the nearest was just a few towns away, and they, indeed, did have a high-pressure safety valve.

Another fine source is Thomas' Register of where to get stuff. This is found in your local library. Also ask your friends as you will be surprised at the mass of junk some people know about.

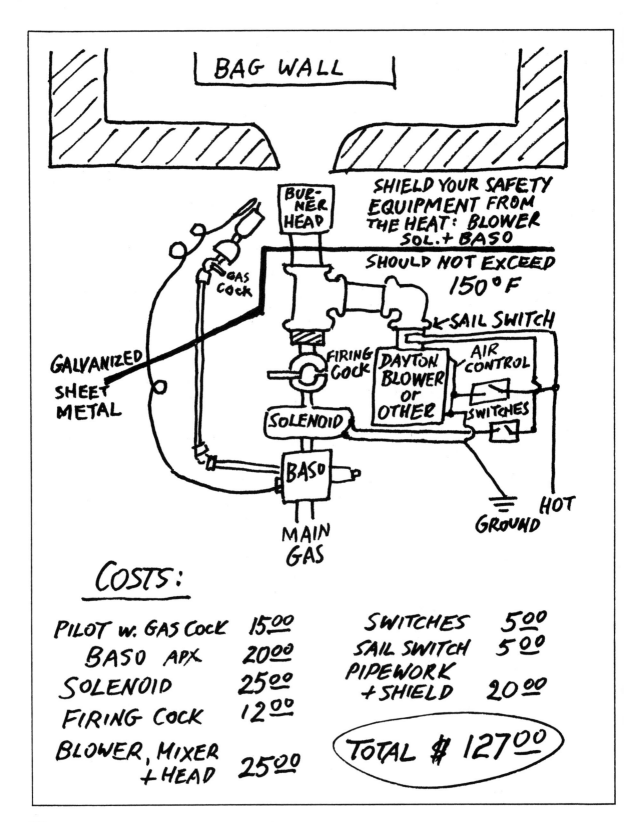

BAG WALL

BURNER HEAD

SHIELD YOUR SAFETY EQUIPMENT FROM THE HEAT: BLOWER SOL. + BASO SHOULD NOT EXCEED 150°F

SAIL SWITCH

GALVANIZED SHEET METAL

GAS COCK

FIRING COCK

DAYTON BLOWER OR OTHER

AIR CONTROL

SWITCHES

SOLENOID

BASO

HOT

GROUND

MAIN GAS

COSTS:

PILOT W. GAS COCK   15.00

BASO APX   20.00

SOLENOID   25.00

FIRING COCK   12.00

BLOWER, MIXER + HEAD   25.00

SWITCHES   5.00

SAIL SWITCH   5.00

PIPEWORK + SHIELD   20.00

TOTAL $ 127.00

Sources of materials

1. Penn-Baso Company
   Consult your local
   plumbing and heating supplier

2. Local electrical wholesaler

3. Ransome Torch & Burner, Inc.
   2050 Farallon Dr.,
   San Leandro, CA

4. The Glassworks
   Box 202
   Warner, NH 03278

5. Auto Ponents
   Grant & 30th Aves.
   Bellwood, IL

6. Maxon Burner Co., Inc.
   Muncie, IN 47302

7. Denver Fire Clay Co.
   Denver, CO

8. Buzzer Burners
   Chas. Hones, Inc.
   Baldwin, NY 11510

9. Your local plumbing and
   heating supplier

10. Your local general machinery
    company

Products they make

A. Safety valves 0-25 psi. #H19TA-3
B. Safety valves, other medium and high pressure valves, consult.
C. Pressure regulators, consult.
D. Thermocouples, varied lengths to fit your requirements. Ask your dealer.
E. Low-pressure safety valves.
F. Solenoid valves.

A. Relays, switches, or magnetic relays.
B. Momentary switches (for fancy stuff) and plain heavy-duty toggle switches.
C. Sometimes Dayton blowers.
D. Sometimes solenoid valves.

A. All manner of burners, venturies, burner heads, torches (as plumber's torches), and they can get Baso valves for you if you give up on your own.

A. Send 25¢ for Catalog #3-73 which describes in some detail where to get most everything to set up your glass furnaces.
B. Ceramic burner head, US Pat. 3697000 will design flame configuration to fit your needs. Six basic designs. Send for catalog above for details.

A. "N-20-B" needle valve, high quality.

A. Ask for their catalog, good burners and nozzles.

A. Burners, gauges, premix units, big blowers for schools and large studios, stuff for foundry furnaces, kilns, etc.

A. Venturi burners.

A. Don't underestimate these guys. They service all the general heating equipment in your entire community. Chances are they will have some of the following: pipe, pipe fittings, solenoid valves, Baso valves, gas cocks, needle valves, thermocouples, main gate valves, pilot states, furnace blowers, and of course pipe for your Alfred mixer.

A. Dayton blowers, valves, pressure gauges, needle valves, solenoids, relays, switches, etc., inquire.

Remember, when you go to these various dealers take a sketch of what you want to do. They will usually put an engineer on the project who can sometimes really solve your problem.

CHARCOAL-FIRED RAKU KILNS

by Harriet Brisson

Raku may be fired in kilns using gas, oil, kerosene, or wood for fuel. Charcoal is also an excellent fuel and it produces unique glaze qualities as a result of the reduction atmosphere within the sagger during firing. Iron glazes are soft green, coppers are red or metallic, and carbon shadows can be maintained. These are a few of the qualities that interested me in using charcoal and in experimenting with the design of kilns made from different materials and methods of construction.

The first charcoal-fired raku kiln that I built consisted of: (1) an outer wall of hard firebrick, (2) a sagger with a cover to protect the pieces from the burning charcoal during firing, and (3) a cover for the kiln. The charcoal was burned under the sagger and in the space between it and the wall. The firebricks were arranged in a circular wall, which was 4'' larger and higher than the sagger when it was in place on two firebricks in the base of the kiln. Three spaces were left in the first row of brick for air intake and ash removal. The cracks between the bricks were calked with fire clay to help provide better insulation.

The sagger was a cylindrical fire clay container 12'' in diameter and 10'' high with straight sides ¾'' thick and a cover which could be removed easily with tongs during firing. It had an opening in the middle with a removable plug, so that the progress of the glaze melt could be seen without taking off the whole cover.

The sagger was made from:

Fire clay	75%
Grog	20%
Talc	5%

The first one was thrown, but some built later were made of separate slabs held together with heavy wire. Holes were made in the walls for direct heat transfer as well as to allow the flame to burn inside. It was then bisque fired to c/09.

To start the firing the charcoal was lighted in the bottom of the kiln and when it was burning well the sagger was put in place before too much heat had built up. The space between the sagger and the wall was filled with charcoal to the top of the sagger, but not covering it, and a piece of metal with an opening in the middle was put on top of the kiln.

After the charcoal had burned slowly for an hour, forced air was used to promote better combustion and increase the temperature faster. An old vacuum cleaner set on reverse was used for this by directing its air flow into one of the air intake openings. As the charcoal burned down, it was tamped and more was added keeping the space filled up to the top of the sagger. A piece of metal 3' long bent 3'' from the end to form a right angle was used for tamping and ash removal, both of which were essential to maintaining a hot fire. Good quality hardwood charcoal should always be used; briquets sometimes have fillers such as hickory chips and do not burn as hot as the hard wood type.

At the end of the firing the air intake openings should be covered with bricks and the top of the kiln covered with a solid piece of metal so that the fire will burn out slowly. This is done to prolong the life of the sagger since the cooling period, as well as the initial heating, should be gradual to prevent its cracking.

Through experimenting with different firing procedures, I found that the use of an air blower cut down on the reduction in the sagger. But more importantly, I discovered that it was possible to fire without using forced air at all and to reach temperature about as easily and quickly as with it. This was accomplished by designing the location of the kiln and air intake openings so that they took maximum advantage of any wind no matter how slight. At this point I decided that the walls of the kiln should be designed to provide better insulation than did the circular arrangement.

With this in mind I experimented with a series of kilns constructed from various materials and shapes, all of which were fired with natural draft. One of these was a kiln built out of firebrick in the shape of a cube, which eliminated the V-shaped spaces made by the circular arrangement of the bricks in the first kiln, and resulted in much better heat retention.

From the results of previous charcoal firings, I had found that at least four air intake openings spaced at even intervals around the base were better than the three used originally. Two of the openings were placed opposite each other and lined up with the two bricks supporting the sagger to take advantage of the main direction of the air movement. This provided a direct flow of air through the kiln giving the charcoal an excellent supply of oxygen and it burned with a hot flame. The other two openings were placed at right angles to the first two. No forced air was used at all in these firings. With the change in the placement of the air intake openings and bricks supporting the sagger, this kiln heated up very well within two or three hours depending on the amount of wind. All four air intakes were usually left open except for very windy days when some of them had to be covered to slow down the fire. This was particularly true when adding or removing pieces from the sagger as the flame, when fanned by the wind, was extremely hot.

Firing this kiln with natural draft produced good reduction inside the sagger as shown by the glaze results. However, since lead glazes bubbled, they had to be eliminated in charcoal firings in which no forced air was used. The cubical arrangement of bricks proved to be better than the cylindrical one in terms of heat retention and as a result required less fuel.

Another kiln was designed with the primary purpose of cutting down on the cost of materials for the exterior insulating wall. A castable was used instead of brick. It can be purchased for $16 per hundred pounds and will take temper

CROSS SECTION OF CHARCOAL BURNING KILN

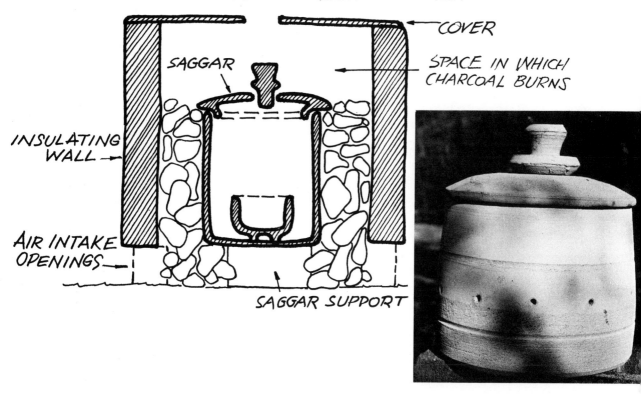

COVER

SPACE IN WHICH CHARCOAL BURNS

SAGGAR

INSULATING WALL →

AIR INTAKE OPENINGS →

SAGGAR SUPPORT

atures up to 1350°C or it can be made from the following:

Portland cement	2 parts
Alumina hydrate	1 part
Pea grog	4 parts
Fire clay	4 parts
Sawdust	2 parts
Vermiculite	3 parts

This figured out to about 11 cents per pound if the pea grog was purchased. A further saving was had by making the pea grog from old soft firebrick, cutting the cost to about 6½ cents per pound. I constructed this kiln at the lower cost using 80 pounds of castable plus 10 firebricks.

The kiln was cast in three separate pieces in the shape of a cylinder, since I considered curved sections to be stronger than flat ones and they could fit together tightly as they were being cast for this specific purpose. They were formed on a heavy cardboard barrel which was covered with grease to prevent the castable from sticking to it. Since the castable material must be packed or rammed onto the form, it was necessary to build walls along the rim of the barrel and at the vertical separation lines. Two-by-fours were nailed to a board at each end of the barrel and held securely in place by C clamps. The castable was mixed with water to just thoroughly moisten all of the material, so that it would hold together in a crumbly mix. It was not wet enough to pour,

but of a consistency to be scooped up with a trowel and packed against the form. It was built up and rammed to a thickness of 2″. Then it was left to cure covered with plastic to keep it from drying too fast or unevenly. This took between 36 and 48 hours, after which the second and third pieces were made.

When these had cured, the cardboard was removed and the sections were left to dry out completely. Then they were assembled into a cylinder in a vertical position and held together by two wire straps placed horizontally around the form. This was put on top of 6 firebricks with the two main openings lined up in the direction of the main air flow as described for the cubical kiln, thus making it possible to modify the air intake in accordance with varying wind conditions. The castable kiln fired extremely well without using forced air and proved to have excellent insulating properties so that it reached firing temperature in a couple of hours.

The most economical kiln that I have built so far was made of a mixture of equal parts by volume of fire clay, sand, and sawdust. The sand and sawdust were free. The fire clay cost $5.00 per 80 pounds, and that was the total cost of this kiln. It could probably be built for less, perhaps for free, where local clay is available. The clay, sand, and sawdust were mixed with water to a workable condition and a cylindrical wall was constructed out of fat coils leaving four openings at the base for air intake. It took several days to build as each layer of coils had to firm up somewhat before

127

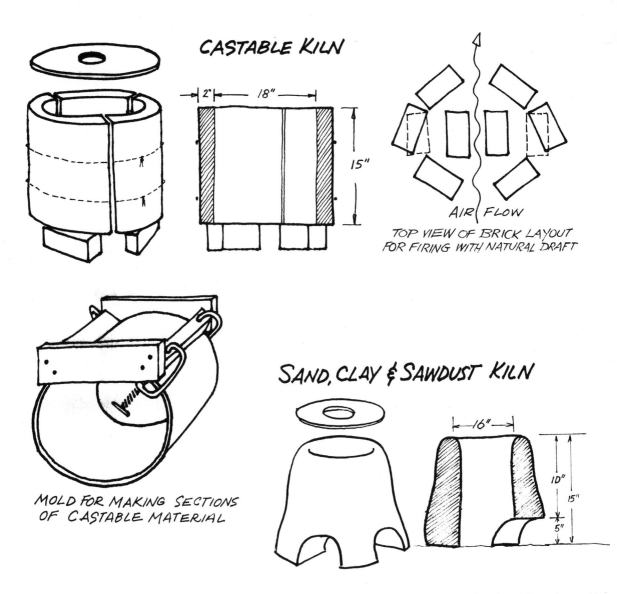

CASTABLE KILN

2" 18"

15"

AIR FLOW

TOP VIEW OF BRICK LAYOUT
FOR FIRING WITH NATURAL DRAFT

MOLD FOR MAKING SECTIONS
OF CASTABLE MATERIAL

SAND, CLAY & SAWDUST KILN

16"

10"

15"

5"

the next layer could be added. When finished it was 15''
high with an inside diameter of 18'' at the base.

Unfortunately the wall of this kiln cracked, even though it
was thoroughly dry when it was fired. Probably this was due
to the uneven heating that occurred when the fire was
started inside. It was still possible to fire this kiln a number
of times as the irregularity of the cracks served to bind the
pieces together like a jigsaw puzzle and there was no appreciable heat lost through the cracks. It, too, was fired
without forced air, reaching temperature in a couple of
hours, and its insulating properties were as good as those of
the other kilns; thus, it would seem to be as viable for charcoal firing as those which cost considerably more.

Cutting down on the cost of building material was the
primary consideration in the design of the last two kilns;
however, this was not the prime concern in the design of a

kiln which was insulated with Fiberfrax. The main consideration here was to build a lightweight, easily transportable
kiln which could be used in a variety of locations. The
finished wall had a total weight of 12 pounds, as opposed to 6
pounds per single hard firebrick. As a dividend it had
superior insulating properties which in turn cut down on the
amount of fuel used. Much to my amazement it reached
temperature to melt glaze within an hour of starting the
charcoal fire and this was on a day with very little breeze.

One inch lo-con Fiberfrax blanket was attached to wire
screen with nichrome wire to form a cylindrical exterior
wall, and galvanized wire was used on the inside surface to
protect the Fiberfrax from being abraded as the charcoal
moved when it burned down. This wire on the inside may
break apart with repeated firings, but it can easily be replaced as it is not attached to the Fiberfrax. The kiln was

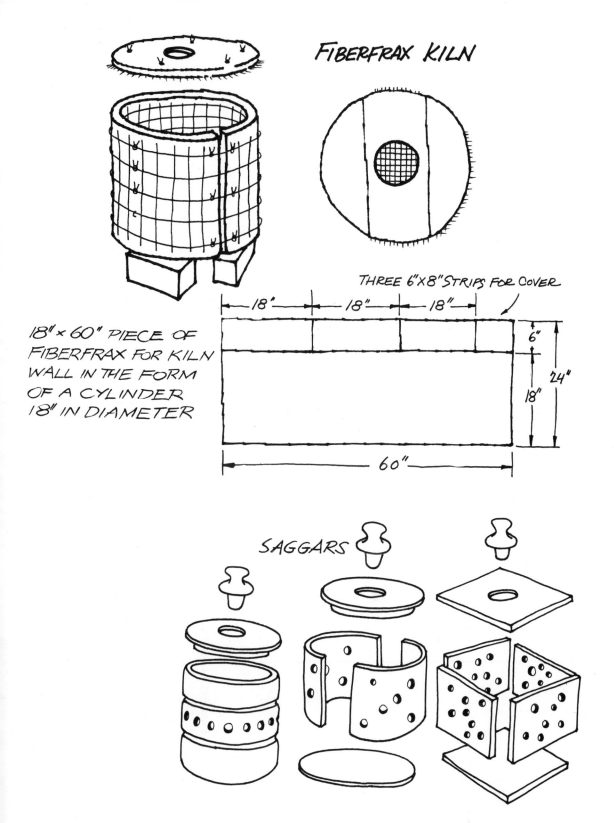

FIBERFRAX KILN

THREE 6"x8" STRIPS FOR COVER

18"x 60" PIECE OF
FIBERFRAX FOR KILN
WALL IN THE FORM
OF A CYLINDER
18" IN DIAMETER

18'   18"   18"

6"

24"

18"

60"

SAGGARS

covered with a piece of metal with a hole in its middle and a piece of Fiberfrax was placed on top of this. Its total cost was $27:

1'' thick Fiberfrax, 2x5' = 10 sq. ft.
@ $1.60 per sq. ft. = $16.00
Wire screen 2x5', 2 pieces   4.00
Nichrome wire, 4' @ .50 per foot   2.00
10 hard firebricks @ .51 each   5.10
                                        $27.10

The surprising thing about this kiln was the ease with which it reached temperature as well as the fact that the temperature continued to climb higher than had been attained in any of the other charcoal firings. In fact, the concern in firing this kiln was to keep it from getting too hot. This can be done by adding charcoal sparingly and not tamping the fire.

The use of charcoal as a fuel for firing raku has its advantages, the prime one being aesthetic. The reduction atmosphere within the sagger and the gentleness of the fire produce excellent glaze results which had not been obtained with other fuels. On the practical side, it is possible to construct an exterior insulating wall at low cost; there is no need to invest in gas or oil burners; and the firing can be done safely in a variety of situations and locations.

General Information for Successful Charcoal Firing

1. Hard wood charcoal of good quality works best.
2. Space between sagger and insulating wall must be at least 4''. A smaller space than this will not be sufficient for a good fire and will make it difficult to reach temperature.
3. Air intake openings should be at least 4'' high and wide.
   A. There should be at least four openings. The two main openings should be opposite each other lined up with the direction of the wind with the two others spaced mid-way between.
   B. Firebricks that support the sagger should be lined up

in the same direction as the two main openings.
   C. Have extra firebricks available to cover air intake openings, if there is a strong wind, to cut down on draft through the kiln, or in case the fire gets too hot.
   D. Close air intake openings when removing or adding pieces to kiln.
4. Firing suggestions
   A. Fill the 4'' space between the sagger and the wall with charcoal up to the top edge of the sagger, but not covering it.
   B. Let this burn down to the mid-point of the sagger before adding more charcoal.
   C. Tamp fire before adding charcoal.
   D. Remove ashes if they accumulate.
5. Kiln Cover
   A. Should be easy to remove during firing.
   B. Should have an opening in middle to provide draft through kiln for good combustion of charcoal.
6. Sagger
   A. When made of separate slabs it will last longer without cracking than one which is thrown. If the sagger cracks, it can be held together with heavy duty wire.
   B. Bisque fire the sagger to c/09, if possible. Otherwise fire it very slowly in the charcoal kiln.
   C. Place the sagger in the kiln as soon as the charcoal in the base of the kiln is ignited and before the fire becomes too hot. Slow heating prolongs its life.
   D. Close the air intake openings with bricks and cover the kiln with a solid piece of metal so that fire burns out slowly at the end of the firing.
   E. The cover of the sagger should have a hole fitted with a reasonable plug so the ware inside can be seen without removing the whole cover. It should be easy to remove.
7. An air blower will lessen the amount of reduction in the sagger, but will provide a good hot fire.
8. The use of natural draft (no air blower) will increase the reduction in the sagger, and an equally hot fire can be had if the air intake openings and firebricks that hold up the sagger are lined up with the main direction of the wind.

Evaluation of Kilns

	Cost:			Forced Air	Natural Draft	Insulating Properties	Time to Temperature
	Total	Materials	Brick				
Sagger, 20 lb. at 7.5c	$ 1.50						
No. 1 Cylinder	17.85		$17.85	X		Poor	2-3 hours
No. 2 Cubical	19.40		19.40		X	Good	2-3 hours
No. 3 Castable	10.20	5.20	5.00		X	Excellent	1½-2 hours
No. 4 Clay, sand, sawdust	6.00	5.00	1.00		X	Good	2-3 hours
No. 5 Fiberfrax	27.00	22.00	5.00		X	Outstanding	1-1½ hours

SOME THOUGHTS ON REFRACTORIES AND SALT

by Tom Turner

When one starts thinking of building a salt kiln and wondering about refractories, three things will determine the outcome: refractories already available; finances available for purchasing new refractories; and the intended lifespan of the salt kiln. At first I used whatever hard brick I could get my hands on and I coated the interior with alumina hydrate. This retarded the reaction between the bricks and the salt vapors, but eventually the salt won. Then I tried coating the interior with a high alumina cement that I troweled on the surface, but again the salt won. More recently I've been involved with high alumina refractories that would hopefully resist sodium destruction. I much prefer making pots to building and repairing kilns. The chief disadvantage of high alumina refractories is their cost. AP Green Mizzou bricks are selling between $1.25 and $1.50 and the Mizzou castable is a little over $20 per 100 pound bag.

Several years ago I decided to build a high alumina kiln because all indications were that high alumina was the answer for long-lasting salt kilns. The kiln had a complete interior of AP Green Mizzou. The floor and walls were Mizzou straights cemented together with AP Green #36 High Alumina Cement. The fireboxes and arch were cast with Mizzou Castable and the entire kiln was G-23 insulating brick on the outside. The Mizzou material ranges from 60 to 63% alumina and in brick form is very dense, strong, resistant to chemical attack, and very refractory, PCE 36-37. In the castable form, it allows you to mix and use it like concrete to cast monolithic units.

The reasoning behind the castable was to cast monolithic units that would be crack free, therefore eliminating sodium and chlorine seepage into my studio. The same reasoning applied to the fireboxes in preventing liquid sodium chlorine seepage through the floor structure deteriorating the refractories. This happened in the past because prior to vaporization, there is always a period of liquefaction even with super hot burners. The liquid can cause more trouble than the sodium vapors. The reasons for using the castable proved to be as weak as the castable.

First, the arch suffered a construction crack that opened in the firings and sifted aggregate onto the ware. This crack resulted from casting from one side of the arch to the center and then from the opposite side to the center. There was enough time lapse to prevent the material from fusing or sealing together and it acted like a scratch on a piece of glass, a natural breaking line. Aside from the construction crack, there developed a network of cracks which I've learned are quite natural with castables. They will form their own stress cracks if not cast in sections. My concern at that time was twofold. I couldn't allow the large crack to dribble debris onto my pots. I was also concerned that the arch might collapse. As for the fireboxes, they became very soft and crumbly although they were containing the liquid sodium chlorine. So I removed the arch with a sledge hammer to learn several things.

The arch would never have fallen on its own accord. During the removal I could also see that there was a good deal of vapor penetration, even though the arch interior surface revealed no reaction. About an inch inside the arch there was a zone of crumbly Mizzou where the vapors were actually deteriorating the castable chemically. The AP Green representative explained that almost all castables are bonded by cement which is fluxed by calcium. The calcium reacts strongly with any alkali, especially sodium vapor. This brings me to the reason for this article. Several disadvantages of castables are: (1) they will crack in use which permits vapor penetration, (2) they are very porous because they are seldom fired to maturity in a c/10 kiln, and (3) they are fluxed by calcium which reacts strongly with any alkali present. This applies directly to Mizzou castable but relates to probably most others. If you choose a lower temperature castable that will become denser, it will overreact with the salt vapors. If you choose the high alumina castables, they will be extremely porous. Therefore, maybe our concern should be with a refractory's density more than its alumina content. High alumina with high porosity is bad news. High alumina and high density is good. Alumina is a very porous material by itself and firing a high alumina refractory to c/10 is like a bisque firing a stoneware body.

At the recommendation of the AP Green representative I replaced the Mizzou arch with a refractory plastic. A plastic is like an unfired brick with a moisture content of about 10%. Industry uses pneumatic hammers, but you can get by with a three pound sledge hammer if you don't mind beating your brains out. We used the Super Hybond Plastic because it was less refractory and we thought it might become denser and seal its surface from the sodium vapors. A real bad mistake! I spent about six hours beating the plastic into place, removed the arch form as directed and fired the arch in place with a 32 hour curing cycle plotted by the engineer. First problem was the arch sagging and the second problem was the sulphur given off by the plastic. But the biggest problem was the many cracks that resulted from insufficient beating or ramming of the plastic into place.

The sulphur chemically bonds the plastic refractory and the AP Green representative thought it would burn out in the curing cycle. Unfortunately for me it did not. Instead, it ruined a load of stoneware. The sulphur chemically reacted with the salt vapors and the iron in the body and reduced the pots so much that two subsequent oxidation firings could not lighten the color. The pots were resalted in another firing with little change and finally put through a c/9 electric kiln cycle which finally made them look nice. The sulphur has been reacting each time I fired so I'm planning on replacing the arch in the near future. I may try a couple of vaporized copper red salt firings to see if the sulphur might be of some help instead of just a hindrance.

Disregarding the bad experience with the sulphur, the trial with the plastic refractory substantiated my feelings that density as well as alumina content is necessary for the resistance of sodium vapors in salt kilns.

My next arch will be 4½'' of dense Mizzou hard brick cemented together with #36 high alumina cement and backed up with block insulation, equaling 14'' of hard brick relative to insulating ability. An arch like this would be high in alumina and density, lightweight, and I think as permanent as can be at this point in time.

There are other brands of refractories available as well as other types of refractories. This hasn't been an ad for AP Green; these are simply the materials I've been using and am familiar with. If you go below the 60 to 65% alumina range, the refractory will react with the sodium to form glaze on the interior and will eventually deteriorate. If you go above 60 to 65% range you will have problems with porosity as well as increased cost. There is a KX-99 brick that AP Green makes that is about their densest high-temperature brick but it's been cracking because it can't take the quick firings and coolings that studio potters practice.

These are my ideas and experiences with but a few materials and I'm sure many people are experimenting with other refractories and may be having good luck. My concern is that people starting out might avoid the problems that some of us have experienced. Special refractories are expensive, as is down-time for repairing kilns and sore backs.

CASTABLES

by Wally Smith

As a professional potter the first thing that comes to my mind in planning a salt kiln is what the costs will be to build, maintain, and fuel the kiln. Never having had the money to construct the "ultimate" salt kiln, I have made compromises and explored refractory materials which perform well and are reasonably priced.

I was able to find a free source of hard firebrick for my present salt kiln, but I didn't know how they would react in salt. I had seen a salt kiln which incorporated refractory castables in its design, so I decided to do the same.

I constructed a 50 cubic foot sprung arch kiln with 9'' hard firebrick walls and floor. Plywood forms were then constructed inside the kiln and a 2½'' thickness of high alumina castable was poured against the firebrick. During construction, openings were left in the brickwork to allow the castable to flow into the walls and prevent it from pulling away from the walls. The arch of the kiln is a 6'' thickness of refractory castable, with vermiculite poured on top of that for extra insulation. Burner ports, damper lintels, bag walls, and several other special shapes were also cast. It is much easier to cast and shape perfectly than to try to chisel the shape from hard firebrick.

The only bricks exposed to the sodium vapor are those in the door of the kiln. They are Babcock & Wilcox firebrick #80 and are approximately 45% alumina. They have never been coated with alumina and do not stick together after salting. The soaps for shelf supports are the same brick.

The castable used was also a Babcock & Wilcox product. Three thousand pounds of Kaocrete 28-LI (50% alumina) were used in the kiln. The cost then was $140 per ton, which is very reasonable.

Stainless steel rods can be used to reinforce refractory castables if they are first coated with wax, which will burn off and allow the steel to expand slightly without cracking the castable.

The kiln has been used professionally for two years and is completely free of sodium deposits except for the fireboxes, where there is some buildup. I do wash the fireboxes of my kiln each firing with a mixture of 80% alumina hydrate and 20% Georgia kaolin. This is also used on my shelves and posts. My pots are also wadded on this same mixture in plastic form.

Just a word about castables themselves. There are several methods of applying castables. They can be gunned, rammed, or poured. Pouring is by far the easiest for the studio potter without elaborate equipment. Castables come in a coarse aggregate form and are mixed with water. The more water used, the weaker the castable. I found the best results came from adding water until the aggregate almost lost suspension and started to settle. It required a couple of minutes to mix 50 pounds in a five gallon bucket with the aid of a jiffy mixer and a ⅜'' electric drill. The castable begins to harden in about 30 minutes, so entire sections must be mixed and cast in that period of time to be free of seams—this is imperative in the arch! Castables separate readily from wooden forms so there is no need to coat them with a release medium.

I do not know how this castable will hold up over the long run. It is in excellent shape now with 90% of the surface free of any salt deposits at all. Of course, if the castable does break down at some point in the future, the present lining can be taken out and another cast in place, yielding an essentially new kiln for about 10 to 25% of the cost of high alumina brick. Or the kiln could be taken down and the bricks used in some other type of kiln because they are free of salt.

Building a kiln with castable refractories at Franklin Pierce College. Rindge, N.H. Erected by David MacAllister and friends. While not a salt kiln, this illustrates the building method used with castables.

Another big advantage to the professional potter is that a kiln of this type uses the same amount of salt each firing, yielding uniform results.

The only disadvantage in using castables is the extra time required to construct the forms.

There are many other types of refractory castables available, ranging from 40 to 95% alumina. The higher the alumina, the higher the cost.

Insulating castables are also available for use in reduction kilns. Arches and doors can be cast in one piece. They will have tremendous strength, be free of sag, and have high insulating properties.

I have always found the refractory company engineers to be very helpful in calculating amount of castables required per job, arch thickness, etc. Before calling a company for information, always have exact dimensions of your proposed kiln, including span of arch and arch rise.

NOTES ON CASTABLES FOR A SALT KILN

by Richard Leach

Kiln building for the ancients wasn't as simple as with the plans, kit kilns and quality controlled commercial refractory products available today. When I saw a scove kiln constructed of the same material being fired, clay being mixed, blended, and formed and the rows of drying adobe brick at one site, I began to wonder about the necessity of depending or having to depend on rather expensive refined resources for kilns. The technology for building the kiln is present in the knowledge of blending clays and forming pottery. Primitive peoples tempered their clay with a grog of whatever was available and with an organic binder, usually

finely chopped manure or straw and grass. The primitive pottery dries quickly, is fired fast and has excellent thermal shock resistance when used directly in the fire.

After having come in contact with southwest Indian pottery and primitive potteries in Mexico, I decided to try some mixtures of inexpensive (cheap) locally available materials to construct or cast a kiln suitable for stoneware temperatures. Bricks made of locally available clay, refractory filler, and organic binder were rammed and tested. These tests were brick shaped blocks of clay placed *in* the *wall* of a test kiln—the tests were not fired in the kiln. The addition of a small amount of Portland cement holds things together and a measure of alumina hydrate to the mix approximates a refractory concrete such as Lumnite made by Universal Atlas Cement Company.

Of the four climbing test kilns I built at Albion in 1970, the first two were without alumina. The kilns cast were catenary arch, monolithic construction (one continuous casting). One could cast brick of conventional size or in larger sections. It would be helpful to key large horizontal or vertical sections so the kiln could be taken down, moved, and reassembled. All kilns are still functioning after seven years, but show signs of wear. Kilns 1 and 2 are used only for stoneware.

The climbing kilns are crossdraft with three Pyronics #10 atmospheric burners using natural gas at 6 to 8″ (propane works as well). Chamber #2 has been built using two atmospheric barriers to finish it off or one "Alpine type" burner (60 cfm blower with three ⅜″ orifice holes). Each works well.

Kilns 3 and 4 were built with 4% alumina or about ½ measure by volume in a 1:6 or 1:7½ ratio.
Parts by volume:

    1 Portland cement
    2 Fireclay
    2 Grog, or crushed bisque, used kiln doors
    2 to 2½ sawdust and/or vermiculite
    ½ alumina

The vermiculite is expanded mica sold as insulation under several brand names and may be obtained at lumber companies or an insulation contractor.

Kiln 3 is for stoneware and kiln 4 for salt. After over 100 firings, kiln 4 is in better shape than chamber #3. Neither has secondary insulation and both retain heat as well as a K23 IFB. Following are some suggestions for a successful cast kiln:

Cast the arch on a base of castable. If hard bricks are used as a base without tie irons, the base will shift causing the arch to sag and fall. If hard bricks are used as a liner for the firebox, place them on a layer of alumina to facilitate replacement.

Incorporate a measure of Portland cement to the aggregate in the ratio of 1 to 6 or 1 to 7½ at the most, as it is a powerful flux and the arch will melt and deteriorate rapidly. One-half to 1 part of alumina should be added to any kiln.

Fifty per cent of the particle size of the aggregate should be ¼″ or smaller with the maximum size aggregate roughly ½″. Crushed biscuit ware screened through hardware cloth works well for the wall, stack sections, or floors. A hammermill will reduce old doors or kilns needing rebuilding to particle size of P grog and the material can be recycled into new kilns (Phoenix I, Phoenix II, Phoenix III, etc.). An earth tamper will work as well, but much slower.

Dry mix the aggregate by mechanical means or in a batch box with shovels.

Use a fairly dry mix. We used about 5½ gal. water to a batch of 160# (the volume measure was a 2½ gal. pail and 1 part or 1 pail of fireclay weighs 30 lbs.), one to 1½ parts crushed corn cobs or sawdust, 1 part vermiculite, 2 parts fireclay, 2 parts grog, 1 part cement, and ¼ to ½ part alumina.

If a portion of the mix placed next to the form be dampened more and the dry mix rammed from the outside, a more smooth and dense surface will result on the inner lining of the kiln. Too wet a mixture makes for a dense arch that will soak up heat too quickly, prolong the firing, use more fuel, and break up easily. It will act as hard brick construction. Too dry a mix will not possess initial dry strength to maintain shape. A correctly mixed batch will maintain its shape after being squeezed.

Cast against oiled flashing, roofing felt, or tar paper on the inner form. Do not use plastic-covered cardboard. The cardboard swells and makes removing the form impossible or very difficult without destruction of the form.

Build forms for catenary construction of durable materials. Three-quarter inch exterior plywood will allow forms to be used many times over. One form was used to build and rebuild over 30 kilns. The door form is still in use.

A high alumina fireclay is to be preferred over a fireclay high in silica if the kiln is to be used for salt. AP Green DM Mo. fireclay plus a high-heat-duty grog, high in alumina (AP Green P grog) is preferred for the same reason. It may be worthwhile to make your own grog by high-firing crushed bisque to c/6,7,8 or by calcining a rough-ground fireclay. Check manufacturers for analysis and mesh size of local materials. Again, we have been having very good luck reclaiming broken doors and kilns in need of rebuilding by substituting the crushed and screened material for the grog portion.

Curing the kiln doesn't make too much difference. Some kilns have been fired within 12 hours of ramming the arch, back, and doors.

Up to a point, the more times the kiln is fired, the better insulation the wall becomes. After 100 firings in one kiln tested, the temperature was 300°F less at a point halfway through a 4½″ wall than in the original six firings.

The cast arch can be further insulated with a mixture of clay, vermiculite, and cement after it has been fired enough times so the chemical water and carbon have been driven off the original casting.

Lumnite has been used in several of these kilns. There does not seem to be any difference in the lasting quality whether used for stoneware or salt.

Sawdust from a chain saw or saw mill is better than table-saw sawdust. It provides a more porous texture for better insulation.

Oat, wheat, or rice chaff is an excellent substitute for sawdust and is preferable if it is available.

Alumina is added to materials used in casting wood-fired kilns for the same reason—to resist ash deposits.

This mixture has been used in casting blast furnaces for bronze casting. One still in use was cast five years ago.

Great American Kilns: Karen Karnes' Salt Kiln 1976

Solar Kiln in action. Zeljko Kujundzic's finished model 4 kiln in operation with the two pound firing chamber.

PART FOUR
ENERGY

ANOTHER BALL GAME

by Paul Soldner

A few years ago, a new fire and safety inspector called me to the kiln room at Scripps College in an extremely agitated state of mind. As I entered, he pointed to a kiln in reduction and accused me: "There are flames coming out of that." At the time I was almost amused by his naiveté. "Of course," I answered, "that's the way it's been with potters since before recorded history. That's what it's all about."

Since then, that same inspector has found additional infractions in the equipment, technique, and philosophy I have always practiced and taught. Just last week, with the authority of the fire department, the power of a stack of OSHA regulations, and the voice of DOOM, he threatened me with the possibility of shutting the ceramics department down completely if he wanted to! Today he is no longer amusing.

As I travel around the country visiting schools and potters, I have become increasingly aware of their growing concern that the tradition of potterymaking may be in serious trouble. The evidence can be found in both the questions they ask and in the facts they relate: "We've been told to cut back our firings by fifty percent." "The gas company refused us a new kiln connect-up permit." "They shut our salt kiln down a year ago." "The head of the department just informed me that the equipment cannot be used nights and weekends anymore."

"I can't get the fuel company to deliver oil out here." "Is it true that Joe wasn't allowed to rebuild his kiln?" "How do you get away with smoking pots?"

Although most of these episodes occurred in large population centers, it is not limited to a specific area. It is happening all over, to all of us, right now. As a result, we are being forced to examine the future of 1984 years earlier. In effect, we are being asked to forget the values of our traditional past and are being forced to re-evaluate the very role of a potter in the future.

Although many of us have been aware that the day of the village potter has been over for some time, we have nevertheless felt the importance of carrying on in a new way the making of pottery related to our 20th century needs. To make pottery as an expression of our culture, to reflect its rapid change, and to somehow enrich the lives of our fellow man with what we make. We have expressed belief in the right of the individual to "go it alone" as an artist, separate but still connected with his time. It has not been easy, yet because it seems right, more and more people are apparently willing to make the effort each year.

Perhaps the question now is, can we cope with the shortages, the restrictions, and the regulations of society without giving up the creative freedom we believe inherent in every person? We have doubts. For example, must we give up reduction firing because of the smoke? Must we stop glazing with salt? Must we lose the tradition of lead glazes, even on the outside of pots? Will our traditions, like an exterminated animal, vanish from the earth? That will happen certainly if we choose to give up.

Somehow, however, I am optimistic enough to think that art and artists will always continue to find the ways and means to survive. As can be seen in this chapter, we are already beginning to seek out our future. Sometimes, it will be by giving up one concept of beauty to declare a new one. In this sense, we may learn to value the garish colors of an oxidized metal rather than the more subtle ones of reduction. We may need to accept and use technological advances like nuclear and solar energy, or to make our own fuels from the decomposition of wastes. Even the indirect conversion of hydrogen from water with electricity produced by a wind generator is a possibility.

On the other hand if new technology seems alien to our thinking, we can always return to the methods of the past. We may choose to fire with wood, brush, or grass, which is really another form of obtaining energy from the sun. If done well, we can "grow" more fuel than we use and in the process, give back to earth moisture and the minerals used in the growing cycle. For those who find the combination of fuels to be in conflict with their personal pollution ethic, other nonfired agents can be explored. Just as primitive man once learned to make watertight his porous vessels of fiber, clay, and leather with glues, resins, and organic matter, so can we.

Not to be forgotten in our struggle to remain creatively free is also the right to resist the encroachment of Big Brother. For some, the refusal to comply with bureaucratic regulation will be the only way. They will need to organize, to lobby, to find ways to change laws, to call attention to their plight, to advocate the importance of their cause. For them, the rights of the minority and freedom of the nonconformist will be as necessary to preserve as will be the survival of the pot or potter.

Each potter will be affected, one way or the other. Each must find his own solution. In the end, I believe art will not vanish so long as man lives.

WOOD

by William C. Alexander

In terms of solid fuel for kiln firing, wood has always been regarded as the most desirable. It is relatively pure (i.e., it has in its composition no materials which are detrimental to the ware such as sulphur compounds, etc.); it burns with a long flame which is helpful in producing even kiln temperatures; it leaves little residue; and it is capable of reaching the highest temperatures used in pottery. Historically, wood was the normal fuel and was used by most cultures until recent times.

The length of wood flames is sometimes dramatically illustrated during the course of a firing. The flame path in the kiln I am currently using is approximately 20 to 24 feet which includes the height of the stack. At top temperature, a single piece of wood 1x18'' can send flames out the stack to height of a foot or more. Under these conditions the chambers are completely filled with flames, and the firings tend to be very even in heat distribution.

When compared to other solid fuels such as coal, wood leaves very little residue. When I first built a wood kiln, I thought that I would have a ready source of ashes for glaze material. This has not proven to be the case. The ashes left in my firebox after a stoneware firing are sometimes so minimal that I do not clean them out before the next firing. In no case have I ever had more than approximately two gallons of dry ash remaining. Even though the draft in my kiln is rather lively, no great amount of ash is deposited on the pots. Even that ash which does remain in the firebox is not ideal for glazes in that it is quite hard (refractory) with a granular texture. Wood of the same type, spruce in this case, burned in an open fire usually produces a soft, fluxing ash of almost a fluffy texture. The difference is that the extreme heat of the firebox seems to volatilize the alkalines in the ash in much the same way that salt is volatilized in a salt kiln.

One of the greatest advantages of wood is that it is a non-polluting fuel. Even the heavy clouds of black smoke which may be produced in the course of a firing are not harmful to the atmosphere. Carbon particles cause the black color and while they may blacken surrounding structures, not to mention the kiln firer and the neighbors' clean wash, they settle out of the air quickly and cause no lasting ill effects. The other stack gases consist of water vapor, carbon dioxide, and, under heavily reducing conditions, carbon monoxide which is rapidly dissipated to inconsequential levels. White wood smoke consists largely of water vapor. The concerned citizen who drives an automobile to the site of a wood kiln to complain about the pollution undoubtedly does more damage to the atmosphere by the simple act of driving than could even a prolonged wood firing.

Very high temperatures are possible with wood if it is properly managed. Until recent times the c/16 porcelain of Sèvres was wood fired. (#1) Japanese high-temperature stoneware and porcelain is still fired in wood kilns as is the salt-glazed stoneware of Germany.

In the United States, wood is seldom used as fuel today due to the ready availability of gas. In areas where gas is not easy to come by, wood may still be the best and cheapest fuel available. Any potter living in an area which has a saw mill should certainly investigate the possibility of a wood kiln, since slabs are sometimes to be had for the asking.

In much simplified terms, wood burns in two stages. Since the charring temperature of wood is below its ignition temperature, the first stage of burning is really the combustion of volatile gases driven out of the wood during the charring processes. The resin content of wood contributes greatly to these gases, and the greater the resin content, the greater the heat release in this initial combustion.

Since this stage of the burning is dependent upon gaseous products, longer flames are produced. (#2) Finely divided droplets of resin are also driven out of the charring wood, and these do not ignite until they have migrated far enough to find sufficient oxygen for combustion. Their energy is released at that point. In a wood kiln this may occur in the chamber itself rather than in the firebox.

The second stage of combustion is from the nonvolatile, but combustible coals or charcoal. On a pound for pound basis, charcoal has a higher calorific value than wood since it is almost entirely composed of carbon, all the hydrogen and oxygen content of the wood having been previously expelled during the charring process. Since charcoal burns with a short flame, its heat release is localized and it contributes less to the heating of the chamber than do the volatiles. Like all carboniferous materials, charcoal requires oxygen to burn. As the bed of coals builds, the oxygen requirement for proper combustion increases proportionately. After a critical point, the *glows* may use so much of the available oxygen that the volatile gases are unable to burn and pass through the kiln without releasing their energy.

Wood varies in calorific value from species to species. The heat worth is also affected according to its condition of dryness, its age, and to a lesser extent to the part of the tree which is burned. On the average, wood has a basic composition of carbon 50%, oxygen 44%, and hydrogen 6%. (#3) As with clay and feldspar, this is an unfindable norm; every sample varies to a degree, but not enough to explain the disparity in calorific value among the species.

Hard wood gives less heat on a pound for pound basis than soft wood, (#4) as is demonstrated in tests done by Gottleib. His figures are as follows:

Type of Wood	Calories	BTUs
Pine	5085	9153
Fir	5035	9053
Beech	4774	8591
Birch	4771	8586
Elm	4728	8510
Ash	4711	8480
Oak	4620	8316

(#5) Tests done by other experimenters have yielded slightly different results, but all prove that soft woods, particularly those from coniferous species, have a greater calorific value than hard woods. This is in sharp contrast to the old rule-of-thumb that hard wood is the preferred fuel for fireplaces and wood stoves. The difference lies in the divergent purposes of household and industrial heating. The former seeks a slow and even release of energy over a period of time whereas for industrial and semi-industrial purposes such as kiln firing the immediate release of as much energy as possible is required.

The advantage of soft wood probably lies in its greater resin content. (#6) This is borne out in tests run by Slosson on knot pine, a very resinous wood. His experiments showed a calorific value of 5770 calories and 10,386

btus/lb., the highest figures I found. (#7) Another point in favor of soft woods is their lower specific gravity which exposes more surface per unit of weight, thereby speeding combustion. In general, then, it can be stated that soft woods, especially coniferous varieties, are to be preferred as kiln fuel and that the greater the resin content, the greater the heat value.

Any kind of wood must be thoroughly dried before it can realize its optimum heat potential. As a rule-of-thumb, wood should not be used until two years after it is felled, but this varies radically according to the climatic conditions in various parts of the country. In Colorado, for instance, where the humidity is usually very low, wood may be dry enough to use as fuel only six months after having been felled. Drying is greatly facilitated if the logs are cut into shorter sections immediately. Hard wood with its tightly knit structure takes a bit longer to dry thoroughly than does soft wood.

It has been demonstrated that wood containing 20% water (a normal figure of air-dried wood) uses more than one-third of its energy for water vaporization. (#8) Rotten or very old wood on the other hand has a lower heat value as do thick bark or roots. (#9)

The type of wood used in a firing can have an effect on the atmosphere in the kiln, and the amount of smoke produced is not always an indication of what is happening to the ware. Bernard Leach mentions this phenomenon in *A Potter's Book* with regard to the findings of Katherine Bouverie. She feels that elder, ash, oak, and elm produce better reduction than do horsechestnut, apple, and walnut. She further states that thorn produces little smoke, but reduces well while spruce smokes a great deal, but tends to oxidize. (#10) Most of my wood firings in Colorado have been done with spruce, and I, too, find that, unless carefully controlled, the kiln gives off vast quantities of smoke yet produces only indifferent reduction.

Firing with wood is an exciting, but exacting, experience and requires the ultimate in rapport between firer and kiln. Wood kilns tend to be temperamental and the slightest change can cause them to lose hard-won temperature. The rhythm of the stoke is extremely important and, unfortunately, there seems to be no single rule which will fit all cases or kilns. Each wood kiln is an entity in itself and the only way to determine proper procedure is by experimentation, experience, and some educated guessing.

Most wood kilns are stoked intermittently, i.e., a quantity of wood is stoked at one time and allowed to burn to coals before fresh fuel is introduced. Leach indicates that this is the method used for all but the last chamber of his three-chambered kiln at St. Ives. (#11) A system of constant light stoking is less frequently used, but it has been my experience that it is sometimes the only method which will give a steady rise in temperature. I have built and fired two two-chambered kilns and both have responded better to constant stoking of one or two pieces of wood at a time.

Both of these kilns are built on the same plan although one is almost twice as large as the other, and both have exhibited a peculiarity which is most helpful in firing them. When a soft, flickering flame can be kept extending at a constant 12 to 16'' above the stack, both maintain a constant temperature rise in moderate reduction. This works for both chambers. For this reason, I try to arrange my firings so that the last period of the fire from about 2100°F is done at night when the flames are more easily seen.

Kilns built on other plans may also give some sort of indication as to how they are doing. It is a good idea to have a pyrometer handy for the first few firings so that the firer can experiment with various techniques to judge which is most effective.

Overstoking is probably the commonest error of inexperienced firers. In theory at least, it seems logical to assume that the more fuel, the more heat, but there are other factors involved. Most wood kilns operate on the natural draft of a stack which dictates a relatively constant air supply. When more fuel is stoked than can be burned by the available oxygen, inefficient combustion results and much of the heat worth of the fuel goes out the stack in the form of unburned gases. The remaining coals continue to consume oxygen so that the next batch of wood is even more oxygen starved and the coals continue to build. If the glows increase to the point that the flues or air intakes become clogged, the air supply is reduced and even less efficient combustion is the result. At this point if not before, the kiln generally begins to lose temperature and the firer must choose between raking the coals, which cools the kiln and stirs up the ashes, or stoking very lightly until they have burned away to an acceptable level which usually both cools and oxidizes the kiln.

Also important is the size of the wood used. For high-temperature firings the wood should be very thinly split and toward the end, when every successive degree is increasingly difficult to attain, it may need to be almost splinter size. The advantage of finely split wood is that it exposes a large surface area per unit of weight causing faster combustion and a quicker heat release. Pieces about 1'' square and of a length appropriate to the firebox are ideal, although larger pieces are also usable.

Thick pieces and blocks should be avoided. They produce lots of smoke and impressive coals, but little else. Likewise, small chips are best left alone. They are a nuisance to get in the kiln, and once in, they usually fall through the grate bars adding only to the pile of coals in the ash pit.

The advantages of wood as fuel have already been touched on briefly. There are also a number of disadvantages, and these, too, should be carefully considered before building a wood kiln. Economy is an important consideration in any discussion of fuels, and with wood this has several ramifications. As stated earlier, scrapwood can sometimes be had for the asking. But it has to be loaded, hauled, and stored, and large quantities are needed. (About three pickup loads are needed for one stoneware firing in my kiln of about 50 cubic feet, and it fires very economically.) And, too, such windfall wood may or may not be dry enough for use and is almost never the right size. Hours of chipping may be needed for every firing.

Time is also an important factor with every potter. In a wood firing, regardless of the technique used, the firer must stay with the kiln until the last cone has fallen. Unless the kiln is fired by a team which rotates stoking duty, the firer can count on a long stretch of concentrated effort. Team firing is a dubious method. In my opinion, it is better to have one fire master and one or more assistants to fetch and carry whatever may be needed. At best, a day which might have been devoted to other labors is lost for every firing. Sometimes another day is needed to recuperate.

Other disadvantages are the smoke, the smell, the splinters, the sparks, and the spectators. In residential areas, the smoke and sparks send all but the most placid neighbors racing to check their insurance policies and may bring the fire marshall or even a fire truck to stop the firing. Be sure to check local regulations before building! The splinters are almost less of a nuisance than the spectators who seem to be as inevitable as death and taxes. Everyone wants to help with the stoking but generally shies away from the more useful activities of chopping and carrying wood.

It would seem that there is a streak of pyromania in all of us (usually a bit overdeveloped in potters) and nothing satisfies that urge like the flames, smoke, and excitement attendant at any wood firing. And, too, it makes for great pots!

References

1. **Leach, Bernard.** *A Potter's Book,* p. 179. London: Faber & Faber, Ltd., 1945. Transatlantic.

2. **Wise, Louise & Jahn, Edwin C.** *Wood Chemistry,* 2nd. ed. New York: Reinhold, 1952.

3. **Schorger, Arlie W.** *The Chemistry of Cellulose & Wood,* p. 32. McGraw-Hill, 1926.

4. **Poole, Herman.** *The Calorific Power of Fuels,* 3 rd ed., p. 85. New York: Wiley & Sons. 1918.

5. **Poole,** p. 246.

6. **Wise & Jahn,** p. 822.

7. **Wise & Jahn.**

8. **Poole,** p. 822.

9. **Jako, Geza.** *Keramische Materialkunde,* p. 123. Steinhopff.

10. **Leach.**

11. **Leach,** p. 189.

KILN CONSTRUCTION
AND SOME THOUGHTS ON FIRING A CLIMBING KILN
by Fred Olsen

There is probably no experience in pottery to match the thrill, excitement, and anticipation of firing a wood-fired climbing kiln. Smoke billowing forth from the kiln every four to seven minutes; the smell of sweat and pine in 180°F. heat; stoking and then waiting and watching for a loud "oui" and stoking again on and on for seven hours. This was the scene, three times a month, every month, for three years as I fired my chamber in the big Kyoto climbing chamber kilns. Each of the seven to 10 chambers measured about 4½' wide, 6' tall, and from 14' to 20' long, containing up to 5,000 cubic feet.

You really feel that by your hands, knowledge, and intuition you are controlling the outcome of the pottery in the kiln. The neighbors are thinking: "Bloody pyromaniacs! Covering the sky with black smoke and the neighborhood with soot, all because those potters are directly challenging the maker of pottery, the devil fire, in the chamber kiln."

Those beautiful old kilns now lie dormant in Kyoto, crumbling into grog. The reasons are simple: lack of wood, its cost, smoke pollution, and alternative kilns such as gas and electric, making life easier and more efficient for the potter. Since the opportunity of firing these large chamber kilns has all but disappeared, the following description will give an idea of how it was done.

Firing the chamber kiln was, to say the least, work. Weeks in advance, the preparation of the wood was begun. Pine wood that had been drying for a year was split and tied into 1,200 bundles of kindling. Each bundle measured 15" in diameter and 18" long, containing pieces no thicker than 1". All the bundles were stacked around the kiln shed. The split logs for the firebox were piled around the firebox and completely filled the front of the kiln shed. It took the potters three days to stack the kiln and brick up the chamber entrances. The chamber kiln is now ready for the firebox firemen.

The firemen start the kiln's fire by building a tepee of kindling and logs on the ash pit floor. (Fig. 1.) As the coals build up and the flames grow, small pieces of kindling are fed onto the grate. Once they begin to burn well, bigger logs are added, until 85% of the stoking is done on the grate area. After eight hours the firemen throw the logs up the side of the firebox as far as they can, filling the firebox except for the upper area. By this time the coals in the ash pit must be raked and cleared. When the logs burn down to a short flame and the atmosphere is clear, the firebox is filled again. During the burning-down period, the grate stoke hole is covered with a swinging metal plate, forcing the air supply to come up through the grate from the ash pit. A continuous rhythm of stoking must be maintained until the first chamber reaches 1000°C. The firebox stoking usually takes from 15 to 18 hours.

A few hours before the finish, the first chamber stokers arrive. They stack the necessary number of wood bundles next to the chamber on both sides of the kiln. About a half an hour before the firebox is finished, the stokers begin to stoke a quarter bundle per side every seven minutes, thus beginning the transition from the firebox to the first chamber.

The first three or four chambers of the climbing kiln are used for reduction firing. The next two chambers are middle fire chambers and the last two or more chambers are excellent oxidation chambers. For reduction, the wood must be piled high in the firebox to produce the reducing atmosphere, and never allowed completely to burn down. To facilitate the reducing atmosphere, the grate bricks along the chamber's firebox are omitted and the door stoke hole is placed 27" above the floor. In oxidation and middle fire, the grate bricks are used along the floor of the firebox to keep the wood off the floor, thus enabling the draft to flow up through the wood with ease. The wood is allowed to burn down between each stoking, allowing the atmosphere to clear up. The door stoke hole is placed about 33" above the floor.

The reduction chambers are stacked mostly with saggers and shelves on top. The oxidation chambers use saggers in the front settings and about half-way up in the back setting. Kiln shelves are used the rest of the way up. The chambers are stacked leaving a 9" wide firebox up the front wall and a 4½" wide firebox between the front and back settings. From the top of the kiln settings down the back wall to the exit flues, a minimum of 3" must be maintained. In stacking the kiln saggers, a space of an inch or more is kept between them to allow flame passage.

The stoking of each chamber is done simultaneously from both sides. During the first hour, a quarter bundle of wood per stoke is used on each side. A few pieces are tossed into the center of the chamber, shortening the toss each time closer to the door, with the last pieces dropped just inside the door again.

The stokers can tell by the flames coming out of the blow holes along the backside of the arch if they are stoking the wood evenly through the chamber's firebox. Every hour the amount of wood per stoke is gradually increased. The second hour about a half bundle per stoke is used on each side. The third hour, three-quarters of a bundle, and the fourth hour one bundle is used per stoke on each side. The stoking rate during the fourth hour on will be 43 to 44 minutes for oxidation. During the last two hours of stoking, two bundles are used per stoke per side. The same chamber stoking pattern is used on all the chambers. However, the more efficient burning of the wood in the oxidation chambers causes the chamber to fire off in less time.

To prevent the plugging of the inlet flues when firing the reduction chambers, a long steel rod with a hook on the end is used to rake the embers along the firebox.

During the firing of the chamber, the main firebox air sup-

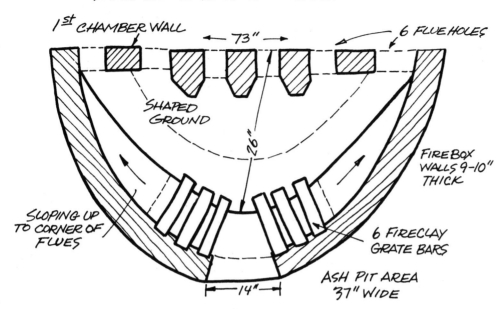

SMALL CHAMBER KILN FIREBOX

1st CHAMBER WALL
6 FLUE HOLES
73"
SHAPED GROUND
26"
FIREBOX WALLS 9-10" THICK
SLOPING UP TO CORNER OF FLUES
6 FIRECLAY GRATE BARS
14"
ASH PIT AREA 37" WIDE

ply is dampered or partially closed. The front half and top of the chamber will reach temperature first. When c/9 is bending on top, the firebox air supply is opened and thinner pieces of wood are stoked in between the settings through the back stoke hole along with the stoking of the main front stoke hole. The increased air supply flows along the floor of the chambers, bringing the bottom temperature up. As soon as c/10 is bending on top, larger hand picked pieces of wood are stoked in the front firebox and the thinner pieces continue to be stoked in the back stoke hole. The thicker wood produces a shorter flame and a more intensive heat through the bottom of the chamber. As soon as c/9 falls on the bottom, one last stoking is done. A 10 minute pause follows and then the stoking of the next chamber begins. The main firebox air supply is dampered back once again.

The firebox illustrated is proportionally reduced in size from the big Kyoto chamber kiln firebox. This particular firebox is designed to accommodate a small chamber kiln with chambers of about 46'' wide, 73'' long, and 65'' tall. One thing to remember in designing a wood kiln firebox is to allow enough grate area for the combustion of wood. The grate area should be 10 times greater than the horizontal section of the chimney.

To calculate the grate area a few rules can be followed:

(1) Minimum size for natural draft chamber kiln flue holes is 4½x9'' or one brick size, spaced 9'' apart.

(2) Basic chimney diameter is one-quarter of the chamber diameter.

(3) Inlet flues equal exit flues.

The above chamber of 46'' wide by 73'' long and 65'' tall will have six flue holes with a total of 243 square inches (Rule 1). One-quarter of the kiln's chamber diameter would give a chimney diameter of 12'' (Rule 2). The flue hole square area will be the minimum square area of the chim-

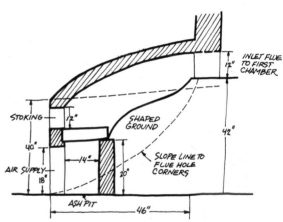

STOKING 12"
40"
14"
AIR SUPPLY 18"
ASH PIT
SHAPED GROUND
SLOPE LINE TO FLUE HOLE CORNERS
20"
46"
INLET FLUE TO FIRST CHAMBER 12"
42"

ney. One dimension of the chimney is 12 or 13½'' to the nearest brick size. Therefore 13½x18'' equals 243 square inches for the chimney section, which equals the flue hole total square inches. The chimney section times 10 will give the area needed for the firebox, or approximately 2340 square inches. The firebox measures 73 by 46'' with about 30% loss due to the shape, giving approximately 2350 square inches of firebox, which coincides with the calculations. It is always better to be a little oversize than too small in calculating grate areas and chimney cross sections.

One important factor in determining the chamber dimensions is to know the kiln shelves available for your use. The chamber illustrated was designed to use six kiln shelves 11 or 12 by 18'' in the back stacking and four such kiln shelves in the front stacking. (Fig. 2.) It is important to leave the 9'' space along the entire length of the front wall for the

143

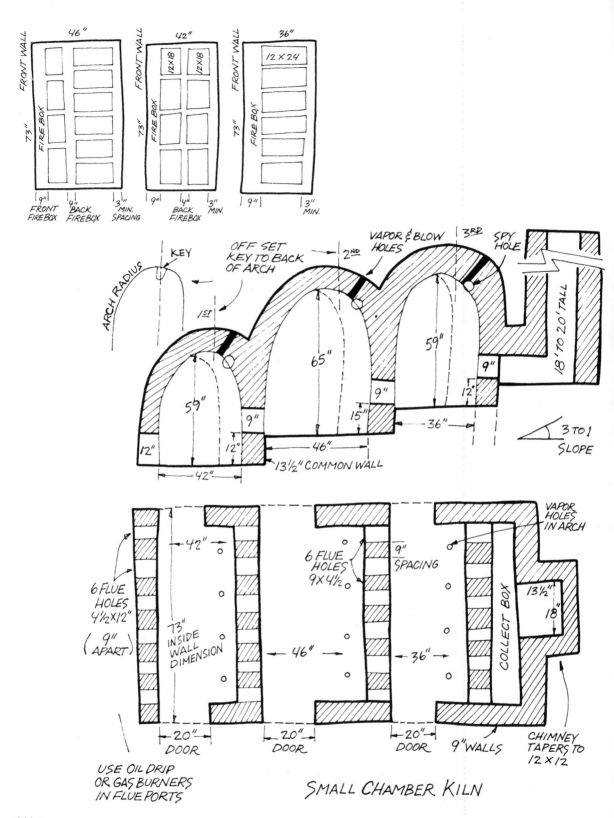

Top row (front wall / firebox plans):

FRONT WALL — 46"
FIRE BOX
73"
9" FRONT FIRE BOX | 4" BACK FIREBOX | 3" MIN. SPACING

FRONT WALL — 42"
12×18 | 12×18
FIRE BOX
73"
9" | 4" BACK FIREBOX | 3" MIN.

FRONT WALL — 36"
12 × 24
FIRE BOX
73"
9" | 3" MIN.

Middle row (section view):

ARCH RADIUS
KEY
OFF SET KEY TO BACK OF ARCH
2ND
VAPOR & BLOW HOLES
3RD
SPY HOLE
1ST
59"
65"
59"
18' TO 20' TALL
9"
9"
12"
15"
9"
12"
12"
13½" COMMON WALL
42"
46"
36"
3 TO 1 SLOPE

Bottom row (plan view):

6 FLUE HOLES 4½×12" (9" APART)
42"
73" INSIDE WALL DIMENSION
6 FLUE HOLES 9×4½
9" SPACING
VAPOR HOLES IN ARCH
46"
36"
13½"
18"
COLLECT BOX
20" DOOR
20" DOOR
20" DOOR
9" WALLS
CHIMNEY TAPERS TO 12 × 12
USE OIL DRIP OR GAS BURNERS IN FLUE PORTS

SMALL CHAMBER KILN

SIMPLE OIL DRIP SYSTEM

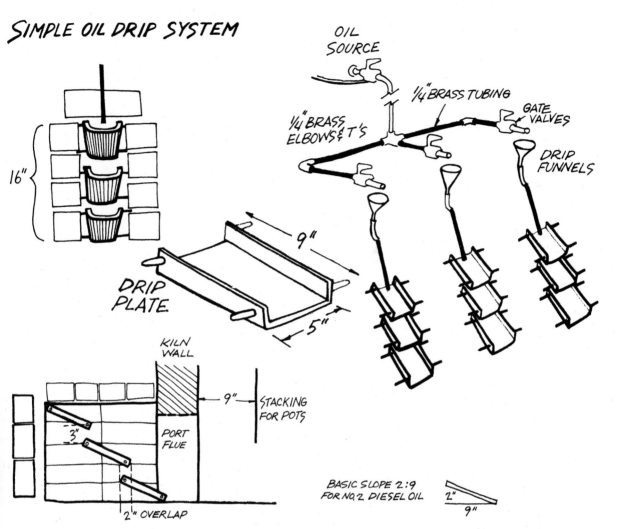

OIL SOURCE

¼" BRASS TUBING

¼" BRASS ELBOWS & T'S

GATE VALVES

DRIP FUNNELS

16"

DRIP PLATE

9"

5"

KILN WALL

9" ← STACKING FOR POTS

PORT FLUE

3"

2" OVERLAP

BASIC SLOPE 2:9 FOR NO. 2 DIESEL OIL

2"

9"

chamber firebox. A 4'' space must be left down the entire back to insure the proper flame movement through the back exit flues. A 4'' space must be left (3'' is absolute minimum) between the front and the back stackings for the back firebox. Two other smaller chambers are illustrated that I have built, and they work extremely well. The smaller chamber is excellent for the last chamber of the kiln and is normally used for bisque. In my chamber kiln, however, I use it as the salt glaze chamber.

The slope of a small chamber kiln is usually 3 to 1. (Fig. 3.) The exit flues are placed from 12 to 15'' in step above the chamber inlet flues. The minimum chimney height for the natural-draft chamber kiln should be equal to the slope of the kiln itself. I use the last chamber and add 3' of chimney for every foot of chamber height and 1' of chimney for every 3' of horizontal length from the inlet flues to the center of the chimney. This usually gives a small three-chamber kiln a chimney height of 18 to 20'.

In all the chamber kilns I have built, the firebox is completely omitted, and I fire directly into the first chamber.

For instance, on my Denmark chamber kiln, I used a simple three-plate per flue inlet oil drip system. (Fig. 4.) At my Pinyon Crest studio, I use four Eclipse 2'' double-compound injector burners (Model TR-80), firing with propane. Bernard Leach, years ago, switched from the wood firebox to a forced-air oil burner similar to the Denver burner. In all instances, hours of labor are saved in getting the first chamber up to stoking temperature, and all the effects obtained from wood firing are retained. Once the first chamber is fired off, the alternative fuel is completely cut off and the second and third chambers rely totally on wood. The transition from the alternative fuel to wood is just a matter of a slight cutback in the amount of fuel used. The secondary air ports are opened slightly and the steady rhythm-stoking is begun, just as described for the big kiln.

It takes weeks to make enough pottery to fill up a chamber kiln. It seems nearly an impossible chore to stack. And then one challenges it to a firing! But the chamber kiln is more than just a kiln: it is a monolithic sculpture that lives, and breathes fire. It is truly a thing of beauty.

BUILDING AND BURNING A GROUNDHOG KILN

by Vernon Owens

The first thing to consider when building a groundhog kiln is water drainage. It should be possible to get drainage away from kiln in all directions. If you have a hillside it will make a lot less work in getting the hole ready to start the kiln, starting the front at the foot of the hill and digging back into it. This way part of the chimney will be underground. Level ground works just as well as far as the kiln is concerned (keeping drainage in mind). If you build the kiln on top of the ground, brace the sides with iron posts, then fill in the stacking chamber with dirt up to the level you want the floor.

Shelter Kiln shelter ought to be at least 3' wider than kiln on each side. If kiln is built where ground freezes deep, chimney should also be sheltered. Build shelter 10 to 12' past front of kiln for storing wood and working space.

Size and Materials We have built several different types and sizes and have found large kilns too hard to heat to high stoneware temperatures. In firing earthenware you can use a longer kiln and do your bisque in the back. Since a groundhog kiln is fired from one end it will always get hotter at the front. This is a problem in salt glazing because you may get pots too hot in the front and not hot enough at the back. In burning glazed pots, these kilns work good because you can use a lower melting glaze at the back.

I think a good-size kiln is 12' long, including the firebox which is 4' long and 5' wide. A good smaller size would be 4' by 10' with a 3' firebox. Since you don't use shelves in these kilns it should be built as low as possible. A 22'' center from flint stone is a good height. With a 12'' wall this gives a 10'' arch rise. (Don't get afraid of getting in and out—I am six feet tall and I can do it.)

Draft: Grate, Fan Since these kilns have nothing but natural draft, it is a good idea to put some kind of grate for the wood to burn on. The grate has to be either cast iron or fireclay brick or large blocks. I think the large blocks are called "car-tops" and made to go in tunnel kilns. You would need to get this material secondhand if possible. It is expensive new and don't last long for a grate. Another way to keep the draft going good is to put in a small (squirrel cage) fan and pipe air under the grate. Not too much air, as this will blow too many ashes back on the pots. Keeping a good draft is the main thing for a good firing.

Bracing Good solid supporting walls should be made on each side to hold the weight of the arch. These should be at least 6'' thick. Use Portland cement, as brick cement will sometimes crumble. A good way to cut down on cost is to throw old brick or small stones in the cement when you are pouring it. You can build the frame to pour the concrete supporting wall with scrap boards or plywood. Use tar paper to cover cracks to keep cement from pouring through. Make

sure forms are about 10'' higher than you want the kiln walls—this supports the arch. Supporting wall ought to be made 12 to 15'' longer at the front than the kiln walls. This supports the side of the kiln front.

Kiln Walls The kiln walls will do with one row of firebricks (hard). Some people think this ain't enough but I have seen walls like this outlast two or three arches.

Arch Arch boards can be cut from 1'' boards or ¾'' plywood. Run a 2x4 along each side against each wall and block up with brick or short wood blocks to within 2'' of the top of the wall. Then tack arch boards about 24'' apart. Put 1 x 1'' or 1 x ½'' strips covering arch boards. You can leave ½'' cracks between strips to save on cost. Tack these strips just enough to make them stay in place until the arch is on. The 2x4s should be left ½'' away from the sides. This will let the forms fall down without catching when you knock out the props.

After strips are on the arch boards raise the whole form up so that the bottom strip is even with the top of the kiln wall. The arch brick should be laid lengthways with the length of the kiln, narrow part of brick up. This will make the arch 4½'' thick. If you turn length of bricks down it will take twice as many brick and after a while the ends will break off and fall through. It will get mighty hot with brick used this way, but you can insulate the arch to stop this. If the kiln is 12' long it ought to have six or eight 2 or 3'' holes left on each side to pour the salt through.

Everybody reading this may already know how to finish an arch in the middle, but using hard brick it is harder to make them fit. I have found the best way is to use a high-temperature refractory that won't shrink. Bring the arch up on each side to anything less than one brick thick. Make up refractory pretty dry and use a hard-wood wedge and hammer and drive it in the crack. Let refractory dry before knocking out arch boards.

Chimney A groundhog kiln must have a good draft. The chimney should be the same width as the kiln for at least half its height. We have never built a chimney over 12 or 14'. But don't think you have to worry about getting it too high — no way, because you will give out and say this will have to do. After you get 3 or 4' above the arch you can taper it some. I think 12'' narrower at the top is enough. You ought to use firebrick from the ground up on the inside walls. The chimney must be double-rowed almost all the way. Red brick (common) will work fine for the outside row after you pass the arch.

Front and Door The front will last longer if it is built three bricks thick, using firebrick on the inside row and red common on the two outside rows. The front must be braced in

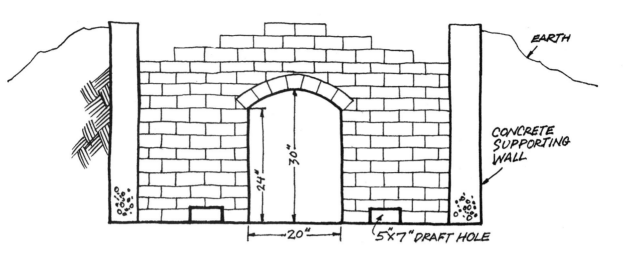

EARTH

CONCRETE SUPPORTING WALL

30"

24"

20"

5"x 7" DRAFT HOLE

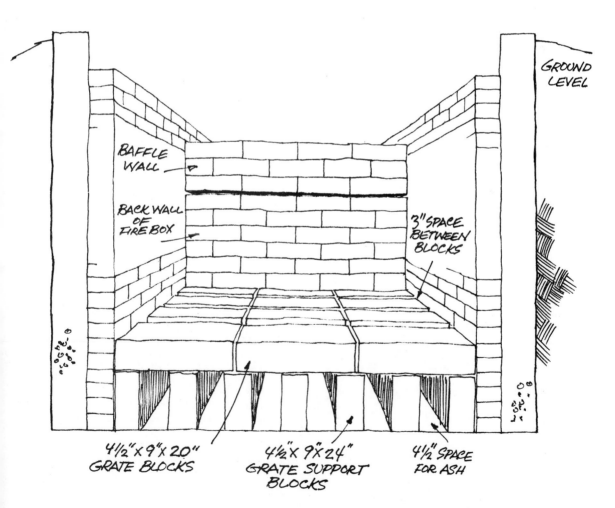

GROUND LEVEL

BAFFLE WALL

BACK WALL OF FIRE BOX

3" SPACE BETWEEN BLOCKS

4½" x 9" x 20" GRATE BLOCKS

4½" x 9" x 24" GRATE SUPPORT BLOCKS

4½" SPACE FOR ASH

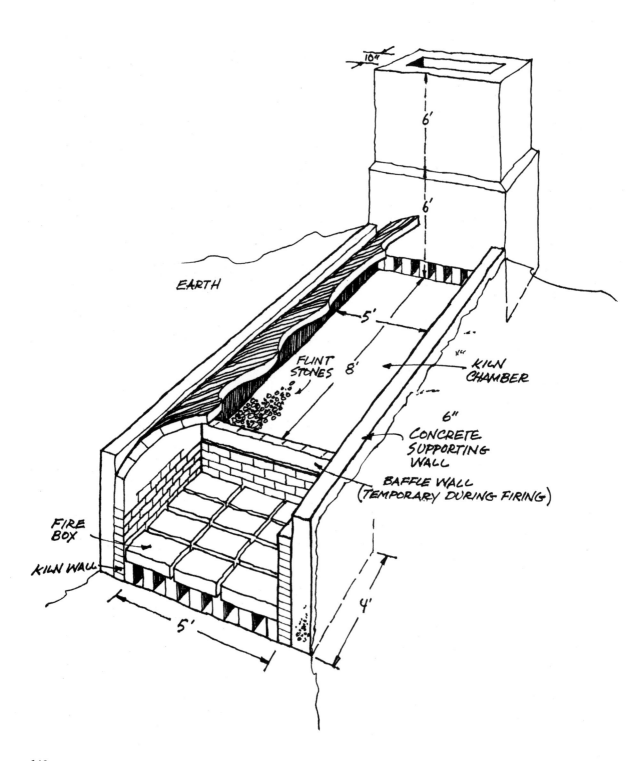

EARTH

10"

6'

6'

FLINT
STONES   8'

5'

KILN
CHAMBER

6"
CONCRETE
SUPPORTING
WALL

BAFFLE WALL
(TEMPORARY DURING FIRING)

FIRE
BOX

KILN WALL

5'

4'

148

some way. If it is not it won't hold the arch in place and the bricks will separate. All you need for a door is a piece of some kind of sheet metal. Use something as light as possible so it won't be hard to lift off and on. Use scrap metal if possible because it won't last long.

Floor The floor ought to have about 1½'' of small white flint stone (quartz). I don't know if it is possible to get this just anywhere or not. If you can't find it crushed, find white flint stones from 3 to 8'' in diameter, burn them out in the kiln to about 2,000°F, then hammer and beat them down to small stones ½ to ¾''. After each burning it is a good idea to tamp the flint stones with a brick to keep them from sticking together. After 15 or 20 burnings add some new flint to keep the floor in good shape. I have seen other kinds of floors in groundhog kilns but I know without a doubt flint is the best for saltglazing because you have a glazed bottom on the pots due to air and salt circulation beneath them.

Burning The Kiln

Stacking Small pots go in the back third of the kiln, then larger pots to within 24'' of the front, and finish up at front with small pots. If you are using flint stone floor make a little mound of stone for each pot to sit on. This keeps the stones from sticking to the sides of the pots. If you are burning salt glaze, put pots with small openings under the salting holes to prevent salt accumulating in bottom of open pieces.

After stacking kiln build a bag wall at the back of the firebox to extend it upward 8'' (approximately). Build of brick laid loose to protect pots from direct flames.

Preheating It is a good idea to build a fire in the kiln the night before you burn. Get the kiln hot enough to be warm the next morning. This way you can fire up a lot faster without cracking the pots.

Burning The length of time it takes to burn a kiln depends on conditions and type of wood and on whether pots are raw or bisque. Burning raw pots you must fire up a lot slower. But under any conditions, heat from wood is a dry, hot heat (quite different from oil or gas) and the kiln should always be heated up slowly.

You need hard wood (logs)—oak, hickory, maple, etc., and it must be dry to do a good burning. You burn this wood for seven to eight hours, then you need small wood to burn for another hour or two. For the last hour small wood that will burn up fast ought to be used.

If your kiln is burning well you should be able to run the blaze solid through the chamber and out above the chimney 10 to 12' for the last two hours of burning. Of course, the flame will fall back between firings of wood, but when the flames die down you know it is time for more wood. In hot weather there ought to be at least two people to do the burning. It can get mighty hot. Sometimes your clothes may smoke a little, but don't worry, you will be alright. Just keep plenty of cool drinking water in a salt-glaze mug close by. Just let the kiln take its time.

Burning a wood kiln is not like burning with gas or oil. Wood don't always burn the same. Just keep it burning, letting the wood burn up so you don't get large chunks bedded down in the bottom of the firebox, which cuts off the draft.

The best wood for finishing a kiln is rich pine—we call it "lightered," sometimes called kindling wood. Most of what we get is old tree stumps that have been dead for 75 or 100 years. Sometimes it is possible to get scrap pine lumber from a lumber planing company that has a lot of heartwood. This is where the tar or pitch is that makes the fast heat and black smoke that make a good salt glaze. A 5x12' kiln should burn out with one or one and a quarter cords of wood.

Cones and Salting I have heard different stories about how cones work in a wood-burning kiln. Some say they will work and some say they won't. I say they will *and* I say they won't. But I think we have figured a way to use cones in a salt kiln that works pretty good. If you want to burn to c/12, put in a set of 8,10,12 cones, and burn till you have the c/10 down plum flat, then salt for the first time. A 5x12' kiln ought to have 25 to 30 pounds of salt. Use about 15 pounds the first salting. Since the salt will cool the kiln down it may take one or two hours to get the c/12 to bend. I think that after salt has been put in the kiln, the cones no longer work as accurately, so if the highest cone don't go down in two hours quit on it. Then do the last salting and put one more firing of wood in.

Cooling After you get the kiln done, prop the door tight against the front and stop up the draft holes. If it is cold, windy weather it is a good idea to cover the chimney about an hour after you are through burning. Opening the kiln too quick after burning can cause air-cracking. We let a kiln cool for at least 36 hours.

Note

I am not trying to say this is the only way to build and burn a groundhog kiln. There have been many different kinds built in the past two centuries. What I have said is what I have found to work best for us. I have been helping to build groundhog kilns since I was 10 years old. My father, M.L. Owens, built the kilns here at Jugtown Pottery for many years before I came to work here. I think most people wanting to build groundhog kilns now want them for saltglazing.

I think wood-burning kilns make good-looking salt glaze, but I won't say it is easy to do. I have burned and helped burn many kilns of salt and I think one good kiln can make you forget five bad ones.

We have fired 12 or more good kilns in a row, then all at once they go bad and these bad burnings can last and last. I think that sometimes when the firing is good, you let up some on the heat because you think you have it made. Then a bad kiln just goes to show you, when you think you know something, you don't know nothing.

FURTHER COMMENTS ON WOOD BURNING

by Malcolm Wright

I would like to add my observations on wood burning, based on my experience here in Vermont. I am an advocate of wood burning kilns, but instead of providing another design (there are potentially thousands) I would like to make some general observations.

First, make the kiln large enough. There are two reasons: 1. A wood flame is many times the volume of a gas flame. Thus a void or open area between stacks and pots is necessary to avoid choking the flame. Up to one-third of the total volume is good. 2. Because of the time it takes to preheat the kiln and to achieve a strong enough draft for high temperature, build a second chamber—or more. You can easily double the capacity with two or three extra hours firing time and wood consumption.

Second, the chimney should be large enough with no tight spots. The friction of gas flowing through a tube is significant. Thus I believe the diameter is more important than the height. Propane tanks 14″ in diameter, welded together should be a minimum; 16 to 18″ in diameter is better. Also, between the kiln and the chimney (especially on small kilns) an after-burning chamber will help prevent expanding gasses from choking off the pull (or push) in the chimney.

Third, the size of the flues between chambers is very important. There is a venturi action that takes place here. The draft-volume is constant at any given phase of the firing. If you decrease the area of the flues, the draft speed must increase. The limit is reached when there is too little air permitted. It is the increased air speed in the firebox that creates faster burning and greater temperature increase.

Fourth, (this is a more general consideration), when and how much to stoke. We use three things to decide stoking times: pyrometer, blow-hole flames, and atmosphere near the exit flues. When you stoke, the temperature falls, back pressure at the blow holes makes a flame several inches long, the atmosphere is cloudy, and the kiln is in heavy reduction. As the wood burns down, the air-fuel ratio comes into balance and the temperature rises; there is still light back pressure at the blow holes and the atmosphere is still cloudy. The flame is more neutral, tending to oxidation. At the moment the temperature levels off, back pressure ceases and the atmosphere clears. Stoke! If you wait, the kiln is losing heat and oxidizing. If you stoke too little wood, you will not get enough BTUs to create a temperature increase, and you will get too much oxidation. If you stoke too much you will not get a net temperature increase because of the large decrease in temperature at the start of the cycle caused by too much reduction.

Fifth, I do not use a damper in the chimney. Instead, I use an adjustable air port at the base of the chimney. Open, the chimney pulls in secondary air through the port; closed, it pulls all air in through the primary air ports. If, after stoking, there is no back pressure at the blow holes, it means the draft is too strong. Open the adjustable air port at the chimney to balance the fuel-air ratio. (Allow enough room for burning embers so that the primary air is not cut off.)

Lastly, this spring we discovered that the primary air control is very important. By adjusting the primary air port between 60 square inches and 180 square inches we can control the length of the flame as well as the length of the firing. The smaller the hole, the shorter the flame and the faster the firing. Also remember the shorter flame is more oxidizing, and the longer flame is more reducing.

To those starting out with wood burning, I hope these observations will help avoid some of the problems that will arise. Most of all, learn to be sensitive to what your kiln is trying to tell you.

OIL-BURNING KILNS

by Paul Soldner

The use of oil as a fuel for firing pottery kilns has interested me since 1964. Prior to that time, I had experience only with gas and electricity as fuels. With my move to Aspen, Colorado, I was suddenly thrust into a situation where natural gas was unavailable and the price of propane was prohibitive. So I began to look to oil as an alternative.

About this time I had also been asked to investigate oil as a fuel for firing in underdeveloped countries. I first met this need from teaching I had done for the Peace Corps while training volunteers to improvise pottery firings in countries with limited resources of gas, wood, or coal. Oil in some form was found to be the most universally available fuel throughout the world.

The difficulty in burning oil is that it is a liquid which needs to be converted to a gas before it will burn well. The making of this liquid oil into a gas can be accomplished in several ways. One method is to atomize the oil into very fine droplets. This can be accomplished by pumping the oil, under high pressure, through a small orifice. This will result in a fine spray and is the method used by the common home oil furnace burners as well as by large steam heating and generating plants. However, the machinery involved is complex. Also, the orifice is small and so is subject to clogging, thus requiring much maintenance. There is another factor as well: the fuel must be as thin as possible, and this eliminates the heavier and therefore cheaper types of oil.

Another method of burning oil is with the familiar weed burner. Here the oil is heated, by its own flame, in coils until it vaporizes into gas. However, the boiling oil develops enough pressure so that it must be contained in a pressurized tank to prevent vapor locking in the supply lines. This system does work well when there is no electricity available, but some means of pressurizing the oil tank is necessary. This can be accomplished by a gasoline-driven air compressor or by a handpump. A minor inconvenience of pressure burners is the fact that they must be operated "wide open." This results in a very hot, oxidized flame. Therefore, to prevent a rise in heat which is much too fast during the early stages of firing, the burner must be located some distance from the burner port. Gradually, the burner can be moved closer to the port as the kiln heats. The clogging of the orifice is also a constant problem and the building of a pressure requires specialized engineering.

I have found that the simplest method of burning oil is the louver and pot type of firing. Each is a separate kind of burner. Both of them depend upon the heating of oil by radiation in the firemouth, resulting in the vaporizing or cracking state. This results in a heavy vapor which then is drawn into the kiln by natural draft and is eventually combusted. My experience with the louver and pot burners is that they are both excessively smoky during the starting period. They require much attention throughout the firing and are inefficient in fuel use until a good red heat is reached. At that point, they are somewhat slower than is desirable. Furthermore, the design of the firebox, kiln, and particularly the chimney, is critical. I believe that such burners are adequate in very primitive situations where electricity is not available.

After trying to adapt these various systems to my kiln, I became interested in an advertisement which purported to sell a device capable of burning any fuel, from gas (propane or natural) to crankcase motor oil. Intrigued by such a claim, I invested $75.00 in The Ursutz Hi Temperature Burner. I was amazed by the simplicity of this "burner" and pleased by its ability to produce a really big, hot flame which could be regulated as needed to fire kilns. It consisted of a motor-driven, high-pressure, paddle-wheel blower and a refractory-lined, steel-shelled evaporator. The operation was to be started by igniting a rag which had been soaked in kerosene and placed in the evaporator. Within a few minutes, the flame was hot enough to ignite small quantities of heating oil, which was dripped into the air path from the blower. This worked. By making proportional increases of both oil and air, an intense heat was created in the evaporator which then issued out the opposite side as a very long, bushy, high-temperature flame. After the initial start-up, heavier oils could be added to the evaporator to provide a cheap, efficient heat source.

Although it was conceivable to direct the flame from the evaporator into a kiln firebox, it occurred to me that the firebox itself could be thought of as the evaporator, thus eliminating that component and thereby simplifying the machinery necessary. To prove my concept, I started a fire (by oil-soaked rag) in a kiln firebox. Then, while directing air from a vacuum cleaner (blowing instead of sucking air), I dropped fuel oil into the air stream a little ahead of the air hose. The result was as I expected: the oil evaporated into a gas from the heat of the firebox, then burned as a flame on into the kiln.

Since these experiments, I have modified the equipment to some extent so as to facilitate the correct metering of both oil and air.

It is important to keep in mind that this is not really a "burner" in the sense that it produces no flame by itself. Rather, it is more like a carburetor, which breaks the fluid into small droplets. These are then combined with air and directed into the firebox evaporator where it finally breaks down into a combustible gas.

I have used this method of burning oil exclusively since 1965 for firing all types of kilns from salt firing, c/10 reduction to raku. I have since discovered that Mr. Roy Cowan of New Zealand has simultaneously been working with the same concept and has improved the efficiency of the system by providing a better atomization of the oil before it enters the evaporator stage. (See the magazine *New Zealand Potter,* 1965, and 1971.) Mr. Cowan quite correctly calls this

Soldner Carburetor for Oil

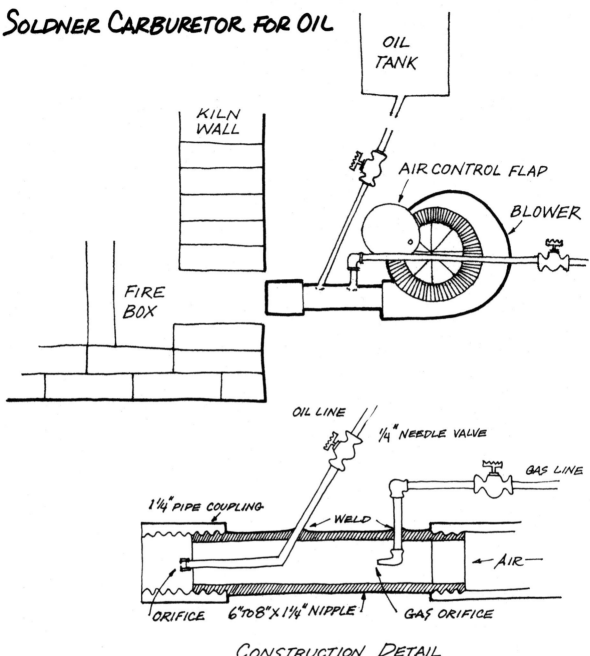

OIL TANK

AIR CONTROL FLAP

BLOWER

KILN WALL

FIRE BOX

OIL LINE

1/4" NEEDLE VALVE

GAS LINE

1 1/4" PIPE COUPLING

WELD

AIR

ORIFICE

6" TO 8" X 1 1/4" NIPPLE

GAS ORIFICE

CONSTRUCTION DETAIL

system a "jet burner" because the principle is the same, although more primitive, as that which drives jet engines, i.e., the burning of kerosene (oil) with compressed air.

Mr. Cowan also uses a pot-type burner to preheat the kiln before introducing the jet burner, resulting in a cleaner start-up.

My experience has resulted in a few discoveries and tips which I feel are worthy of mention to those who wish to try this method:

1. To prevent carbon "clinkers" in the firebox, keep it relatively small. The firebox should be not larger than 8" square. Do not attempt to direct the oil under a floor or down a long wall, as the clinker builds up at the point where the flame is too cool to completely evaporate and consume all of the carbon.

2. To burn as cleanly as possible, go slowly in feeding oil.

Keep in mind that the hotter the kiln becomes, the more combustion will be complete. Also, always start a cold kiln with the lighter fuels, then add heavier fuels as heat is built up.

3. Be sure to use a needle valve to meter the oil. A water valve or gas cock simply will not be accurate enough.

4. Secondary air is not important because of the forced draft.

5. Do not try to use a squirrel-cage blower for the air supply. It would be fine for gas but does not have enough force or volume for the heavier oils. In this context, a vacuum cleaner of the old (big blower) type is good, but better yet is a paddle-wheel, high-pressure blower, powered by a ⅓ horse power, 3400 rpm motor. The best source of such a blower is from WW Grainger, located in most US cities. A 2x8" wheel diameter will be fine for one carburetor.

6. Gravity feed from the oil tank should be between 2 to 4' high. If the height is greater, too much adjustment must be made because the oil weight drops with use. Oil lines can be steel pipe or copper or plastic tubing.

7. The orifice of the oil burner tip can be drilled anywhere from 1/16 to 1/4". If very heavy oil is used (such as crankcase) use the larger orifice. Because oil stored in tanks is quite safe, they may be stored inside. If tanks are outside and if temperatures are below 0°F, oils which are heavier than #2 or diesel fuel, may not flow easily. In this case, either insulate the lines or bury them underground.

8. In place of a rag saturated with oil to start the jet burner, a piece of soft brick can be substituted to act as a wick.

9. Because the blower is of high volume and pressure, it is easy to use too much air. This may result in a flame-out if the oil is cooled below its evaporation point. The visual quality of smoke coming out of the kiln will determine if more or less oil is needed. If the flame turns a bluish gray, accompanied by a strong acrid, eye-smarting smell, too much air or too little oil is the problem. Briefly, if the smoke is black, less oil or more air is indicated. If a flame-out does occur, it is better to wait for all smoke to disappear before attempting to relight the kiln. To prevent any serious explosion, which might occur early in the water-smoking period, be sure that dampers are open at least halfway and, as an additional safety precaution, don't close the door completely until red heat begins to show. This is good advice for all kiln lighting.

10. There is another method of burning oil which is different but related to the technique described in this article. I call this oil assist. It works in conjunction with a high-pressure propane burner. In practice, the kiln is fired on propane burners up to a good red heat. At that point, oil in the form of #1, #2, or diesel oil is dripped into the flame just ahead of the propane burner tip. Both the heat of the flame and the high-velocity air rushing into the burner port quickly convert the oil to a gas, which mixes with the air, and burns easily. The advantage of this system is that it adds extra BTUs from the oil to the propane at the end of the firing. This is the time in the firing when propane becomes most expensive to burn, when excessive drain of propane causes the tanks to freeze up, and when a stubborn firing needs to be concluded quickly.

DRIP FEED OIL/WATER BURNER

by Ann Stannard

My work over the past years with primary school children, and later student-teachers, prompted me to search for more direct and economical ways of firing kilns. In 1959, after exploring wood and sawdust as fuels, I visited John Reeves's studio in England. He introduced me to a "sump oil" burning step ladder, excellent for my purpose.

Sump Oil

Sump oil may be a puzzle. In England, this can be collected free from garages (the drainings of car sumps after an oil change). The oil requires cleaning. The sediment should be allowed to settle at the bottom of a large container fitted with a spigot inserted about 6" from the base. After several days, the oil is slowly filtered through a sieve into another container, ready for use. Alternatively, #2 fuel may be burned.

Kiln Design

Most oil burners have a forced-draft element built into their design which pushes the flames through the kiln. It is important to understand that the flames flowing from the step-ladder burner require "pulling" through the kiln. To create a pulling draft it is necessary to build a chimney with the following dimensions: minimum 9" diameter and a height of at least 12 to 15'.

Firing Process

Preheating. To induce a pulling draft through a cold kiln, preheat the chimney flue by building a wood fire in the 9x9" opening constructed at the base of the chimney.

Controlling Velocity of Draft. Removable bricks at the base of the chimney enable one to vary the velocity of the pull

DIAGRAM 1

OIL & WATER DRIP SIMULTANEOUSLY INTO FUNNEL AND FIRE FROM TOP STEP

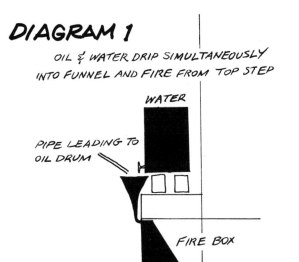

WATER

PIPE LEADING TO OIL DRUM

FIRE BOX

DIAGRAM 2

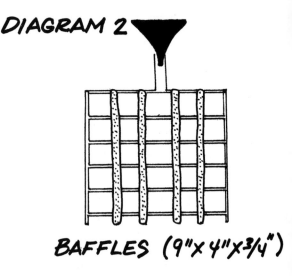

BAFFLES (9"x 4"x 3/4")

through the kiln, particularly during the initial stages of lighting the burner when the flames are often tentative. Replace bricks in fire opening after each stoking, otherwise air is sucked in at the base of the chimney, thus reducing the strength of the pulling draft from the front of the kiln. Continue feeding the fire at the bottom of chimney until the kiln is pulling confidently.

Preliminary Stages of Firing. (1) Build a temporary wood-burning firebox in front of burner as an extension of permanent structure. Step ladder should be in situ. Light wood fire to preheat burner metal and kiln in general. (2) After about 30 minutes, while continuing to stoke wood fire, turn on oil to permit a steady dripping on the top step of the ladder (approximately one drip per second). Then, when oil is burning, turn on water (approximately one drip per five seconds). The addition of water to the oil vaporizes the oil to promote more efficient combustion. Too much water will cool the metal and extinguish the flame. (diagram 1) (3) When oil and water flow is balanced so that the flame is burning strongly off the top step and a little off the second step, allow the wood fire to burn out. Slowly remove the temporary firebox.

General Principles. Throughout the firing, the following pattern of burning should be maintained:
(1) With each increase of oil (and water) gray smoke will be emitted from the chimney. As the temperature in the chamber rises, the smoke emission will gradually clear giving the signal for the next increase of oil/water. (2) It is essential always to keep the oil burning from the top step. As the oil/water flow is increased, a downward progression of burning off the second step, followed by the third and fourth, etc., should be achieved. Too much water, at any time during the firing, will cool the metal of the burner, thus causing the flame to leave the top and burn only off the lower steps. This allows unheated air to be drawn into the chamber through the top of the ladder, subsequently causing a drop in temperature. To bring flame back to the top

step, turn down the oil and water for a short time until burning is re-established.

Too little water prevents efficient vaporization of the oil, thus causing incomplete burning of the fuel and black smoke emission. (3) At about 1100°C (c/1) the temperature is sufficient to burn the oil efficiently without vaporization by the water. The water should be turned off gradually. (4) Watch for carbon deposits accumulating on the sides of the firebox forward of the step ladder. They constrict the throat and prevent free passage of flames to the chamber. Accumulations can be scraped off the wall with a metal rod. (5) In the early stages of the firing, four baffles (scrap kiln shelves on edge) should be placed in front of the step ladder (see diagram 2) to decrease the amount of metal exposed to cold air being pulled into the kiln.

Conclusion of Firing

If salt glazing is desired, salt can be thrown through the steps of the ladder, at top temperature, to be vaporized by the flame running through the throat. Repeat as necessary.

When required temperature is reached, turn off the oil, remove step ladder from the firebox with tongs, and brick up the opening.

Disadvantages. Smoke emission from the chimney, owing to incomplete combustion of the fuel, cannot be avoided in the early stages of the firing. It is also necessary to pay constant attention to the kiln during the first four hours or so.

Advantages. The step ladder can be made at minimal cost (see diagram 3); the consumption of oil is low (approximately one gallon per hour); the system is independent from other sources of power (e.g., electricity for blowers); and there is the enticing possibility of using free sump oil for fuel, certainly an economy.

In conclusion, I must say that we had great success with both reduced stoneware and salt-glazed firings.

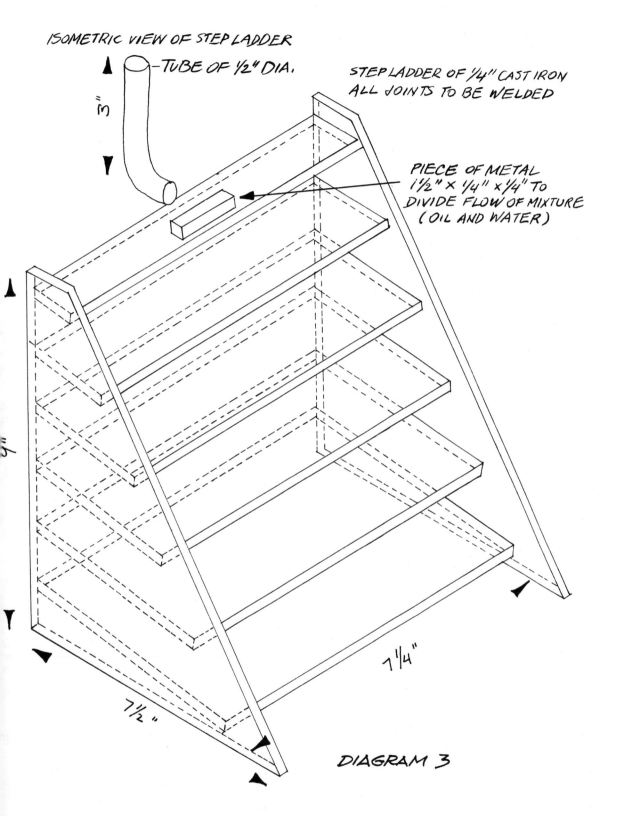

ISOMETRIC VIEW OF STEP LADDER

TUBE OF ½" DIA.

3"

STEP LADDER OF ¼" CAST IRON
ALL JOINTS TO BE WELDED

PIECE OF METAL
1½" × ¼" × ¼" TO
DIVIDE FLOW OF MIXTURE
(OIL AND WATER)

9"

7¼"

7½ "

DIAGRAM 3

155

ADAPTING FUEL OIL BURNERS TO CERAMIC KILNS

by Joseph Mannino and Marcia Selsor

Our interest in fuel oil began the day our propane distributor informed us that he could not supply us with gas for our newly constructed kiln. The kiln was designed to use propane, and at the time we felt it would be easier to convert to oil rather than wood. We began experimenting with drip systems and high-pressure air carburetors but never seemed to get them to work satisfactorily. Then we obtained several discarded domestic furnace burners from junkyards and heating contractors. There was something wrong with each of these burners. So we immediately went to the library and borrowed books on oil burner service and repair. The 1940s and 1950s copyrights were the most informative. Almost all the motors and pumps on these burners are interchangeable and with the handbooks as guides, we began putting two working burners together.

Burner

The burner consists of an electric motor which drives a fuel pump and a squirrel-cage blower. The oil is pumped at 100 pounds pressure through a small orifice in the nozzle, producing a fine mist which is mixed with the forced air for combustion. The system is highly complex compared to a propane weed burner but quite efficient. Since the orifices are of a fixed BTU size, and drip or spurt at any pressure under or over 100 pounds pressure, there was no way of regulating the burner without changing the nozzle periodically during a firing. Playing with a hot nozzle in the middle of a firing was not our idea of an efficient system. Somehow we came up with a simple solution. Instead of having one nozzle permanently mounted in the burner, we installed three. Each nozzle is controlled by its own valve from the pump. To change the BTUs per hour one valve is turned off and another turned on. The three nozzles are held together with a screw hose clamp in the draft tube.

The burner nozzles ($1.25 each) consist of an orifice and a swirl pin which are machined to spray a specific amount of fuel oil at 100 pounds pressure. They are rated according to output of gallons per hour: .5 gal./hr., 1.75 gal./hr., 2.5 gal./hr., etc. To convert gal./hr. into BTUs/hr. multiply the nozzle size by 138,500, which is the average BTUs per gallon of #2 fuel oil (compared to 93,000 BTUs for propane gas). The nozzles are also rated for the width of spray. Wide-flame nozzles are rated at 90° spray, medium at 65°, and narrow at 45° or 30°. Since the walls of a combustion chamber on a kiln are thick, it is necessary to use the more narrow spray nozzle. The oil spray must not come in contact with the sides of the combustion chamber. If it does, carbon clinkers will develop and decrease the efficiency of the flame.

The nozzles screw into an adaptor ($.75 each) which is threaded for ¼'' pipe. Copper tubing (⅛'' interior diameter) is run from the adaptors to brass valves ($2.25 each). Don't be cheap about the valves. Make sure they can hold 100 pounds of oil pressure. These valves are then connected to a brass cross ($.80 each) which has three leads to the valves and one to the oil pump.

The pumps are usually of the gear and crescent type and can handle 10 gal./hr. (some can handle 20 gal./hr.). The fuel oil is piped from the bottom of a tank, through an oil filter and into the pump. A second oil line runs from the other side of the pump back to the top of the oil tank. This return line is to relieve excess pressure in the pump and make it last longer. Our tank is over 50 feet away, so instead of running two pipes, we plugged the return line. A pressure gauge with a scale over 100 pounds is attached to the bottom of the pump by removing a ¼'' plug. The pressure is regulated by a screw which is found under a cap on the side of the pump. After the burner is wired, and all the nozzles are set up, open all three valves, turn on the motor and adjust the pressure to 100 pounds (clockwise to raise, counter to lower).

The burners are mounted so they can be moved an inch or so during the firing. The draft tube should be at a slight angle (¼'' slant) pointing down into the burner port. So if a nozzle started to drip, the oil would run into the combustion chamber and not into the burner. A 2'' collar of Fiberfax or asbestos cloth is wired around the draft tube. This is used to seal off secondary air during the early stages of firing. An asbestos board (transite) is placed over the draft tube to protect the motor from the radiating heat of the burner port.

Our kiln is a 30 cubic foot hard brick catenary, and we felt that 900,000 BTUs/hr. would be necessary to power it to c/10. We chose to use two burners with the following nozzles in each: .75, 1.5, and 3.0 gal./hr. The two 3.0 gal./hr. nozzles produce 831,000 BTUs/hr. Later, we found, after the kiln has reached red heat, two or even all three nozzles can be used at the same time. This gave our burners an overkill of 1,454,250 BTUs/hr. A better choice of nozzles would have been a .5, 1.0, and 2.0 gal./hr. giving a total output of 7 gal./hr. or 969,500 BTUs/hr.

Since the oil pump and blower depend on the electric motor, if a power failure should occur the entire system would shut down. For the last two years, this is the only safety precaution we've taken. Once the oil spray has been lit (using an oily rag on the burner port) we have never had the flame go out. Recently, we purchased two used burners ($8 and $15) with operating transformers and electrodes. We mounted the electrodes over the smallest nozzles, as pictured. This gave us a self-lighting burner similar to a spark plug safety system. Now we can sleep a little sounder during an overnight preheat. A further precaution can be taken by rewiring a master oil burner control switch. This switch will not allow the electric motor to run unless there is a spark going across the electrodes.

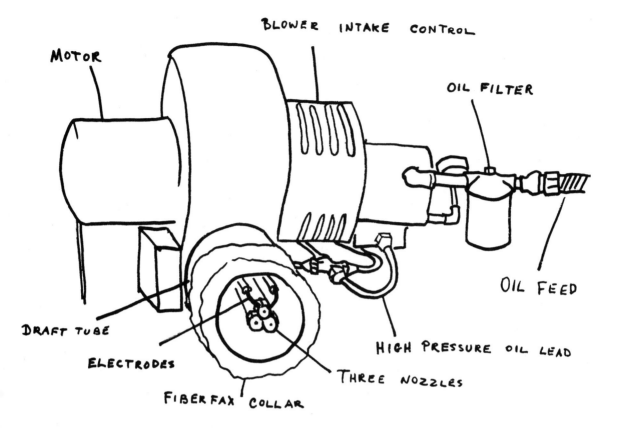

MOTOR

BLOWER INTAKE CONTROL

OIL FILTER

OIL FEED

DRAFT TUBE

ELECTRODES

FIBERFAX COLLAR

THREE NOZZLES

HIGH PRESSURE OIL LEAD

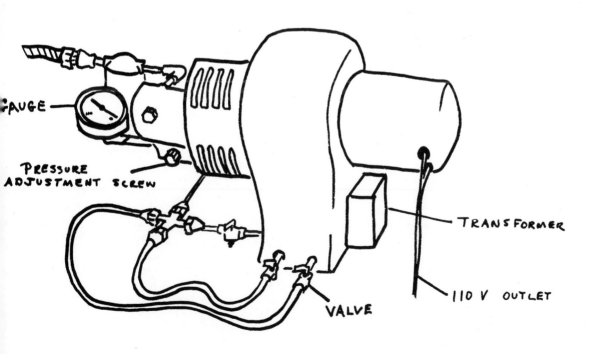

GAUGE

PRESSURE ADJUSTMENT SCREW

TRANSFORMER

110 V OUTLET

VALVE

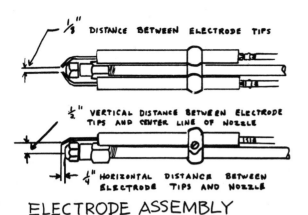

ELECTRODE ASSEMBLY

Combustion Chamber

It took us almost a year to realize that these burners need a combustion chamber far greater than that of gas burners. Using a cross-draft system, our combustion area is between our catenary arch and bag wall. The important dimensions are: the distance of the nozzle to the bag wall, the distance of the nozzle to the kiln floor, and the width of the burner port. These are chosen according to the largest size nozzle in the burner, not the total output of the burner. The whole kiln becomes a combustion chamber after red heat. However, the force of spray from the largest nozzles can still create clinkers if the area within the bag wall is not sufficient to keep the oil spray from coming in contact with the walls of the chamber. See the chart for dimensions of the combustion chambers.

We made two burner blocks out of 3,000° F castable. These blocks were 9'' wide x 10'' high x 7½'' in diameter. The burner port was a conic section of 5'' diameter increasing to 9'' diameter. These blocks could be made by substituting four stacked 3000°F insulation bricks and cutting a 5x9'' conical section out of them. The oil flame is incredibly hot and corrosive on refractories. We found 3000°F insula-

tion bricks to be excellent for lining the chamber. They heat up quickly and help produce a nice, even flame from the start. Our bagwall is made of high temperature firebricks (except at the top where we cut soft bricks for radiants). It is solid for the first 9'' and then the bricks are increasingly spaced for the next 18''.

Firing

Firing with these burners is very different from our experiences with gas. A great deal of smoke, soot, and smell is created. The burners produce an incredible amount of pressure. During the reduction, the whole kiln throbs and the long oil flame licks between the pots (similar to a wood flame). A slight back pressure must be maintained on the burners to produce an efficient flame. To start the firing, all peeps are plugged and the Fiberfax collar is pushed tight

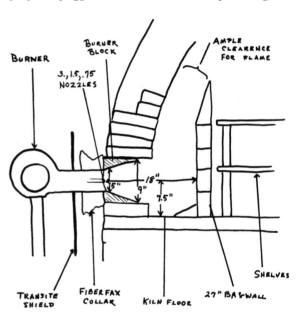

around the draft tube and burner port. This is to seal off secondary air from entering and cooling the combustion chamber. A cool combustion chamber makes an inefficient flame creating a lot of carbon and smoke. We use one burner with a .75 gal./hr. nozzle as an overnight preheat. The air intake is almost completely closed to produce a nice, round red flame which can be seen through the back of the burner. The damper is adjusted until there is a slight pressure on the bottom peep (level of the first shelf). In the morning, everything in the kiln is covered with soot which later burns off with no effect on the glazes. Each time the nozzle size is increased black smoke is produced at the stack but quickly disappears. During most of the firing the kiln burns clean. A heavy, black smoke is not necessary for a good reduction.

After using these burners for two years, we are very pleased with the results. Our copper red glazes never looked so good! We used on the average 50 to 55 gallons of oil per glaze firing.

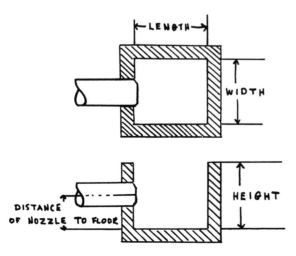

Kiln Log

Time	Burner	Flue	Comment
11:30 pm	One burner at .75 nozzle, air intake almost choked off, Fiberfax tight on burner port	½ open	Black smoke from stack. Slight pressure at bottom peep
12:00 am	Adjust air intake for round flame	½ open	Gray white smoke from stack
6:00 am	Both burners on .75 nozzles, air same, Fiberfax tight	⅝ out	Everything in kiln is black from soot. Slight smoke, later gray white from stack
9:30 am	Both burners on 1.5 nozzles, Fiberfax pulled back slightly to allow secondary air to cool burner, adjust air intake	⅝ out	Color on top of kiln & over bag wall, soot on pots in middle & bottom of kiln
12:30 pm	Both burners on .75 and 1.5 nozzles, Fiberfax pulled back further on draft tube	⅞ out	Good color all around; soot burned off
2:15 pm	Burners on 3.0 nozzles, Fiberfax pulled all the way back, burners pulled 1″ out of ports, adjust air to create slight reduction	⅝ out	c/08 on top & middle down, start reducing for one hour, damper & air cut a little, black smoke at stack, heavy back pressure on burners
3:15 pm	Both burners on 3.0 nozzles, adjust air for oxidation	⅞ out	No smoke from stack
6:00 pm	Both burners on .75 and 1.5 nozzles, air cut	⅝ out	c/8 going in middle; c/6 starting on top & bottom, reduce BTUs; heavy back pressure on all peeps & burner ports; black smoke at stack not real heavy
7:30 pm	Both burners on 3.0 nozzles, adjust air for reduction	⅝ out	c/9 going on middle; c/8 going on top & bottom, still heavy back pressure and reducing
8:15 pm	Both burners on 3.0 nozzles, adjust air intake open	⅞ out	c/10 flat & c/11 bending in middle, c/9 flat and c/10 bending top and bottom. Clear kiln for 15 minutes and shut down, close damper and cover burner ports
8:30 pm	Turn off burners		

159

FIRED FREE

by Dennis Parks

There are three reasons for firing kilns with drain oil: ecology, economy, and aesthetics.

Road and Track magazine, April 1976, says: "The experts report that approximately 370 million gallons of used oil are probably dumped in this country every year, oil that could be re-refined and put to good use."

In the 16 years of my clay career, I have had only the necessary interest in firing kilns and almost none in technical innovation. But with diesel oil prices more than double what I started paying, I have subversively switched my allegiance to drain oil.

It is my experience here in Elko Country, Nevada, that the service stations, garages, and auto dealerships casually but regularly drive past the city limits and empty 55 gallon drums full of drain oil behind a sagebrush (the state flower). Even hauling away over 200 gallons of free oil a month for my kiln, I cannot keep up with the supply.

When speaking of the aesthetic advantages of anything, we place ourselves out there standing firmly on a floating island. For a moment accept my view. I see a richness scale of fired ware varying according to the heat sources:

Regal

    wood
    drain oil
    diesel oil
    gas
    electricity

Common

There are undeniable differences in body color, glaze surface, and happenchance if the same clay with the same glaze is fired in kilns burning different fuels. My aesthetic heart keeps telling me my pots are prettier when fired with oil or wood. The glazes appear deeper, more buttery, and the body toastier. Now to the technology of drain oil-diesel firing. The sample kiln shown here (a 30 cubic foot, downdraft one), single fires to c/10 on plus-or-minus 50 gallons (15 gal. diesel and 35 gal. drain oil) in 18 to 24 hours. The diesel is burned in the early hours because it ignites more readily (flash point 170°F). Then, when the firebox starts to glow, instead of increasing the diesel, I begin dripping a little drain oil (approximate flash point 475°F) into the funnel where the two mingle before entering the burner. By the time the drain oil valve has been turned up to allow a steady stream through (instead of a series of droplets), the diesel can be gradually decreased with the subsequent compensating increase in drain oil.

The most serious problem of firing with drain oil is maintaining a steady flow. Having been discarded, it is dirty. It has a residue of impurities: bits of bearings, gaskets, piston rings, etc. It is far from being homogenized. It is predominantly crankcase oil, but seasoned with gasoline, brake, and transmission fluid, grease, water, and godknowswhatelse. The stuff is black, thick, and viscous. This last condition gets worse when the temperature outside the kiln drops, approaching the consistency of Jello at 0°F. In order to use drain oil as a fuel these disadvantages must be overcome. Every time I transfer this oil from one barrel to another, and from the final barrel to the burner, I use some simple system of filtering.

The businesses that save their used oil for me store it in 55 gallon drums. Because a full drum weighs in the neighborhood of 500 pounds, I pump up from their drums on the ground to mine in the back of a pickup truck, using a Charle Heavy Fluid and Grease Pump (SV-55, cost: $50). It can be operated by hand or with a ½" electric drill. A square of 30-mesh window screen is wired over the pump inlet, and a kitchen sieve sits in the 2" bung hole of the drum receiving the oil.

When I return to Tuscarora, again I pump the oil—this time from the drum in the pickup to the storage barrels near the kilns. And again the oil flows through a sieve. Operating the pump with a ½" drill, the process takes less than 10 minutes.

The final "filtering" of the oil is completed when the oil is flowing toward its destination from the barrel via a sediment bowl to the burner (see diagram g). My needle valves have never plugged up, using this basic system. This pleases and surprises me. When I took off on this adventure, I had feared that I would have to develop a higher level of technical sophistication.

The problem of flow due to the thickness and viscosity of drain oil also had a simple solution. The winters in northeastern Nevada are similar to New England's. When the temperature drops down to 10°F, even your diesel oil gives you enough trouble to make you wish you were a weaver. Slush and ice may form in the lines, congesting at the needle valves. A preventative dose of gasoline anti-freeze routinely poured in the diesel oil barrel eliminates this inconvenience.

Diesel's bastard cousin drain oil, on the other hand, will refuse to flow on a cold night. Heat seemed the obvious tonic.

One day I was in Leo's Radiator Shop in Elko. Not being burdened by knowledge of kiln design, Leo simply reached under his workbench and came out with the device I am using today: an electric automotive block heater, the type installed to preheat car engines (see diagram f). He correctly reasoned that since it appeared I could not avoid drawing some electricity I would demand less by preheating with the block heater for even six hours than by plugging in an electric pump for 18 or more hours.

I now religiously plug in the block heater before starting to candle the kiln. A built-in thermostat cuts the voltage off when the oil entering the heater reaches 170°F, safely below the flash point. After about four hours of percolating heat, the element comes to life only intermittently. Still, by c/10, the temperature of what drain oil is left in the barrel reads 150°F (see diagrams a and h for insulation).

The question of smoke is almost as quarrelsome and personal as that of aesthetics. My oil kilns are smokier than any gas kilns I have ever witnessed. At a workshop recently a student who had helped me fire the demonstration drain oil kiln said: "You know that firing of yours smells just like a goddamn Greyhound station!" She was right, too.

Free and smelly is my choice. Since I now live in the country my fuel options are the greatest; in suburban Los Angeles I could debate between gas and electricity, and earlier, on a second floor in Washington, D.C., restrictions forced me to go electric. The future of firing in cities does not appear any less limiting. Rural America may no longer be a backwash or pastoral retreat. It is looking more and more like the front lines.

Possibilities exist for eliminating the worst of your oil smoke if you are willing to surrender a degree of simplicity in the system. My burner is most inefficient, i.e., smoky, in the early stages of the firing, up to red heat.

If a potter had even a limited source of wood, I feel sure a firebox could be converted to accept that renewable resource in the early hours and burn rejected waste oil later. This modification looks environmentally sound. Even if the kiln is just as smoky, it will certainly smell better.

A civil engineer visiting Tuscarora last summer stated that heavy carbons in black smoke, though certainly more visible, are actually less harmful than the invisible pollutants emitted by more refined fuels, since the former settle out of the atmosphere sooner. I certainly want to believe this theory. He even went to the extreme of suggesting that ugly, black smoke, in limited amounts, may act like a charcoal filter attracting passing pollutants and taking them down out of the air as the smoke rapidly settles. A very attractive theory if you fire an oil kiln, but don't expect your E.P.A. inspector to be up on it.

Coming up is an idealized firing schedule which is included only as an outline, to guide and encourage. Tinker with it freely. The assumption is that any of you who might try firing with drain oil have already had experience firing with gas.

An oil kiln demands more attention in the early hours; the liquid fuel is temperamental in igniting and slow to red heat. Later, all those BTUs may melt the cones faster than you are accustomed to seeing. On occasion I have pulled a peephole brick and watched a cone gradually lie down.

Reduction is not as simple as I would like it to be. When I previously fired with straight diesel, the regime I settled on was basic. Reduce: unplug blower and shut damper. A problem with drain oil under this program is that it cools too rapidly, pools, seeps, and soon floods ominously outside the kiln. I am not proud of doing it, but presently I revert to diesel during each reduction. This revisionism is not expensive in diesel terms, but it is a step backwards. A small price to pay.

By now you can see that "The Modified Tuscarora Drain Oil-Diesel Combination Burner System, as illustrated on a one-burner downdraft salt kiln," is not truly firing for free as

Close up of burner tip.

Block heater and sediment bowl.

the title would mislead you to believe. But don't knock a 70% cut in your fuel costs. Drain oil is not snake oil.

THE MODIFIED TUSCARORA DRAIN-OIL-DIESEL COMBINATION BURNER SYSTEM

as illustrated here on a one burner down draft salt kiln

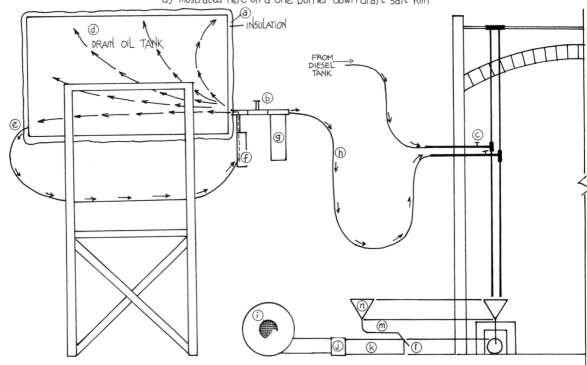

a – Roll wall insulation, 3"thick, covered with plastic
b – Gate valve
c – Needle valves
d – 55 gallon oil drum
e – Oil exit connection. Must be drilled and fabricated
f – Engine block heater (1000 watts)
g – Sediment bowl (Wicks Fuel Filter #24389 [filter removed]).

h – Heater hose covered with roll pipe insulation,
    wrapped with green plumbers tape
j – Blower (Clements Cadillac HP 3)
k – Pipe (2"diameter, 16" long)
l – Welding rod, attached to lower lip of oil pipe
m – Oil pipe (3/8" diameter)
n – Funnel

Hours	Comments
6 hour preheat for single firing.	Candle kiln. Start paper and wood fire around the mouth of burner. Drip diesel on fire. Stay with it until adjusted to lowest steady flame.
1st to 8th	Increase diesel every 20 minutes. Avoid making a pool of oil larger than an Eisenhower dollar until kiln has color.
8th to 12th	Start blower with gate valve open ¼ inch. Every 20 minutes alternately increase air, then oil (chimney exhaust should reflect change from relatively clear to smokier). Continue process until c/1 or air is on full, whichever comes first.
12th	With luck the kiln will have a mild glow. If you haven't already begun, now is the time to start introducing drain oil. With a glow in the kiln, stop looking in the firebox (regulating the oil flow by puddle size) and become concerned with nurturing a rich atmosphere within.
12th to 15th	During this period, as the drain oil is gradually increased, diesel is gradually phased out.
15th	C/1 down. If the cone doesn't want to fall, work at tuning the oil valves where the kiln sustains a murky atmosphere with the cone pad barely visible.
16th	C/5 down.
17th	C/8 down.
18th	C/10 down. Kiln off.

Fred Elliot installing system.

EXPERIMENTAL SOLAR KILNS

by Zeljko Kujundzic

There is nothing new under the sun! Archimedes is said to have experimented with solar projects, and the Carthaginians burned Roman ships entering their harbor with the Archimedes mirror in 214 B.C.! (An Archimedes mirror is constructed of flat reflector strips arranged in a parabolic curve.)

Lavoisier, the 18th-century French scientist, designed lenses, and St. Gobain Glass Works made them for him, which he filled with white wine. With the solar energy thus generated he conducted all the experiments in his laboratory. A printer from Paris constructed a solar collector in 1853 which was the power source for a small steam engine that he used to run his presses.

Solar homes utilizing low-temperature solar energy are now becoming quite common in the United States. Almost everyone has heard or read about them. But to those of us in the field of ceramics and metal crafts (I like to call them the Fire Arts), it is of far greater importance to utilize solar energy for high-intensity solar kilns.

Indeed, if we look again into the past to examine what other people have done in this area, we will realize that. For example, at Odeillo, France, the world's largest solar furnace has been in operation for over 20 years and has been developing over 6000°F. It has been used to smelt steel, etc., for industry. It is possible, as some more recent experiments have shown, in Japan and in France, to construct a solar furnace with a smaller, precisely ground reflector around 60'' in diameter to produce comparatively high temperatures (around 3000°F).

Large solar distilleries have been set up in Greece, Chile, Colombia, and Australia, some of them decades ago. They have been producing great quantities of drinking water, some as much as 4,000 gallons a day. In fact, the future of solar energy probably lies not so much in the use of "direct" solar energy, but in distilling alcohol on a large scale from surplus corn, grain, and other vegetable matter. Plants convert solar energy into sugars, starches, and cellulose, all of which yield alcohol, methanol or ethanol. Perhaps there is no need to point out that alcohol as a fuel is superior to gasoline.

Each square yard of the earth's surface receives about 1,000 watts of power during sunlight hours. This gives us a fair idea as to how much energy we are wasting daily. To translate this into "power" language, we should know that one horsepower roughly yields about 700 watts. So we receive more than a horsepower per square yard in terms of energy from the sun.

My own experiments in this solar research are mainly to prove that one does not have to have an enormous background of thermophysics in order to construct a practical and compact device that will produce solar energy. It is also obvious that this source of power does not have to be used for ceramics or metallurgy exclusively. I leave it to your imagination to come up with other ideas.

I constructed in the spring of 1971 a small experimental solar kiln. It was simply made out of plywood with a sliding back running between a couple of ½'' wooden rails and two wingnut bolts, so that the collected sunlight can be focused precisely. A 12'' fresnel compound lens from an opaque projector was used in the second solar kiln that I built a year later to concentrate the power of the sun into the area where the kiln is placed. This was made out of a coffee can which was cut to the right size and with an opening on the top just big enough to allow the light beam to enter. It was carefully lined with Fiberfrax, a Carborundum product. The edge of the tin which protrudes about ¼'' had been ground into a soft K24 brick so that adequate absorption would be provided for the heat that entered to be retained.

I had all kinds of difficulties at first. Because I had no success in firing ceramic samples to maturity, I was almost ready to discard the whole project. I realized, however, that I had to learn a bit about astronomy and find out the angles at which the sun moves along its daily path at different times of the year. The axis marked on the front of the collector must be aligned to run parallel to the axis of the earth in order to have the sun's rays fall on the collector at 90° angles. Otherwise even a small deviation will decrease the efficiency.

The best results were eventually produced during the longer days in the late spring, and were even better in the summer when the sun was almost directly overhead. Even then only a short period of the day would be effectively used for producing temperatures that are required to melt low-fluxing glazes, such as c/04, 1940°F. The best time of day of course is from about 11:00 a.m. until about 2:00 in the afternoon.

In firing, of necessity, small pots have to be used. Even though high temperatures can be reached, only a small amount of this heat can be put to practical use. I found that by focusing the lens in such a way that the beam of light enters directly into the inside of the small pot, I got excellent results. The refractory material keeps absorbing the heat until it reaches maturing point. Initially I made pottery ¾'' in diameter. Later none of it was bigger than 1½'' diameter. The soft focus at the start heated the objects in the first 15 to 20 minutes. By focusing more precisely every 10 to 15 minutes, and also manually moving the solar collector in order to track the sun, one can complete the firing in about two hours. But keeping up with the 15° per hour movement of the sun on its path across the sky is a demanding task.

An astronomer friend has given me a small motor and information for constructing an automatic tracking device which will eliminate this problem eventually. In Pennsylvania, where I live during a good part of the year, it is of no use to try to experiment on the days when it is cloudy, even to a small degree, because when the kiln is almost hot enough to start fusing the glaze, a 5 to 10 minute cloud cover could cause a drop in temperature.

Other factors have to be taken into account. Even on the sunniest day, a small amount of wind is enough to frustrate the firing project for the day because of its cooling effect. But under ideal conditions, sheltered from the wind, I was able to produce temperatures close to 2000°F.

Considerable difficulties were encountered in firing ceramics very rapidly. The excessively fast temperature cycles tend to crack the pots.

I rectified these problems, with good results, by developing new clay bodies. Mainly by mixing additives such as petalite (Li_2O-$Al_2O_3 \cdot 8SiO_2$) and/or wollastonite (Ca-SiO_3) in various proportions in order to make them withstand the heat shock.

This small prototype kiln has in fact proved its worth. It clearly demonstrated that a larger kiln may be constructed using two- or four-collector lenses in a battery, and yield greater amounts of useful heat at higher temperatures.

At the Kern Graduate Center at Penn State my solar kiln aroused considerable curiosity and interest. This led to my receiving a grant from the Office of Academic Instruction for Commonwealth Campuses. With some private support as well, I was able to spend the summer of 1975 on San Juan Island, off the west coast, where I undertook to design and construct a larger reflector-type solar kiln, capable of developing temperatures around 3000°F, and with a greater firing capacity than I had done heretofore.

I already had a parabolic reflector, which was a private donation towards my research project. It consisted of a 62''-240 lb. component cast in bronze, and polished to 4000-1'' precision.

Since Egyptian times bronze has been used in manufacturing mirrors of great perfection and beauty. But in our age slave labor is not available to keep this mirror polished at all times. Therefore I thought of combining it with 20th-century technology: electroplating the surface with chromium, as this would protect the sensitive mirror with a tough, durable, permanently reflective surface—like the car bumpers which take a tremendous punishment. This seemed to work very well.

The building of this furnace had to be done in several stages:
1. A perfect horizontal platform had to be constructed to ensure accurate alignments and smooth tracking of the sun.
2. A simple cradle constructed for suspending the collector, with a good amount of maneuverability so that any work and experiments could be conducted without added problems.
3. A strong tripod made with an adjustable and versatile suspension system for attachment of the firing chamber or for a secondary reflector mirror to reverse the beam and reflect the concentrated light behind the primary collector (through a 10'' center hole).
The use of a secondary reflector was my ultimate goal for the present kiln, in order to make it possible to build a larger firing chamber without obstructing some of the light and thus increase the efficiency of the collector. It all took more time and more parts and adjustments than originally esti-

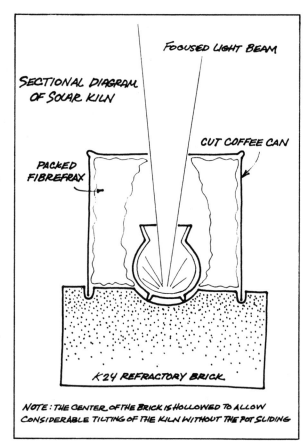

SECTIONAL DIAGRAM OF SOLAR KILN

FOCUSED LIGHT BEAM

CUT COFFEE CAN

PACKED FIBREFRAX

K24 REFRACTORY BRICK

NOTE: THE CENTER OF THE BRICK IS HOLLOWED TO ALLOW CONSIDERABLE TILTING OF THE KILN WITHOUT THE POT SLIDING

mated to assemble and refine the mechanics and procedures to a workable system. I was advised by other solar experts to retain the original one-pound coffee can as the standard unit for the firing chamber. This would in fact give me a comparative value for measuring the speed and efficiency of this and the previous kilns that I built.

I found this to be true. My first test firing proved that this new furnace was vastly superior to the small experimental kiln I used before.

The chamber heated up to 2000°F within seconds, and it was possible to raise the temperature to 2800°F in five minutes. I was able to soft focus the light beam on my piece of pottery and the firing cycle was completed in just over an hour. Encouraged by this success, I changed the kiln chamber to a two-pound coffee can lined again with Fiberfrax and I repeated the process the next day with equally good results. It took seven minutes, however, to reach maturing temperature and another pot was fired in a little bit more than an hour.

I changed to a three-pound coffee can on my following experiment and again the temperature rose within seconds to 2000°F. This kiln was three times the size of the one I used on the first attempt. I had no difficulty, and reached the melting point of the glaze in just 15 minutes. The pot was fired and matured in an hour and a half.

At this stage I decided to switch to using the second

165

reflector mirror and move directly into the final stage of the testing, intending to use the three-pound capacity kiln chamber as a starting point. I did expect somewhat less efficiency through this reversal process and I was anxious to find out to what degree. (Estimated loss of efficiency is approximately 3%.) I installed the mirror and made all the necessary adjustments for the subsequent firing.

The sun was unfailing day after day. For two months I seldom saw even the smallest cloud on the horizon. But now it happened—a few clouds appeared suddenly, and shortly showers forced me to cover the collector with a tarpaulin that I held in reserve for such an event.

The sun emerged again a few days later in all its splendor and fire. I was eager to resume the experiment. I lined up everything and let it go. But after a minute or two it became obvious that this was not going to be satisfactory. The needle on my temperature gauge hardly moved at all. When I decided to check the problem at the source I suddenly realized that the secondary mirror was smoking. On closer examination, I realized it was melting from the fierce heat! I immediately swung the cradle around. But it was too late: the mirror was ruined.

I was upset and dumbfounded. What was wrong? Did I install it badly? I checked everything step-by-step. I could not find a logical explanation for this failure. I dismantled the mirror and decided to examine it with a powerful magnifier. The surface of the glass was melted.

Then it occurred to me that I should have used a highly polished metal surface as a mirror, and not glass. The concentrated light beam, particularly the short waves coming from the primary collector, produce a considerable amount of heat passing through the actual thickness of the glass, since the silvered surface is on the back side.

Just to find out if this was the real reason for the disaster, I decided to cover the curved glass mirror with aluminum foil and test it again. Even though the surfacing of the mirror was wrinkled and imperfect, when I aligned it, it did in fact reflect better this time and the surface did not get too hot, as it did previously when it was just glass.

So this was the real problem. Having identified it, however, did not help too much except for the peace of mind. I had no means to manufacture a new metal mirror with the great precision essential if this experiment was to be continued.

My time had run out. I had to think of dismantling the whole collector, tracking system and all, and packing up to return to Penn State. It was apparent to me that it will require more sustained work and time to further develop this aspect of the solar furnace.

A few words of caution. At no time should one experiment with lenses or reflectors without wearing protective glasses; not just dark glasses, but welders' goggles with at least a #3 filter lens. Also asbestos gloves. Because if I forgot to put my glasses on for just a few seconds while I was adjusting the focus on my solar kiln, I would be seeing spots for the rest of the day. This is obviously harmful for it is very easy to damage the eye with such a powerful concentration of sunlight. It is also easy to inadvertently burn one's hands. It is hard to get used to the idea of the tremendous heat in these small furnaces. It is also a good idea in case of an emergency to have a blind ready, or just a piece of cardboard, that can be pulled over the lens to immediately stop the supply of sunlight.

I expect many potters will be experimenting with solar kilns in the near future, trying their luck with the production of solar pottery. In order to avoid disappointment, the best ceramic material to start with in solar kilns is Egyptian paste, with a low fusing point. After achieving success here, work towards the higher temperatures. I have a five-foot reflector lens which I intend to use for building a larger and more powerful solar kiln capable of producing temperatures of around 3000°F. I think this should produce some very exciting results.

Solar energy is the only totally nonpolluting, environmentally congruous, and free source of unlimited power. We must learn to harness or perish.

FIRING WITH SUNLIGHT

by Tom Fresh, Chip Garner, Bob Connors, and Pat Keyes

During the summer of 1972 up here, some potters, an artist, and a few engineers thought about what a good thing it would be to fire pottery with sunlight. The rising cost of petroleum fuels and the growing scarcity of wood have since made the idea more attractive. Since that time, a few of us have been working on this idea with varying intensity depending on free time, availability of spare change, and the weather.

The basic parameters we have to work with are the amount of power per area of sunlight, the condensing of the sunlight, the daily apparent motion of the sun in the sky, the transfer of light to heat, the containment of the heat, and the cost of materials. These factors determine the size of the kiln which can be fired and the temperatures which will be achieved.

With these ideas in mind we mounted a mirror that focused sunlight on a tracking mount, and built a small kiln with a window to be placed at the focal point of the focusing mirror. At first the kiln was made to move as the mirror maintained its direction toward the sun. But this proved inconvenient as the pottery in the kiln would be moving about. So a second mirror, called a heliostat, was constructed. This mirror was made to track the sun automatically, always directing its light to the focusing mirror, which did not have to move. This was more practical—the kiln could then be placed stationary at the focal point—although less efficient and more costly due to the extra mirrors involved. A crude kiln was made of cement, perlite, and vermiculite with a 4'' square opening in the front for a Pyrex glass window. The focusing mirror was a surplus parabolic collector of spun copper with nickel-rhodium plating 5' in diameter. The little test kiln was about ⅓ cubic foot in volume.

We tried several different clays in the focused sunlight and in the kiln. The ideal clay for solar firing seemed to be one which was low fire and could withstand thermal shock. Discontented with commercial clays, we took to hunting for geological sources of clay in our area, particularly in the desert washes. These clays were better suited to withstand the extremes our simple experiments required. Later we learned about Indian firing techniques and their similar temperature requirements—it was no coincidence that the clay used to make *ollas* could also be solar fired.

Measured with a commercial pyrometer, the tip inserted through a hole in the rear of the kiln, the kiln reached nearly 1400°F, enough to bisque the few small pots inside. Glazing was done in the focal point directly, or near to it. This is where the clay had to withstand thermal shock, as it was moved in and out of the light. Also it was difficult to obtain an even glazing since only a spot as large as the focal area could be glazed at one time. But part of the interest we had in solar firing was to explore its unique possibilities, and this problem could ultimately be an asset. The technique proved useful for rakuing, especially beads, which were more readily acceptable according to the size of the focal area. Another problem with this setup was encountered with the Pyrex window. Although it would work for a few firings, eventually it would crack and finally break. The window problem will have to be solved before higher kiln temperatures are reached.

At present we are working on a larger, more simplified setup, one more practical for the potter's craft. This design will give us inside kiln temperatures capable of firing pots of more usual sizes to stoneware temperatures. It would appear that without getting overly expensive and grandiose solar firings will be limited to comparatively small-sized kilns. The present design calls for a 3 cubic foot kiln with the focusing mirror constructed at a cost of $2 per square foot. The aim here is to make firing practical enough that repeated daily firings could make up the same yield of pottery over a given period of time as conventional kilns. Hence we see the individual potter who eventually depends on solar firing techniques operating at a different rhythm than today—one aligned more with a day-to-day firing interval. For example, according to our present design criterion, a modular 3 cubic foot kiln fired say 10 times during two weeks would yield an equivalent of a 30 cubic foot kiln fired once. The obvious advantage would be that once the kiln is built the fuel cost is nil.

All in all, we find learning to fire bits of the earth with sunlight a satisfying and enlightening process, particularly now as the larger kiln nears completion.

CLEAN HEAT

After our initial attempt we built a larger and more successful solar kiln, red-firing several burnished pots to 1500° or 1600°F. We constructed a 5 x 10 ft. mirror that focuses 47 square feet of sunlight into a 6 x 18'' rectangle. The focal length is 14'. The kiln is cylindrical, 6'' in diameter and 16'' long inside (see drawing). It is insulated with 1'' of ceramic insulation and a 3x14x¼'' Pyrex window. Since the focal area is larger than the window, we don't know how much of our 47 square feet of light is entering the kiln.

The mirror is mounted on a movable axis parallel to the earth's axis (pointed toward the North Star). The kiln is up on a tripod. Our tracking mechanism consists of adjusting the mirror and inching the kiln along as the earth turns, to keep the sun, kiln, and mirror aligned. We set the pots on the fiber insulation "floor" and let the light coming through the window strike them on one side. The fire is surprisingly even with this arrangement; only a few pots have come out fire-marked on the sunny side. A good firing takes about 1½ hours up to 1550°F (so as not to blow up the pots), 1 hour soak at 1550°F, and 1 hour cooling time. This kiln has proven a fairly economical (it's hard to compete economically with cow dung) and very enjoyable method for low firing pottery.

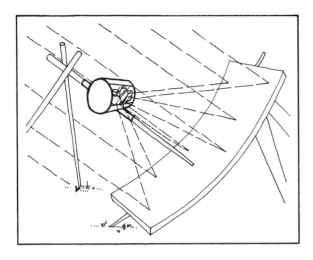

By tightening up the system and using better materials, larger low-fire and higher-temperature solar kilns are possible. Rough estimates indicate that it would take between 50 and 150 square feet of sunlight to fire a 1 cubic foot kiln to c/10 with the methods we are using. To purchase a 3 cubic foot electric kiln and fire it 500 times to c/10 can easily cost $3,000. If a 200 square foot focusing mirror proves sufficient for firing 3 cubic feet, a competitively priced solar kiln can be constructed. Pottery can be fired to temperatures just under 1600°F (where Pyrex windows start to slump) cheaply with sunlight. Whether or not solar kilns will be built, solar firing is an enjoyable and ecologically clean process.

SOME PROPOSALS CONCERNING THE USE OF WASTE HEAT

by John Glick

It is no doubt absolutely essential that potters and glassblowers must immediately seek workable alternative solutions to their fuel needs. We have all long since come to know that "cheap fuels" no longer exist and that as time passes we will be substituting for or eliminating whole technologies that are based on fossil fuels. This upheaval will surely come, and we must prepare to live with the changes it will bring. While we must focus our attentions on new technologies, we can, as in the case of wood-fired kilns, return to entirely practical, low-technology solutions based on replenishable resources. Certainly the timetable of the approaching fuel supply problem appears more or less frightening depending on your choice of expert opinion. Estimates range from highly optimistic "never in our lifetime" projections to speculation that we will, indeed, exhaust several major fuels (including "real" natural gas) by the year 2000. I must choose a moderate attitude, one that keeps me from total depression and helps me to work toward some partial solutions to supply and conservation on a private level as it directly concerns me.

Users/Abusers

What very much concerns me is that, as a group, potters and glassblowers have consistently been the greatest primary consumers of fossil fuels in the entire craft spectrum. Just as obvious is the fact that very few of us really gave much notice to this fuel consumption until price and availability yanked our attention directly to our checkbook as fuel bills skyrocketed and overhead costs followed. But all this is

a well-known set of factors now. No matter how we alter our work approach (short of stopping) we are, for the most part, rather securely stuck in an energy-consuming manner of working.

Heat Conservation

Sadly, little has been done to recognize the major role that conservation and careful use of waste heat can play in making the required adaptations to change less painful in a fuel-starved world. Stop and think how many times you have warmed yourself next to a glass furnace or kiln, marveling at the satisfying, radiated warmth that penetrated your backside. Think further how hard we work to keep adjoining work spaces comfortably cool and how we really have come to regard this radiated heat as an offensive nuisance. For the summer perhaps this is justifiable, but for the winter we will have to rethink our whole attitude about heat.

Simply stated, there is absolutely no reason that a potter or glassblower should ever have to heat his studio or his home with any other source of heat than his own waste heat byproduct from normal kiln and furnace use. There are, doubtless, exceptions to this blanket statement; there always will be. If a craftsman was thinking along these directions when he planned his geographic location, building placement, and equipment design, then the potential shortcomings in the heat-saving systems would be greatly minimized. But, even for craftsmen already situated, there is much to be done to take proper advantage of waste heat.

I see the necessity of two distinctly different approaches

when considering the equipment used by glassworkers compared to that of potters. The basic differences exist because potters usually fire periodically and glassblowers usually run furnaces around the clock.

Potters' Kilns

Think of a kiln as a gigantic radiator of heat. Even with a wisely insulated kiln wall, there is a massive quantity of heat radiated from the kiln walls starting about midpoint through the firing cycle and certainly continuing through the early stages of the cooling cycle. Let us use this as a starting point, a "no technology" system. In my studio the kiln is situated in a separate kiln room (Fig. 1) to isolate it from me during the firing cycle (fumes and noise from blower burners). When this layout was originally planned those convenience factors were the only facts I considered. Now, in cold weather I use a 24″ window fan hung in front of the kiln during the cooling cycle (after the burners are off assuring that no combustion fumes are present) to blow warmed room air into the main studio space. I can heat 1,350 square feet of space for up to 36 hours in Michigan winter weather. Cost is in pennies to run the fan motor and the studio furnace never goes on the whole time. Duration is the obvious shortcoming of this simple system since I fire at best twice each month and would get a maximum of 72 hours of "free" heat. The idea would function more smoothly in a studio where two or three kilns were fired on a daily basis. Even with this tiny step toward heat saving we are beginning to move in the right direction.

The Chimney as a Heat Source

The following heat extraction and storage proposals are not yet in general use (at least not in my studio, as yet). I offer these considerations in the hope that if the ideas are not totally practical as they now stand, then through discussion, experimentation, and exchange of ideas, we may help each other solve some of our most pressing mutual problems.

Look at what happens with the kiln chimney during and after the firing process. From the start it shunts vast quantities of heat (and money) to the outside air. The unwanted combustion fumes are certainly not a desirable commodity to consider for our purposes for obvious health reasons. So, we must devise ways to tap the heat that exists in the flue stream. Heat-exchange devices that are built directly into the chimney brick structure are the first consideration. The "Fuel Saver" (Fig. 2) is an example of a type that employs metal probes to absorb heat and transfer it through the brick to an exterior chamber where a fan system directs an air stream past the external, radiating members. This device functions well in flue temperatures in the hot (1000°F) range. The relatively short span of effective use (the last stages for a firing cycle) would be the most serious limitation with this type of extractor.

Now consider the stack as the kiln cools. Most dampers leak enough heat to make a constant, hot updraft throughout the entire cooling cycle. Later when we open the damper to help the kiln to cool further, more heat passes up and away. We need not consider this lower (below 1000°F) flue tem-

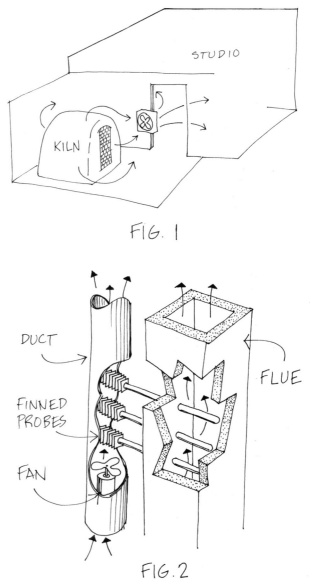

FIG. 1

FIG. 2

perature as lost heat. By testing the flue draft temperature with a thermocouple probe we may find that we are dealing with about 900°F and below. A simple diversion system (Fig. 3) would shunt this valuable heat to a secondary stage heat exchanger. The "Torrid-Air Heat Saver" is another kind of heat exchanger, one designed for use in flue systems (wood and oil stoves) where temperatures are more moderate. A thermostatically controlled fan provides a forced draft through a series of safely enclosed heat-exchange tubes. This is what you could expect to gain from this device according to the manufacturer: flue temperature before entering exchanger 840°F; flue temperature after going through exchanger 610°F; air temperature at output end 155°F; flow rate 210 CFM; BTU/hr. 19,139.

With this particular unit, 840°F appears to be the highest operational figure from a durability and safety standpoint. One could construct a larger, more durable device to accomplish this job. In general, the bypass shunt/damper would come into play at a flue temperature below where built-in exchangers (such as the "Fuel Saver") could provide useful function. Both exchangers could be easily connected to existing ductwork to deliver warmed air to distant rooms. Some very exciting heat exchanger work is being done by Paul Sturgis of Stone Ridge, N.Y. His concepts center around high efficiency, passive (no fan used), multiple-tube clusters that could very well be applied to kiln or furnace reclamation situations.

Finally, we can tap the last remaining portion of heat available in the flue when temperatures drop below the 300°F range by shunting the entire flow of air into a duct system and mixing it with cooler room air for service to other areas of need. Common sense will tell us that if any of these last two systems are treated foolishly—that is, allowing excessively hot air into ducts and systems not designed for high heat—then we can predict rapid deterioration of metals and fire hazards. One does these things wisely or not at all.

Storage Water Transfer

Up to this point we have only dealt with ideas that use waste heat as it is produced from kiln walls or lost through the chimney. Now we can turn to the most valuable potential of all, that of heat storage. One possible direction involves heating water and using it as a transfer medium to other spaces requiring heating. We can literally wrap a copper tube around the chimney (Fig. 4) and also apply an insulating jacket around the resulting heat absorption coil and pass heated water to a storage tank for distribution to finned baseboard heat radiators. Recycled auto radiators work very well for this purpose. Another concept would involve suspended collector panels (Fig. 4A), not unlike solar collection panels, erected overhead in kiln room situations where a warm air cavity exists continuously due to frequent firings in several kilns. Above my kiln, for example, I have an insulation shield of galvanized sheet metal and ¼" asbestos board to act as a heat deflector and ease my mind about the nearness of the kiln to a wood roof. Why not substitute a water-filled collection panel in that space as temperatures up to 160°F are often reached as the firing progresses? The major drawback to these water systems may well be the sporadic nature of the firing schedule, at least as I experience it. For a potter firing three or four times a week in a series of kilns the water system could work well, coupled properly with a thermostat-regulated pump for circulation and an insulated storage tank equipped with a pressure-release valve to handle any accidental steam-induced overload to the system. Certainly domestic hot water for nonheating needs could be easily obtained in this system.

Storage/ Air Transfer

What intrigues me much more, however, is the concept of moving hot air as the transfer medium. Compared to hot water systems, the ductwork required for air transfer is essentially leak proof and should connect easily to existing hot-air heating systems in buildings or homes. The basics of the proposed hot-air transfer and storage system come from adaptations I have projected from solar energy systems as discussed and outlined in *Harnessing the Sun* by John Keyes (see References at end of Chapter). His book is dedicated to the development of a practical solar heat collection principle coupled with the "rock crib" heat storage principle. This system employs washed river gravel of uniform size (about 1" to 1½" in diameter.) Various solar heat storage systems have employed rock as a primary storage system or as a supplementary storage device (an insulator of sorts) in connection with large water tanks. Keyes has focused his research on an advanced, highly efficient collector panel of his design and a circulation system that washed air across the collector face and subsequently into the rock crib for storage and eventual use. Space will not permit me to explain the design and operation of his "Solar-Aire" furnace, but to understand the fullest potential application of this approach I strongly advise that you read his book and also write for literature on his furnace as licensed through International Solarthermics Corporation (see References at end of Chapter for address).

The Kiln Foundation

For the moment let us turn our attention back again to the kiln as a heat source. This time we will focus on the foundation since it is there that we can expect to extract great quantities of heat over a long period of time. The collection principle is based on the common use by many potters of cinder block as a kiln subfloor (Fig. 5). I personally use 4" hollow block under my kiln and I have had occasion to discover just how very hot the space under the kiln gets during a firing. Using 4" block (with holes lined up to form air passages across the entire foundation), two layers of insulating brick, and a final setting floor of 2½" hard brick, I place the temperature in the center of the air space beneath the kiln at about 450°F during a c/10 firing. More importantly, once hot, this massive amount of brick and block keeps on radiating a steady supply of heat as the firing ends and cooling begins. It is the last place to cool even several days after the kiln is empty. In the case of my kiln (which occupies a floor space of 64 square feet) the potential heat gain time from this honeycombed foundation mass covers a 36 hour period starting from the time the burners are turned off until the foundation would be too cool to serve a further purpose. Any potter designing a new kiln would do well to consider heat storage and collection when he plans the kiln foundation since this is such a marvelous heat trap.

A Collection Manifold

Next we require a manifold (Fig. 6) running the entire length of the kiln foundation. Essentially this is an extension of the block foundation and might be constructed of galvanized sheet metal backed up with fiberglass insulation. The function of the manifold is to collect heat from the entire understructure of block and concentrate and direct the flow of hot air to the storage area. The open face (the opposite side of the foundation) could be thought of as the cold air return since air must flow under the kiln to carry heat away. Positive draft would be provided by a belt-driven blower. Placement of the blower and motor in this system should be somewhat more exacting than the solar applications outlined in the Keyes book since we are dealing with higher temperatures, at least at the beginning of the collection cycle. Placement of the blower in a position in front of the manifold location (a cool area) to push air through the storage system would probably insure against motor failure due to overheating. A series of thermostatically controlled switches would tell the collection fan system when to push warm air and when to shut down (when the highest safe storage temperature had been reached).

The Storage Crib

The most logical way to approach the storage crib (Fig. 6A) is by seeing it as a heat pool. This will be where we expect to store waste heat until it is needed elsewhere. To act as a successful storage chamber the crib must be well insulated. Although some designers for solar storage needs suggest the use of polystyrene block insulation of 4 to 6'' thickness to handle the potential peak temperatures of up to 350°F, it is quite possible that the material may suffer from deterioration under continual use at that range. In this instance, with a possible input range in excess of 450°F, we might well go to a more durable combination of wool or asbestos materials or fiberglass batts, at least, for the innermost core (Fig. 7). Since the combustion point of wood is in the 450°F range, we must take pains to isolate any wood members well away from the inner space. Possibly the material order should be (from the inside) aluminum foil, steel-reinforced galvanized sheet, mineral-wool block insulation or fiberglass batts and possibly asbestos of some type, and finally the wood exterior sheathing.

Reclaimed hard brick (firebrick) or even red building brick could form an excellent material for the core of a heat well. Stacked in such a way to allow heat flow (probably by updraft) the heat retention capacities of such a well would be considerable. Even moderate-sized broken brick rubble would do a good job, providing the material had been washed well to remove the dust. It may be tempting to think of placing a heat well underground. If this is planned, then several considerations that should be well researched are whether there is ground water to deal with and whether the duct connections will be made more difficult than a ground-level installation. Additionally, access to the internal structure for adjustments or repairs would not be made easier by a below-grade design.

Moreover, I cannot see why the collection crib could not be made to function as a solar heat unit and a waste heat device at the same time. With proper southern exposure the same structure should easily serve both functions, assuming care was taken to properly insulate the solar collector face and air-circulation blowers from the potentially higher internal temperatures when the crib was receiving waste heat from a firing. This (hybrid) design should help span the days in between when no kilns are in use but when the sun may

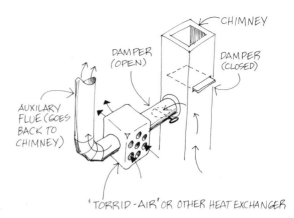

FIG. 3

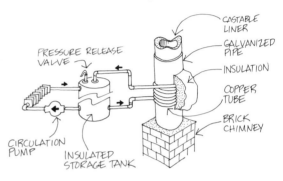

FIG. 4

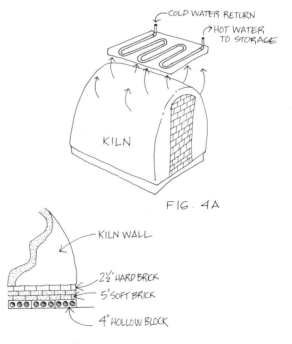

FIG. 4A

FIG. 5

171

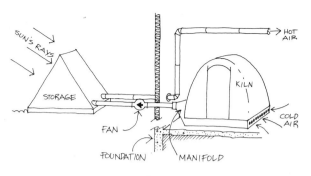

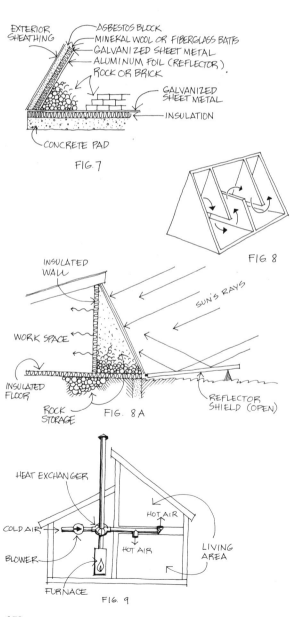

SUN'S RAYS
HOT AIR
STORAGE
KILN
FAN
COLD AIR
FOUNDATION
MANIFOLD

FIG. 6

EXTERIOR SHEATHING
ASBESTOS BLOCK
MINERAL WOOL OR FIBERGLASS BATS
GALVANIZED SHEET METAL
ALUMINUM FOIL (REFLECTOR)
ROCK OR BRICK
GALVANIZED SHEET METAL
INSULATION
CONCRETE PAD

FIG. 7

FIG 8

INSULATED WALL
SUN'S RAYS
WORK SPACE
INSULATED FLOOR
ROCK STORAGE
REFLECTOR SHIELD (OPEN)

FIG. 8 A

HEAT EXCHANGER
HOT AIR
COLD AIR
HOT AIR
LIVING AREA
BLOWER
FURNACE

FIG. 9

be shining. Certainly it would be quite logical to provide all the necessary domestic (wash) hot water one needed with the same storage unit merely by integrating a pickup coil in the design. It would be worth the experiment time to solve these dual functions since under even the best circumstances a separate waste heat crib and a solar unit would be unnecessarily costly and space consuming.

The rock crib could be a variety of shapes unless the dual system was the goal. Then it would seem the "A" frame configuration Keyes has developed would be the best since it provides for a proper attitude of orientation between collector face and sun. Further, if both functions are expected to be incorporated, then a cold air return (Fig. 6) is required to serve the crib when it functions as a solar unit so that the return air is not (cold) outside air but relatively warm air returning from the structures to be heated. The kiln foundation collector duct could well serve as a cold air return since when solar heat collection was in process it would be because waste kiln heat was not flowing in at that moment. These functions would be regulated by a series of heat-sensitive switches that would decide which heat input was the greater and thereby cut out the undesired component. To promote proper internal circulation of heat to all parts of the crib Keyes has designed internal baffle walls to direct the air flow (Fig. 8).

There are many potentially useful design possibilities that would combine collection, storage, and studio design into one unified whole. The southern-facing wall could be thought of as a massive combined functional unit (Fig. 8A). The exterior face would be angled at the correct attitude to the sun's rays for your particular latitude. A rule of thumb for this angle is: collector tilt toward sun equals latitude of your site plus 10° for winter considerations. However, since in all likelihood this collector will not be adjustable to accomodate to spring and fall sun angle differences, a better optimum choice must be to use latitude plus 5°. A blower would collect accumulated heat from the collector face and also, when necessary, pull heat from the waste heat lead duct from the kiln manifold. The interior wall insulation thickness would be calculated to provide the desired amount of gentle, radiated heat to the immediately adjacent work space but would be designed to retain the bulk of the accumulated heat load for use throughout the entire building (or other buildings) which would be serviced by forced air circulation means. The storage function could occur as well in a subfloor location by transferring the heat load there for storage, radiation up through the floor, and later movement to other locations needing heat.

Further, it would be necessary to consider a backup heat source (wood burning stove with Torrid-Air Heat Saver?) for days when no firing had recently fed the crib or when no sun appeared. Or, one could plan firings to occur in a concentrated pattern over the worst of the winter months. Perhaps this is not a convenient thing to consider, but neither is the entire energy-related situation in general. If the backup system was a conventional furnace, then the existing duct work could very likely be used for a large part of the total distribution system. The controls of the solar/waste heat system and the standard furnace would be interfaced so no unnecessary overlapping of heating duties would occur.

Storage Crib Capacities

There is an essential bit of figuring that has to be done to compute the heat loss from a structure we desire to heat. In order to know what performance we can hope to gain from our stored heat we must know the Degree Days of the specific climate locale. In the Detroit area of Michigan, for example, we have about 6232 Degree Days. These figures are achieved by the following method: When the outside temperature is 0°F during the day and the inside temperature is 65°F we refer to this relationship as a 65°F day. In a five day period of like temperatures we would have 5 x 65 or 325 Degree Days. Keyes' book and many other solar heating texts list accepted Degree Day figures for the entire country. Michigan in the Detroit area is in the high median zone of Degree Days (coolish).

Next, we should consider the nature of the structure to be heated (insulation, windows or not, size, etc.) so we can reach a conclusion about heat needs. We want to reach an answer about how many BTUs will be required to heat for each degree of temperature difference between inside and outside. A small, well-insulated building with storm windows might use 500 BTUs per degree. If we had only a 10° difference between inside and outside temperature we would need 10 x 500 BTUs or 5,000 BTUs to maintain the difference (to heat that particular building). Applying this concept to the Detroit figures using the same theoretical small house, we would have 500 BTUs x 6232 Degree Days heating season x 24 hours/day, giving somewhat less than 10^7 BTUs per heating season. Since there are about 10^5 BTUs available in one gallon of fuel oil, we would require the equivalent heat of about 900 plus gallons of oil to do the job of heating the structure. Most solar heating texts will show you how to measure your individual structure and arrive at an approximate BTU requirement for your Degree Day location.

Assuming we will design a dual system, then these facts will be very useful in determining how large (tons of rock) we can expect to build our heat-well. If you live in a relatively moderate climate with good sunshine (quantity) over the winter, then you may be talking about a relatively modest crib. But the exact size could not be easily predicted without actual test data. My guess is that we might well be talking about a volume of rock in the 20 to 50 ton range if the structure was large or the climate harsh or the potential heat sources great. The efficiency of a rock storage system quickly drops off as it becomes saturated with heat. One way to offset this problem is to increase the overall capacity by increasing the sheer volume of the material to be heated for storage. Then, as the heat being carried to the storage area is absorbed by the greater mass of rock, a longer interval will exist during which some appreciable efficiency in temperature gain can be experienced. Or to say it another way, before the return air leaving the storage crib is so close to the input side of the loop in temperature that no great gain will occur.

Remember, these are projections, not hard facts. But they are based on a great deal of well-documented research and performance testing with Keyes' "Solar-Aire" device and many other related projects across the country. Additionally, we have been speaking about solar only without considering the added imput of waste heat. In any event, the specifics of the structure being heated (size, type, and quantity of insulation, numbers of doors and windows, exposure) will, coupled with geographic location, help determine your requirements.

Here is a conservative projection of my expectations for a heat conservation system based on the known facts of my local weather and heating season, my normal kiln firing cycle and simple data so far gained from experience. In order of logical occurence I expect (already do get) 36 hours total heat needs from warmed kiln room air beginning immediately after firing. Collections from stack and foundation systems placed in rock or water storage (or both) for use beginning immediately after kiln room air cycle ends—at least three days for each kiln firing. This would bring the total expected heating days to about four and a half days per firing. Over the entire eight-month heating season in Michigan, I fire an average of six glaze and perhaps five bisque kilns, giving a total expectation of 4.5 days x 11 or 50 days "free" heat. The severe winter days would be the greatest drain on this estimate, while milder spring and fall days would lengthen the period of function of the system. Loss in transmission and storage can only be estimated until actual experience is accumulated. These estimates do not allow for the possible additional use of solar input for the sake of a basic understanding of waste heat use.

Other Sources of Heat

Briefly recall the two types of stack heat exchangers and now project a duct system that could feed from them directly into the rock crib. Perhaps the "Fuel Saver" which operates at a high stack temperature would be the best choice since it can safely operate while the kiln is still firing even before the foundation is hot enough to yield heat.

Summer Considerations

In summer, the storage crib would naturally not need to function as a heat storage location. The supplementary reflector shields (Fig. 8A) used in connection with solar collection would be closed, effectively blocking the collector panels from the sun's rays. The waste heat pickup system would not come into use because no rooms would need heating. However, the storage capacity of the rock crib could be employed to store "cold." The blower system could be designed to draw in relatively cool night air into the crib which would lower the temperature of the rocks as much as 20° to 30°F over the daytime high temperatures. During the day, room air would be drawn into the crib for cooling and returned to the areas needing "air conditioning."

Glass Furnace Considerations

If waste heat production were the only factor used in deciding whether to be a potter or a glassblower, I would have to choose glass as a profession. I cannot think of a better, daily

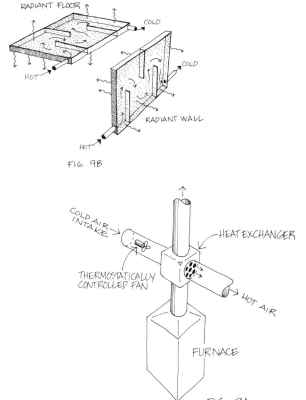

FIG. 9B

FIG. 9A

COLD AIR INTAKE

HEAT EXCHANGER

THERMOSTATICALLY CONTROLLED FAN

HOT AIR

FURNACE

RADIANT FLOOR

COLD

COLD

HOT

RADIANT WALL

HOT

source of heat for storage and use than the 24 hour cycle most glass studios employ. The glassworker who cannot heat all his work and living space "free" is missing a big bonus.

Most glass furnaces I have seen use a vent hood that collects expelled, updraft waste combustion products (and heat) and directs it up to the outside. Because room air is pulled into this system the temperature in the duct above the furnace is not in the heat ranges we see in stoneware kiln flues. Since the area immediately around the furnace usually needs no additional heat, even in winter, we should employ methods to serve those places where heat is needed.

Updraft Principle

Why not take proper advantage, first of all, of the natural updraft caused by rising hot air? Suppose we are in the planning stages for a new glass studio and can control the orientation of living quarters to work space. I would make sure the living quarters were on a second level, if possible. Then I would design a double-walled heat pickup manifold (Fig. 9), to occur at a convenient point around the exhaust vent duct. Allow for a feed duct coming from a distant pickup point where no combustion products are present but where the air is still warmer than outside air. This is the makeup or feed source for the updraft flow, which will move naturally to any space higher than the point of beginning (the hot ex-

haust duct pickup manifold). Where required, a simple blower could draw from the main hot supply duct to service areas not logically reached by the updraft flow.

Heat Extractor

Where undraft flow is not sufficient for the needs we could employ a device similar to the "Torrid-Air" unit (Fig. 3) or possibly a Sturgis Exchanger. Or, since glass furnace ducts are not round or small enough to make use of such a unit, why not salvage and modify a gas furnace (or other) heat exchange unit (Fig. 9A)? Essentially these are hollow tube structures designed to pass hot gasses through while an air flow extracts the radiated heat and feeds a heat circulation duct. If no exchanger is available or suitable then a fabrication of stainless, thin-wall tubes of 2 to 3″ diameter should handle the job, coupled with a blower capable of the proper air displacement for your needs. The fan motor would be thermostatically controlled from remote locations in other buildings or adjacent rooms and the total effect would approximate the same function as any forced-air furnace. This notion is hardly new to industry where every effort is usually made to save and use any exhausted heat.

Storage

There may well be circumstances of building location and weather that would make storage of waste heat equally sensible for the glass studio situation. The rock crib idea could easily function for storage if fed through a duct directly from the heat exchange unit.

Another idea that seems potentially valuable is to build a hollow, internal "wall" (Fig. 9B), within a living or work space that would act as a radiant wall. A feed duct would supply this rock-filled cavity and internal baffles would move the air flow through all areas of the wall until exiting at a baseboard location. Thermostatic control would govern the quantity of heat placed in the wall so that it would not become too hot but would supply only a gentle radiated heat from its entire surface. Such a wall would require more than casual engineering to handle both the heat and the weight of the rock within.

The same general principle could apply to a floor storage system (Fig. 8A) where a cavity filled with rock absorbed the input and released the heat as a gentle, radiated updraft.

Certainly hot water systems could be easily devised with a heat coil pickup in the exhaust duct system. This water could serve both domestic (washing) and storage and radiator needs as well.

Conclusion

I strongly believe we must immediately break away from our complacent attitudes and begin to experiment with waste heat utilization techniques. If these generalized ideas are in any way useful or lead to more specific, functioning systems, then the intention of these comments will have been more than fulfilled. In the meantime, for those who are deeply concerned about alternative energy systems and conservation of existing energy supplies, I urge you to acquire and read the books listed below as a start (if you haven't already done so). There is so much we can do as individuals if we are willing to try and then, in the spirit of exchange, to share our experiences. Much has been done with solar heat; much more is to come. Much is in progress with wind power and methane production. And then there is the exciting subject of heat exchange devices that actually use hot air or water for cooling purposes.

References

Keyes, John. *Harnessing the Sun.* Colorado Book Store, 1111 Broadway, Boulder, CO 80302. $1.25 plus 50¢ handling.

International Solarthermics Corporation, P.O. Box 397, Nederland, CO 80466. Send for descriptive brochure.

Other books and pamphlets of interest:

Producing Your Own Power, Rodale Press, Book Division, Emmaus, PA 18049. (Organic Gardening people)

Handbook of Homemade Power, through Mother Earth News, P.O. Box 70, Hendersonville, NC 28739.

Electric Power from the Wind, by Henry Clews. Solar Wind, P.O. Box 7, East Holden, ME 04429.

Energy Primer, Portola Institute, 558 Santa Cruz Avenue, Menlo Park, CA 94025.

Additional Notes:

"Fuel Saver" heat exchanger: Corsiglia Heating, Greenfield, MA 01301.

"Torrid-Air Heat Saver": Torrid Mfg. Co., Inc., 1248 Poplar Place S., Seattle, WA 98144; and dealers elsewhere.

Sturgis Heat Recovery, Inc., P.O. Box 397, Stone Ridge, NY 12484.

BUILDING WITH ADOBE BRICKS

by Richard Masterson

Adobe is a sun-dried building block made of clay and sand. It is also a term used to describe the clay/sand mortar used to lay up the block, and the word adobe also refers to any structure built of this material.

Adobe is the traditional building material for the part of the country where I live. There are New Mexico buildings in use that are over 200 years old, and there are remains of Indian adobes much older. Before the recent concern for energy conservation, adobe was often used mainly for aesthetic considerations and, at least for the building industry, was considered an expensive material compared to frame-stucco or concrete block. For the person building his own structure, however, with a low budget and/or a concern for economy in a larger sense, adobe has many advantages. While it requires large amounts of labor, it doesn't require highly skilled labor. It is a low-energy material which doesn't use the irreplaceable resources that are required for the production and transportation of cement blocks, fired brick, fiberglass, or lumber. As oil prices increase, adobe may become much more economical even for the commercial builder.

In relation to solar energy, adobe blocks are sun baked as opposed to fired brick, chemically hardened building blocks, or milled lumber, all of which require large amounts of conventionally produced energy. If produced on the building site, adobe also saves the oil used in transporting the other material to mill or factory, from there to retailer, and then to the site. If used in solar-heated buildings, adobe can become a heat sponge and aid in heat storage.

There are certain climate limitations—it is much easier to produce adobe blocks and construct an adobe building during hot, dry weather. Adobe, unless stabilized, must be protected from running water. With properly designed roofs and foundations, however, adobe can be used outside the usual desert climate.

Stabilized adobe is the same material, made by the same process, with the addition of asphalt emulsion or other ingredients to increase water resistance. While there are some practical applications for stabilized adobe, it hooks the process into the oil industry again, and most of the advantages of stabilized adobe can be achieved with regular adobe by careful planning and design.

For the potter, adobe is a natural, basically clay process with very plastic possibilities. It can be used for studios, housing, wind breaks, low-temperature kilns, and outer layers of stoneware kilns. The labor factor is not necessarily a drawback for those potters whose lifestyles are evolving toward more independence and who are used to putting in long hours at their work.

Making Adobes

To make adobes, build a frame out of 2x4 milled lumber,

with openings 10 by 14″ inside and 3½″ deep; a multiple frame with four or five compartments is best. Nail the frame together (square on the corners) with 16-penny coated nails. The frames can be oiled with linseed oil or motor oil, or simply wet down with water before each filling. Next, run some tests with the soil near the building site. Mix in a

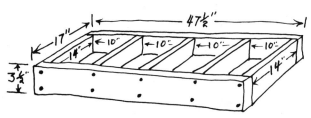

adobe frame

trough, pit, wheelbarrow, or cement mixer until wet enough, but not too soupy, to dump into the forms and screed off evenly with a minimum of effort. Finished adobe blocks should be tough enough to pick up without crumbling or breaking. There should be no deep cracks in a good adobe.

For your tests, try the easiest possibility first—unscreened dirt from the immediate area, throwing out only the rocks that are too large to fit the frames. Next, try the same dirt screened (dry) through ½″ mesh. Third, try screened ½″ mesh dirt with a small amount of straw (a handful per wheelbarrowful) mixed in. Mark your tests and keep them out of the rain to dry. Drying cracks are the most common problem, and in very hot, dry weather, this is sometimes solved by shading the fresh blocks during the first day or two, but uncovering them from evening to early morning. The next possible solution to cracked or crumbly adobe blocks is to add sand. So run a new series, unscreened, screened, screened with straw, and try sand proportions from 1 to 10 up to 1 to 1 if your soil has a high clay content. The next possible problem at this stage is that there may be too little clay in your soil, in which case the blocks usually will dry well but will crumble when picked up. In this case, run a series as with the sand, but substitute local clay. Scratch the proportions and other information in the wet adobe blocks for future reference. In all of the above tests and in later production, pull the frames off the blocks as soon as the blocks will come out without slumping (two to four hours in this climate). Leave the blocks flat for one or two days, then gently turn them on edge to sun dry and harden for one or two days before stacking to cure.

The object of these tests should be to utilize, as much as possible, the local soil with a minimum amount of steps. The best possibility is to be able to use the material from the building site. Determine the total volume of the walls to be made out of adobe and excavate an equal amount of soil, adjusting for the addition of any material not taken from the site (clay or sand). If additions of sand or clay are needed, these should be established before any excavations are

started, and the building placement can be adjusted to save labor. In some cases where the sand and clay balance is off, a test hole can be dug and the needed material found at a different level on the site.

To begin production, figure approximately 150 frame openings per person on the crew, and plan on filling twice a day (or 200 to 300 adobes per person per day). One person should have about 38 frames, with four 10 by 14″ openings each. Try to schedule during a dry season, and allow enough flat area for drying, where runoff from any rain will not flood the production site. Lay the frames out in rows on level ground with no vegetation. Frames should be tight against each other to allow screeding from frame to frame. Aisles should be left between rows of frames for access. Usually by the time all the frames are filled, the first frames can be pulled, laid out, and refilled.

At this stage, rain on the blocks in the frames does no harm except to slow down the drying. Fresh adobes out of the frames, however, are particularly vulnerable to water. Plywood, sheet metal, plastic, or tarps should be available before starting, since at any one time there may be three days work spread out on the ground. A good plan is to figure out the roofing materials for the building (such as corrugated metal) and have this on hand before starting production. This will have to be purchased anyway, and two functions are served by getting it early. Also, unlike sheet plastic or polyethylene, which will wear out after a few rounds of covering and uncovering, the metal roofing is undamaged. It can be used to cover the stack of curing adobes and then to roof the building.

The "green" adobes must be cured about four weeks, depending on the humidity, in order to completely dry and harden. They should be stacked on edge, up on pallets or boards, in single rows, 14″ side vertical, with walking space between rows, and about 5′ high. Plan these stacks close to the proposed building, but not in the way of footings or access for pouring these, since moving the adobe blocks is the second largest labor factor after mixing (3x10x14″ adobes, cured, will weigh anywhere from 25 to 40 pounds each).

Adobes can be produced by soaking a large pit containing the correct proportions of clay and sand, and then using bare feet to work up the mix. Wheelbarrows and hoes and shovels are a large improvement, since the mixing can be done in a comfortable position and then wheeled directly to the frames. A cement mixer is a real labor saver and, in this process, probably the place to use some purchased energy.

Building Adobe Houses

Foundations for the walls of a building can be of reinforced concrete, cinder blocks, or local stone—the idea being to support the weight and keep the adobes up from any moisture. A great many old New Mexico buildings are on top of very simple rock foundations put together with mud. New adobe buildings usually have reinforced concrete footings and block foundations approximately 8″ above grade. The best mortar for laying adobe is the same mixture that is used for the blocks. This mortar, spread about 1″ thick, may be applied with a shovel, large masonry trowel, or bare hands, working directly from a wheelbarrow until the walls get high enough for scaffolding. Then mud boards are placed so that the mortar can be shoveled up onto them. As with any other brick or masonry construction, courses of blocks should be bonded, meaning that the joints between the blocks should not line up with the joints in the course below. Depending on the drying conditions, about four courses can be laid up per day, and, if the walls get too rubbery during construction some temporary support may be necessary.

Lintels over doors and windows may be wood or reinforced concrete cast in place, always allowing for the considerable weight of the material.

For roofed structures, some sort of bond beam is needed. Again, reinforced concrete is good, with bolts cast in to hold on the framing; or a double 2x10 lumber plate spiked into the adobe wall with 12'' rebar spikes will work. Overhanging roofs are a good combination with adobe, making it unnecessary to protect the walls with stucco and also shading southern windows or solar collectors in summer months. If a finish coat is wanted, the same mortar may be used, screened through ¼'' mesh and usually with sand added, troweled on and later floated down with rubber floats. Various local clays can also be used in this manner for color.

Cement and lime plasters are commonly used to coat adobe walls, but the objection to this combination is that when water does get behind this layer it can do much more unobserved damage, washing out the walls under the plaster skin. It is not always necessary to protect unroofed walls, depending on the climate; and, in many cases, if the top course is not disturbed after a rain, it hardens again without damage. Protective caps on exposed walls can be of poured concrete, brick, tile, or fired adobe, allowing an inch or two overhang so that running water does not go down the adobe wall.

Adobe Kilns

Adobe kiln construction is certainly not a new idea; primitive kilns still being used are made of this material. There is probably no firm dividing line between primitive adobe kilns and high-temperature insulation brick kilns, but rather a refinement in brickmaking technology and kiln design. There are stoneware potters today making kiln bricks in wooden frames essentially in the same manner as adobes but with fireclay and grog. At the moment, it would be hard to rationalize this in terms of economics or function. It is possible, however, to utilize adobe as described here for kilns. Probably the easiest way to find out if the locally produced adobe will function as a low-temperature kiln material is to build a small kiln and fire it. In most cases, the adobe will work fine within earthenware temperatures but will tend to turn to glass very quickly as it gets into stoneware range.

Stoneware kilns can utilize adobe as an exterior wall, support for protective roofs, and windbreak walls. In the actual kiln wall, two separate walls are laid up—the inside of 4½'' of firebrick and the outside of 10'' of adobe, with 1½'' between. This space between the two walls should be filled with vermiculite. Firebrick should be taken around door openings, burner ports and flue openings. The two walls

should be bonded together approximately every 12'' in height, with a rowlock of firebrick extending over into the adobe wall. In a large kiln, this system can save a lot of firebrick and, with the vermiculite insulation layer, result in better insulation than 9'' of refractory brick. (When a stoneware kiln constructed in this manner was torn down

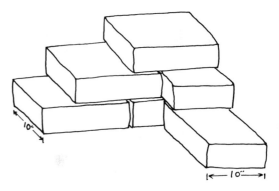

this year, the inside of the adobe showed some sign of heat, turning from the usual tan to slightly orange, but this fired color was only on the surface.) The disadvantage of this system is in the time and labor required to lay up two different materials and bond them carefully together.

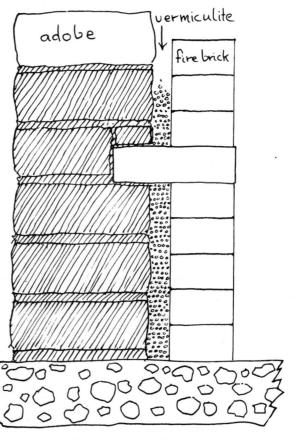

Adobe brick high temperature kiln.

Tools for making and laying adobe. Left to right: mixer, inclined screen, wheelbarrow, masonry tools, hoe, shovels.

In New Mexico, and most of the Southwest, adobe construction is ideal in many respects. It is ecologically sound and economical, can usually be produced from materials found on site, is strong and versatile, and is a good insulator. Whether used for a room, a building, a kiln, or part of a kiln, the process and the material can be adjusted to suit climates which are not so dry as much of the Southwest. It is the ideal material for use in combination with solar heated structures.

Masterson's Solar Heated Pottery Studio in Northern New Mexico

The collector panels and front wall are framed up of 2x6 lumber. The panels are glazed outside with one sheet of double-strength glass. Inside the panels are four layers of black metal lath (the expanded metal used in plastering), spaced ¾'' apart; this is backed up with corrugated metal roofing painted inside with black roofing mastic. There is a 6'' space top and bottom in the corrugated metal for circulation. The 2x4 grate is spaced with 2x4 blocks to allow the warm air into the rock storage. The rocks vary in size from 4 to 10''. The floor grates are left open in the back or north end of the room and usually are closed in front to force the warm air through the rock storage.

A lot of heat is taken in directly through the studio windows during the day, and closing the sliding doors at night in the winter is necessary to keep down heat loss through those windows.

The rock storage maintains an average around 68°F and the studio has never gone below 50°F even when left closed up during freezing weather.

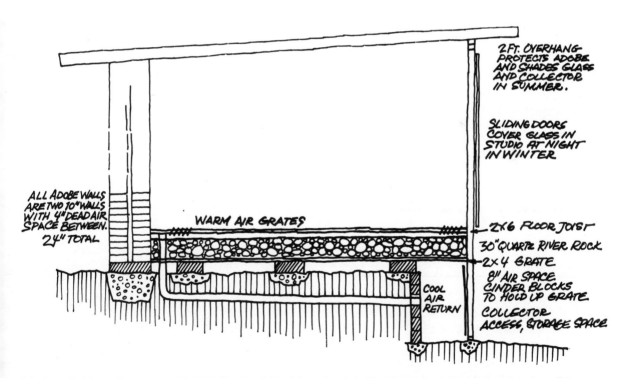

Solar heated adobe studio constructed in 1972. Two foot thick adobe walls, cinder block foundation and two-foot roof overhang. Solar collector below, shaded in summer by catwalk, which is access to barn doors which are closed during winter nights.

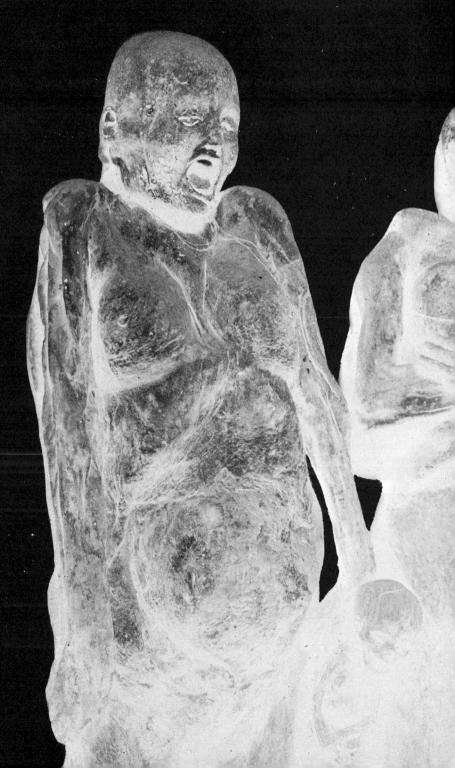

CERAMIC TOXICOLOGY

by William C. Alexander

Considering the number and variety of ceramic materials available to the contemporary potter it seems inevitable that some of them would be toxic. A surprisingly large number are, but more alarming and perhaps more dangerous to the studio potter are the many materials which cause pulmonary disorders when inhaled. These are seemingly inert and benign materials and cause no immediate effects. Symptoms are slow to develop and as a rule there is no dramatic or noticeable change from week to week or month to month. Hence, the person affected may not discover the illness until it has caused permanent damage which may result in permanent disability. Materials in this category will be considered in the first section of this chapter.

A number of materials are actually poisonous if taken into the system and will be reported in the second section.

Inhalants

Many of the materials used in ceramics are not poisonous in that they may be taken internally with no detrimental effect. Kaolin for example is used medicinally in such products as Kaopectate and in some kinds of pills where it serves as a binder. The danger in these materials lies in the damage they may do to the lungs if inhaled. As a rule, one exposure is not particularly dangerous but repeated exposure over a period of time compounds the buildup and very serious effects may result. Silicosis has long been recognized as one of the occupational diseases associated with pottery and other dust-producing industries and most potters are probably aware of its dangers to some degree. It is contracted after inhaling finely ground silica dust. Usually an exposure of 10 to 20 years is needed to produce really severe symptoms, but disability has been reported after only six months' exposure. Factors regulating the length of exposure necessary to produce symptoms are the concentration of silica dust in the air and the size of the silica particle. The higher the concentration and the smaller the particle size, the shorter the period needed to produce the disease.

Silicosis is rarely fatal in and of itself, but those suffering from it are more susceptible to other pulmonary diseases and are less likely to survive potentially fatal diseases such as pneumonia due to their already weakened condition. The pathological evidences of silicosis are nodulation and fibrosis of the lungs. The external symptoms are shortness of breath, chronic cough, pain in the chest, and, especially, decreased vital capacity or in lay terms, decreased ability to perform work requiring physical exertion.

Unfortunately, the damage to the lungs is permanent and so the disability is also permanent. Medical science can offer a certain amount of relief by treating the symptoms, but no treatment for the disease itself has ever been proved effective. As a rule when silicosis is diagnosed, the patient is urged to remove himself from further possible contact immediately. Past middle age, when silicosis is most frequently diagnosed, it is very difficult to change jobs, particularly when a complete change is the only answer. The mental distress brought on by a forced career change in later life may be worse than continued exposure at a reduced rate.

Almost any of the nonsoluble materials in a potshop will produce symptoms similar to silicosis in varying degrees of severity. Some even produce diseases common enough to have names.

Alumina produces a disease known as aluminosis. To the layman it is practically indistinguishable from silicosis, with shortness of breath, cough and decreased vital capacity being the chief symptoms. Like silicosis, there is no cure, but some remission of symptoms can sometimes be effected by complete avoidance of further exposure.

In recent years, studies of the medical histories of asbestos workers have revealed alarming results and have shown how extremely dangerous this material is. As mentioned earlier, silicosis is rarely fatal, but asbestosis is one of the commonest causes of death among workers who deal with asbestos fiber regularly. In addition to its debilitating effect on the lungs, it can cause skin irritations and "asbestos warts" and it has now definitely been established that asbestosis can lead directly to lung and other forms of cancer.

Diatomaceous earth is composed primarily of silica and sufficient exposure leads to silicosis.

Feldspar of any sort leads to a condition known as pneumoconiosis. It is not critical in itself, but weakens the body in resisting other more dangerous diseases.

Fiberglass produces effects very similar to asbestos fiber.

Gum Arabic has been associated with asthma and may produce asthmatic conditions where none were present before contact. In addition it may cause eye inflammation called conjunctivitis. Anyone already suffering a pulmonary disease should avoid contact.

Iron oxide produces a disease called siderosis which refers to the mineral siderite or iron carbonate. It is less serious than silicosis and may have no permanent effects.

Kaolin and china clay cause kaolinosis if inhaled. The highest acceptable concentration is 50 million particles/cubic foot of air. This seems high but is really quite low considering the submicroscopic size of the clay particle. The symptoms are the same as silicosis except that it may also lead directly to emphysema and tuberculosis. The disease comes in stages beginning with minor nodulations of the lungs and progressing to severe fibrosis. The disability may be permanent.

Mica, including muscovite, vermiculite, and lepidolite, leads to lung irritation but is less dangerous than silica.

Ochre causes pneumoconiosis.

Talc inhalation leads to a disease common enough to have been named talcosis. It is evidenced by granulation and fibrosis of the lungs and symptoms similar to silicosis. It may lead directly to emphysema.

Most of the materials listed above have been in common usage in the ceramic and other industries for years. It stands to reason that diseases and disorders directly traceable to them would have been discovered and documented by now. But what of the many newer materials which are not listed? Is inhaled nepheline syenite any less dangerous than feldspar, or ball clay less debilitating than kaolin? One can only doubt those conclusions. Surely any particular substance in sufficient concentration would have some effect on the lungs, perhaps even to the extent of causing diseases and disabilities such as those listed above.

It is important to note that there is no known positive cure for any of these pulmonary diseases. The treatment most usually suggested is "symptomatic and supportive," meaning that the best that can be done is to offer some relief from the miseries of the symptoms and support the rest of the system to produce as good a state of health as is possible. More research has been carried out on silicosis than the other named diseases due to its prevalence particularly in the mining industry, and some effort has been made to treat the actual disease rather than simply relieve the symptoms. Positive pressure breathing designed to increase lung capacity and various decongestants have been tried but the results so far have been inconclusive.

In every case, the preventive measures for these diseases list dust control measures as being of paramount importance. "Adequate ventilation" usually heads the list; filter respirators are often suggested; and under severe conditions, "wet methods" (meaning that all materials are kept damp at all times) may be called for. At the very least adequate vent fans should be installed in any area using these materials. Almost equally important is some provision for cleaning floors and work areas *by a method other than a dry broom.* Regular hosing is the ideal, but is frequently impossible. In areas which cannot be hosed periodically, a sweeping compound such as oiled sawdust designed to entrap dust particles before they are stirred up into the atmosphere is a viable alternative if frequently and generously used.

Toxic Materials

Many ceramic materials are dangerous not only for the physical damage they may do in the lungs and respiratory tract, but also for purely toxic effects caused by absorption into the system by whatever means. Some, such as lead and arsenic oxides, have long been recognized as dangerous to life, but a surprising number of seemingly benign materials are toxic, some dangerously so.

Lead poisoning has long been regarded as the classic potter's disease. By the late 1700s movements were underway in Europe which would bring regulations on the usage of lead glazes. Today nearly every country in the Western world has stringent rules regulating lead glazes in industry. The artist-potter remains one of the few as yet unaffected by such regulations—a freedom which also makes him susceptible to the very dangers they were designed to prevent.

Unfortunately, nearly all lead compounds, with the exception of certain frits, are poisonous. White lead, the usually preferred material for raw lead glazes, is no less toxic than litharge or red lead.

Lead is classed as an accumulative poison and may be stored for years in the bone structure. Fortunately, only about one-half of all lead taken into the body is absorbed and much of that is later excreted. Even so, over a period of time, the fatal dose of absorbed lead has been determined to be as low as ½ gram.

Inhaled lead is relatively more dangerous than ingested lead and the symptoms appear more rapidly. Acute poisoning from inhalation has been known to cause death after only two days of exposure. Symptoms are characteristic of many other forms of poisoning: abdominal pain, vomiting, black stools and diarrhea, retention of urine, collapse, and, in terminal cases, coma.

The aspect of death aside, chronic poisoning is worse in its effects than acute forms. There is a variety of symptoms including lassitude, loss of appetite, weakness, headache, constipation, stomach pain, and so on. All of this, unpleasant though it may be, is nothing compared to the fact that brain damage may also be occurring. About 25% of all those who incur brain damage as a result of lead poisoning die as a result of it. Most of those who survive show permanent mental deterioration. Even less severe cases require one or more years for complete recovery.

Lead, however, is a known threat, and hence, perhaps less dangerous than some of the other materials used but not recognized as toxic.

Arsenic trioxide is the commonest form of arsenic used in ceramics and is certainly one of the most dangerous materials ever found in a pot shop. Most literature on the subject of arsenic poisoning refers to criminal or suicidal usage or accidental poisoning from commercial rodent poisons. Arsenic is occasionally used medicinally as in the treatment of amoebic dysentery. Under carefully controlled conditions a certain immunity can be established. Personal tolerance to arsenic varies radically, but as little as 0.12 grams has been known to be fatal.

Symptoms of acute poisoning from inhaled arsenic begin with headaches and chest pains, particularly around the heart. After that, symptoms, regardless of manner of intake, are much the same. When taken internally there is usually a three to four hour delay before any symptoms are noticed. After that period vomiting, severe diarrhea, and nausea begin, leading to eventual collapse, coma, and often death. If the arsenic is inhaled, these are accompanied by a severe foamy cough.

Chronic poisoning produces serious and lasting effects including anemia, cirrhosis of the liver, and kidney damage. Patients who survive as long as one week usually recover, after a period of six or more months.

Antimony trioxide produces symptoms and results similar to arsenic in most ways. Although fatalities are rare, 1½ to 3 grams may be fatal. As with arsenic, recovery is slow.

Acute poisoning has lasting effects due to hemorrhages in liver and kidney tissue. Survival for more than 48 hours usually indicates that recovery is possible.

Barium carbonate is the usual source of Ba in ceramic usage. It, along with barium chloride and barium hydroxide, is partially soluble and may be a deadly poison. If completely absorbed into the system, as little as one gram can be fatal. The first symptoms are tremors followed by convulsions, and in terminal cases death is due to cardiac and/or respiratory failures.

Inhaled barium compounds are also dangerous, but are not usually absorbed into the system and, hence, not fatal. They produce "Baritosis," a form of pneumoconiosis associated with barite.

Beryllium compounds can be taken into the body by ingestion, inhalation, or through cuts. Cuts coming in contact with beryllium compounds may become ulcerated and require months to heal. Beryllium oxide is a strong sensitizer and the dust may cause dermatitis similar to first and second degree burns.

About one-quarter of all beryllium taken into the system is deposited in the bones and becomes permanent.

Inhaled dust is by far the most dangerous. It causes a granulation of the lungs and symptoms similar to silicosis. A single massive dose could cause death almost immediately, or the reaction may be delayed for weeks. Small amounts taken in over a period of time can produce Be pneumonia or allergic sensitivities. Again, the reaction may be delayed for up to 15 years.

Boric acid, Borax, and Sodium perborate are all poisons according to Moeschlin. Fatal doses taken internally vary from 2 grams for infants to 20 grams for adults, but individual tolerances vary widely. A fatal dose could be absorbed through a cut or skin abrasion. An acute dose leads to vomiting, diarrhea, and sometimes collapse and hemorrhaging.

Chronic poisoning can cause a variety of symptoms, including anemia, delusions, diarrhea, and skin disorders similar to psoriasis.

Cadmium oxide can be taken into the system by either inhalation or ingestion. The latter may produce symptoms in as short a time as 30 minutes. A massive dose could cause death, although this is very rare. The most usual form of absorption is through inhalation, which causes pulmonary lesions leading to emphysema. Damage to the liver, the kidneys, and bone marrow are also proven byproducts of cadmium poisoning.

Carbon monoxide is a colorless, odorless, toxic gas that is a byproduct of incomplete combustion of all sorts. In the process of firing ceramic kilns under reducing conditions, a certain amount of CO is inevitable. Most of this exits through the stack and is dispersed into the atmosphere in nontoxic concentrations. Kilns situated in small or unventilated rooms and fired with considerable back pressure may exhaust CO in sufficient amounts to cause potentially dangerous situations. Concentrations as low as 50 parts per million can cause marked drowsiness and impaired vision. As the concentration increases, the symptoms become more severe and 1,000 parts per million is considered lethal.

CO is heavier than air and the concentration at floor level may be markedly higher than at ceiling level. The danger lies in carbon monoxide's affinity for the hemoglobin in the blood, which is reported as 300 times as great as that of oxygen. All symptoms including possible death are a result of oxygen starvation.

Simple precautions in proper ventilation will prevent accidental asphyxiation due to CO.

Chlorine gas is one of the waste gases produced in a salt-glaze kiln. Its dangers have long been known. Chlorine poisoning is rare in any case and the likelihood of a damaging dose while firing a salt kiln is very remote. Even so, care should be exercised, since personal tolerances vary and as little as one part per million in air can have an effect. A heavy dose causes the formation of H Cl in the lungs, accompanied by acid corrosion of lung tissue.

In no case should a salt kiln be built and operated in a small, tightly closed room. Even large structures should be equipped with suitable vent fans.

Chromium compounds, including potassium bichromate and chromic acid, are known to be poisonous. Inhaled chromium compounds lead to acute pneumonia and are definitely associated with some forms of lung cancer. The most usual form of absorption is ingestion and a fatal dose has been variously reported at from one-half to five grams. In a case of acute poisoning the patient suffers severe stomach pains, bloody diarrhea, vomiting, kidney damage leading to retention of urine, and usually dies in a state of complete collapse. Those who survive this stage usually die within 10 days as a result of uremia. Even contact can be dangerous, since chromium is irritating and destructive to all cells in the body.

Cobalt is an important trace mineral in the human system, but overdoses can cause an imbalance leading to irritations and allergies.

Copper is rarely involved in poisoning and only copper sulfate and verdigris are considered dangerous. Copper sulfate can cause death in a matter of hours in surprisingly small doses. Copper carbonate has yet to be fully researched, but it is sometimes used in insecticides and should be avoided. Neither cuperous nor cupric oxide is thought to be harmful according to current knowledge.

Ferric chloride is not fatal, but can cause gastric upset. It can also cause a permanent discoloration to abraded skin.

Ferrous sulfate on the other hand can be fatal and should be avoided.

Iron chromate inhaled may lead to acute pneumonia and has been definitely associated with some forms of lung cancer.

Lanthanum is little used in ceramics; it is quite rare in other industries, also, and consequently little is known about it. It has been associated with headaches and nausea and should be used with care.

Lithium carbonate is partially soluble and when ingested may cause severe lesions in the bone marrow and symptoms similar to pernicious anemia and leukemia. It is usually not fatal.

Manganese dioxide is more dangerous than is commonly thought. It can be absorbed through either inhalation or ingestion. It is an irritant and may cause an overgrowth of the connective tissues in the brain and degeneration of certain of the motor functions of the central nervous system. Inhaled MnO_2 gives rise to a variety of difficulties including stammering speech, muscular discoordination, paralysis, and spastic gait. All may be permanent. Three months to two years exposure is sufficient to cause any or all of these.

Complete cures are rare, due to the brain damage involved, but the progress of the disease may be successfully halted.

Molybdenum compounds are toxic only in massive doses. Repeated small doses are apparently harmless, since these materials are readily excreted from the body.

Rare Earths, due to their scarcity, have not received much research but it is known that *Cerium, Yttrium, Lanthanum, Praeseodymium,* and *Neodymium* all have some toxic effects.

Selenium compounds are for the most part poisonous, but selenium dioxide is one of the most dangerous. Even simple contact with the skin can cause serious burns. Acute poisoning is similar in its symptoms to arsenic.

Thallium compounds are all poisonous. As little as one gram of ingested thallium may be fatal. Thallium compounds are used as rat poisons and depilatories. They are rare in studio ceramics, and, considering the dangers involved, are best left alone.

Vanadium pentoxide is absorbed by inhalation. The human body shows very low tolerance and as little as one microgram per gram of tissue causes serious disturbances. It has been connected to emphysema and severe irritations of the nasal and bronchial passages, leading to a chronic cough.

Zinc oxide has been reported as being toxic, but the reports are in older treatises and the effects cited are more likely to have been from contaminations from lead or mercury. Even so, ingested zinc oxide may cause temporary illness.

This treatise does not presume to be all-inclusive. I have gleaned the information from the references which follow.

My concern is that some of the materials used in contemporary ceramics are not used in other industries and may not have been completely investigated. All of this points to the fact that all materials should be treated with respect. Every effort should be made to avoid ingesting ceramic materials, particularly those used in glazes. Smoking or eating in glaze laboratories should be discouraged and great care should be taken to clean hands and clothes before meals.

Perhaps even more important are complete dust-control measures. Potteries are inherently dusty and it has been demonstrated that the dust from a wide variety of materials can cause permanent pulmonary disorders.

Considering the fact that a cure, i.e., complete remission of symptoms, is often impossible, adequate preventive measures are most emphatically indicated.

References

Moeschlin, Sven, M.D. *POISONING, Diagnosis and Treatment.* New York, London: Grune and Stratton, 1965.

Fairhall, Lawrence T. *Industrial Toxicology.* New York: Hafner Publishing Company, 1969 Revised.

Dreisbach, Robert H., M.D., Ph. D. *Handbook of Poisoning.* Los Altos, CA: Lange Medical Publishing Company, 1969.

Plunkett, E.R., M.D. *Handbook of Industrial Toxicology.* New York: Chemical Publishing Company, 1966.

This paper was originally presented to and published by the National Council on Education for the Ceramic Arts at its annual meeting in the spring of 1973 and is reprinted here with the permission of the Council.

TOWARD A NEW AESTHETIC:
THE ROLE OF THE CRAFT HISTORIAN
by Gerry Williams

It has been only 25 years since Bernard Leach came to America and candidly remarked that except for the Indians, there were no real potters in America.

Coming as this did from an eminent British craftsman, it was a grievous blow to our ego. And he may have been right. There weren't very many of us, except for a traditional enclave or two, and crafts were pretty simpleminded.

But it seems unlikely the charge could now be made to stick. Crafts in America have changed. They ain't what they used to be. A whole new generation of craftsmen has grown up and gone to work. Now there's hardly a town in the country that doesn't have one. Indeed, we view with astonishment, if not awe, the size, grace, energy, and versatility of the craft movement.

We are in the midst of a feast.

It's strange to think of crafts as being anything but a part (minor) of Art History. But a host of factors has contributed to a new maturity that tells us otherwise. The craft movement is now a major phenomenon which needs to be examined on its own merits.

It is quite apparent that unique cultural, artistic, and social events have had a bearing on this development. We must, however, put it all into perspective if we are to understand who we are as craftsmen and to relate that knowledge more effectively to our work.

The vast dislocation of the Second World War, for example, began to make profound changes in American crafts. Timid and safe, they were soon under vigorous influence from new aesthetics imported by G.I.s returning from Europe and Japan. These aesthetics were soon incorporated into our educational experience. The most singular result was the rise of the American university as the center for craft learning. Alma Matrix: Alfred, Ohio State, Cranbrook, Berkeley. Super teachers were superstars, and daily dealt us delicious blows with their abstract expressionism, pop, funk, social commentary, and porn. Universities have become the ultimate breeding ground for the craft hipoisie.

Concurrently came the craft organizations. Essentially nonacademic, they aided by forming markets for craftsmen and in publicizing crafts. The Boston Society of Arts and Crafts, the League of New Hampshire Craftsmen, the Southern Highlands Handicraft Guild—a dozen others. The American Crafts Council (a mighty swell bunch!). And lately the National Endowment for the Arts, sprung from Rockefeller loins, dispensing grants and prestige.

Perhaps the most important phenomenon has been the increasing number of professional craftsmen in America. Options now open to the current generation of students on the lam from academia are much greater. Instead of all becoming teachers, many have chosen to make it on their own as craftsmen. They enjoy a high degree of technical sophistication, and are supported by an appreciative public. It is this economic viability at the base of the craft pyramid which is most encouraging of all. Without it crafts would lose touch with reality.

If crafts are manifestations of a social consciousness, then the study of craft history is an important guide to where we are going. While old traditions like Bauhaus and *Mingei* will always be with us, their clarity fades. Principles must be regenerated. Like the Phoenix, the past must arise to live again.

We now need a new aesthetic for the crafts. Such new guidelines can only come from a deep understanding of the relationship of our crafts to all others. This is properly a study of history.

As a first step we urge the establishment of a new discipline called Craft History. Its focus should exist primarily within the academic environment, but can also be independently developed.

The formation of such a discipline will aid in our search for a perspective from which to view the new aesthetic. It will greatly strengthen the growth of American crafts and assure their continuity in the years ahead.

THE FIRE'S PATH

by Garth Clark

It is a potter's truism that nothing must be allowed to obstruct the fire's path. In this spirit Michael Cardew has led an extraordinary life, working to clear those restrictions which both man and nature place in front of the potter.

The route has taken him across four continents: reviving the slipware tradition in England; marrying stoneage tribal pottery with stoneware technology in Africa; teaching his craft to Aborigines in Australia, and crisscrossing America to give lectures and run workshops.

He has also written extensively, producing *Pioneer Pottery,* a classic of ceramic literature, and many articles. And he has made pots. Not as many as he would have liked to have made—but enough to comprise one of our richest contemporary examples of the universal and traditional values of the potter's art.

Cardew at 75 is still a practising potter and the vitality which distinguished his earliest Winchcombe work is still evident in the 30 pots that he has just completed and shipped to his retrospective exhibition at Boymans Van Beuningen Museum in Rotterdam. They are subtly different from the rest of his work, somehow saying more about form and less about function than at any other state of his work. They do prove however that a good potter, like a good wine, matures, rather than declines, with the passing of the years.

One of the reasons why Cardew has managed to maintain this sense of life about his clay is because of what Charles Counts refers to as his "contagious humanity." It intrudes throughout his work, breaking down the mannered formalism that traps so many of the so-called traditionalists.

For instance Cardew does not see himself as a craftsman in the strict sense of the word: "I am simply not careful enough for a craftsman. After Bernard Leach, I must be the world's worst thrower. But you see, carefulness can be a terrible virtue. In fact it is a vice. It destroys recklessness and somehow one feels that there is a bigness in being reckless."

Cardew feels that there is something greater than great craftsmanship and this is "saying something." This can be seen as the element that distinguishes his work from most of his contemporaries', the extent to which Cardew will "go" with his clay. All sensitive potters respond to the nature of the clay under their hands but there is a point where head and hand take over. Cardew delays this intrusion as far as possible, which results in forms that are unconventional in that they say more about the medium than about the "Golden Rule" aesthetics of balance and proportion.

This special affinity for clay is evident whenever Cardew talks or writes about his medium. In a recent issue of *Tactile* he spoke about the significance of one's first contact with clay. Kneading, he contends, places him in the mood to make a pot by introducing him to the character of the clay, thinking of what he will make and how it will fit.

Winchcombe 1935 Earthenware Lidded Jar. H. 7½". Coll. the Artist.

"Otherwise what you are doing is pouring some suitable lubricating liquid on this assemblage of strangers which is the clay and expecting them to work harmoniously together. A lot of modern pottery methods seem like a cocktail party. You collect together a lot of mortal enemies, and you invite them into the same room and expect them to get on. They hardly know one another and the little they do know they do not like. And with the aid of alcoholic drinks (the heat of the kiln) the party goes very well."

In order to retain an intimacy Cardew is wary of perfection, referring to it as an intellectual invention as "nature is absolutely innocent of perfection." It is the Lorelie of the potter's art resulting in pots that are "perfect yet stillborn." There was a period in Cardew's career when this rock seemed to be seductively close to his work, between 1949 and 1950 when the first stoneware came out of Wenford.

As objects these pots are superb, the flawless glaze, immaculate finish, and generous decoration being repeated on both sides of the lid, inside and outside the bowl and even

Winchcombe 1937 Teapot with sliptrailed decoration. H. 10'' -
11''. Coll. K. Pleydell Bouverie.

Wenford Mid-50's Stoneware. H. 7''. One of the earliest forms to
evolve from the traditional Gwari casserole.

under the foot. But it was uncharacteristic and ultimately not as convincing as either the Winchcombe slipware or the African stoneware. It was Cardew being careful.

Another of the potter's traps is technology, for this is where the craftsman's gluttony is most often indulged. It was Aldous Huxley who noted that "only an artist of exceptional austerity can make temperate use of a highly developed technology." Cardew is such an artist. His restraint is not born so much out of a dualistic and conscious aesthetic discipline but it flows naturally from the route he has chosen to follow in his craft.

His best views on this are contained in a lecture he gave in America in 1972:

"So more and more people like to become potters, or at least part-time or amateur potters. Most people at first choose to do it the easy way: you buy the clay ready mixed in plastic packets, you get ready prepared glazes, you buy a prefabricated kiln. Then you have to learn the making part—and goodness knows even then there are plenty of difficulties. But if you remain at that stage, the pots will only be partly yours. Their character will be conditioned by that of the clay, the glaze, and the way they are fired.

"And since all these things—clay, glazes, and kilns—are fabricated and standardised, the pots will be less satisfying than you expected. If they are deprived of half their personality by all their shortcuts, a sensitive potter, feeling there is something missing, will probably try to replace it by what I call 'a deliberately willed injection of personality.' But it's a mistake because the something that is missing is in fact a very mysterious and elusive thing, which cannot be pinned down and captured by direct assault."

Creativity, Cardew believes, must be stalked by an indirect route, i.e., craft. In Cardew's case this has resulted in a rugged workshop philosophy allowing all the impurities and imponderables that returned life to this art. But even that is too glib a description. His route was more simple, a search for truth.

In England at Winchcombe Pottery from 1926 to 1939 he concerned himself less with the science than with the physical problems of bringing a pottery back to life after it had lain derelict for 12 years. He used a traditional technology and his energies went into the physical release of production throwing, filling a 600 cubic foot bottle kiln three times a year.

It was Africa that broadened his horizons. There he brought a stoneware technology and the desire for it to grow and live from its environment. At Vume, in what is today Ghana, he set up his first independent stoneware workshop and for three years (1945 to 1948) sought the indirect route. Bauxite for his clay came from a mine miles away, refractory earth from the bottom of a 60 foot well that he located eight miles from Vume. Fuel was collected and brought back (from territory up the Volta river) in a sailing canoe Cardew had acquired. Glazes were compounded from a local feldspar, clay, and oyster shells! This process of living as a pioneer potter was extended when, as the Nigerian Government's pottery officer, from 1951 he established the Abuja Pottery Training Centre on the Iku River. Vume had been run on a small scale and was more experimental than

Wenford Bridge 1975 Lidded Jar. H. 22''. One of the pieces for the Rotterdam Retrospective.

Abuja 1960 Pair of Hot Water Jugs. H. 7'' - 8''. Coll. M. O'Brien.

Vume Dugome 1947 Teapot in olive celadon breaking to bright
rust. Coll. the Artist.

productive. At Abuja he set out to create a productive pottery that could live efficiently from its own resources. His ingenuity and growing knowledge of geology achieved this. Clay arrived rather noisily and colorfully thanks to 50 to 100 women from nearby villages who gathered the clay in pots and brought it to morning markets where it was purchased.

Other raw materials like limestone required a week-long expedition to Kabba Province by jeep, river ferry, and the final 16 miles on foot. Kaolin was located on the Jos Plateau and brought 250 miles by truck. In some cases Cardew salvaged necessary materials like Albite and potassium feldspar, economically enough, from the spoil heaps of nearby tin mines. Tirelessly Cardew's geological detective work produced clues to sources of supply that were purer or more accessible.

In this way, and by the sheer force of what Cardew calls the "cussedness of the individual," he has managed to avoid those traps into which so many of the traditionalists have fallen. Cardew's view on this is that a potter who knows his tradition will, if he is "alive," be constantly innovating.

"But," he warns, "his innovations will be largely unconscious. So the artist who is an innovator is also the only true traditional artist. The others, the 'practitioners' who call themselves traditionalists, are really the traitors of the tradition. They murder it in order to be able to take the measurements of the corpse."

The difference between the practitioner and the true traditionalist is the difference of being ego-bound and esoteric and, in short, falling in love with yourself. The traditionalist, no matter how well formed his ego may be (and Cardew's is certainly healthy, in fact elemental to his success), cannot allow this indulgence in his craft. Cardew explains that "the form that first excited you and goaded you into trying to recreate it must be something impersonal, outside you and beyond you, altogether other." "If it were not so you would not have fallen in love with it. It is something before which you prostrate yourself and which you worship—by struggling."

Part and parcel of Cardew's belief that flows from this is a different sense of reward to the norm. Collectors sell his pots, particularly his '30s Winchcombe period, in the rarefied air of London's Sotheby's and Christies' sales rooms. A 7/6 (37 cents) plate from Winchcombe recently sold at Christies for $760. Yet about half a mile away at the Craftsmen Potters Association one can still buy his current work for less than £25. In common with many English artist-potters (Lucie Rie, Hans Coper) he is simply not prepared to cash in on his celebrity value.

Cardew acknowledges a just price and a natural price. The just price is the one a potter deserves for his labor, the natural price is that price he can receive in the marketplace. In order to remain the master of his situation the potter must decide on a meeting point between the two. As important, Cardew prefers his pots to have the natural mortality of functional ware and so charges prices that allow the pots to be used (if with a touch of reverence) rather than being frozen in glass cases because of their value.

Cardew does not expound this view because of an ascetic attitude to life. He enjoys creature comforts with the rest of us. It is a matter of retaining one's judgment. If one follows the market price, one begins to follow market influences as well and integrity is slowly but inevitably eroded.

The answer is to be judiciously selfish: "I have always made pots for myself first because the potter does not merely follow what his public wants but leads it, so that in the end they want what he wants. He will often have to wait a long time before he is accepted. He makes life hard for himself at first, but later on his public will come to him because in his workshop the potters' art is alive."

Yet Cardew is always ready to share that life, a generosity that springs from his "contagious humanity," not from a missionary zeal:

"Why have I spent so much of my life teaching pottery to non-Europeans—West Africans and Australian Aborigines? I think the reason is that art—any art, but especially pottery—is in some way universal; its springs and origins are rooted in the prelogical part of our mind. You are dealing directly with material substances, not with abstractions. You don't merely tell yourself verbally that the human race is one race; you know it by a direct perception, because the stuff you are dealing with—not merely the clay itself but what you are doing to it—is universal and belongs by equal right to everyone."

Abuja 1958 Stoneware Storage Jar. H. 13''. Coll. W. A. Ismay.

Cardew Biography

1921-1923 While studying classics at Oxford University learned to throw at Braunton pottery, run by W. Fishley Holland, grandson of Edwin Beer Fishley, one of the last great rural potters.

1923-1926 Accepted as Bernard Leach's first European apprentice at St. Ives, producing mainly slipware. Worked briefly with Shoji Hamada, later joined by Tsuranoske Matsubayashi, and by apprentices K. Pleydell Bouverie and Norah Braden.

1926-1939 Revived a pottery on a farm in Greet, near Winchcombe, which had been producing agricultural hardware for over 100 years until its closure in 1914. Joined by Elijah Comfort, Sydney Tustin, and Ray Finch. Annual output of 12 to 15 thousand functional pots in loosely translated slipware tradition.

1939-1942 Purchased Wenford Inn on Bodmin Moors, Cornwall and established Wenford Bridge Pottery.

1942-1945 A pottery instructor to Achimota College, near Accra, in what is today Ghana, Cardew was in charge of Alajo Pottery. Alajo floundered, largely due to a lack of regularly available raw materials.

1945-1948 Moved 70 miles away to a traditional pottery village, Vume Dugame, on Volta River. Set up a small stoneware pottery with Kofi Attey and Kwami Agbedanu.

1948-1950 Built an additional chamber to the Wenford Bridge kiln with help of Ivor McMeekin and produced stoneware.

1951-1965 Abuja Pottery Training Centre was begun in August 1951, introducing the Nigerian potters to stoneware. The work of this center has become internationally known, particularly the work of Ladi Kwali. Assisted in establishing Jos Pottery with Kofi Attey.

1965-1976 Cardew returned to Wenford Bridge, potting there ever since between his travels and writing:
First United States lecture tour 1965
Published *Pioneer Pottery* 1969
Taught pottery to Aborigine students in Darwin, Australia, 1967
Received MBE 1965
Tour of U.S.A. with Ladi Kwali and Kofi Attey 1972
Touring retrospective exhibition opened in Rotterdam at Boymans Van Beuningen Museum 1976

References

Cardew, Michael. *Pioneer Pottery.* London: St. Martin's Press and Longmans, 1969.

Bouverie, Katherine Pleydell. "Michael Cardew." *Ceramic Review* No. 20, April/March 1973.

Lowell, Christopher. (Len Dutton) "Cardew at 75." *Tactile,* pp. 2-14, 1976.

Cardew, Michael. "A View of African Pottery." *Ceramics Monthly,* February 1974.

Cardew, Michael. *Potters and Amateur Potters.* Monograph published by National Council on Education for the Ceramic Arts (undated).

Ross, Sylvia Leith. *Nigerian Pottery.* Introduction by Michael Cardew.

Clark, Garth. *Michael Cardew: A Potter's Search for Order.* Japan: Kodansha International, 1976.

Films
Pottery in the Gold Coast. 1944.
Pottery in Abuja. Alister Hallum. 1965.
Mud and Water Man. Arts Council of Great Britain. 1974.

LEGENDS OF AHIMSA

by Daniel Rhodes

In the foothills above Lake Pancil, and a few minutes walk from the village of Karuna, was the pottery known as Ahimsa.

The pottery had been there as long as anyone could remember. Its workshop, kiln shed, dwelling, and storage buildings were nestled under the trees and almost invisible until one approached closely. When the kiln was firing, the steady rise of white smoke could be seen from the village.

The master potter, a quiet man with broad shoulders and a kindly face, was seen from time to time in the village trading his pots for goods at the market. He was a respected member of the community, but his retiring manner and the rather distant relationship between Ahimsa and the rest of the village gave rise to much gossip. The two apprentices, Joco and Boso, were looked upon with some suspicion.

"Those two are so dirty! Their trousers are always caked with clay."

"They say that the apprentices do all the work and that the master never goes near the wheel himself."

"They say he imitates the potters at Lamasa, and never originated any forms or colors himself."

"Why do they fire the kiln at night?"

"Someone who was over there recently said the clay smells like rotting cabbages."

"They say his pots are famous and fetch very high prices in the city."

"Impossible! We are using two of his pieces for pickling jars."

The Master worked nearly every day at his wheel, and the apprentices became used to the steady flow of strong, full shapes which at the end of the day stood in impressive rows on the rack. But one day, the pots seemed stronger and more beautiful than usual. The apprentices stopped their work and watched him in awe.

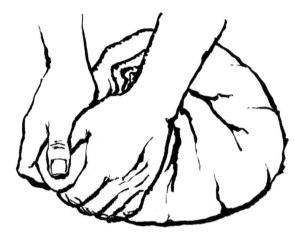

"Master, is that some special new clay you are using? It is a different color than our regular clay."

"Yes. I got this clay from my friend at Lamasa. It is a discarded batch—pots made from it crack in the fire."

The Master returned from the city where he had gone to sell his pots. The sale had been a great success. In fact, all but one of the pots were sold. The Master tossed the unsold pot carelessly under the table without comment.

But the next morning the apprentices were surprised to see the leftover pot placed on the shelf above the wheels where special pieces were kept for study and emulation.

"Look," said the Master. "Look well at this pot. Study the subtlety of its surface and the energy of its form. Penetrate its mystery. It is our new standard."

The pottery received a large order from an important client. Everyone knew that the reputation of Ahimsa was dependent on the successful completion of this group of pots. The Master and his two apprentices went to work with great energy and determination. They wedged up the oldest clay, greased the wheels. All day long and for several days they threw and trimmed. The Master worked on the more important forms and he directed, criticized, and cajoled the others as they worked. At last all was finished and ready for the fire.

But the next day when the apprentices entered the shop they were astonished to see that there were no pots on the racks. At first they thought the Master had set the kiln during the night, but it was empty. Then in the slaking pit they saw their efforts melting into the slime; every pot had been discarded. Some lids and handles could still be seen above the wet surface.

The Master entered the shop rubbing his hands. He put on his apron.

"The warm-up is finished," he said. "Now we begin."

Of the two apprentices, Boso was the most skilled, the most expert thrower. His pots were always straight, symmetrical, and perfectly formed. He had received much praise and encouragement from the Master. But gradually the favorable comments became more infrequent.

One day, the Master stopped at Boso's wheel.

"Your pots are too straight and perfect," he said.

"How can I change them?" asked Boso.

"Stop trying so hard! Relax! Let the clay do what it wants to do."

Boso then began to work at loosening his style. He encouraged irregularities and saw to it that each piece had something a little out-of-round or off center. He was sure that he was making progress, but for a long time there was no comment from the Master. But finally the Master stopped again at Boso's wheel.

"Your pots are too crooked, too eccentric," he said.

"But how shall I change them now?" asked Boso.

"Stop trying so hard! Relax! Let the clay do what it wants to do."

The apprentice Joco was of a philosophical turn of mind. He had pondered on a problem for a long time, and finally mentioned it to the Master.

"Master, how can the two characteristics of clay be reconciled in a pot? Clay when plastic is soft, slippery, and easily manipulated. But when fired it is hard, brittle, and rocklike."

The Master answered, "A state of unity must be obtained by doing away with the two polar and contradictory states. Remember that *saja* is always realized by transcending the dualities. One must realize a synthesis between notions of formal existence and the unformed. *Yoni* and *lingam* must become as one."

"I don't understand," said Joco.

"Get back to your wheel! Stop mulling!"

Joco was making saggers. Such tiresome work; the shape was just a cylinder, and the clay was so coarse it hurt his fingers.

The Master usually reserved criticism until the end of the day, but today he kept interrupting.

"Make them a little higher. Thicken up the edge. Clean up that sloppy bottom! Don't let the form belly out! Too thin! How can we set pots on that rough bottom? Watch the texture!"

Joco became really exasperated. These were only saggers!

He burst out, "Why are you so particular about the shape of these saggers? We don't sell them, and no one ever sees them!"

"That's just it," said the Master. "The pots are sold and gotten rid of. But these saggers—we have to handle them, look at them, and live with them for months or even years."

The Master seldom reminisced, but one day Boso asked him how he had acquired the ability to make pots so filled with energy and life. He replied by telling a story.

"When I was a young apprentice, I struggled at the wheel, like everyone else. I made good progress, but I was always dissatisfied, and sometimes discouraged. My pots seemed good to me while they were still on the wheel, moist, soft, and glistening. But later, when they began to dry—awful! And after the fire, worse still!

"My master, knowing that I was discouraged, offered suggestions, advice, and encouragement, but nothing seemed to help.

"Finally, to my surprise, he ordered me to stand on the wheel head. He then began coiling thick ropes of clay around my feet. Then he coiled around my ankles, my legs, and then my body and my neck. I was covered with coils of clay! I stood on the wheel transformed. I was the space within the pot! Then he took a paddle, and as the wheel slowly turned he beat the coils against my legs and my body, shouting, 'foot, foot (smack), belly! belly! (smack) (smack), shoulder! shoulder! (smack), neck! neck!'

"After that day, my pots changed."

The Master had apparently gone mad. He was glazing pots for the kiln, but instead of the usually orderly process of stirring, dipping, decorating, chaos took over. The Master mixed different glazes together, coated pots over twice or three times, scraped off parts of the glazed surface, dribbled and splashed glazes, swiped at pots with the studio broom instead of the brush, dusted on clay and sweepings over the glazes, hurled ashes from the kiln into the buckets of glaze, sprinkled salt on the shoulders of jars.

The more he worked, the more bizarre were his methods. But at last, all the pots were glazed and the kiln was set.

"This will be a disaster," said Boso as they sat that night slowly feeding the fire. "We are wasting our time, because the Master has ruined all of these pots with his mad glazing."

But the next day, the Master insisted on a meticulously

correct firing, and the kiln advanced to white heat just as usual. After the stoking ceased, the glowing rows of pots could be seen through the spyholes.

When the kiln was opened, the worst fears of the apprentices were confirmed. Pots were stuck to the shelves. Glazes were crawled and cracked. Colors were muddy. Surfaces were crusty and dry, or runny and glassy. It seemed that each pot which was brought out was worse than the last one. The Master threw them one by one onto the dump, where each made that special crashing noise which signifies the death of a pot.

But as they delved deeper into the setting, they reached one large jar, standing at the back of the kiln. A masterpiece! Its color, a mysterious gray green, was luminous and deep. Around the shoulder a band of deeper color encircled

the pot, and near the lip the glaze was flecked with minute pinpoints of gold!

The Master studied the pot a long time as it lay on the ground at the kiln door. He took the paper from the prayer stick and put it in his pocket, then carried the pot towards the shop.

"Good firing!" he said.

Joco asked, "Why do we never sign our pots with Ahimsa, the name of the pottery?"

The Master replied, "Those who value our pots recognize them instantly without the aid of a mark. Those who do not value them would not be impressed with a mere signature. Furthermore, those who would imitate us cannot do it by forging a mark. They would have to breathe the same fire into their work as we do, which is impossible."

The Master's former apprentice Soba was visiting. He said, "Master, would it be too much to ask if you would give me the recipe for that green glaze?"

"Of course not," said the Master, and wrote it out for him.

Later, Soba came back. "You remember that green glaze? It looks entirely different when I use it."

"When I gave you the glaze, it became yours. Why do you now complain because it looks like your green glaze instead of mine?"

One day while Boso was out of the shop, the Master slipped one of his own pitchers onto the board holding Boso's morning production of pitchers. Boso returned and began to put handles on the pitchers. But when he came to the pitcher the Master had made, something went wrong. He made several handles, but none of them worked, and each time he cut them off.

"Master," said Boso, "I can't make a handle which looks right on this piece. What is the matter?"

"Throw it into the scrap," said the Master. "There is at least one bad pot in every batch."

Joco was restless, and thought that his skills had reached the point where the Master would grant approval for him to leave and to establish himself as a master potter. But the Master was silent.

Finally Joco broached the subject.

"Do you not think that my training should be coming to an end?" he asked. "I can do each job in the shop perfectly. And my pots fit perfectly into the production here. Some of them have even been mistaken for yours."

"Be patient," said the Master. "Your training is not complete. It may be nearing completion when you are no longer able to make pots which fit perfectly into our production here."

Joco's day did arrive. The Master, with a twinkle in his eye, drew Joco aside and said, "Time for you to leave! I caught myself imitating one of your pots!"

MICHAEL FRIMKESS

In Conversation with Tim Crawford

All my life I've been in clay. I've always had clay around ever since I was a baby. My father was an artist. For some reason I always had clay around, wet clay and also plasticene. I didn't start into pottery until I had a vision: I was throwing a pot when I had never thrown a pot before. I knew intuitively that it was a pot that I was throwing. So I signed up the next day, and I have been a potter ever since.

Nowadays apprentices don't come like they used to. Now they're not often raised in the ceramic business. An apprentice might have been raised by a servant, or is very wealthy, and they're just not used to serving people. They might help you so far and then figure— well he can take it from here. This isn't the right attitude for an apprentice. An apprentice helps and keeps helping until he's ordered to change the job, or until the job is completed. He leaves the master's mind free to continue to work.

Perhaps I'm not old enough or they just don't make them the way they used to. I might not deserve the master type treatment yet. There are a lot of people who are just beginning who shouldn't be apprenticing. I need someone who's further along but yet is willing to submit to my orders. So I don't have to explain things and then get back talk. I don't mind creative ideas but they have to watch my time and be in my service.

Most of the apprentices that I had were just here to use the studio, to indiscriminately use the place and humiliate me. When I was an apprentice to Peter Voulkos I was very helpful. When Voulkos told me to jump, I jumped. I looked ahead for his welfare. He's the kind of person that demands and gets that kind of treatment because he looks like Anthony Quinn. People treat him like that—he's lucky that way. When they see me they figure well, this guy's not. My looks stand in my way, and my voice doesn't have that authoritarian ring. It just doesn't work for apprentices. I say do this and they do that.

The reason I'm studying the classical shapes of pots from all over the world is that I've always had this feeling that this generation, the time that we're living in, needs someone, somebody, somewhere, to try to learn as much as possible about cultures around the world. Things have to fall that way nowadays. The work of a true artist is to express the time that he's living in. The classical pots and shapes will someday help to communicate to people in other countries.

I've always been concerned with social commentary in my artwork. I haven't been getting too far with recognition on the philosophical side of it. It hasn't been too well received. I had a black news commentator that I made for a sculpture in 1960 before they had black people on television. That was a very new idea. People hadn't thought of it before. It hadn't occurred to people that black people weren't on television. It was five years ahead of its time. As an artist you have to be ahead of how things are shaping, and contribute straws to the camel's back.

If potters of future generations were to take what I'm doing and go a step further, then they wouldn't be going a step further unless they were following in my footsteps morally and consciously, and not merely technically. They should go the whole route. If they always take what they want and ignore the rest of the message that I want to leave behind, I don't feel that they will be going a step further. If they study classical shapes from all over the world, they should go the whole route. Take the whole thing and paint the stories on that have helped to create peace in the world, and see the whole foundation that I'm trying to establish in the ceramic art. This, I feel, is my main contribution.

When in 1960 I conceived that black news commentator —that bronze sculpture I did—I also sculpted some dying trees on the television set—a lot of symbolic extrasculpture to illustrate what I thought the time was going to be like and what our obstacles would be. I've always been concerned with that kind of stuff. And now it's considered corny or old-fashioned but that's not going to stop me, because that's illustrating the times.

I've always been concerned with the way animals treated their fellow animals and how they were treating nature. An artist should be feeling those things, and nowadays it's out of the artist's hands you might say. But when I first started thinking about it and painting these things on the sculptures, it wasn't out of the artist's hands—it was very new. I still think that it isn't over yet. It's just beginning.

The artist could help a great deal, making people aware over the whole world. If he makes a Chinese shape, if he's great enough it will be displayed in China. When the Chinese see the artwork on it they'll know that the artist in the USA has a certain amount more freedom than they have, because of their political limitations. But at the same time they should also know that Americans are not as advanced on many levels as they are. Then a Chinese potter should be able to get through all of that bullshit and create something that can communicate to American potters.

Pottery is a very functional medium. The Oriental people regard pottery like we do rock and roll, and it serves many more functions than to drink out of or serve tea from.

Megdalena Frimkess

BEATRICE WOOD

In Conversation with Tim Crawford

I had no intention of becoming a potter. I was in love, which has been the motive of all my activities probably even today. I was in Europe, I went to hear Krishnamurti. I was going through museums and suddenly it occured to me, My God! I'm engaged, I must get something for my new home. So I immediately went into an antique shop and bought six luster plates. It was the first time I had ever looked at a craft.

I had always been interested in paintings. (This was around 1940.) When I returned to America I wanted to find a teapot to go with the beautiful little luster plates. And I couldn't. A friend suggested that I go to Hollywood High School—the only place they were making pottery—and make a teapot. So the next day I went and made two plates—an abomination—and two little figures, and a friend bought them for $2.50. So I said to myself—I had no money in those days—well, maybe if I make a few of these things I'll make $10.00 or more a month. So that kind of awakened my interest. Then I became hooked.

I heard that Glen Lukens had started a class and I went to him twice a week for two years at USC. I was the worst student in the class because I'm not naturally a craftsman. This is a great advantage because a great deal of talent can be a handicap, as it doesn't give one discipline. Things come too easily. I had to struggle and struggle.

When I moved to Ojai I had enough money to carry me three weeks. I just took a gamble. I moved March 3, 1948. My place (which the Heinos now have) was a rock pile—nobody wanted it. It was a square acre. I slept in my exhibition room and ate in my workroom. After 26 years, working with my own hands, it became a showplace and the Heinos love it.

I sold for several years to all the finest stores: Phillips Wilshire, to Neiman-Marcus, Marshall Field, Gumps, all of them. Even in those days I was getting rather good prices. I was making on an average $800.00 a month of which I netted only $175.00, because the stores keep one-half of the retail. I'm not price conscious. I often think prices are high but the museums don't necessarily think so. I don't know what to say. I keep out of it.

I tried once to work in partnership with a man who was a chemist; he would do glazing and the business side. It didn't work out. I realize now it's very hard unless you're married, legally or illegally, to get a person to work with you.

I tried to make this place go in a conventional way and then I gave up. Now I'm not under pressure. The Zachary Waller Gallery has put on in the last year four gallery shows, which sold, and I keep my hands out of it. They do whatever they wish. They come every few months and pick up what they want. I walk out when they price the things. I don't want to know and they take care of the invoicing and for me it's very happy.

I hesitate to give advice to young potters because each one of us has a unique experience. I can only speak for mine.

The fact that I've had all these great difficulties has been most helpful to my character. And also being somewhat of an artist temperamentally—when I was younger I went to all museums but now my extravagance is art books—my eyes are titillated by art from all centuries, from the beginning of man to the end. I'm fascinated by what the human race has achieved. So I would say two things: if a person wants to be just a potter let him go to the best school and get a fine technique. If he wants to be what is called an artist-potter then he should expose himself to art. If he's responsive to it something will happen. I think it's terribly important that we should do our own thing.

Now I had invitational exhibits in Tokyo and the Japanese greatly responded to what I did because I was not doing Japanese pottery. (The reason is that I didn't know enough; but that's neither here nor there.) One of the papers said that I could teach the Japanese. Of course when I read that as flattering I laughed because it was funny.

I've often said I believe so in discipline. I had an agent when I started out. She went on vacation and I delivered 15 pots. The store said where's your invoice and I said what's an invoice and the lady said it's a list. I said Madam, I'm not a typist, I'm an artist. She said, sit down. How do you expect us to pay you. I assure you, it was a great revelation in my life, that I saw then, if I wanted the privilege of working at something I loved, that I related to society, I had to conform to society. •

I think the great tribute of my life was that three museums where I had shows went out of their way to say I'd given them the clearest invoices they ever had. Now to me, to make a beautiful invoice is as important and creative as making a beautiful pot.

JOHN SCHULPS

In Conversation with Tim Crawford

How it started was like this. I was trying to get into a major university, and they put me in a ceramics class with this guy named Ataka. I was continuing along in my college football career. After obtaining my B.A. at Valley State College in 1963, I played professional football with the Vikings, and continued to be a potter in the off-season.

I worked on my masters at U.C.L.A. while playing pro football. The M.F.A. was in design, with special emphasis on ceramics. I studied with Laura Anderson, Ed Traynor, and Bernard Kester.

Then I came to a crossroads. A leg injury, and a feeling that I needed more time with my ceramics, made me quit football and concentrate on ceramics.

In 1966 I opened a store in Malibu called the Sunspot. From there I moved into Calabasas and a larger studio. Then we did this big operation last year.

We use 8 to 10 tons of clay a week. We make our own stoneware clay using all natural California clays. We make clay similar to Swedish style white clay.

Clay is made every other day and the excess is sold to schools, potteries, and individual potters. I'm constantly working on some new clay body, as I feel not enough work and research has been done on it. One clay can't suffice for all a potter's needs. A sense of change of clay is a nice awareness.

We've been using Brent wheels, but except for the gear-driven models they've been breaking down. Now we're going to Lang-Lion, made in Hermosa Beach, California. In February I'm going to Korea to set up a national pottery, and I'm developing a wheel that we'll be using there. It's a two horsepower motor, slip-clutched with a direct drive, and a table on it.

I throw double-sponge in a weird way. I use Japanese *keai* sticks. I developed a technique where I throw sponge-to-sponge. We use this real heavily grogged clay that would wear your hands off. You make 10 pots and your sponge is gone. The grog is called 401—larger than 30 mesh, with some pumice. We fire to c/9. We're bringing it down through. Probably c/7 to save gas.

Production is geared to sales and seasons. Some items outsell others in our catalog, and these items are made without current orders. Other items which move slower are made as the purchase orders dictate. Three potters work on just the faster selling items; one potter on specialties. Two potters and I throw the large pots.

Really, the forte of our whole operation is that we make pretty large stoneware pots, 50 to 75 pounds of clay. We have one girl who makes the tableware. It's all handthrown —no jigs. I personally sell at the fairs.

We do two 300 cubic foot kiln loads a week—two bisque, two glaze firings. There are two glaze days a week during which outside help is brought in, mainly college girls who make excellent glazers.

I have around 20 employees. Most of my apprentices stay with me. I've had one boy for six years. They get paid. I encourage them to make their own stuff. They really learn. It's better than a school situation because they have to throw so much. So many things happen, you just don't get that kind of exposure elsewhere.

It takes a kid about four or five years before he can really throw well. I can teach a kid in three days how to throw, but as far as what's coming out of him, it needs developing. Throwing is like a mechanism in your hands—a relationship of curves and such. A lot of it is connected with an inherent sense of design.

Art schools get rather didactic. For a long time the northern art schools were just doing this low-fire stuff that you need to walk on—abstract expressionism. You just couldn't sell it to the public. If you're Pete Voulkos, you know, it's fine. But the average guy, he can't do it. There's no way he can support a family. People don't understand it. It is really hard to merchandise.

The public acceptance of pottery has grown considerably in the last few years. But I don't think in one sense that there's been a true renaissance of crafts. I don't know how many craftsmen are really making an adequate living. I mean as compared to a guy working as a white-collar worker.

In the beginning, the physical aspect of making pottery appealed to me, probably due to my interest in sports and playing football. It seemed to tire me physically and relax me mentally. I feel that the discipline encountered in sports has helped me as a potter to start and finish projects.

We have a 300 cubic foot envelope kiln with two platforms, the car moving over the ware. Excellent for stacking large pots. Being big, the kiln is actually cheaper to fire than several smaller ones. It seems to hold the heat longer and spread it more evenly. Gas consumption is cut down and more ware produced. It fires with few hot spots and no flashing.

A lot of teachers say that large kilns can't get the results. I think that's a fallacy. They haven't fired big kilns. A lot of teachers in universities really don't like the studio potter, which is suprising. They get a check from the state. It's different when you're not supported from teaching alone.

We're now getting a 400 cubic foot kiln. This next kiln is going to be safer. We're going to a double-fold door to get away from the guillotine doors. Our present kiln weighs close to 30 tons. It was moved in on a flat-bed. It was really something to see. I've been really happy with that kiln.

BERNARD LEACH

In Conversation with Fred Olsen

Many of you perhaps, in America, are taking part in the new wave of making pots which I hear of from John Reeve, my old student in Canada, and from Warren MacKenzie of the Twin Cities.

Warren writes in his letters that having taught for 27 years he went out to see what effect his teaching had had within a radius of 50 miles. To his astonishment he found that not a few dozen but hundreds of potters have found a new public who want to use their pots and enjoy them, as the makers themselves have enjoyed and probably used them.

Their own hearts' sake! That's grand! It came as a new wind across the Atlantic that potters in the United States, in the new world, should be catching this idea which came from Japan.

I had been taken one day [in Japan] to a party which offered the entertainment of decorating pots. A pot had been put into my hand and in broken Japanese I'd been asked to write a poem on it. I said, "No, I don't think I can write poems." (These brushes are awfully difficult to write our alphabet with, you know.)

I had drawn a pattern—not my own pattern, I had not used the word before. A pattern. It made me think—what is a pattern? What do you paint on pots? Do you have to paint pots with patterns of pictures or photographs or anything of this kind? Is it a voluntary matter? I was trained as an artist and the idea of making a pattern was something new and exciting.

What is a pattern? It's like a song, a tune, a dance. Only it's a painting or scratched or resisted with wax on the surface of a pot. Which meant that you could use colors.

In that case I remembered a pot I had seen in a museum in Tokyo and it excited me. I did what I could of a parrot sitting on this stage—or, what shall I call it—framework, with a little cup on one side painted in blue on the white porcelain. It was probably of the Ming dynasty, way back 400 to 500 years ago. On the other side there was a pot for water—it has to eat and drink.

So there you are. And as you climb up, it could climb up on to a framework, which made the parrot the center of the framework in a circle of a plate.

These elements of abstract forms and observation of the life of a parrot holding its food and nibbling at a seed in its mouth, standing on one leg, with its rounded beak, made to my mind my first moment of looking at the pot—really looking—and the idea of a pattern.

I didn't remember exactly what I had seen, but I made up what I couldn't remember. Within an hour of being painted that pot was in my hand, warm in rags. I was so excited that I said, "This is what I came to the East to do. This I must find a master to teach me."

That master turned out to be the 6th Kenzan. I've written a book called *Kenzan and His Tradition,* and if you want to tell all about that you can read that book—it's still obtainable. It's quite an interesting book. I took a long time and an immense trouble because involved in it was a very big question as to whether there had not been a very big discovery of the first Kenzan's work when I was in Japan about 10 years ago.

I've always believed that the pots now called Kenzan's, of which I have several in this room, are real, not fake, although Japan is full of fakes. No man has been copied as much as the first Kenzan. The first Kenzan and his great uncle Koetsu were the two first artist-craftsmen of Japan, long before we had any of what we now call artist-craftsmen in England. Something to think about. Something to dig into. Something to read about if you can.

But what I want to go back to is what John Reeve in Canada and Warren MacKenzie in the United States could do. They have brought me news about the kind of pot I came back to try to make in England, which seemed to me right for an artist-craftsman.

I was trained as an artist and I fell in love with potting. I wanted, as William Blake and his friends of the English Arts and Crafts Society wanted to do as educated men, to make things for our own delight or use.

Now, in a machine age, that you should move away from the one-of-a-kind pot in the United States and go back to the usage and pleasure of people around you in making and using things, gives mankind the opportunity to use heartbeat in his work. A machine does not do that. And that is why you and we are slave people—the modern slaves.

Don't be slaves!

I'm delighted to hear this news. I hope it's true. We're moved that you have leaders, because you must have pathfinders in the world of art.

The traditional kind of work which preceded our [world of art was] when people made dances and tunes—it was the art of the people, the Tom, Dick and Harry for all men. The juice that went up that tree—the sap that went up—has now died because it's being displaced by energy that has gone into the machine world.

But you've got to put some of it back. That you want to do it, I hope and believe.

Goodbye!

Goodluck!

Michael Boylen

PART SEVEN
GLASS

BASIC GLASS BATCHING

by Robert D. Held

"If any workman conveys his art to a strange country to the detriment of the Republic, he shall be sent an order to return to Venice and, failing to obey, his nearest relation shall be imprisoned. If he still persists in remaining abroad and plying his art an emissary shall be charged to kill him" (Council of the Law, 1474)

Times haven't changed much in 300 years, it seems. Although modern industrial chemical research and techniques are available, and are being used by corporations, the contemporary individual glass craftsman seems to find the entire area of glass batching bewildering. In the old days, it was necessary to jealously guard the source, quantity, and quality of the raw materials used in making glass. Since most old glass formulas were arrived at through tedious trial and error methods, it is no wonder these secrets would be subject to extraordinary protection. There were no patent laws then, so nothing was protected from stealing, and one can understand the great importance of the glass industry to the economics of the country that had the best crystal glass. There are old stories of Italian glass workers being kidnapped from their beds and tortured in Western Europe in order for France to economically compete with Italy for the world glass trade.

This ancient secrecy in glass started for basically economic reasons and has tended to pervade the glass world, from the 15th century up to this very day. I know of an offhand glass factory in Ontario, Canada, where only the two owners know the formula and will not allow any workmen to be in the building when they mix the lead crystal batch. The workmen simply blow the glass and don't know what is in it, nor are they allowed to.

Over the past few years "batching" has become one of the main interests to the individual offhand glassblower. Many glass craftsmen who started with the revered "475" marbles have found that they are personally limited in quality and workability.

Mark Peiser, one of the pioneers in individual glass batching, has said that he never melted a batch of glass that wasn't better than 475, even the ones right out of Scholes' book. Five years ago 475s were about the only thing that studio blowers knew and loved; but once you have tried batch, there is a yearning to find out more about it.

Before you attempt batching from raw materials, you should ask a few questions with regard to what you want from a glass. What are the qualities of your "ideal" glass? There are many types of glasses, from special optical to cheap beer bottle glass, and each type has been formulated to work in a certain way and have certain visual properties. Some of the qualities that you might want in an offhand working glass are these:

1. The glass has a long "life" or "workability" (sometimes called "out of tank time").

2. The glass has a good factor of actual workability or maneuverability.

3. Glass should melt rapidly and "fine out" (no bubbles in melt) quickly.

4. The glass should have a good color range potential.

5. The glass should have a high index or refraction that gives it a brilliancy and sparkle.

6. The glass should have properties that will make it durable to weathering.

7. Perhaps the glass should have a high viscosity at low temperatures.

8. The glass should have a gradual "cut off" working point and not an abrupt setup point.

9. The glass should anneal easily.

10. The glass should not deteriorate the furnace lining too rapidly.

11. If possible, the glass should not be too expensive.

There is no glass that has all the qualities listed above, but there are some that have most of them. The person who wants to attempt batching from the basics should do some research before dumping some chemicals together and attempting to melt them. Some older glassblowers have advocated many years of study and research before actually getting into batching. Personally, I feel that batching does not require long years of tedious research, but has become one of the most exciting areas of my glass experience. We started batching three years ago and I hope I'll continue to develop better and better glass batches. Bottle, cullet, or marbles just don't have the qualities that good batch glass has. Armed with a few reference books, a little chemistry knowledge, a good dose of common sense, and a yearning to go and experiment, you are well on your way to developing a batch glass just for you.

I have broken batch research methods into three types:

      A. Patent medicine approach
      B. Line blend studies
      C. Calculations and research

A. Patent medicine approach is simply testing known or existing glass recipes, one at a time. Once you have determined a number that seems promising you can do further research by making simple additions and/or subtractions to these known recipes. My suggestion is to add or subtract only one material per test, so you know which material causes the change.

B. Line blend studies are a step towards a more scientific approach to glass batch research. Line blends have been used in ceramics for years and methods are applicable to glass research. Starting with a simple basic glass formula, you make additions of one material in that formula and determine the differences. The next stage is to make additions of one new raw material at a time to the simple formula. For example, a simple batch of silica 100; soda ash 35; whiting 25 will give you a basic glass. To this glass you can make ad ditions of 2, 5, 10%, etc., of one of the raw materials in the batch, i.e., whiting. The next step is to make additions of new materials or substitute similar materials such as a direct substitution of dolomite for whiting. By keeping careful records you can empirically determine what raw material is causing what reaction. The line blend technique is certainly the simplest "kitchen" method to explore color variations in additions to batch experimentation. A further development of the simple line blend is the triaxial blend. The triaxial is really the combination of three line blends into one. The illustration will give a simple explanation of the triaxial. Batches A, B, and C make up the corners of the triangle, and midway between each basic recipe is a 50-50 mixture. The other points on the triaxial diagram represent varying portions of the three batch recipes of colorants. For a more detailed explanation refer to **Rhodes, Daniel.** *Clay and Glazes for The Potter.* Rev. ed. Philadelphia: Chilton and London: Pitman, 1973. One further note on line blends and that is the experimental methods of decolorizing the basic batch with chemicals such as manganese, cobalt, selenium, nickel, etc. Through the systematic line blend of decolorizer additions to the basic batch you will be able to narrow the amounts with a few tests. Every batch will react differently and therefore the proper amount of decolorizer needed will vary accordingly. Also, the type of decolorizer can vary from batch to batch, and a line blend of different materials should be the first step in determining the best decolorizer to use for your particular batch.

C. The most precise method of batch exploration is, of course, the use of calculations. Once you have attempted the line blend and the patent medicine approach you will soon find the limitation of each method and perhaps desire a more scientific method to determine your batch. Chapter VIII of S. Scholes' book *Modern Glass Practice* is one of the best available sources for learning batch calculations. If you have had some experience in glaze calculation, then glass calculations will come much easier. In general you will find that you must be more precise in glass composition than in glaze composition. If you know how to use a slide rule it will cut the calculation time down considerably. The process of batch calculations is a number of relatively simple mathematical steps that are in themselves not difficult, but seemingly difficult when lumped together. If you take the time to go through the steps, the results may prove to be well worth the energy and time. Once you get into batch calculation you are in a much better position to understand and use similar mathematics for calculating the coefficient of expansion of different glasses so that they will fit. You should learn the steps in calculating batch to formula and formula to batch. Once you are familiar with these calculations you should be able to make important changes in the basic batch while keeping the glass relatively stable. Alterations for quality, new or different raw materials, workability, etc., can be undertaken with confidence. By almost eliminating the guesswork from batching you eliminate the secrecy and have less fear; that will usually lead to even further batch and color exploration.

An area of glass that has held a special interest to glass blowers and collectors is that of opal glass. The glassblower can find many opal batch recipes, but the old problem of the opal fitting the basic crystal batch seems to cause many problems. There are two major types of opal glass, fluorine opal and phosphate opal. Phosphate opal has one major advantage over the fluorine opal in that the fit problem is greatly reduced. We have used fluorine opals for three

years and continually have the disconcerting problems of dangerous fumes, severe attack on the refractories (particularly crucibles), and the real problem of fit. The very different workability of flourine opals from the basic crystal batch is another factor that must be dealt with in blowing thin-walled pieces. Once we decided to try a phosphate opal, many of the old problems disappeared but a few new ones appeared.

Technically, opal glass is defined as: "glasses of the light diffusing type which do not directly transmit light" (from Scholes, Samuel. *Modern Glass Practice.* 7th rev. ed. Boston: Cahners, 1975). This is caused by minute inclusions in the glassy matrix that have a different index of refraction than the basic glass and therefore scatter the light instead of allowing it to pass uninterfered through the object. These inclusions cause the light to travel four to eight times the thickness of the object wall. Phosphate opals can be classified as solidified emulsions whereas flourine opals are classified as devitrified glasses.

The two major raw materials that are used in phosphate opal glass are mono- or tri-calcium phosphate, $Ca_3(PO_4)$ (see S. Scholes, *Modern Glass Practice,* as cited above) and bone ash. Generally, the best results are obtained using mono-calcium phosphate. Proper melting procedures are also very important in achieving the best results. Through experimentation and research we have come upon the following melting procedure:

1. Melt hot

2. Reduce temperature to just above liquidus for overnight

3. Raise temperature to blowing consistency

4. Turn down at night

5. You can run much hotter with bone ash than you can with any flourine opal

Blowing requires certain simple changes in order to obtain the opal. We have found that you must cool each opal gather until it is very cold. After cooling you must heat the opal gathers until they are very hot. After some experimentation you can start to control the opal effect to the point of having an opal bowl and center of the foot on a goblet, while the rest can be graduations from opal to clear. So, in general, the longer the reheat, the more opaque the phosphate opals become. Some phosphate opal batches have continued to strike opal after three weeks. One nice thing is that the burned out phosphate opals become very clear and have a very good index of refraction.

A few notes of caution on phosphate opals are:

1. Make sure that the bone ash or calcium phosphate is thoroughly crushed and dry

2. Screen it through a 30-mesh screen

3. Mix it very well with the entire batch

4. Stir the melt periodically to keep opal distributed (phosphate opals tend to separate into layers after standing for extended periods)

The amount of calcium phosphate needed to produce an opal varies from 4 to 8% of the total batch. We are using 6% and the opal is very white for about two weeks and slightly burned out after that. Some experimentation has been done with varying the amounts from 10 to 30 parts for each 100 parts of silica, with good results. However, care should be taken with additions of over 15 parts because of the change in the coefficient of expansion or fit of the basic crystal batch.

Personally, I have tried a combination of cryolite and mono-calcium phosphate in the same batch in an attempt to get the best of both, and I have had good luck so far. However, more research and testing is needed. It seems that a low-potash basic batch gives a better phosphate opal. Also, additions of arsenic and antimony tend to change the opaque to a translucent opal.

Add 6% mono-calcium phosphate of total batch weight to the following batch formulas that should strike opal on reheating and should fit the basic glass.

In hopes that more glassblowers will experiment with batch and add to the general wealth of knowledge for all other glass people, I list a few of the glass formulas that I have tried with some success.

Sheridan School of Design, R. Held, 1972

Silica	33 lbs.
Soda ash	12
Whiting	5
Potash	5
Borax	2
Arsenic	20 gm. approx.
Manganese dioxide	small pinch

R. Held, S.O.D., 1974

Silica	45 lbs.
Soda ash	16
Dolomite	10
Whiting	5
Potassium carbonate	3
Alumina A 10	1.5
Borax	4
Barium	1.5

Zinc Batch, Dick Huss, 1973

Silica	100 lbs.
Soda ash	30
Potash	20
Zinc oxide	10
Lime 1	5
Fluorspar	6
Barium carbonate	3
Antimony	2.5

Giberson, 1972

Sand	100 lbs.
Soda ash	41.5
Potash	6.25
Lime	15

R.I.T., G. Thiewes, 1973

Cullet	35 lbs.
Silica	20
Soda	8
Lime	7
Potash	4

Penland, 2B

Sand	33 lbs.
Soda	12
Lime	6
Potash	5
Cullet	50

K. Ipsen, 1973

Silica	100 lbs.
Soda ash	40
Potash	5
Dolomite	4
Barium carbonate	4
Zinc oxide	4
Borax	1

Table of Crucible Formulas from the Notebook of Dudley Giberson.

These crucibles can be used for melting glass, iron, brass, bronze, and aluminum.

Source of Information	Fire-clay	Ball Clay	Grog	Kaolin	Al_2O_3 & SiO	Other Stuff	Other Stuff	Whatever
Yeoman's Dictionary of Everyday Wants 1872	1. 1 part weight	—	1 part weight	—	—	Graphite 1 part weight	—	Multi-metals
	2. 1 part weight	—	—	—	—	Graphite 2 parts weight	—	Multi-metals
Elements of Glass & Glassmaking by B. Biser 1899	3. 7 parts volume	—	—	—	—	—	Burnt clay 8 parts volume	Handbuilt glass crucibles
	4. 6 parts volume	—	3 parts volume	—	—	—	Burnt clay 4 parts volume	Handbuilt glass crucibles
"A Study of Glass" by John Karrasch Aug. 1964 Attrib: Ceramic Industry	5. —	Tenn. ball 5 parts	45 parts weight	28 parts weight	Flint's 4 parts weight	Spar 3 parts weight	Ill. Bond clay 5 parts	Glass crucibles
"A Study of Glass" by John Karrasch Attrib: Saugger	6. —	English ball 10	Fine grog 55	Georgia kaolin 35	—	—	—	Glass crucibles
Modern Glass Practices by Scholes	7. 40	—	60	—	—	—	—	Glass crucible ugh!
Tony Packer Studio Potter	8. —	10	reg. grog 20	15	Al_2O_3 50	Talc 5	Bentonite +1.5% of total weight	Glass pot
Mark Peiser and Alfred University	9. Water 8 qts.	Tenn. ball 18 lbs.	Sodium silicate 2 ozs.	—	Mullite* 200 mesh 21 lbs.	Mullite* 325 mesh 21 lbs.	This a highly reliable slip casting formula for glass or metal pots	
Iron-Melting A.S.M. P.800 Rec. formula	10. —	Some ball clay	—	—	Some Silica sand	Some Graphite	—	American practice iron-melting
Ranges from page 801 Dated 1939	11. It is claimed on p. 801 that the English still use a "Clay pot" for the melting of iron: Huntsman process							English practice iron-melting
Glass Art February 1974	12. —	Tenn ball 10	Kaolin grog 20	Kaolin clay 20	Al_2O_3 50	—	Bentonite 1.3% of total weight	Glass pot
Glassblowing by Frank Kulasiewicz	13. 50	—	50	—	—	—	I doubt it but he claims this makes a good pot for glass melting	
My Favorite Hand-building Formula by Dudley Giberson	14. AP Green Mo. Fire-clay 4 parts volume	Tenn #9 2 parts volume	AP Green Fine grog 4 parts volume	—	Mullite* 200 mesh 4 parts volume	Water as little as possible to make it shrink less	This formula is good for glass or metal pouring crucibles. Also good for making high-fire kiln furniture, etc.	

*Available from Kyanite Mining, Dillwyn, WV

GATHERING ON GLASS

by Dale Chihuly

The glass drawings are made up prior to the blowing process out of thin glass threads which we pull from Kugler color rods. The drawings are fabricated by using a propane torch—in this case by Flora Mace and in the earlier pieces by Kate Elliot. It usually takes anywhere from one to eight hours to prepare the drawing. The cylinder itself takes from one to one-and-a-half hours to blow.

Flora and I are in the process of setting up a drawing on the marvering table. The drawings are often three or four layers deep and for this reason the glass needs to be extremely molten.

One of the more serious problems that the potter and glassblower have to deal with is how surface design relates to the vessel. In the case of the Blanket Cylinders, I wanted the designs to wrap around the cylinder like a blanket. The drawing becomes at least as important as the cylinder.

A quote from Kahlenberg's and Berlant's *The Navajo Blanket* has had a nice influence on this series: "No matter

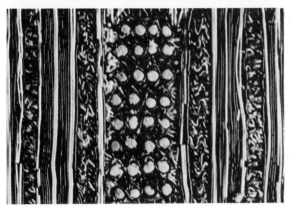

how the blanket is worn, its design suits the body and de-emphasizes its physical reality presenting an idealized being."

This sequence gives a good description of how the pickup is made. The molten glass is dropped directly onto the drawing and left in this position for about 10 seconds. This is the most critical stage in the aesthetic development. At this point the drawing can be distorted, which is purposely done in the case of the Blankets.

I work with a number of assistants. They are normally my students, in this case Erica Friedman, Michael Glossip, and Ben Moore. I find them a tremendous aid in the blowing process and give them as much responsibility as possible. I feel this is by far the most effective method for teaching. I find it much more enjoyable to work with people than to work by myself. Most of my work in the past six years, with the exception of the cylinder series, has been done in collaboration with Jamie Carpenter. Our ideas are similar. Both of us are primarily interested in exploring new aspects of glass, a material which has been dominated by industry and commercial usages since its discovery. I have also worked with other artists and nearly always find these collaborative efforts stimulating and productive. It's unfortunate that more artists in the 20th century don't work together. It can be very rewarding.

SAFETY IN THE GLASS STUDIO

by Dominick Labino

The contemporary glassworking studio has a unique position in the glass world. Working with hot glass in a factory situation was always a team effort. The assembly-line method was necessary in order to assure uniformity and speed up production. The contemporary studio-glass craftsman is in a different situation. He designs what he intends to produce, and then he executes it, working alone. Yet while this atmosphere of solitude may stimulate his creativity and underscore his individuality, putting a personal stamp on his work, it becomes at the same time a potential safety hazard. Carelessness, thoughtlessness, and lack of concern have no place in a studio where hot glass is being worked, and where dangerous chemicals are being handled and stored.

There are inherent hazards in many of the aspects of studio glassworking, and these hazards necessitate care and caution in the very setting up of the studio:

• The location and structure of the studio, and its layout for space.
• Furnace construction and hook-up, gas piping, and safety controls.
• Safeguards against accidents and first-aid in the event they occur.
• Chemicals—their labeling, stowing, and use.
• Safety of finishing equipment; grinding, cutting, and polishing wheels; sand-blasting, acid-finishing, and electroplating. There are other hazards resulting from poor work practices of the craftsman:
• Personal safety in the area of clothing and body protection.
• The handling of the hot glass.

Since the most obvious thing about hot glass is that it is worked in its molten state at very high temperatures, care should be taken to locate the studio away from other buildings, especially dwellings, in order not to subject them to noise, fumes, or the danger of fire.

If the studio is to be located in an urban area, it is wise to investigate and find out whether there are zoning restrictions or fire department regulations which should be met. The building itself should be as nearly fire resistant as possible, either of metal, brick, or concrete block, with floor equally fire resistant.

The working space in front of the furnaces should be large enough for the craftsman to move around safely when he is handling hot glass. A working space of 400 square feet is a bare minimum for an individual studio. (It should be larger, of course, for a class in a college arts course, where several people may be working at the same time.)

The equipment should be well designed and located so that the craftsman can work comfortably and efficiently without endangering his safety. My design of a triple-hinged swinging door on my glass-melting furnaces works so effortlessly and safely that it has been copied many times. The handle is of wood, making the use of a glove unnecessary for opening and closing the door.

The piping and hookup for the furnaces should meet the standards of local codes. This is not the place to use poor fittings or makeshift connections. Natural gas is the best and safest fuel. If this is not available, the next best is fuel oil. Propane gas is the least desirable because of safety hazards. For, if a leak should occur at a loose connection, the propane, which is heavier than air, will settle to the floor and create the possibility of fire or explosion. All furnaces should be equipped with safety controls which will automatically close off the fuel supply valves in the event of interruption of either the fuel or power supply. Manual control valves for air and gas pressure should be placed where there is sufficient room to adjust them without having to crawl around furnaces and run the risk of setting fire to your clothing. Consult your local gas company and be sure that you are meeting the specifications of the Associated Factory Mutual Laboratories.

In the event that you do not have a spark plug ignition for lighting the furnaces, a safe practice is to use a rod or copper tubing at least three or four feet long, having a wick soaked in oil, to be used as a torch to light the main burner.

When gas is used, there are times when valves which you thought were closed were in reality open or leaking. An accumulation of gas in the furnace will cause an explosion when you light it. It is best therefore to be certain that you are using good, safe, gas-tight valves.

The furnaces should be provided with a good ventilating system. A satisfactory arrangement is a 36'' high-volume slow-speed fan which is almost noiseless, used for venting the hood over the furnaces. This runs continuously and provides circulation of air which takes out the fumes discharged from the furnaces.

A showerhead in the furnace area is a precaution in the event that clothing catches fire. Also, a garden hose connected to the water supply is a good idea. A first-aid kit should be in the same area so that local burns or cuts can be attended to immediately.

The personal safety of the craftsman is a matter both of precaution and of safe working practices. Protective clothing is most important for work near the furnaces, and particularly when handling hot glass. The very best material is wool, because it is slow to ignite, and so protects against fire and body burns. Next comes 100% cotton. But, under no circumstances should synthetic materials of any kind be used; no rayon, orlon, nylon, or dacron. They do not blaze, but they melt with the heat and stick to the skin, causing severe burns and possible skin damage. The hair should be cut short, or if worn long, it should be tied away from the face. Trousers or slacks should not have cuffs which will trap hot glass and catch fire, and they should cover the shoe tops. Safety shoes are best, but any sturdy work shoes which

cover and protect the feet will suffice. Avoid the use of sandals or open or loose shoes; they are hot glass traps.

Protective flame-resistant asbestos gloves made of durable Underwriters' Grade basketweave cloth with wool lining will meet safety requirements for hand protection. These gloves can be used when handling a piece of glass which is ready to be placed in the annealing oven. Or asbestos-covered tongs can be used for this purpose. Safety glasses should be worn at all times in the glass studio. They are particularly necessary for work near the open furnaces to protect the eyes against harmful ultraviolet or infrared rays from the furnaces. But they are also necessary at other times to protect against flying fragments. Most protective lenses are still made of glass, especially if they are used near furnaces. There are various kinds for specific uses. Protection against harmful rays require lenses which will transmit an adequate but not excessive proportion of the visible light, and which will effectively stop ultraviolet and infrared radiation. *Calobar* lenses protect against glare, effectively screening invisible ultraviolet and infrared rays, and are made in three shades, medium, dark, and very dark. For furnace work, the medium shade is recommended. If you have a special vision problem, consult your ophthalmologist before making your selection of protective lenses.

Because the craftsman is handling molten glass, casual observers should be kept away from the working area near the furnaces. They could sustain injury, or burn themselves, and they could also endanger the safety of the craftsman who is at work.

Personal safety, as well as the safety of a group, is really a matter of common sense and wise precautions. In the matter of handling hot glass, the beginner is often tempted to use spectacular movements which show off the behavior of the molten glass. One example of this sort of thing is the whirling of the blowpipe in a circular movement over the head to show the hot glass as it stretches away from the end of the pipe. This is one of the most dangerous maneuvers possible if the craftsman is not familiar with the behavior of hot glass at various temperatures. He may have heated it more than he realized, and the hot mass may sag and come into contact with his hair or clothing or skin. The stretching action can be shown just as well, and even better, by swinging the pipe like a pendulum, accomplishing the same goal but much more safely. A glass studio is no place for horseplay.

The air hose is another auxiliary tool which should be handled with extreme caution. Its use should be forbidden for beginners, since it is possible to shatter a piece of glass and have pieces flying in all directions. This is especially likely to happen if the air hose is being used on a piece of glass which is too cold and has a thin spot in the wall. Even the experienced craftsman is cautious in using it.

There are certain safety measures which apply to the setting up and use of finishing equipment, such as cutting wheels, grinding wheels, and polishing wheels and belts. All cutting, grinding, and polishing wheels and belts should be equipped with guards to protect the hands and body from injury. And goggles or safety glasses should be worn at all times when working on finishing equipment or cutting wheels.

A very specialized, air-tight chamber is used for sandblasting, and no part of the body ever comes in direct contact with this interior. Special heavy rubber gloves and a view-window are built into the face of this chamber. It should be near an outside wall so that the exhaust dust can be piped outside into a dust collector. Needless to say, one should not breathe this dust.

All chemicals should be treated as if they were poisonous. They should be kept in closed containers, and should be properly labeled for identification and safety warning. When the containers are opened, care should be taken to avoid contact with the skin, eyes, nose, and mouth; and there should be protective covering when highly volatile chemicals are being handled. It is best to avoid smoking when handling chemicals or mixing batch; and by all means, wash your hands after handling chemicals or mixing batch, whether they seem to need it or not!

When the studio movement began, most craftsmen were not mixing batch, but were remelting cullet or marbles. They were unfamiliar with the chemical requirements of glass formulation, and they wanted glass which would melt quickly and which was reliable. Now, they are endeavoring to formulate glass batches, some of them without an adequate knowledge of glass chemistry. This is a case where technical knowledge is of the utmost importance. Some of the chemicals which they are using can be very dangerous to them if they are unaware of their potential for toxicity. One of the most common dangers, and one which is least likely to be taken into account, is batch dust. A glass batch is a dry mixture into which toxic elements may have been introduced. Therefore, the batch should be put into the furnace very carefully, not dumped in abruptly. And, in this case, the ventilating system should be operating efficiently to take out all of the dust and toxic elements which escape.

While many chemicals are toxic to the skin upon contact and are therefore dangerous to handle, some present other hazards and should be stored in isolation. For example, cyanide compounds and solutions give rise to special hazards in the presence of acids. Therefore, all cyanide salts should be stored in locked rooms or closets away from the possibility of contact with acids.

The use of chemicals to fume a piece of hot glass to produce iridescence should be done with extreme caution. Actually, some of the older formulas for iridescence are almost the same as those for making gunpowder! These fumes should be applied in the area close to the ventilating fan so that the excess fumes will be carried away from the craftsman and out of the building.

In acid cut-back, the use of hydrofluoric acid is common; and hydrofluoric acid is extremely dangerous to handle without proper equipment and protection. Electroplating, as well as acid cut-back, is so specialized that extra precautions should be taken regarding both the chemicals used in the process and the protection of the body during the process. Protective covering over the clothing and face should be worn at all times for both of these. There are coveralls, masks, and gloves designed especially for this purpose.

There are also instructions and warnings concerning the handling, storing, and use of the chemicals involved in these two treatments of glass. (See References at the end of this Chapter.)

There is no intent here to cover the possible mixtures of chemicals which will cause explosions or fire. Therefore, if you are not familiar with chemistry, don't try to mix chemicals until you have taken the time to learn about their potential hazards. This is not something which can be mastered quickly. It requires the knowledge of a competent chemist. As an example, a fining agent for glass is recommended by Dr. R. Charan in his book *Handbook of Glass Technology*, page 45: "Ammonium nitrate: NH_4NO_3 — It gasifies entirely and it is available in a very pure state and thus it is free from any harmful residues. It is wrapped in a piece of wet paper and is thrust deep into the glass by means of a fork." Since this book was written, there have been some disastrous explosions caused by ammonium nitrate — a whole ship was blown up. It is even used as an explosive. It is cited as a disaster hazard in *Dangerous Properties of Industrial Materials*, page 432: "Ammonium nitrate: Disaster hazard; dangerous, heat and confinement may explode it. When heated to decomposition, it emits highly toxic fumes of oxides of nitrogen; can react vigorously with reducing materials." There is no substitute for a knowledge of chemistry when you are mixing all of the possible chemicals that can be used to formulate glass.

There are chemical hazards which exist without the mixing of chemicals. An example of this is the excessive use of salt cake without the proper amount of reducing agents, thus creating pools of molten sodium sulphate (called "salt-water") on the surface of the molten glass in the furnace. This salt-water in contact with plain water creates violent explosions. In the event that it leaks through the furnace wall, it will even cut steel bars in two.

References

A good source for ordering safety and protective equipment is: *M S A Catalog of Industrial Safety Equipment*, Mine Safety Appliance Company, Pittsburgh, PA.

Reliable references on chemical dangers are:

Graham, Kenneth A. (editor). *Electroplating Engineering*, chapter 12. Van Nostrand Reinhold Company; New York, NY.

Steere, Norman V. (editor). *Handbook of Laboratory Safety*. The Chemical Rubber Company; 18901 Cranwood Parkway, Cleveland, OH 44128.

Sax, Irving N. *Dangerous Properties of Industrial Materials*, 2nd ed. Reinhold Publishing Corporation; New York, NY.

The cautions and advice in this article are not intended to discourage the craftsman from working with hot glass, but to protect his safety so that he will be around to enjoy it!

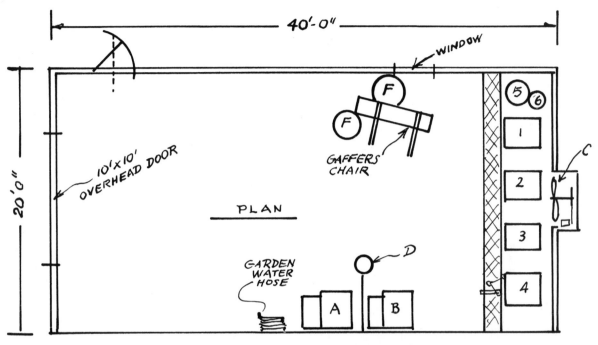

40'-0"

20'0"

WINDOW

10'X10' OVERHEAD DOOR

F

F

GAFFERS' CHAIR

PLAN

GARDEN WATER HOSE

D

A   B

5 6

1

2

3

4

C

A - B - ANNEALING OVENS
1, 2, 3, 4, - FURNACES
5, 6, - SMALL POT FURNACES
C - EXHAUST FAN 36" 1/3 HP 10,200 CFM
   (W.W. GRAINGER INC. STOCK NO 2-C204)

D - PULL CHAIN SHOWER HEAD
E - INSULATION (REMOVED DURING
   WINTER MONTHS) FOR FURNACE HOOD
F - WATER TUBS FOR WOOD BLOCKS
G - MAKE UP AIR OPEN IN WINTER MONTHS

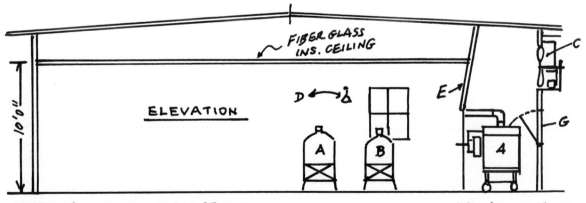

FIBER GLASS INS. CEILING

10'0"

ELEVATION

D

A   B

E

C

4

G

WORKING AREA FOR GLASS STUDIO

D. LABINO - 10-5-73

THE GLASS FURNACE: AN ALTERNATIVE METHOD

by Lynn Mucken

"Glassblowin' to me, it is no secret to it. And why people hold it, I can't understand. If you know somethin' about glass that can help me, why not tell me, and then we'll go out and get it mastered and make the best of it . . .

. . . what I know about glass I care to tell anybody. If it will help them out, that's good, and maybe they can work it like I do or maybe they can do it some other way." (Everett, Shorty, Finley, A Blenko Gaffer, "Glass Art Magazine," October, 1973)

When Anthony Parker and Mike Nicholas began making plans for a new glass furnace at Portland State University, they really wanted to plan something new. Tony and Mike, Ray Grimm's graduate students at PSU, were looking for an alternative to the brick furnace made popular in the 1950s by Harvey Littleton and Dominick Labino. Funds were not provided by Portland State to build a furnace in the Littleton-Labino method. The facilities and utilities are provided by the school, but studio equipment is built as class instruction.

Extensive planning went into the project. Both Nicholas and Parker have degrees in graphic design and both are working toward their Masters' in Ceramics at Portland State, Mike working in clay and Tony in glass. Their talent and knowledge blended well. Nicholas, who had built a glass furnace before, approached construction from a potter's side. Parker provided the input from the glassblower's viewpoint. Both ceramists emphasized the importance of planning the project carefully. Although actual construction was trial and error, and minor changes were made during the building, the design and construction plans were carefully worked out beforehand.

First came the crucible. Any potter capable of building a large pot could handle this part of the project. Basically the formula, developed by glass people Dan Schwoerer and Ray Ahlgren and used extensively in Oregon, breaks down to a combination of 50% alumina, 15% kaolin, 10% ball clay, 20% grog, and 5% talc; materials with the least iron content. Approximately 200 pounds of wet clay were used for the crucible, which, because of its size, was coil-thrown on a wheel, adding rings of clay one at a time.

Prior planning was especially important in constructing the dome, which was built in the same manner as the crucible. Parker, seeking a cold-faced furnace with a hotspot on the glass, says the height of the dome is roughly double the depth of the crucible. The width of the dome should be constructed as close as possible for the dome to form a parabolic arc. The closer to a true parabolic, the more efficient the furnace. An additional 200 pounds of clay was needed for the dome.

The burner port was thrown to the diameter of a Dudley Giberson style burner. The wet port could be a quarter of an inch larger than the burner, but the clay body they used showed no sign of shrinkage from wet to bisque fire.

A couple of hints in the clay construction: Parker and Nicholas say build it fast and dry it slowly for seven to ten days. Before drying, however, cut the door, flue, and burner port holes. The door hole should be 9'' wide and 11'' high in an oval shape. The crucible should be whole from the bisque fire, but the dome can be cracked or even broken after bisque firing. AP Green #36 refractory cement makes an excellent mortar.

Expansion cracks may appear in the dome and crucible. Don't worry about the cracks. There is no difference between them and the seams of a brick tank.

The location of the flue and burner port holes and their relation to the door are essential to efficient firing operation. The flue opening is placed to the rear of the tank, behind and under the burner port and 3'' above the water line. The burner port enters from above and behind the door. The flame path crosses the door and should hit the dome above the glass line, with the door closed. It is then sucked around the dome to the flue. The flame path crossing directly behind the throat eliminates cold air from the door. Radiant heat from the dome, rather than a hotspot on the glass, melts the glass.

After the clay was completely dry, it was given a high bisque firing up to c/1. This clay body should be fired slowly because of the wall thickness. Nicholas and Parker then made a floor of two layers of brick. The first layer (farthest from the crucible) was of soft insulation brick and the second of regular, hard firebrick. The crucible was set on these bricks and the dome joined to the crucible by refractory cement.

Next a form was built which provided approximately 3'' of space all the way around the dome and crucible. Into this form, AP Green Mizzou was poured. About 400 pounds of Mizzou at $20 per hundred pound bag made this refractory material the single most expensive item in the furnace construction. A brick throat for the door and a Mizzou flue chamber to the brick chimney were attached with refractory mortar. After the Mizzou had dried and the form had been removed, Parker and Nicholas added another layer of insulation in the form of 1'' thick pieces of soft insulation brick attached to the Mizzou by refractory cement. An angle-iron frame was built over this layer of bricks, as a framework for the final insulation layer and as something from which to hang the door. The final insulation layer was 5'' thick, made up of five parts perlite (vermiculite would do) to one part aluminate cement. The furnace door was made of Cast-O-Lite 3000 (another AP Green product) and hinged off the angle iron.

For the best results from these multi-castings, force-drying should not begin for three days. Nicholas and Parker brought their furnace up to 150°F for two days to sweat out moisture in the soft brick. Then they fired it slowly, like a kiln, to c/13 before putting glass in it.

After one school year, this new furnace used the same amount of natural gas as the previous tank, but yielded three times as much glass. During that year it melted batched soda-lime crystal, fluorine and phosphate opals, and fluxed cullet. The furnace shows little wear. Parker and Nicholas see no reason why it won't be used next year.

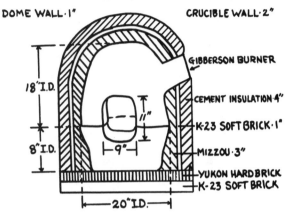

Materials Used and Cost (based on Portland, OR, prices)

400 lbs AP Green Mizzou	$80.00
25 lbs aluminate cement	4.00
1½ bags perlite	4.50
3 Yukon splits	1.62
20 Yukon hard brick	10.80
20 K-23 soft brick	14.00
1 Box k-23 splits (1″ thick)	21.00
20 sq′, 6″ reinforcing wire, 20′ angle iron	5.00
400 lbs wet clay body	67.00
Dudley Giberson burner	40.00
15 lb can #36 AP Green refractory cement	5.30

If you need further information, write:
AP Green Refractory Products
Mexico, MO 65265

Dudley Giberson
P.O. Box 202
Warner, NH 03278

Anthony Parker
Art Department
Portland State University
Portland, OR 97201

PART EIGHT
COLOR PLATES

FIGURE OF A HIPPOPOTAMUS
from the Metropolitan Museum of Art, New York, New York

by Fong Chow, Assistant Curator

One of the most admired ceramic sculptures in the Museum's collection is the charming hippopotamus, widely published and once the subject of a delightful story in the English magazine *Punch*, and affectionately known as "William." The piece shows not only keen observation of nature but its successful translation in terms of ceramics by an unknown ancient potter of great imagination and poetical disposition. The turquoise blue figure, decorated on the head and body with buds, flowers, and pads of lotuses drawn in black outline ingeniously suggesting the aquatic habitat of the imperturbable beast, is a remarkable example of early blue Egyptian faience.

Egyptian faience (the term "faience" is a misnomer since the name was derived from the lead- and tin-glazed earthenware made at Faenza in northern Italy during the Renaissance) refers to a type of glazed ware made from a body material composed mainly of gritty quartz held together with a binding material. The glaze is a potash or soda lime silicate similar to glass, either mixed with the body or applied onto the surface of the piece.

The glaze ingredients are mixed in soluble form with the porous body material, and during the drying process the glaze-forming substances migrate to the surface through capillary action and form a glaze coating after firing. In other words, the ware is self-glazing and needs to be fired only once. This type of self-glazing ware represents one of the earliest glazed ceramic materials in the world. The attractive brilliant turquoise blue color of the glaze results from copper oxide.

Detailed discussions and basic formulas for modern rendition of blue Egyptian faience can be found in Charles F. Binns, Myrtle Klem, and Hazel Mott, "An Experiment in Egyptian Blue Glaze," *Journal of the American Ceramic Society 15* (1932), pp. 271 to 272; Daniel Rhodes, *Clay and Glazes for the Potter,* Philadelphia: Chilton, 1957, pp. 190 to 191; Joseph Veach Noble, "The Technique of Egyptian Faience," *American Journal of Archaeology 73* (Oct. 1969), pp. 435 to 439.

Egyptian
XII Dynasty, ca. 1900 B.C.
Height: 11.43cm.
Acc. No. 17.9.1

225

MOCHICA PORTRAIT HEAD FROM ANCIENT PERU
from the Dallas Museum of Fine Arts, Dallas, Texas

by John Lunsford, Curator

Among the varied ceramic-producing traditions of ancient Peru, that of the Mochica is notable for the variety of subject matter expressed in effigy vessels, of which the portrait heads are an important class. The north coastal Mochica culture was already several centuries old when the majority of these head effigies were produced. Although their exact use is uncertain, it is probable that they represented leaders and other important persons whose effigies could by this means be distributed to followers as marks of favor or perhaps to show clan connection or political allegiance. In some instances a number of similar vessels survive, either made from the same mold, or made in different sizes of the same individual. There are, for instance, two identical smaller vessels in the Rafael Larco Herrera Museum in Lima, Peru, which represent the same individual.

Most examples of Mochica ceramics which survive come from burials, which indicates the ritually related nature of at least a certain number of these vessels. There are indications, in fact, that the stirrup-spout shape may have been reserved primarily for ceremonial use. While this shape occurs sporadically in other parts of the world, it had its most numerous and longest use in ancient Peru, where from at least as early as 1200 B.C. onward it was the prevalent ceramic form in the north coastal valleys, where it continued in use until the mid-16th century A.D.

By the time this vessel was made, Mochica potters were using mass-production methods for most of their vessels. Ceramic master molds were made, from which replicas could be produced by pressing the evenly textured, sand-tempered reddish brown clay into the front, patterned half. When this had hardened enough for removal, it was combined with a separately molded and usually far simpler back half, and the whole was finished off by hand, details being sharpened and sometimes varying ear or headdress ornaments being added to the same basic mold. When the vessel was leatherhard, the separately produced stirrup-spout was added. The vessel was then slipped, normally with reddish brown and cream slips, occasionally with a third color (brown or orange red). Here again variety might be introduced through the application of different patterns of facial paint to various examples from the same mold. The vessel was finally burnished. As far as is known, firing of the thin-walled, evenly potted vessels was done by the simplest methods, very much like those used in the American Southwest today, to produce an evenly fired, oxidized ware. A post-firing black pigment was also used at times.

While there is no certain evidence in the form of contemporary representations showing potters at work, it is the feeling of many specialists in Peruvian studies that the potters were probably male craft specialists, just as it is even more certain that women were the specialized producers of textiles. For several centuries these specialists produced works in a style unusually naturalistic for the New World and expressive of the vigor and purpose of the culture whose leaders, activities, and beliefs these ceramic sculptures have preserved until the present.

Peru Mochica
ca. 200-500 A.D.
Acc. No. W113
Height: 33.3 cm.
Width: 18.5 cm.
Nora and John Wise Collection, loan.

YUEH "DRAGON" BOWL

from the Metropolitan Museum of Art, New York, New York

by Fong Chow, Assistant Curator

This magnificent bowl is a splendid example of Yüeh ware, a type of gray-bodied, densely fired stoneware with a grayish green feldspathic glaze derived from iron oxide fired in a reducing atmosphere. The ware, named after its principal place of manufacture, Yüeh Chou, the ancient name for present-day Shao-hsing in Chekiang province, represents the culmination of a long and fascinating tradition of celadon or green-glazed stoneware, which began at least as early as the 16th century B.C. By the 10th century A.D. Yüeh reached the peak of excellence and was reserved for the exclusive use of the Princes of Wu-Yüeh, who sent large quantities of the ware to the Imperial court. After the 10th century, Yüeh was supplanted by Lung-ch'uan celadon, with its thicker glaze, more attractive color, and more jadelike quality.

The beautifully potted, coupe-shaped bowl, with a graceful, uninterrupted profile, was thrown on a potter's wheel. A minimum amount of trimming produced a slightly hollowed foot rim. The outside of the bowl has been left unadorned.

The inside, on the other hand, is deeply carved and delicately incised, probably with a simple bamboo knife and comb. Two spirited dragons pursue each other around the inner rim, while a third one emerges from the surging waves near the center. A limpid grayish green glaze covers the entire piece, accumulating in the carved and incised designs, creating the illusion of these marvelous supernatural creatures actually sailing over the waves. It is a masterpiece of the potter's art.

Chinese
10th century A.D.
Diameter: 27.18cm.
Acc. No. 18.56.36

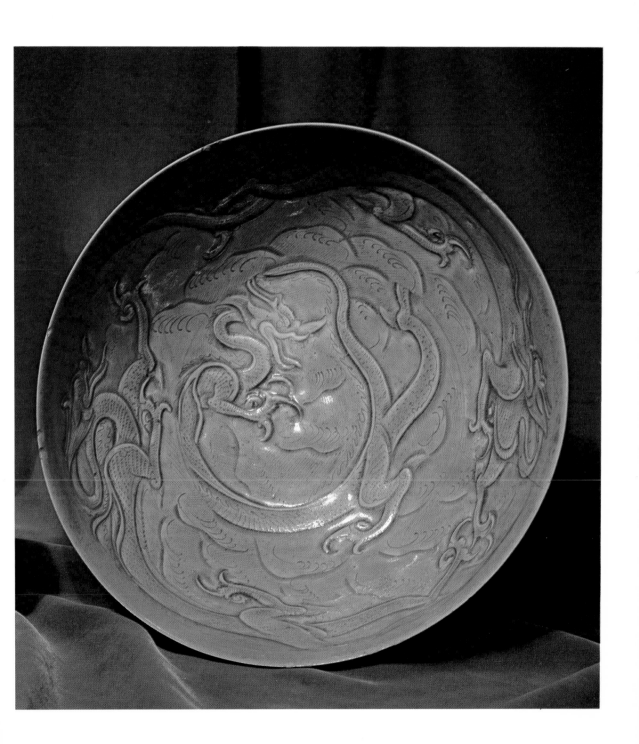

WATER JAR FROM SAN ILDEFONSO, PUEBLO, NEW MEXICO
from the Denver Art Museum, Denver, Colorado

by Richard Conn, Curator

Today, San Ildefonso is best known for its black-on-black pottery made famous by Marie and Julian Martinez. The village has, however, always made a variety of ware.

This piece was made in about 1909 by Tonita Roybal, and was typical of the pottery of that day. The pot has been covered with a brownish red slip, and overpainted with a black slip. The curvilinear black designs are often seen in San Ildefonso painted ware. Like all Pueblo Indian pottery, it was not glazed but well polished before firing.

The shape—a globular body surmounted by the conical neck—has been a standard Pueblo form since at least the 17th century. In function, the constricted neck helps safeguard the contents of the jar, while the body mass augments the quantity of water or dried food it can hold. When such jars are used for water a fine film of moisture soon appears over the exterior surface. The slow evaporation of this moisture helps keep the stored water cooler.

San Ildefonso Pueblo, New Mexico
ca. 1909
Catalog No. XI-116

SOUTHWESTERN PUEBLO INDIAN DOUGH BOWL
from the Museum of New Mexico, Santa Fe, New Mexico

by Betty T. Toulouse, Curator of Anthropology Collection

This bowl was produced in the early years of the 20th century by an unknown New Mexico Indian woman who lived in the Pueblo of Santo Domingo, located 30 miles southwest of Santa Fe.

The bowl was formed by coiling rolls of light grayish red clay around and around, upward and outward, from a small, flat base. The clay was obtained from clay beds near the village, tempered with fine gray volcanic sand, and kneaded until ready for use.

The vessel was started in a moveable shallow pottery dish as a base. Although this base revolved as the coiling advanced, it was in no sense a "wheel."

The sides of the bowl were shaped and smoothed as work progressed with a small oval section of gourd rind, frequently dipped in water. The potter worked from the inside, steadying it from the outside with the left hand. After a short period of drying it was scraped and smoothed on the exterior with the same gourd rind.

After the bowl was dry it was slipped with light gray bentonite (also found near the village), prepared for use with the consistency of a thin fluid and applied in several coats. While the surface was still damp from the last application of slip, it was smoothed with a soft, dry cloth or polished with a small, fine-grained pebble of black quartz, jasper, or other siliceous stone.

The decoration was painted on, freehand, using a thin syrupy solution of boiled Rocky Mountain bee plant or *guaco (Peritoma serrulatum)*. This paint carbonized during the firing to become permanently integrated with the slip.

Primitive measures prevailed in the firing. A permanent kiln has never been used in the Southwest. The fuel, wood or animal dung, was piled around the vessel in a kilnlike structure, after the dry ground was thoroughly heated with a large wood fire. Additional fuel was added as the firing progressed. A maximum temperature of 700°C was reached, which took about an hour. The vessel was removed from the coals while still very hot, ashes were wiped off with a greasy cloth and the making of a bowl was completed. The slip had turned a creamy white, the *guaco* plant paint decoration was an intense black or very dark brown and the vessel was ready to use for the mixing of the next batch of bread dough.

Santo Domingo Pueblo, New Mexico
ca. 1900-1910
Height: 30.48cm.
Width: 55.88cm.

MAYA BOWL
from the Dumbarton Oaks Collections, Washington, D.C.
by Elizabeth P. Benson, Director

Like all Pre-Columbian pottery, this bowl was not made on a wheel but was formed from coils of clay. Two bowls were pressed together at the lip to form a double-walled vessel with a space between the walls at the bottom of the bowl; in this space there are rattles of stone or clay. Small holes in the bottom of the vessel allow the sound to be heard more clearly. The top border consists of a series of indentations, possibly made by a thumb. A band of glyphlike elements surrounds the next plane of the vase, and below are four widely spaced bosses. The base of the bowl consists of a double-swirl design, half of which is fluted and polished; the other half is carved and incised with glyphlike designs and contains the small sound-emitting perforations. The surface is highly polished, and there are traces of cinnabar, or mercuric oxide, on some of the incised areas.

The bowl was probably made around 600 to 700 A.D., a period which produced fine pottery of different styles and decorative techniques all over Mexico and Guatemala. The provenence of the bowl is a puzzle, for its style does not clearly indicate its origin. Half-and-half swirl designs appear on vases from Teotihuacan, near Mexico City in the central highlands, but this bowl form is not typical of Teotihuacan. Double-walled bowls were made in Veracruz, on the Gulf Coast of Mexico, and the glyph that is depicted around the top of this bowl also appears on sculpture in Veracruz. However, somewhat similar decorations have been found on pottery from the Maya highlands of Guatemala; the form and the ware of this bowl seem to be Maya; moreover, there are other instances of Maya bowls with their major decoration on the bottom; the bowl is called Maya, therefore, although it is not typical of the style.

It has been suggested that both the carved designs and the rattle sound are rain-associated. The bowl may have been used in rain-controlling ceremonies.

Mayan
ca. 600-700 A.D.
Height: 18.08cm.
Width: 12.19cm.

SLIPWARE CORONATION DISH

from the Nelson Gallery-Atkins Museum, Kansas City, Missouri

by Ross E. Taggart, Senior Curator

Made in Staffordshire, circa 1661, by William Taylor, this 16½''-diameter dish exhibits a buff clay body, decorated with cream-colored base slip and trailed designs in brown, orange, and cream-colored slip.

Slip decoration, a technique as old as creative man, enjoyed enormous popularity in Staffordshire, England, in the late 17th and early 18th centuries. All manner of objects were thus ornamented (a vast majority, simple kitchenware long since broken and discarded) but the commemorative dishes or chargers are of special interest. On them was lavished the potter's greatest skill in manipulating trailed, jeweled, and painted slip, and proudly and boldly did he sign them.

William Taylor (who also signed his dishes "Talor") has depicted on the dish illustrated here a current event of great significance— the Coronation of Charles II by the Archbishop of Canterbury in 1661. This event ended the religious oppression and austerity under the protectorate of Cromwell.

The dish itself is of the roughest kind of marl— thick and heavy. But the sprightliness of the design and the childlike innocence of the concept raise it to the level of a coveted work of the ancient English potter.

English
ca. 1661
Diameter: 41.9cm.

RAQQA BOWL

from the Metropolitan Museum of Art, New York, New York
Bequest of Horace Havemeyer, 1956,
the H.O. Havemeyer Collection

by Manuel Keene, Research Associate in Islamic Art

To a very marked degree, historic Islamic pottery served as yet another surface for the Islamic artist to cover with decoration (presumably the painters of pottery at least sometimes were not the potter himself). The decoration on Islamic pottery, like that on Islamic architecture and other types of "decorative arts," falls into four broad categories: epigraphic, geometric, floral (most usually "arabesque patterns"), and animal and human figural motifs. Among the most graceful and accomplished animal paintings on Islamic ceramics are those of Syria in the 12th and 13th centuries, beautifully exemplified by the present piece with its peafowl, which exhibit a marvelous combination of careful observation and free artistic stylization; and, typically for Islamic work, the decoration is masterfully fitted to the form and surface to which it is applied.

The glaze (like that of many of the other Persian and Syrian pieces which have alkaline glazes) has unfortunately deteriorated badly during its period of burial in the earth, interfering with the transparency of the glaze and obscuring some of the details of the painting. The black is applied as a stain to the white composite, largely manmade body. This "artificial paste" or, as it is sometimes called, "faience" body came into usage in the Islamic world in the late 11th or 12th century A.D., representing essentially a rediscovery, since it closely approximates in general nature the siliceous paste or faience bodies of the ancient world. The Islamic wares are never self-glazed but indeed were often doubly glazed for enhanced whiteness or brilliance of color.

The artificial body in large measure (but by no means entirely) supersedes natural clay in centuries subsequent to the making of this piece. This artificial body presumably must contain considerable amounts of clay, considering the fineness and control of the potting, particularly that of 12th- and 13th-century Iran. (See Hans E. Wulff, *The Traditional Crafts of Persia,* Cambridge, MA: MIT Press, 1966, p. 165, where the formula for modern "stone paste" pottery bodies is given as 70 to 80% white quartz or flint, 10 to 20% of a bentonite-type clay, and 10% frit of the same composition as that for the glaze.) The body is seldom fired to maturity, as kiln design in western Asia, like that of Europe, was not such to produce the required temperatures. As is well known, China's downdraft kiln was a secret which, unlike sericulture and paper/printing, did not reach areas to the west until comparatively recent times.

Syrian
Late 12th-early 13th century A.D.
Diameter: 28.57cm.
Acc. No. 56.185.6

STUDIO MANAGEMENT

by John Glick

In the beginning, while people are still in school or just starting to think about studio potting, they seem too often to arrive at the conclusion that studio potting is not possible. I think it's sad that many people cannot imagine inventiveness and personal integrity going hand in hand with productivity. There is an old, tired notion that full-time potters must, by the nature of things, deal with a lowest common denominator. Well, I just don't think this is so. The inventive personality can always find ways of making and selling his pots for a living, yet preserve his integrity in the process.

I strongly believe the craft community is weakened in direct proportion to the lack of specific information about what might be expected in the life of the practicing craftsman. I feel that it is up to those craftsmen already in the field to make their experiences available to those who need to know, before it is too late. All art students and apprentices are not destined to become full-time professionals. But how many potentially great craftsmen are we losing each year through nonfunctioning avenues of communication?

To this end I have assembled a few thoughts concerning work in the studio based on my own experiences and the observation of others in their studios.

Location

I look on location as the key to anyone's approach. It can be divided into three basic choices: the city, the rural area, and the mountain retreat.

In the city, one of the first problems to crop up is the zoning code. Before you go to City Hall, check with other craftsmen to find out what kind of problems they have dealt with. People at City Hall can react with indifference, confusion, or fear that you are going to disrupt something, which can harm you later on. I know many instances where craftsmen have gotten totally involved with leases and rentals before they checked on zoning, only to find out that they simply couldn't do what they wanted. So look first.

Another key factor would be whether you intend to sell on the premises. I have run into cases where a craftsman is allowed to work in a certain location as long as he does not intend to have a retail outlet. This may simply require a more modest emphasis on signs, advertisement and showroom windows.

Other considerations are: ease of communication between you and your customer, and delivery of raw materials from companies who service you with fuel, etc. Art galleries can also be very important for your development if you intend to rely on them as a major sales source. On the other hand, if you intend to sell in your own establishment, you become a source of potential competition to these same galleries.

A second basic approach to location might be the rural area or one of mixed environment on the fringe of the city. This combines peace of mind in isolation while still retaining an acceptable communication with the city.

Certainly travel for you and your customers will be in a reasonable range, and this would also hold true for delivery of materials. Zoning in these mixed areas is usually much freer. I still advise checking first and looking into the general descriptive title of home occupation or home industry, in effect in some rural areas. This usually would cover the kind of activity in which craftsmen are involved.

A third category might be a romantic kind of forest or mountain retreat, where you can hide from the world and do your thing. Obviously, the maximum amount of isolation and peace are available, but I would strongly advise against being lulled into thinking that this is a cure-all for the craftsmen's problems. First of all, raw materials and general services are going to be much more expensive; indeed all expenses will become compounded. If you have a family, schooling could be a problem. Most importantly, it will move you towards wholesaling and towards art fairs to sell your work. Now, this may be ideally suited for your personality but consider it realistically before you make a commitment to buy 500 acres in the lovely boondocks only to find you eventually can't afford it because you're selling your work at half-price and shipping it all away.

My own choice of location for a studio pottery in the Detroit area was highly affected by school experiences. I was a graduate of Wayne State University and later of Cranbrook Academy, and in both instances I'd had good sales response at student exhibitions. In 1962, right after completing a masters degree at Cranbrook, I was drafted and sent to West Germany. There I was exposed to German family potteries, particularly small ones run by the father and son, with the mother perhaps helping in the showroom. I was very much impressed with the continuity of this lifestyle, and the fact that all of the activity existed on one piece of property.

So when my wife and I returned to the Detroit area in 1964, I decided to rent for a short time, literally to try out the idea of a studio pottery. That year-and-a-half's experience was very promising. We had a good deal of sales response right in the studio showroom and it encouraged us to make our location permanent. We looked carefully and found a one-acre property in Farmington, a suburb of Detroit. On it was an old Michigan farmhouse with a 30x30 farm building, which we converted into a studio. The location's essential advantage was that it was only an hour's drive for approximately five million people in the greater metropolitan Detroit area. It is an area that has a great many schools, two or three specialized art schools, a number of universities, and a community which has been exposed to art for years and years.

In our Farmington location we had to apply to the zoning board. We obtained a variance which recognized us as a home occupation and allowed us to make pots on our property as long as selling was not a prominent feature, and as

long as we did not have a sign out saying, Pottery For Sale. We have since become very happy members of the community, and I feel we're looked on as an asset. We have a great deal of interchange with community groups such as Scouts and Brownies, and any interested visitor or group can make an arrangement with me to tour the studio.

Financing the Studio

The best possible advice is: don't start in debt. It's just not necessary to equip the studio with the best and most expensive equipment. In my situation I simply could not have afforded it, and I really didn't know how to appreciate it. The personal development of the artist and his understanding of tools and materials will go hand-in-hand with the eventual need for larger and more complex devices to help him.

The question, however, still comes up: how to finance a studio with no capital. In our situation it was possible for my wife, Ruby, to work for two or three years during the setup period, so that the income situation was not a frightening one. This is terribly important, because the kinds of work that you're going to do as a potter are researched and begun during those first few years. It's important to make sure that you don't start off with the notion that speed and quantity are the primary goals and that personal desires come second. I felt insulated against this simply because I did not fear for our weekly food money. Thus, an outside income could be of positive assistance in getting a firm foundation under your studio.

Grants are another source of finance worth investigating. While I was still a graduate student of Cranbrook, Tiffany grants were available for generalized purposes in the arts.

In 1961 I applied for a grant to be used in starting a studio, and received $1,000, which I set aside during my entire Army experience and used while setting up my first studio in 1964. Presently the Tiffany Foundation is awarding grants promoting apprenticeships, and in 1972 my apprentice Rostie Eisemont and I applied for and were given a $4,000 grant for a year. He received $3,000 and I $1,000. So, although they've changed the format, this is a worthwhile form of financial aid. The National Endowment is also available. And of course there are times when borrowing money from family, bank, or the government (small business loan) is the only way to get started. Whatever the loan involved, I recommend that it be very small. You eventually have to pay it back, and meanwhile the interest charge cuts away at the recovery period.

Another interesting approach exists at Penland School of Crafts, North Carolina. They invite four to six craftsmen to take up studio residence in a building set aside for that purpose, and to operate as if they were in their own studios, producing work, getting marketing experience, and really finding out what the pressures in studio life are, without full commitment of renting, owning a building, or assembling equipment. Peters Valley, New Jersey also has such a residency program. In these Artist-in-Residence programs, the craftsman is in a way isolated from some of the worst starting blunders, and the hope is he'll be able to learn and benefit from others' experiences on an intimate day-by-day basis. I think this is a good alternative to teaching. I hear a lot of graduate crafts students talking about how they'll teach for a while and use that money to set up a great studio. All too often they're lulled into remaining in teaching

243

because of its stable income. The pressures teaching brings to bear are not those of the studio. And this is sad because once one has lost that momentum towards one's own studio it's extremely difficult to get it back.

I think the key to success is to start small, with a very conservative amount of equipment, and let that equipment earn your way so that you are not overwhelmed with a beginning burden of debt.

Equipment

I'd like to point out that I do not have any particular mechanical ability, and therefore am not deeply into building equipment. For example, I did not build my wheels or clay mixing equipment. But I do build kilns and benches and make building improvements. If a person is going to build complex equipment he should do it with a great deal of care and with the best advice he can get, because maintenance of even the best commerically available equipment is a problem. I know several potters who admit to spending up to one-third of their time repairing breakdowns, or trying to improve things they've put together.

Time is what you have a lot of in the beginning, and one of

the most consuming problems in the studio is clay preparation. Yet I think you should start off with a very simple approach. And one of the best I can think of is with several old bathtubs set up on blocks, with plaster bats to dry out the clay that you mix in them. It's quite simple to put in a predetermined amount of water and sprinkle in the clay, feldspar, grog, or whatever layer by layer. After a day or two of slaking, use a plaster-mixing hoe with holes in it and simply mix that thick liquid up, ladling out onto plaster bats later. One way the bat system can be improved is to obtain soil-heating cables or elements (used in greenhouses to force plants in hotbeds) and cast these right into a large plaster bat. They are very low voltage and dry the bats quickly, eliminating the need for putting the bats near the kiln or outside in the sun. I know of one production studio that did this successfully for three years. When I used the bat method I only had small ones which had to be dried constantly. So I made two sets: one in use and one drying.

I oppose the system of buying ready-made clay. In your first year or two of studio work it represents a tremendous cash outlay. You're buying water, for one thing. Next, you're buying labor. It can be a tremendous drag if you're investing $200 or $300 in clay every so often, when for the same price you can get a backlog of raw materials that you yourself can mix. And all the time you're learning how to do without equipment. Furthermore, if you're in rented facilities and have to move, it's easier to transport a bathtub and bats than heavy clay-mixing equipment.

After about two years of mixing by hand in the bathtub system, we realized that it was time for a change. I ran across a typical piece of equipment potters use when they can get it: a used bread-dough mixer. Mine was one that could hold 250 to 300 pounds of wet clay. We mixed two to three batches a week and this seemed enough clay for that time. I had also acquired an apprentice, so we were using clay at a faster rate than I was during the first few years by myself. Other machines of this general type are the Bluebird, which is based on the dough-mixer concept and the Soldner mixer, a revolving-drum type. These batch mixing machines are relatively easy to load and unload, and give 200 to 300 pounds of clay per mix.

As our needs have increased in the studio, we have moved on to a pug mill. We acquired one from the Paoli Clay Company, owned by Dave Jacobs. Mixing clay is his primary business. He makes these machines on a one-at-a-time basis, and his product is very strong. It's essentially a pug mill and a mixer. Using dry raw materials and water it's possible to achieve a one-time-through mixture that is very close to being de-aired. It extrudes 800 to 900 pounds of clay an hour in a well-mixed consistency requiring very little wedging for use.

We lay bags of our two main clays up on the machine and cut open the ends, pulling out the clay with left and right hand. We have a barrel of premixed additives (grog, feldspar, flint, and ball clay, mixed in a barrel with a wooden baffle, and tumbled on the floor), and scoop this into the pug mill in direct proportion to the clay. Water is brought in through an overhead hose. With this pug mill we mix about 4,000 to 6,000 pounds of wet clay. This lasts us about two months, and is stored in plastic bags under work benches. I clean out the pug mill after each use so it doesn't rust.

We still use our dough mixer, though. Its primary function is in mixing occasional batches of porcelain and a specialized ovenware formula. I prefer to keep a single formula involved with the pug mill, and then use the dough mixer for the smaller test formulas. So we do have two ways of mixing clay now. I like the idea of having one piece of equipment to back up the other in case of mechanical failure.

Storing unfinished ware is one of the biggest problems potters encounter. My first approach to this was a dead-storage or built-in shelf concept. At that time I felt I had to have the kiln right in the middle of the studio, and it was sensible to cluster shelves around the kiln so that as pieces were finished they could be placed near it. But this is possible only when travel from wheel to kiln is a short distance. As my studio changed, and we moved the kiln some 60 feet away from the potter's wheel, it became necessary to acquire ware carts. I drew up an idea of what I wanted and had them fabricated by a steel outfit in Detroit. This was cheaper than if I had purchased them commerically. If you're good at welding, fine, weld them yourself. I recommend you use 5 or 6'' diameter medium hard-rubber casters—one set of swivel casters, and one set of fixed casters. Now I am able to judge the kiln capacity by the number of ware carts filled with biscuit ware. It is possible now to move a whole month's production from the throwing area to the kiln in less than five minutes, instead of thousands of trips with small quantities on a ware board.

The potter's wheel is obviously an important piece of equipment in the studio. I think that the potter's own personality is crucial to the choice of equipment here, as almost any potter's wheel can be used and enjoyed. I find when you come right down to it, most potters tend to like what they originally learned on. I have two Americanized versions of the Leach treadle wheel, built here in Michigan by Anthony McNeill. I do a great deal of throwing on them. My apprentice uses one, and I use the other. We like the control and intimacy these wheels provide. They are very quiet, which makes it possible to listen to music while you're working. I used a hydraulic wheel composed of an electric motor driving a World War II bomber turret component for six or seven years until it was irreparable. Later I acquired a Soldner belt-drive wheel. In both cases the power wheels were used to make smaller pots where speed could be an asset. I think, however, it's almost worthless to recommend specific wheels, because you have to try them and see how you relate in terms of size, noise, power, speed, and so on.

The kiln is the major factor in any studio. All the kilns that I've been involved with in my studio have ben fired with propane. My first kiln was built with bricks dug up from an old kiln site and pried out of the ground in midwinter with a crowbar. I took them back, dried them out, and scraped off the old mortar. With them we built a 60 cubic foot downdraft catenary kiln in 1964. There weren't any books on kiln building, so after talking to some engineers, we put forward our best thinking and built as it seemed logical. The kiln was fired with four medium-pressure L.B. White tar kettle burners, and c/10 was reached in about 24 hours, with a fuel cost of about $25. It was a very successful kiln, firing quite evenly. But after a year-and-a-half we left the rented building so we tore it down and salvaged the bricks for another kiln.

The next kiln developed out of the misguided notion that 60 cubic feet was too large for me. I built a 35 cubic foot hard firebrick catenary, thinking I could cycle the studio with shorter work periods. At the same time that we built this kiln I acquired an apprentice who suddenly contributed a great deal to the throwing output of the studio. It was soon apparent that the 35 cubic foot kiln was inadequate, as we were constantly two or three bisque fires and three or four high fires behind. It was not a wise choice to move down in size.

Consequently in 1967 I built a 60 cubic foot soft firebrick kiln, this time with a sprung arch. It had a crossdraft firing concept using four Denver Fire Clay block burners, and it fired to c/10 in 18 hours—more acceptable than the 24 hour hard firebrick cycle. The c/10 firing cost of this kiln was about $20. However, in about two years, increased productivity led to the conclusion that we needed a larger kiln.

In 1969 we added an extension to the studio in which to

house a larger kiln. We built a 100 cubic foot catenary kiln with soft brick. The interior is 7x7' and is 7' to the arch crown. It is fired with two Johnson Burner Co. blower-type burners equipped with pilot and safety shutoffs, and reaches c/10 in 28 to 32 hours, depending on the type and density of the load. With the safety equipment we can sleep during part of the firing cycle. The cost to c/10 is $30 to $35, and the kiln holds about 350 pots. It has had a kind of final influence on my work cycle, allowing a four to six week throwing period followed by bisque, glaze, and high fire. The yearly number of firings to glaze temperature has varied from 6 to 12.

In addition to the large kiln, in October 1972 we built a 30 cubic foot vapor kiln to use with bicarbonate of soda or soda ash, approximating salt firing but eliminating the chlorine problem. We are just beginning to become involved in its use. I have a top-loading 15 cubic foot soft brick kiln, with a cast solid Fiberfrax roof that can be lifted off. We use this kiln primarily for bisque firing when necessary or for medium temperature work which Ruby does. Finally, we have a 6 cubic foot top-loading electric kiln, also used for bisque firing when we need a small addition to complete a high fire.

When choosing a kiln, I suggest you keep in mind your particular approach in making pottery. Obviously if a person is doing very small constructions, it would be senseless to have a 20 cubic foot kiln, as it would take forever to fill it. But for someone using standard throwing and slab techni-

ques, working in fairly productive ways, an intelligent size for a kiln would be 40 to 50 cubic feet of interior space. (Be sure to equip the burners with some kind of safety system, so you can sleep in peace during night portions of a long firing cycle.) Then if your productivity goes beyond present capacities, you still have a chance to go to a larger kiln, or build another medium-sized kiln to switch off to. My feeling is that a kiln under 30 cubic feet is a bad move unless you're in the very beginning stages. Lastly, build kilns without mortar during the first few years so you can take them apart for rebuilding.

Studio Layout

The personality of the potter, ease of movement, and the resulting traffic pattern are key factors in thinking about studio configuration.

When I first started, I had a 30x33' building with a very low ceiling. The walls were six feet high, and at the peak there was nine feet. I had very little choice about where to put the kilns. They had to go in the center of the building, towards one end, underneath the highest section of the roof so that there would be a safe space between the hot kiln and the roof structure.

Our traffic pattern in the early few years of the studio was based on the location of that kiln and storage of ware around it, and all movements were based on the kiln's being right in the midst of studio activity. The building additions that we did later were designed to improve the space relationships in the studio: to increase the safety factor by eliminating that hot, smelly object from the middle of the studio, as well as eliminating some of the boondoggles of storage and raw material access.

What we have now is a main work area with 1,000 square feet for all the throwing, glazing, ware cart storage, clay storage, small woodworking shop, a small office space, plus the 350 square foot addition for the kiln building and pug mill room, located in a separate area through a door. It is adequate for one potter and one apprentice under most normal conditions. We have dual-use areas in the main working space. The throwing area is used for raw ware during that part of the cycle, and during the glazing cycle the same benches are used for holding glaze buckets which are stored away during the clay working cycle.

I think if I were to build from scratch and design a building for this specific purpose, I would start with raw material receiving and storage, make sure that I have access to a solid road so that I could back trucks to unload without having them sink into the mud, and have the storage area adjacent to the clay mixing area for minimum moving of heavy sacks of raw materials. And I would also try to store the mixed clay in that vicinity, then move it directly to the wheel area so that movement of wet clay to the wheel would be minimized. Then, considering access to the kiln area, I would locate the potter's wheels and other support facilities around these major primary functions and try to eliminate duplication of effort. I do not mine or gather my raw materials, so all my comments are based on a dependence upon commercially produced clay and glaze materials.

The primary consideration, I think, is to isolate the kiln

for reasons of noise (especially if you have blower burners) and for dangerous fumes that are emitted during firing. I prefer to have the kiln in a heated second room, so it can be easily loaded in wintertime without any discomfort, or without fear of slightly damp raw ware developing freezing cracks. I think the overall aspect of analyzing and organizing a studio is to see what your personal movements are by drawing a model floor plan on paper, and trying to make it easy to go where you need to be most often, locating the sink for example right next to the wheel and not 40 feet away. It's mostly learning to develop a sense of the grace of movement within those spaces you define for yourself, and to eliminate or change the things that get in your way. The goal should be to become completely unconscious of moving and working in your studio. Just learn to remove obstacles that aren't necessary so that you have peace of mind when you're working.

Work Cycle

The kiln size is one of the main points in evolving a work cycle. It's a fixed size and you can use it to determine the evolution of your work. In a sense, you design your time to yield enough ware for a bisque firing (assuming you're doing a two-fire system). I count the loaded ware carts for a bisque load. In my case it's five ware carts just stuffed full of pots—double and triple high, large things filled with smaller pots, and so on.

The question may come up, "Why do you need a specific approach to figuring out a work cycle?" Well, I feel it gives you a sense of freedom within some logical boundaries. It lets you predict with some accuracy a firing schedule. The

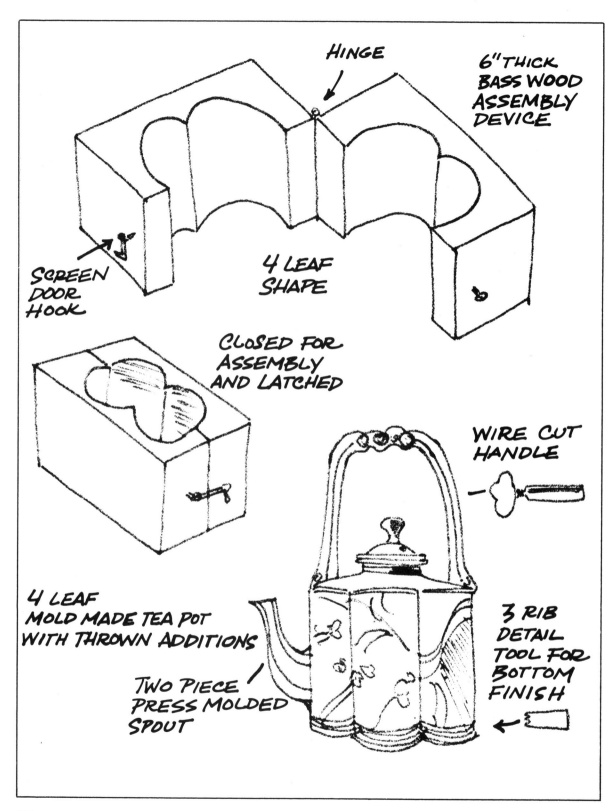

HINGE

6" THICK
BASS WOOD
ASSEMBLY
DEVICE

4 LEAF
SHAPE

SCREEN
DOOR
HOOK

CLOSED FOR
ASSEMBLY
AND LATCHED

WIRE CUT
HANDLE

4 LEAF
MOLD MADE TEA POT
WITH THROWN ADDITIONS

TWO PIECE
PRESS MOLDED
SPOUT

3 RIB
DETAIL
TOOL FOR
BOTTOM
FINISH

times of the month that you'll be able to fire helps you antici-
pate scheduling problems, an exhibition or a sale that may
be coming up, for example. It makes life a little more predictable if you know how long it will take to produce a kiln
load. Interestingly, knowing these factors, I often ignore
them while caught up in the excitement of the flow of fresh
ideas. In the long run predictability tends to take a back seat
to evolution and I try not to box myself into a tight, repetitive schedule.

My approach is to list all the things that I want to make
during a given time period. For me, it turns out to be approximately three or four weeks of throwing and handcon-
struction for a bisque firing. Here's a list of objects that
might be considered in one cycle: Bowls, 40; plates, 60
(thrown type); plates, 18 (slab type); jars with lids, 36;
pitchers, 24; kitchen shakers, 30; planters, 18; teapots, 12;
casseroles, 18; winebottles, 24; hypothetical Jones dinner
set, 12 place settings, with four parts in each setting; miscellaneous slab pots, 50 to 60. This would be looked on as a
general goal for that work cycle, but all the quantities will
vary when the actual work is begun. There's no need to be
exact. It's just a rough estimate. In the end this will usually

yield between 400 and 500 pieces of work, depending on the
comfort and speed of the cycle.

Now, on Day One of a work cycle, assuming a fresh start
with an empty studio, I extract a portion of several of those
listed areas in which to start throwing. For example, small
two pound plates, 18; dinnerware plates for the Jones set,
16; allow some extras for kiln failures. Then for a change of
pace, six teapot bodies and the related parts, and finally, 12
medium planters. This is generally what would be done in
one day and covered lightly overnight with plastic to partially
dry.

I use the highest energy time (for me that's early morning
to midday) for throwing, so consequently do the Jones dinner set salad plates, 16. Now for a change of pace: miscellaneous bowls thrown off-the-hump, 20. Then I trim all the
plates from the previous day, add elaborate feet to the
planter bodies now drying, and assemble the six teapots.
And so on for a six-day week.

A day-to-day breakdown of my time might be this: I usually rise at 6:00 a.m. and come immediately to work for an
hour-and-a-half. At 7:30 I go in and wake the family, give my
two children breakfast, my wife coffee in bed, and then usu-

ally eat breakfast myself. I practice the guitar for half-an-hour, and then finally go back to work around 8:30, and work through until 12:30, when I take a midday break. I may practice guitar again after lunch and then return to work at 1:30. I work through without a break until 6 p.m., when we have family dinner. If I get a break in the afternoon, it may be for some miscellaneous activity: taking care of some special visitor, or even practicing the guitar again if I've missed one of my earlier sessions. After dinner, if necessary, I will return to work for one or two hours, though I'm not a night person. In this way three or four weeks progress.

One consideration: at times it is absolutely essential to shorten the work cycle because of some deadline or other. I then throw the largest and most complex things in the first few days of the cycle. These pots are allowed to dry slowly under plastic during the rest of the cycle. Then I go ahead with smaller and more easily dried things as work progresses. It is also possible to eliminate the slow-drying items and time-consuming things if they're not crucial: for example, teapots which for me take a great deal of time to construct and must be slow-dried to allow parts to accommodate each other. Concentrate on medium-to-large open forms, such as planters and large bowls which, of course, can be filled with smaller items in the kiln. These can be thrown rapidly and dried with some speed, and they fill the kiln rapidly.

All my dinnerware pieces have been worked out over three or four years. I have a large chart that details clay weights and wet dimensions for throwing, so that I know exactly how much clay to select for each size of bowl or plate or mug. This saves a lot of guesswork and refiguring each time I sit down to work. I just glance at it next to the wheel or next to the wedging board and proceed accordingly. I have all other general-purpose ware programmed, so if I want to make a four-quart casserole, regardless of shape, I select so many pounds of clay, and so on. Even though the shapes may vary a lot from month to month, I still know that a basic weight of clay as indicated on the chart will give me a desired volume.

It is important to stress how little time in actual hours is spent on the throwing portion of the work cycle. When I list all those pots I don't mean to imply that it takes three or four weeks of solid work to produce them. My days are broken up with unpredictable things: I'm called away from the studio for a little while, unexpected visitors come, family problems arise, I catch a cold—you name it. But somehow or other it all comes together in that length of time. I rarely can throw more than three or four hours in any 10 hour day. Trimming, decorating, and assembly of things are not what I consider in throwing time.

At the end of the clay-working period, when the last of the wares are dried, we wheel everything into the kiln room and prepare to load a bisque firing in the 100 cubic foot kiln. Every possible corner and crevice is jammed. Every big pot has two or three smaller ones in it, nested medium and then small. I use grog between the pots that are stacked together, and a little bit on the shelf to allow for small movement during bisque shrinkage.

We start a very slow overnight warmup period in the kiln so that even by morning, about eight hours later, we haven't gone beyond 212° F, or the boiling point of water, so we're not in danger of blowing up heavy pieces. During the actual firing day, I may be finishing more raw ware or mixing and preparing glazes that need replenishing, and converting a portion of the studio over to the glaze mode in anticipation of biscuit coming out.

After a day of cooling, we unload, work out what will go in the first high fire (of course it will be less than what was in the bisque), and store the remaining biscuit on several ware carts, covering them with plastic to keep away the dust. Then we proceed to wax the feet, the lips, and the lids. Then I immediately proceed to glaze the entire load over a four to five day period, without a break for any other kind of potting—just glazing, getting the rhythm of the forms and becoming excited all over again by the potentials of decorative techniques started on some pieces, and making glaze combinations enhance what I have done. We need about four ware carts very closely packed with glazed ware, plus three of four large and medium pots to fill out a glaze firing.

I have 26 glazes arranged in two rows, kind of an aisle, where for easy movement I just glide around and dip and pour. I have large catch-basins that I use if the glaze bucket itself isn't sufficient to catch overflow. (These are horse feeding troughs made of strong rubber, available at horse and riding equipment stores.) The glazes are eight basic formulas, most of which I have developed, in a variety of colors. I have two ash formulas with seven variations; four to six matt glazes based on two formulas; and about 12 or 14 celadon glazes from three formulas.

At the end of the glaze cycle, we move all the ware back into the kiln room on the ware carts. It takes us about six hours to place all glazed ware into the kiln. During the glaze session we have marked pots that have heat-senstive glazes with paper slips: blue, tan, and red for cool, medium, and hot zones. These are sticking out of pots, so we know where to place them. By the time you've glazed 300 to 350 pieces it's difficult to tell at a glance which glaze is which—especially when many pots have three to four glazes on them.

As soon as the kiln is loaded, we brick the door up and start the high fire. It's usually late in the afternoon by then. I give it a fairly slow start and then boost the temperature, until by late evening I'm at 1000° F. It's turned up once more before I go to bed. Then I get up several times during the night and boost it again, till by midmorning it's ready for body reduction at 1850° F.

Our overall cycle is 30 hours, depending on the density of the load. The kiln will be firing most of that second day on into the late evening. I never stray too far from the quite heavy reduction after 1850° F that seems to be required for my kiln to achieve a good, penetrating reduction. I like the effect I get, especially on glazes. We have one-and-a-half days of cooling for this kiln—roughly 30 to 36 hours. On Cooling Day I may be cleaning up the studio or storing glaze buckets and washing the place up, doing repairs, running errands, even relaxing a bit, believe it or not!

The next day is Unloading Day, the day to cheer or cry or a little of both. We sort the ware out, make notes on any

glaze tests, and comment on any new results in glaze combinations that my be useful in the future. We begin to move ware up to the showroom in wicker baskets, setting aside potential exhibit pieces that may have shown up in the general run (this may be as many as 40 or as few as one or two). The next day, after unloading, we finish dispersing pots and cleaning up the kiln room, organize things back into a semblance of order, and begin thinking out the next work cycle. By now we're well into the fifth week. Many ideas and fresh thoughts have occurred, and we are ready to start the entire process over again. However, I do often add anywhere from several days to a week to my schedule at this point for extracurricular activities: travel, home projects (constructing a

hot tub, tiling a fireplace), going to dog shows with the family, all fall within this realm.

Apprenticeships

One of the major facts of economic survival for a potter today is the need for some kind of studio help. The apprentice and the employee are two distinctly different types, each with a potential contribution to the studio. Any such person in a studio has a tremendous impact on the potter's approach in terms of time and peace of mind. In 13 years I've had eight people working with me or for me: three female and five male. All have fulfilled some quite different need at different stages of my own development in clay.

251

Jan Sadowski came as a high school student, very advanced in potting, with a lot of personal ambition. He worked with me after school and on weekends. My intent with Jan was to teach him studio throwing so that I could have a certain amount of production from his output, along the lines of the Leach pottery in England.

In two or three months he was able to reproduce my more simple shapes with excellent results, and I began to pay him for piecework. In addition to this he was a general studio helper in the kiln loading, clay mixing, and so on, that we did together. When he worked he was paid $1.50 an hour. This relationship progressed through his junior college for several years until his time was taken up elsewhere. By then he just worked weekends and vacations, and was extremely prolific, earning up to $40 on a weekend of throwing. He threw up to 15 pound shapes very well and started many forms that I would later uncover and coil and throw to extend the shapes.

In addition to these studio activities, he helped sell at art fairs and took part in all related craft activities. He also visited other studios to increase his total comprehension of the craft picture. One of the negative aspects of that relationship was that by having throwing as a dominant goal, his own personal growth was inhibited by the necessity to do my things, with almost no spare time for his own interests. He had an unusually long stay, and I think what held us together was mutual respect and a need being fulfilled at both ends.

After his stay here, I took almost a year's break without an apprentice and I learned some rather interesting things. One was that I could make the same amount of pottery myself. The choice of the ware size seemed to be upgraded; there weren't so many small objects. But my output that year was identical, so that the time I was spending with him on his work disappeared and I made more pots. During that year away from an apprenticeship, Ruby filled in wherever possible with the more tedious jobs, and this was a help, of course.

In 1972 a most unusal type of apprentice arrangement evolved. This was with Rostie Eisemont, a graphics designer from New York. He proposed to give up his job there and bring his family to Michigan and learn pottery for approximately a year. And we applied for, and won, a Tiffany grant. The grant specified that the $4,000 be divided: $1,000 to me and $3,000 to the apprentice. We determined that we would use this as a wage for him, to be paid monthly for living expenses.

This was a different approach. In many ways he was an independent potter learning here in my studio. He fired ware here, and although he was not tempted to establish a marketing procedure until towards the end, he was functioning in many ways as a potter would in his own studio. We mixed clay together, loaded kiln, and did general jobs that needed to be done. But he was in a unique position: rather than spending his time in labor for my needs, he spent most of it making his own pots. Of course, his work was constantly analyzed in joint critique sessions, and we did not keep all that he made.

I would like to emphasize some aspects of how I react with the apprentice in the studio. I never have believed in turning over all the traditional so-called dirty jobs to an apprentice. I prefer to be involved with clay mixing and kiln loading. I want to know what's going on, and in almost every case it's a mutual job. With Rostie there was a tremendous influence on my thinking due to a second productive personality in the shop. It's frankly quite difficult to balance and modify my approach to accommodate two people in a kind of competition for kiln and studio space. Having accepted, however, the basic premise of another person in the studio, there is the responsibility to give him the experience best capable of advancing his career.

Beth Campbell worked for me for over three years. She was not a potter. Her only involvement was constructing slab-built pieces. I did all her preliminary training, primarily teaching her to assemble various slab forms. She worked in her own home and I set up a small facility in her basement with workbenches. We prepared clay here in the studio, sliced it into required thicknesses, wrapped it in plastic and labeled each bundle as to which kind of form it would be used for. I drove these to her home, delivered the raw material and picked up finished pieces that had been done the previous week or 10 days.

She followed a kind of work guide I had prepared for each pot. It described which steps should be performed first, how dry to allow the clay to become, and so on. Then using metal templates as size and shape guides, she cut out the various parts required in groups: all the sides, bottoms, etc. Using the assembly techniques, plus some wooden framework and wooden profiles I had made, she bent and assembled the various parts coming up with the basic forms. She then wrapped them up and set them aside until I came to pick them up and bring more clay. Working this way on a piecework basis, she earned perhaps between $4 and $5 an hour. We went through this process about two times a month.

Using the resources of a second person extends the time in which I can successfully interact with a particular form. Even so, these become very limited editions. In most cases a maximum of maybe 100 to 150 over the course of two or three years, less if the form ceases to stimulate me.

I think the real importance of this relationship is its physical absence from my shop. These activities are out of sight, in another location. As designer I feel the responsibility to put a great deal of time into the preliminary designs, before I would ever dream of finalizing them for my helper. After Beth was done with the basic forms I spent considerable additional time on them, adding thrown parts, decorating, and so on. This was to insure the successful completion of the feeling I had started out with.

In a final view of apprentices as assistants, I think they can be a powerful help and influence. But I cannot deny the large impact they have both in terms of my time which they consume and in the emotional impact involved. Their problems become your problems, and this is a drain. But if you're willing to accept the benefits you should be willing to accept the disadvantages too.

I look on all this as a worthwhile aspect of my role as craftsman: occasionally to be the catalyst in some person's beginning, and to let them see in depth what's going on, act-

ing as a focal point for later growth on their own. I look on apprenticeships as a responsibility a craftsman has towards the larger craft world. These opportunities are generally not available in any school situation. I think all craftsmen in every field should seriously consider whether they could do this occasionally, perhaps not as a steady diet, but as the opportunity comes to do the job well. To experience the truth of the studio artist's situation, rather than going on hearsay and vague generalities that filter out of dry lectures

at school, is a living kind of learning.

Sales Concepts, the Craftsman's Relationship with the Public

The craftsman has to take the lead in directing his selling and distribution. Don't slavishly follow the dictates of the marketplace. One has to be sensitive to outside influences, but not strictly follow commercial pressures. Otherwise personality and inventiveness take a back seat. To get this creative freedom of movement, I feel one must use direct sales as a basic approach.

Our direct sales approach started in our first rented studio. We sent out announcement cards after we were properly set up, saying we were back from the Army and in business. Our showroom was in a separate room in the studio, and sales started off slowly after those cards were mailed. But they doubled monthly for six months before assuming a modest rate of climb.

People came and looked and bought and told their friends. It's an amazing process, and an excellent way to reach people. Having the showroom in the studio was a good education for me. The feedback—both negative and positive—was very instructive. At the same time I began to sell in several galleries in Detroit on a one-third commission consignment, and also became involved in local art fairs, building more business through contacts that eventually followed me back to the studio.

The common factor in most of these involvements was that I got full-dollar return on the sale, and this means greater flexibility. I had a chance to observe on a first-hand basis how my newer ideas were received. I developed the attitude that whatever I was going to do would be the freshest and most challenging and best I could offer.

I have learned it is not necessary to do pot-boilers or rent-paying pots, pieces with low sales resistance factors. Perhaps in the very beginning this might be feasible, but after that it becomes an excuse for not getting deeply involved. In the end people will respond to your best efforts far more consistently than to your quickie notions. Life is far too short to waste time on knock-out items.

One refinement of the direct-sales approach is the Sale with a capital S. We've had two: one just before leaving the rented studio as a prelude to plunging into the conversion of our newly acquired property in 1965; the second in 1969 to help finance the addition of the kiln room and large kiln. We feel, however, that it does little good to overdo these events, unless it's your only major sales event of the year. I feel people get a bit weary of a yearly Sale, and thus it loses its impact as an interesting phenomenon.

Our present showroom is located in a converted one-and-a-half story garage building near our farm house, about 80 feet from the studio. The bottom-floor is divided almost in half. The showroom area is 10x19', paneled in rough cedar, with a burnt red brick floor. It's large enough to hold 70 to 80 pots, and has a small seconds shelf in one corner. The room is separated from the other half of the bottom floor area, which is my wife's studio and a showrom backup supply storage facility. There is a wall running lengthwise with a door and sales window. All sales are carried on through that window. We're open Wednesday through Friday 1:00 to 5:00 p.m., Saturday 10 to 5. That's about 20 hours a week. Of course there is considerable pressure on Ruby to attend to showroom needs while making valiant attempts at holding together family and household, not to mention getting some of her own work done. These drains can be considerable and cannot be ignored in designing a personal sales approach.

I must mention that in addition to taking daily care of the

showroom, Ruby does all billing to customers who didn't pay on delivery or in the showroom. She types and prepares all orders to suppliers and she pays all bills, both business and family. On my end, I prepare a yearly master set of books for my accountant so that he's able to analyze our complete cash situation as far as income and outgo, and prepare our tax records. I also prepare a monthly income tally sheet from all sources of income we have. And I do all business and professional correspondence.

Another major source of selling is the art fair. There are many in the midwest, with a nucleus of good ones. Among those we've participated in, and think very highly of, are the Oldtown Art Fair in Chicago, the Milwaukee Lake Front Art Fair, and the Somerset Art Fair in Troy, Michigan, although we rarely attend more than one each year and some years none at all. I feel it's best to visit a number of them if you're considering entry into the circuit, and try to discover where critical selection of participants has given the look of quality to the event. Usually, open-juried 300 to 500 artist activities are a loss. There is too much clamor and confusion, and no visitor has a way of seeing the overall picture before commiting himself to a purchase.

I'd like to contrast all of this with the wholesale-selling approach. One aspect of wholesaling is the catalog. I must say I would enjoy having a catalog of my work. But has a way of freezing what you stand for in people's minds; in fact, it has a way of freezing what you do because you continue to get orders for work that was perhaps done two or five years before. None of us likes to spend more money, so the inclination is to use the same catalog for quite a period of time. The result can be a stifling of the creative urges, which are subjected to the pressure of following orders pouring in. I think being weighted down by the catalog has a downgrading effect on a creative person.

To get an idea of pricing when I first started producing enough to sell, I simply went to galleries whose taste in crafts I respected and tried to put myself in some perspective with their state of achievement, using these first notions as a rough price guide for my own work. Soon I was able to analyze my own situation: kiln space, ease of techniques, my own state of achievement, and so on. I went so far as to prepare a time-motion study, relating that to clay weight, material costs, and so on. I always came up with some very strange figures! Essentially I learned that many objects which are rapid in production time will pay for such things as teapots and more complex things. It turns out that if a variety of work is done there's no problem with having things even out in the end.

In analyzing my prices over the last six-year period, I've found these facts: in 1967 to '68 during the period with Jan (my throwing apprentice), our average per-piece sale for the year was about $7. Many small objects were being done, and showed his influence on general output. In the 1969 to '70 period, after he left, $11 was the average per-piece price, and in 1972 to '73 it rose to about $20, and in 1974 to '77, the figure is close to $30. Now, this shows that I'm making fewer small pieces as the time passes and more in the $25 to $50 range, or even higher. On most ware it's 25 to 30% higher now than it was partially to offset the inflationary rises in raw material and propane costs, and the result as well of a sense of increased awareness concerning the inherent worth of my own work. As this whole process took over 13 years to evolve, I strongly suspect it's not something you can easily manipulate, or even analyze, in the first years of your studio work. Over the years things become more fluid and you still find that the pot itself is the major reason for buying, not price.

I think it's a great advantage to have a well-designed series of business materials, whether it's a handsome business card only, or a whole package of related articles such as stationery, envelopes, business cards, informational brochures, and so on. The concept of excellent design should influence them all equally, as it does your pots. In our studio we presently use an informational brochure composed of a folding cover that holds up to 10 loose photoprints of pots of recent vintage. Inside is a brief philosophical comment and a statement that says, "this is not a catalog but a representation of what's being done." We have these in the showroom, supplementary to gift giving, and as general information for newcomers. The photos are replenished once a year, keeping the image fresh and up-to-date. Such graphics are not inexpensive, costing us up to 40 cents for each set. At art fairs we don't casually scatter them about, you may be sure! In short, when your work is not there to do a good communications job for you, well-designed business literature should be there instead.

Earnings and Philosophy

Income potentials of a studio pottery are quite flexible. I know of several potters with small potteries that have a yearly income of over $50,000. In each case, however, the net income may be quite variable due to the number of apprentices, location, overhead, and so on. In our location, with direct-sales approach, we find it possible to earn a net income roughly equal to the earnings of a senior faculty member in a university. This figure varies from year to year, but has been relatively stable over the last five years. We have all the usual financial responsibilities of other families, including Blue Cross, auto, home and business insurance, heavy local taxes, and so on. We do manage to save a reasonable amount each year for our future needs, and to help defray college expenses in the future for our children, Margaret and Ian.

What frightens me most of all about this whole subject of studio management is the complete lack of any accurate information on the part of those who should know about it before taking the plunge; that is, on the part of the student, apprentice, or would-be professional. The possibility of earning a reasonable living definitely does exist, without the usual accompanying overlay of commercialism so often thrown into discussions about working artists. It's really up to the individual to sort himself out in a way that deals with the hard facts of earning a living. And with the even harder realities of living with your ego and surviving as some kind of functional artist.

I am grateful each day to be working as a craftsman. Being in my studio and doing pottery has become an almost unconscious act, a natural function of the body and mind. Stopping during these moments to reflect on what I'm doing, I find the same feeling of excitement and sense of challenge in my work now that was present 10 years ago. I hope I may stay equal to this challenge.

Toshiko Takaezu glazing a pot.

STUDIO PRODUCTION: A CONVERSATION

Michael and Harriet Cohen

Harriet: Printing on pots is a very frustrating technique. Every other kiln we fire I say I'm going to give it up forever. Because if you get the slip just a little too thin or a little too thick or the pot is a little too hot you lose the clarity of the decoration. A little too cool and you don't have the right contrast. Technically it's very demanding. But Michael has always been a decorator and always used difficult decoration techniques. He had done a lot of work with complicated and repetitive wax-resist designs but due to the high failure rate he dropped it over the years. He had also done a lot of Japanese-type wax resist. But I nagged Michael out of doing brushwork because I felt that you were either as good as Hamada or forget it. And even if you were as good as Hamada it would still be derivative. I feel that brush work has to be absolutely smashing or it tends to be a cliché. In addition to all the decorative surface techniques Mike had tried, he had a number of plaster and wood stamps that he used to make impressed patterns, and now as I look back on them, I see that many of those designs are related to what he is doing now. Michael was a decorator in search of a technique.

Michael: I went to Toronto to be on a panel with John Glick, Cynthia Bringle, and Mark Peiser and we all brought along objects for a joint show. John had a repeated pattern on one part of a platter and I said, "John, that's fantastic, how do you do it?" It was what I was looking for. I could see the potential for overall patterns and when I got home I immediately started working on it, literally using the next six months experimenting with forms and slips.

Making the stamp is not terribly difficult. First you need polyurethane foam; you can get it as cushions in almost any discount house. The best way to cut it is with an X-acto knife or razor along a ruler; this allows you to cut very precise squares. I use a 3″ cube so that all the designs interconnect. I design a pattern on paper, measure it out very carefully, and transfer it to the foam. I've found that it's better to use a water-soluble marker to draw the pattern on the foam. The indelible-ink markers seem to deteriorate the foam, almost rot it away. Then, using a soldering iron with a pointed tip, I simply burn away the pattern I don't want. It's important to set up a fan to blow the smoke away from you: it is noxious and probably dangerous.

Another way is to make a wire design, heat it with a torch, and touch it to the foam. It's easier to make circles or loops with a heated wire. If I'm trying for clean, tight angles and edges, I'll heat an X-acto knife and cut with that.

I usually test the stamp on paper first to make sure it doesn't make marks I don't want. Then you're ready. I've always printed on top of the glaze. I'm sure you could print on raw work, bisque it, and then glaze it all over. I've limited myself to two glazes and two slips. I think you could go further by using a white slip under a clear glaze. I use either a celadon with a cobalt slip or a saturated iron red with a rutile slip. I find that it is best to decorate as soon as you can touch the glaze. You cannot glaze a whole group of pots and come back the next day to decorate them, because the glaze is too dry and the sponge sticks. Interestingly, Leach talks about this technique in *A Potter's Book.* He says that he has observed rubber stamps being used to imitate handwork or hand brushwork. The examples are terrible—it really doesn't look like handwork. But he sees nothing in the technique itself that couldn't be used in a very beautiful way. The important thing is to test everything. Take your own glazes and slips and combine them. See how they work.

Harriet: A dark slip will work on a light glaze and vice versa. I think there is also a possibility of glaze on glaze, which we have never done.

Michael: That's right. Or take a clear base glaze and print with copper reds. And porcelain—print anything on porcelain under a clear glaze. I think the contrast would be nice.

Harriet: When we started working together, I had a separate studio and intended to make my own forms, use my own glazes which I had tested and brought from Alfred, and fire my own kilns. But one of us was always saying, "can I get a pot into your kiln," and within six months we were using each other's glazes and firing together. We have, however, continued to work separately. Since I was good at casseroles, Michael eventually stopped making covered things except as a one-of-a-kind item. I was never tremendously interested in slab work, so Michael does all that.

Michael: There is always a cross-current of criticism. When you are alone you can experiment in private and fail in private. But when you bring it out into our studio, the other person has a right to express an opinion—tear it apart or praise it. Neither of us is the same after we've talked about it. So next time you try it with these criticisms in mind. When we have a new design or variation worked out, we just put a couple of them on the table and talk about whether they'll fit into the production for the season.

I really dig heavy praise, and when it doesn't come that's the depressing time. But then it makes me really look at what I'm doing. It goes the other way too. Harriet will be doing something that she really feels is a breakthrough and I can see her bombing. Then she will ask me and I have to lay it on her and she defends it and we argue and go back and forth.

Even though the creative process is independent, we do handle each other's pots. Harriet does all the waxing. During this time the apprentice and I will start glazing. He does all the cleaning and then arranges the pots on boards for me to decorate. Harriet will join in glazing when the waxing is

through, so that I am free just to do the printing. I print on both her work and mine.

Harriet: With printing we began to collaborate more closely than ever before. I was very impressed with the results Mike was getting with his new technique and decided to redesign my forms. The new forms were related to my old ones but simplified. Fingermarks were replaced by ribbing so that the surfaces could receive the printing. We also collaborate on the stamp designs themselves. Michael works up designs, and then I pick over them and together we decide which ones we should use.

Michael: I'm allowed to do anything I want for testing on hanging planters. When those come out of the kiln, we talk about them—getting rid of certain stamps; doing more of others and so on.

Harriet: Or reworking the design: "I like this one, but it could be a little stronger, more dynamic, or a little smaller or larger." I have the ability to come in objectively.

Michael: I'm involved in every step of the process and can't be objective about it. Harriet can, which is a good thing. So I'll dump the old stamp, make a fresh one, and start again. We keep refining. Several of them have worn out over five years, and I've redone them exactly.

Harriet: It's an on-going critical interaction which I feel is very fortunate. I think that is one of the things which has helped us grow over the years. It's much harder if you're alone and nobody's there to say, "That stinks" or, "Hey, that's great, do it again!"

Michael: Very often a partnership can be an ego conflict, but between us it is to each other's benefit that we get better. So I watch her plate rims and she watches the depth of my planters.

Harriet: The most interesting division is the firing. When

we were first married, we had terrible fights. He would come over and tell me what to do while I was firing and I would do the same with him. The pots out of each kiln, though, seemed to be about the same. So after a couple of years I decided the quarreling was ridiculous and gave up firing. Besides I hate getting up at six a.m.

We work according to our interests and aptitudes. I think Michael cared more about firing the kiln. If he had been bored with it we would have alternated. It's the same with stacking: I lay out the kiln as I know what we need to fire next.

Michael: I just stand waiting for my orders.

Harriet: I have a good memory of what was in the last kiln, what the stacking was, and whether this kiln is likely to be hot or cold in the same places. But then Michael is much better at getting the most on a shelf. Together we stack the kiln. And usually we unstack together too. I almost never mix clay. The apprentice and Michael do the wet mixing and the three of us pug it. It's physically impossible for me to lift a 100 pound bag of grog. It's pointless for us to do things that we can't do easily. I do all the bookkeeping, all the billing, and most of the correspondence.

Michael: The apprentice plays a crucial part in our production. We have an apprentice four days a week, nine to three, in exchange for use of the facilities, lessons, and a small honorarium. He wedges all the clay and weighs it out for throwing. That could take until lunch, because Harriet and I use about 300 to 500 pounds in a morning. In the afternoon the apprentice might trim hanging planters, or string them for me. When it comes to the heavy labor of mixing clay, we do it together. Harriet and I use about 15,000 pounds of wedged clay a year, and last year we fired 25 glaze kilns. We couldn't do it without the assistance of an apprentice.

Over the years I feel we have had unusually successful relationships with our apprentices. I think the number one reason is that we have never asked anyone to work for free. Number two, we have never had any apprentice live with us. I think it is just too great a burden on any relationship to

have someone stay with you in the studio all day and then get involved with your family problems too.

This is our third studio and the first one we built from scratch. It sits facing north in the middle of 10 acres of land. We have very fine working light and good privacy. The studio is invisible from the road and yet it is within five minutes ride from Amherst. Based on past experience, we figured out our space needs right down to the square foot and designed a flow of clay traffic that works pretty well. The studio is on one floor so that we can roll everything from one area to another as needed. Even our kiln is on a car: we are great believers in putting things on wheels.

First off, we have a large turn-around at the end of the driveway so that a big tractor trailer can back up to the clay storage shed. We stack the clay on pallets in sequence of use: alternating layers of ball and Goldart on one pallet, then grog, Redart, and talc on the other, so there's not much shifting once it's inside. The shed leads to the clay-mixing room. We can mix about 3,000 pounds in a day. The next day we pug it, bag it, and stack it for aging.

When we are ready to throw, the apprentice will wedge the clay and bring it to the wheels. When the large ware racks and two rolling carts are filled with greenware, we fire a bisque. After the bisque, the car of the kiln rolls out into the center of the room where pots are unloaded onto central worktables. We glaze and restack in the same area. Another reason we have a car kiln is the ease of stacking. The three of us can stack a glaze kiln and close it up in an hour-and-a-half. The finished ware is stacked on carts and rolled either into the shipping area or the showroom. The pots circulate easily and quickly through the whole process. Our aim is to eliminate redundant movement.

Here's a summary of my firing schedule. We have a 100 cubic foot catenary car kiln, fired with LP gas, with about 75 cubic feet of stacking space. We stack after lunch. At three p.m. I put on the pilots to warm the kiln up, and by six p.m. it is up to about 100 to 200° F. I then turn the front two burners on to 5 oz. A couple of hours later I turn on the rear two burners to 5 oz. (These are Hones "Buzzer" burners; very nice!) Three hours later (11 p.m.) the kiln is up to around 650° F and I turn all burners to 25 oz. By six o'clock the next morning the kiln is close to 1700° F. I then up the burners once more to 50 oz. Up to this point the atmosphere is completely clear—a wide open primary air and an open damper. At 1800° F I close the primary air control to three-quarters of a turn open, and push the damper in from 4'' to 3'' open. This produces back pressure at both portholes. There is a semiclear orangey flame coming from each porthole—but no smoke there or at the chimney—and I can see through the whole kiln. I leave it at that setting until c/8 starts falling. I now change the primary air setting from three-quarters to one-half of a turn open, and close the damper ever so slightly so that the back pressure is heavier and it is smoking a little bit. From the porthole I have a fairly yellow flame with a little bit of smoke on the end of it. The smoke is barely noticeable from the top of the chimney. When c/10 is about half down (around two o'clock), I shut off the burners. The kiln takes two days to cool. It uses on the average 100 gallons of liquid LP gas per glaze firing.

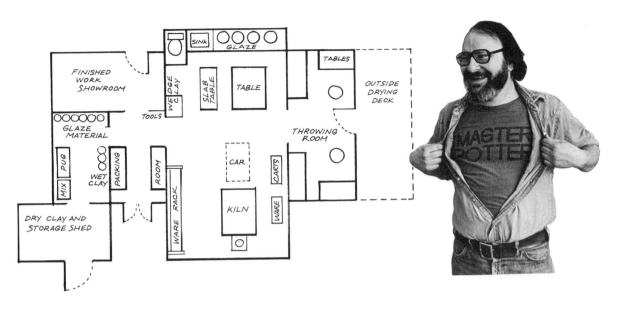

SLAB CASTING

by Ron Burke

I've been making my living as a studio potter for about 11 years now. For the past eight years I've worked a great deal with slabs of clay—I've rolled them, squeezed them, thrown them, and cast them. The method which works best for me is the cast slab. But since I began casting, I have found it a little difficult to come by information on it. When I was in graduate school in Cranbrook, and up until just last year in fact, casting in pottery was looked down upon in the art department. As a result nothing about it was ever taught or written. Recently, however, I have noticed it seems in vogue in a few of the college art departments. There is a great deal of experimenting going on among the students, and quite a few of the teaching potters are now working with it.

I learned about the procedure back in 1961. My family and I were in Penland, North Carolina, in the Resident Craftsman Program, when a small commercial pottery appeared on the market for sale in the Hudson Valley area of New York State. It came fully equipped with kilns, with about 2,000 molds, all kinds of clay-mixing equipment—blungers, tables, and racks. (Most of the equipment I have today came from this pottery.) When we bought this place we got not only the equipment and the building, but also their formulas for casting, moldmaking, and glazes—a couple of thousand oxidation glazes in the c/2 to 4 range. I decided to try casting their primary salable item—a porcelain tile with zero absorption (frostproof). I have continued pretty much their procedure: the porcelain body was poured into molds and then cut into various sizes. They even had cutters made up for handpressing special designs. The only problem was their casting formulas. They were extremely short, fast casting but short. There was no way you could do anything with the slab when it came from the mold other than to cut it into shapes.

It was at this time that I took on my first apprentice, and through his prodding and questioning I began to experiment with a more plastic body. I took my regular throwing body and added some deflocculant and water to it and poured it into one of the tile molds, and lo and behold, I got this fantastic slab out of it that did all kinds of things. From this point on I became less and less interested in throwing on the wheel and more and more interested in building with slabs of clay.

At the time my throwing body was basically this: Jordan, 50 parts; fireclay, 50 parts with a little grog. When I mixed it as a casting body, I took the grog out and had something like this: water, 180 lbs.; Darvan #7 (a deflocculant), 2400 grs.; Jordan, 150 lbs.; North American fireclay (an Ohio fireclay), 150 lbs.; and a clay from England, 50 lbs. It was a satisfactory casting body for a while. It had some shortcomings: it didn't flow properly and had the tendency to gel up when it sat. But otherwise it worked OK. I would like to say it is possible to mix any clays together, but I know there are

some clays that just won't cast. I don't know what it is in their makeup—probably a lot of soluble salts that tend to mess up either in the molds or in the mixing, or in the case of a high-sulphur clay like the Ohio clays, in the firing. Some times you also get bloating because of a high-sulphur content.

By trial and error my casting body has been refined to the following formula:

Water	140 lbs.
Darvan #7 (deflocculant)	1900 grs.
Victoria ball clay	125 lbs.
(Tennessee ball clay)	
Feldspar	16¼ lbs.
Jordan stoneware	50 lbs.
Cedar Heights bonding clay	50 lbs.
Kaiser fireclay	100 lbs.

I've used as many as 10 different production casting formulas and found it quite important in all of them to have a certain percentage of plastic clays. The ball clay keeps the works (the coarser clays, the fireclays, etc.) in solution, increases the fluidity for pouring the slip into the molds, and of course adds greatly to the plasticity of the slab. It has a high shrinkage rate, but I have always figured that the increased plasticity more than offsets this detriment. Though I use Victoria ball and Jordan stoneware, there are many other ball clays you can use—I just found that this combination produced a light-burning clay that I like for its color. The total shrinkage is about 12% —that is, measured from the slab, not from when it's poured into the mold. I happen to be using Cedar Heights bonding clay and Kaiser fireclay. In the past I have used with success the AP Green Missouri fireclay in place of Kaiser, and in fact, I've substituted the AP Green fireclay for both the Kaiser and Cedar Heights of this formula. I use about 5% feldspar. I was having some difficulty earlier in the year with the glaze shivering, but I found that the small addition of feldspar took care of that. I've also had problems with dunting, and the addition of feldspar has taken care of that too. Really you could use almost any feldspar; I'm using a c/6 feldspar because it's inexpensive.

The most critical part of the formula in any casting body is the ratio of water to deflocculant. I'm using 140 lbs. of water and 1900 grs. of Darvan (which is in liquid form) to about 340 lbs. of clay. Almost each time I mix up the slip, there are slight adjustments: sometimes it needs a little more water or the addition of another jigger full of Darvan to get it flowing properly. The batches don't deviate a great deal, but you do have to check it each time. I've started checking the specific gravity of each batch this past year, and that gives me at least a reference point to go by. The batch seems to work best when it measures 1700 on my scale. When we mix the clay in the blunger I usually like to keep it going for at least a couple of hours. My apprentice or I always check

two or three times make sure the clay is off the sides of the barrel and in solution. Letting the slip set overnight seems to improve the fluidity. In that period of sitting around, the particles just seem to soak in more water and become more thoroughly mixed. I think the clay body is really a matter of experimenting with the water/deflocculant ratio. From one of my basic formulas, measure out the amount of water and Darvan and then add the clay proportionally—watch how thick it is in the mix, how well it flows, try it out, and go on from there.

To mix a batch of clay, I use a 55 gallon drum with a removable top lid and a bottom bung. I attach a large metal spigot to the bottom bung. The bung is threaded, so it's just a matter of getting a spigot that has the same thread size. I put a little silicone rubber around the threads when I tighten it to prevent leaks. It is through this spigot that you tap off the casting slip. To mix the slip I have a professional-type blunger—½ hp motor with a gear box that turns about 420 rpm. It has a 1″ diameter stainless steel shaft with two large propellers attached to the end that extends to the bottom of the barrel. The blunger motor attaches to the drum by means of a large belt-in clamp. On a smaller scale I've used a large galvanized trash can with ½ hp motor (1700 rpm). On this one you could use a ⅝″ diameter shaft with two smaller propellers, and basically it will do the same thing. In fact, I find that the smaller blunger is better suited to reclaim scrap, because it turns at a higher rpm and does a better job keeping the large pieces of scrap in solution.

Each mold that we use is made up of two pieces—17x18x1½″. It takes about 40 lbs. of plaster for each one, 20 lbs. to a half. The halves are separated by various thicknesses of wood. We usually place 12 of these molds in a row and fasten them together with long furniture clamps. Then we pour the slip into the top of the molds and let them set for a certain length of time. When the molds are new, this will take, in the case of my thick slabs, about 3½ to 4½ hours. At the proper time we put each one down horizontally on the table, open it up, cut the slab out, wrap it under plastic, and put the mold back up at the other end of the table. When the whole group is completed, we simply clamp them up again and recast them. We can get anywhere from four to six castings from the molds before they have to be taken down, cleaned, and put on a rack to be dried out. You have to be very careful to fit the molds together tightly in order to prevent leaking.

I use pottery plaster for these molds rather than a super-fine casting plaster. I find that with pottery plaster the molds last a lot longer, and that they're far more uniform in their density and absorption. I'm very careful to do a thorough job in mixing the plaster—to have the water temperature the same for each mold and to weigh out the ingredients accurately. A few years back when I called the laboratories of United States Gypsum on Staten Island, they told me that for pottery molds my formula should read 13 lbs. of water to 19 lbs., 10 oz. of plaster, and that is the ratio I use. Sometimes there is a tendency in mixing plaster for molds to use a higher water-to-plaster ratio thinking it will be a softer, more absorbent mix. This doesn't work, though, because what happens is that the molds fall apart

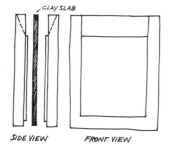

CLAY SLAB

SIDE VIEW   FRONT VIEW

much faster from the soluble salts, the deflocculant, the water, and the various clays.

In the past eight years I have been very, very timid in using what I now consider to be the full potential of this kind of slab. I don't know if it was the fact that I became accustomed to making the porcelain tile, but in the beginning I had a tendency to work very flat, almost like wood or metal. Then I made this one hanging planter that I call my sidewinding planter. It's made from a single slab of clay—quite simple—and I can make them very fast. Until this point I hadn't realized there was much more to this technique than I had let myself work with.

Going beyond this, I have also seriously considered casting some basic shapes, and then doing something to the form—distorting it or adding things to it to lend a little more individuality. I have held back from making a mold of an ob-

ject and casting a finished form from it, because each piece remains the same. That bothers me, but I really can't put my finger on why—it would just become pretty damn boring I think. On the other hand it could be very exciting to get a piece from the mold and work it with your hands: touch it, push it, add things to it, take things away. It could also be a fantastic production technique in which you get a group of basic forms immediately, and then go to work on them. It's clear that casting does have great potential.

I have noticed that most of the objects I make from slabs tend to be clean and crisp in design. I look upon this technique as a way of boiling the design down to its essence. I don't know if it's the uniformity of the slab, or the thickness, or the fine grain size, or what. But my slab pots differ in feeling from my wheel-thrown work, and I try to work from that difference in what I do.

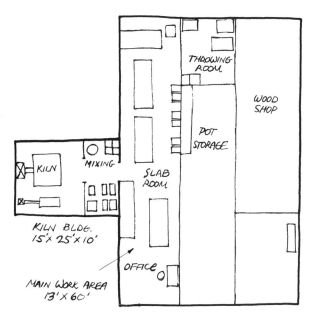

I think this method of making slabs cuts down significantly the time involved—enough in my case so that I can earn a living in a pottery that is devoted almost entirely to slabware. I am also, however, branching out into other time-saving methods of production. I have a woodworking studio next to the pottery where I turn templates, jugs, and various fixtures. As an example, I make a small square dish with two forms—one concave, the other convex. I place a slab of clay 6x6'' between two pieces of cloth, put it between these two forms, and hit the top form with a rubber mallet to squeeze the clay into shape. Then I simply add a foot afterwards. I trained for four years in the industrial arts—metal, wood, graphics, and electricity—before I became a potter, and now I find this training useful in the studio and wouldn't trade it for anything. In fact, it's an ambition of mine to someday work clay and wood together.

I think I'm at the point that these ideas are coming together for me. I can't really say where it's going but my work is in for a big change. I've noticed since we've moved to Maine that I'm much more aware of color. Color is very different up here, and the air much clearer. The view that I have from my studio is just fantastic. I look out and watch the colors throughout the day—especially at sunset, and sometimes even at sunrise. The reflections in our pond and the colors in our fields change from season to season. I see this influencing my work in both form and color. I've never really attempted to do a painterly kind of thing on my pottery, but I find myself doing landscapes on my square dishes—and seascapes and nightscapes.

As a potter I talk with my hands; crafts to me have always been a way to speak visually. I can only sense this new direction, but I'm looking forward to a possibility of saying new things.

268

SLABWARE

by Jeanne Giberson Judson

Making a container shape that is as strong and durable as thrown ware from a single slab of clay presents some interesting technical problems. To do so on a production scale demands a well thought out system and a lot of molds.

The mold itself imposes a very rigid and narrow framework and an efficient production system requires simplicity. The result for us has been very pleasing—the straightforward, unassuming slab pots have an honest character that our thrown ware rarely equals. We feel that this is due to the demands of the production process and the limitations of the materials far more than our own control over design. (Carl Judson)

Materials

Possibly the most important part of our clay body is the grog. AP Green grog-0-30 is a controlled-particle-size grog lacking in fine dust and particles larger than 30 mesh. I experience little warping and minimal loss in drying. The lack of large grog chunks allows for clean cuts when slabs are sliced.
Molding Clay Formula

AP Green grog-0-30	75#
Missouri fireclay	25#
Pueblo fireclay	100#
Sutter	25#
Kaolin	25#
Batch	250#

I use white slip made of 20% ball clay, 40% kaolin, 20% spar, and 20% silica to which is added 1½% each of cobalt carbonate, manganese, and iron oxide to obtain a blue slip. The clear glaze, used over pots which have been slipped and bisqued, is made of 35% spar, 15% lime, 15% fireplace ash, 25% silica, 10% ball clay and 2% bentonite. The refractory clay body used in making kiln furniture for slabware is made of half Pueblo fireclay and half grog-0-30.

Shapes

The most obvious shapes for pitcher molding (slump molding using slabs over bisqued clay molds) are oval and rectangular. Our objectives when deciding on actual shapes were threefold:

1. Advantage in firing: using a shape which would allow boxing or the use of panrings.
2. Corresponding shapes: resulting in nesting bowls, etc.
3. Lack of complication: shapes which were simple enough to facilitate rapid production and thus would allow a freshness of feeling.

Molds

My description of moldmaking would be rather long and, really, the process of making an original mold (negative)—then a plaster master mold (positive)—and from that a clayworking mold (negative) is not an unfamiliar one. For reference, I

would suggest *Pioneer Pottery* by Michael Cardew, pages 124 to 125. However, there are pointers which are sometimes overlooked in making the original mold:

1. I do not find it necessary to use the best clay available for making originals. Scrap clay works fine.
2. Do not overlook shrinkage—shrinkage of clay mold wet to biscuit and of pot from clay mold to fire. For our particular clay, I use 20% as a rule of thumb.
3. Use a plywood bat on which to pound out clay (for making original); outline shape on required thickness of clay and make a vertical cut. Remove the excess from the perimeter of the cut and place a second piece of plywood on top of the clay and flip the plywood/clay/plywood sandwich. This process gives accuracy to the bottom edge of the original.
4. Masonite works well for making the templates used to scrape away excess clay (Drawing #1).

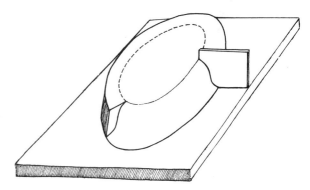

5. I keep all templates and patterns for shapes as these are valuable in case the master mold should break or, more importantly, for reference when I want to add another size with corresponding proportions.
6. Convex detail on the original cannot be corrected once cast in plaster whereas concave detail on the original can be scraped away from the plaster.
7. Solid thrown shapes can be used; however, it is important to have clear (smooth) and precisely thrown sides.

Plaster Master Moldmaking

1. I have never felt it necessary to use the best plaster as these molds get little use.
2. Take care to store the master molds where they won't get wet. This is far more important a factor in their life than the fineness of the plaster used.

Working Molds

1. Scrap clay can be used to make the working molds; in using scrap clays, however, I would suggest making at one time as many molds as you may need and firing these molds

together in the interest of avoiding shrinkage variations.
2. Make molds heavy enough to be sturdy and durable but not so heavy as to be impractical to use.
3. When throwing stems, I make certain to (a) give enough height so trimming tools can be used, (b) remember that too much height merely takes up valuable storage space, and (c) make stems broad enough to keep a mold steady.
4. Take care not to fire molds beyond a porous state.

Tools for Clay Preparation

1. Slats—½″x2″x2′—used when slicing a mound.
Slats—¾″x1″x3′—used when making slabs one at a time. Slats need to be smooth and free of ragged corners which would snag wire when making cuts.
2. Cotton cloth—approximately 3x4″—used only when making slabs one at a time.
3. Metal slats—two pieces of thin strap iron 2″x2′. One piece is used under each stack of slats when slicing a mound of clay. (It is virtually impossible to retrieve the bottom slice otherwise.)
4. Wire—thin piano wire with washers secured to each end. I use three different lengths: one about 12″ long, to use with small mounds; medium length about 18 or 20″ which gets the most use; and a large wire about 25 to 28″ which is used with large slabs.
5. Twisted cord (for slicing)—gives a nice texture, but requires more strength than wire to pull and is apt to break on the very largest slab. When my back started to bother me, I gave up using a cord altogether.

Tools in Making Slabware

1. Wide sheetrock knife—this is used lightly to smooth the slabs before they are removed from the mound.
2. Dissecting needle—for making preliminary cuts.
3. Flexible steel rib—used to smooth outsides of pots while on molds.
4. Fine-toothed comb for scratching surfaces.
5. Rolling pin—used lightly on the bottoms of plates when they are first on the mold to discourage warping by thinning slightly and correcting the plastic memory caused when transferring slab from mound to mold.
6. Cutting bow—for making first bevel while pots are still on the mold.
7. Turntable—molds are used on top of a lightweight turntable.
8. Coggles—sometimes used on the soft clay while pots are on molds.
9. Drying racks—8x18″ made of 1″ slats spaced about ¾″ apart.

Tools for Finishing

1. Clay plane—used for beveling edges; seems most suitable for noncurving edges.
2. Edgers—C.J. has made a variation on Mike Cohen's

edger (see *Funky Tools* later in this chapter) which can be used on inside bevel on oval bowls or top bevel on plates.

3. Edge roller—sometimes pots are not beveled (either on or off molds); an edge roller is used instead. This works well with earthenware.

4. Broken-off fettling knife—used for beveling; same use as edger. Also used after beveling to polish cuts (both inside and out). The principal advantage of polishing is compression which gives added chip resistance.

Slipping/Glazing Tools

1. Comb—made from truck inner tube. This is flexible and has notches in one end. Used to scrape away slip or glaze in a variety of patterns.

2. Slip bulb—with removable tip is best. Also good is one which will fit in the hand and be comfortable to use for extended periods.

3. Turntable—heavy weight, freestanding. For use when slip trailing.

Procedure

Preparing slabs one at a time is a procedure I use only when making very large pots. A piece of strong cotton cloth is placed on the table, making sure that there are no creases. Clay wedged into a flat, oval shape is laid on the cloth and beaten out into shape. If there is not enough excess clay to give a good cut, more should be added so as to have excess thickness of no less than ½''. The slats are laid on either side and the cut is made. The excess clay and slats are removed, the surface polished quickly with the sheetrock knife and the mold is placed upside down on the clay. The cloth is gathered as snugly as possible next to the stem and with a quick motion the clay, cloth, and mold are flipped.

I make sure to set the mold down at the corner of the table which makes it easier to get my hands disentangled after the cloth is removed. A preliminary cut is made to remove the excess clay. This should be done immediately so the weight of the excess clay does not tear the clay on the mold. The clay is pressed into shape using both hands and then polished using a flexible steel rib. Next, using the bow, I cut the outside edge and set the pot and mold aside to stiffen. The large pots are apt to split so extra care must be taken to get them off the mold after they are stiff enough not to sag but before splitting occurs.

I usually keep two cloths and alternate them during the day to allow for drying. It is a good idea to wash cloths and to check them for strength periodically, as it is quite a disappointment to have a cloth split while being used.

The consistency of clay is a major concern to me when making slabs in a mound. Too soft a clay will cause one slab to stick to another in the mounds or droop on the mold (making thin corners) or at best be difficult to polish with the steel rib. Too stiff a clay will crack at the bottom corner when a slab is placed on a mold.

For smaller slabs a mound is bashed out and pounded into shape using my hands, one on the top and one on the side. Using the small-size slats stacked on either side of the mound, I cut the slabs, starting with the top one; remove two slats, make the next cut, and so on. After I remove the excess clay from the top of the mound, I lift a slab onto a mold and the procedure mentioned for making large pots is then followed. The pots, still on their molds, are placed aside while another batch is started.

After the pots have stiffened sufficiently so that their shape will not slump when removed from the mold, a drying rack is placed on bottom of pot and rack, pot and mold are flipped and the mold removed. The pots are placed now in a damp box or on the ware rack, depending on my schedule, to stiffen a little more before I bevel the lip.

Slipping/Decorating/Glazing

Unlike our once-fired thrown ware, most of our slabware is slipped then bisqued prior to glazing. With our clay, the best time to slip is between leather- and black-hard.

Although we do not have a set pattern for decorating, we do have several patterns which we always come back to: a single comb lengthwise; using the comb to crosshatch; a slip-trailed continuous S. Rather than decorate using several patterns with one run, I prefer to take a pattern and use it as a central theme—using it not only for one time but carrying it through all sizes of bowls or all sizes of plates. The only item which is the exception to the above is the largest platter. I have always used a white slip overall and slip trailed a blue crosshatch pattern on the edge.

The pots are left on drying racks from overnight to two days and then are moved to wareboards. After pots are completely dry and when wareboards are in high demand, the pots are condensed—bowls are stacked five or six high and plates are stacked 10 or 12 high on wareboards to await firing.

Firing

One of the principal advantages of production slabware lies in firing. With the exception of very large platters, all slabware can be fired without the use of shelves. The denseness of the kiln charge is immensely satisfying, both economically and visually.

Plates are fired right side up on panrings in columns. Oval bowls may be boxed or fired upside down on panrings, resting the unglazed lip on the ledge of the panring.

Panrings are made from the previously mentioned refractory clay body. An extruded coil of this clay is formed into a 24'' ring on a large bat—the ring is then centered on the wheel and shaped with an appropriate metal template. After the clay stiffens enough to be handled, the ring is cut into 10 pieces. These are numbered in sets of five and rough edges are planed using a clay plane. (Cardew gives a description of molding panrings on page 162 of *Pioneer Pottery,* but we have never used that method as it seemed much slower.)

272

I usually wash the top ledges and the upright insides of the panrings about once a year with regular kiln wash mixed a little thin and I never seem to have any sticking. The pan rings are stored in sets on shelves next to the shuttle kiln.

Without pressing for room, the top of the shuttle kiln is left for plates. It will accommodate 50 to 60 plates, a convenient number, using only shelves at the bottom for support

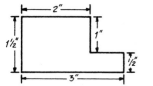 

and waster shelves on top (to keep crunchies out). Columns of panrings and pots may be taken as high as the situation warrants for as long as the stack is steady.

My only regret about the slabware is that we have not felt the prices of our plates were low enough to push the plates into the restaurant market. I would very much like to see the restaurants which use our other pots buy our plates, but we have been unable to beat the problems of price and weight. In normal household use, the weight is no problem and the thickness adds to durability.

TWO-WEEK WORK SCHEDULE

In general I follow a cycle for making slabware, taking number of molds, practical working number of runs, and demand into account.

MONDAY	10 oval plates
	8 round plates
TUESDAY	10 oval plates
	8 round plates
WEDNESDAY	8 salad plates
	12 pie plates
THURSDAY	8 salad plates
	12 pie plates
FRIDAY	8 meat platters
	8 salad plates
MONDAY	4 gowumba platters
TUESDAY	4 large platters
WEDNESDAY	12 #3 oval bowls (smallest size)
	8 small oval bowls
THURSDAY	12 #3 oval bowls
	8 small bowls
FRIDAY	8 medium oval bowls

TWO-WEEK PRODUCTION TOTAL

		With a Retail Value of
20 oval plates	$ 6 ea.	$ 120.00
16 round plates	6 ea.	96.00
24 salad plates	4 ea.	96.00
24 pie plates	10 ea.	240.00
8 meat platters	12 ea.	96.00
4 gowumba platters	30 ea.	120.00
4 large oval bowls	22.50 ea.	90.00
24 #3 oval bowls	3 ea.	72.00
16 small oval bowls	7.50 ea.	120.00
8 medium oval bowls	15 ea.	120.00
	Total	$1170.00

With an average retail value of $117.00 per day or an average wholesale value falling between $70.20 and $78.00 per day based on a five-day workweek.

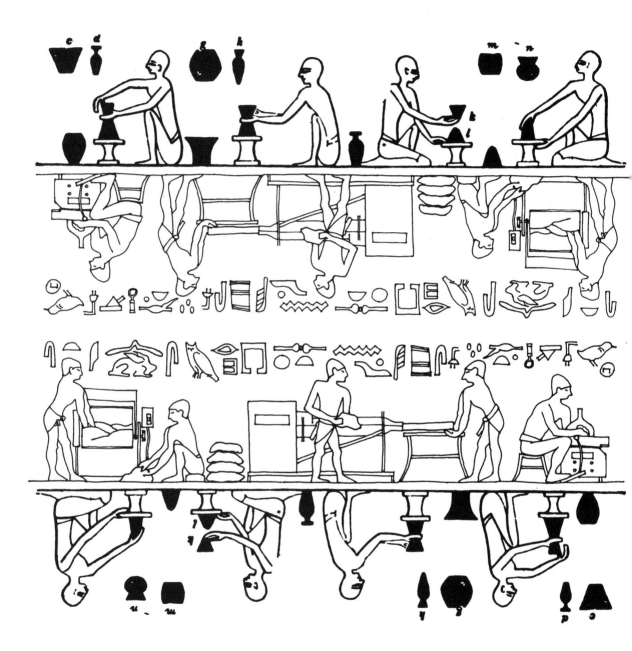

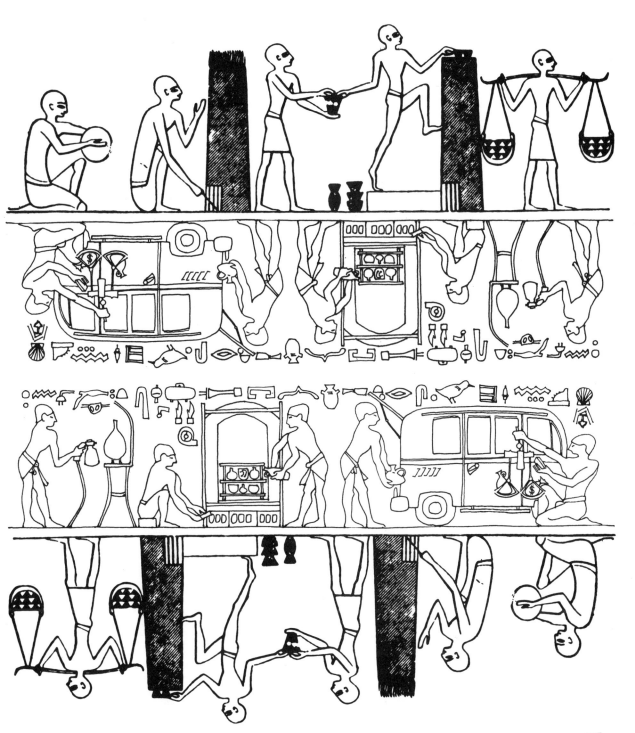

THE ANONYMOUS POTTERS OF THE ROCHESTER FOLK ART GUILD

Our first year was 1957. We began with the difficulties and dissatisfactions of our ordinary lives and only later came to work in crafts. Discontent with our habitual selves gave us the wish to change, and the modern legacy of the work of Gurdjieff brought the means and hope that the difficult work of transforming ourselves into balanced, whole men was possible. A group was formed. Initially, our tendency to intellectualize, dream, and socialize over our situation and possibilities was a danger. This tendency had to be countered by concentrated efforts centered in practical work. So the demand came: "Build a potter's wheel." We didn't know anything but we began.

We did not know if that beginning with a simple wheel in a basement would lead to anything. Our aim was not to become potters but to follow the given task that it might lead us to master ourselves. Working in members' homes on weekends, we began to develop a serious attitude towards the discipline and potential of crafts. We started to see in pottery the total identity between man and the processes of the craft.

By 1967 we had come to a point in our work where our need for commitment to the crafts especially among younger members was greater than part-time work allowed. We needed permanent full-time shops. Considering the influence of nature to be essential, we purchased a farm.

We began the continuing process of constructing buildings for housing and workshops which now include pottery, woodworking, glassblowing, weaving, iron forging, clothing design, printing, and bookbinding. The fields, vineyards, and gardens are worked; the animals tended.

The practice of making pottery in our experiment here will become much clearer if we look at clay from the same point of view that we try to look at ourselves. Looking closely at clay and pottery, we can see a parallel to man and the universe. A teaching is contained within the practiced craft. When a man tries to learn to control, or to master, any medium, he may be able to find relationships between himself and the material, and one day, to master himself.

Look at clay. Clay is a very common, ordinary substance. Farmers don't want it in their fields because it is so miserable to grow anything in. Even an earthworm wouldn't choose to live in clay.

In spite of this, if man has vision he can see in a lump of crude clay the possibility of a finished pot: something that with discipline and training, vision and practice, a different possibility might become a reality from a most common substance. If man hadn't the wish and the foreknowledge that an inherent possibility was in this clay, it might forever remain in a field somewhere.

Clay is so ordinary that it's difficult to suspect that a useful and beautiful pot could ever be made from it. And yet, that transformation can occur, and the clay will no longer be slippery, slimy mud, but a vessel that will hold something.

The potter takes his clay and places it on his wheel. From this moment, the clay has a possibility of becoming something more than it is. The process begins with centering the clay on a spinning wheel that might be called the wheel of life. The wheel's centrifugal force spins outward, trying to push the clay out from the center. To find the center of the clay, the potter exerts a corresponding inward force, or movement. This opposition of forces gives birth to the clay on the potter's wheel of life. It is an invisible place, this center, yet everything revolves around and depends on it. When a man tries to put his finger on the outer circumference of the wheel, and keep it there as it turns, the spinning is so rapid he cannot hold his finger there for a second. However, as he moves his finger toward the center of the wheel, the rate of movement of the wheel around the center becomes less and less apparent. Finally, when his finger touches the center, all motion seems to cease and he can hold his finger there, even though the outside circumference of the wheel spins as fast as it did before.

The experience of centering a ball of clay can't really be measured. To look at the clay, you can't quite tell if it is in the center or not; it can be found only by the sense of what the center truly is in that lump of clay.

And so it is with us when we try to find our own center. We can try to think about it, read books about it, and talk about it. But if the essential quality of the centering isn't felt, and if the head is playing leapfrog with the feelings, then we never really will be centered.

The potter, working on his wheel, finds the center of the clay, and the possibility begins for the clay to take shape. Within that clay, that centered, rounded mass, are contained countless forms and shapes. Under the right hands, it can become responsive to whatever is demanded of it. The final shape is determined by the way the clay has opened. If the vessel is opened unevenly, then the pot will be unbalanced. A broad opening will suggest a platter or plate; a more narrow opening might be a tall jar. Very much depends on how it is opened.

Next, the potter raises the clay into cylindrical walls. He begins to give shape to his pot through understanding the form that the shape represents and by applying pressure, both from inside and outside, that causes the clay to rise almost by itself. In a way, the clay is not so much pulled up into a cylinder. Rather, the conditions are prepared to allow the clay to rise of its own. The potter then finishes the final shaping of this pot into a jar, a mug, a bowl, a spout, or a lid, each according to its function.

The volume, or emptiness, that this finished pot can hold is impermanent. No matter how well the clay was mixed and prepared and wedged, even though the pot might have been perfectly centered, opened, and shaped, if this pot was to sit out in the rain, or if water was poured into it, this pot would once more return to mud, formless and useless, the kind of earth that farmers wish they did not have.

This pot, this vessel, this created thing, needs something more to become permanent, to change forever the very fabric of this common, ordinary material called clay into a permanent vessel. It needs to be able to hold something under all conditions, without the fear of losing again all that had been accomplished to that point. To change the nature permanently of this raw clay pot, it must undergo its trial by fire.

So the potter places his pot in the kiln and begins the fire. The fire is a test for all work up to this point, where every ounce of effort that has been given to the pot might be lost. In 20 or so hours of firing, the pot endures an intensity that rises to white hot heat. When one looks into the kiln at high temperatures, the pots look naked and almost become transparent.

The potter must know when to add more fuel, or less fuel, and the pot is subjected to the pulse of the fire. The potter must understand that the pot has to take its own time to mature. Large pots may require a slower fire because of the mass of resistance of so much clay; smaller pots can be heated up quickly. Pots that are delicate and thin need extra protection from the fiercest of flames. If the rhythm of stoking is too fast, then only the side of the pot nearest the firebox will be done, the other, far, side of the pot left immature and porous. Or, if the stoking is too fast, the pot might crack, making it useless to hold anything. There are innumerable reasons why the proper fusion of clay might never be reached.

With experience, the potter learns how to fire his kiln for a proper fusing to occur, and the pot emerges whole. The clay will never again be reduced to a shapeless mass, nor again be thrown on the wheel. Its nature of impermanence has been burned out of it. A new permanence has been given to this pot that isn't obvious to the eye. The shape has remained the same, but the inner substance has been fused into a form that is irreversible and impervious to change. The pot has the possibility of a life which will last longer than the maker.

The usefulness of any vessel or container, of which man is perhaps a higher form, lies in the volume and quality of emptiness that it encloses. In clay, we consider this to be the substance of the craft; in man, this is the highest art he is capable of.

He models his pot, passes it through the ordeal of fire, and has made a vessel to contain something that has the hardness of rock. The potter participates in a cycle of birth and death, and he gains a knowledge of experience, and experience that cannot come from books, or be measured by one or another yardstick, but must in fact be sensed, felt, and questioned. It is an experience of himself.

While generally working in silence, Guild potters are at certain times required to exercise the discipline of formulating their perceptions of self and materials. The body of these discussions has yielded what amounts to a diary. Excerpts from this diary can give a taste of pottery at The Rochester Folk Art Guild.

When I was first a member in the Folk Art Guild, I had an opportunity to explore many different kinds of work. I worked in the woodshop, in silkscreen, in block printing. I washed dishes sometimes, or helped with meals. And then one day I had a chance to try my hand at pottery..And when that happened, I felt a sense of life that I had never experienced before; and with the centering of a pot, of a ball of clay on a spinning wheel, for the first time in in my life I felt that there was a possibility of a center in me. And ever since that time when I first felt that, I have continued my study in pottery; and now for over 10 years I have stayed with it, and I am sure that it is my life's work. The more I work in pottery, the more I see order, and the more order I see, the more it's possible to see.

We are often asked why we do not sign our pieces. Some shops and galleries who could do very well for us will not take our work for lack of an individual's name. We use our crafts as tools for seeing and, if we are fortunate and persevering in our struggle, for breaking down our egotism. I suffer inwardly as I watch myself feeling proud as others admire my work. I don't need my name to further such attachment, which can only hinder real creativity and growth in the craft. Our pots bear a Guild seal. The pot is not mine to sign—it is a result of my being fortunate enough to work under the conditions created by the Guild, to further the aim of my craft and life, to transform myself as I transform the clay. That my body and senses, and even my heart and mind, are instrumental in the event is only a small part of the creation.

What can pottery teach us about ourselves? How can we come to see that the craft isn't an analogy but that it is ourselves?

There are laws inherent in the craft. Especially in throw-

ing, I have been struck by the fact that the only way to make a pot is to obey the laws which the process demands. It is something impersonal. There is a sense of serving, if you are right in yourself. You are a vehicle of the active force. The clay is passive. For example, when you kick the wheel, the speed of its rotation determines how fast you can work the clay. These two are in definite relation. It I am not in harmony with that law, due to my ego, my idiocy, impatience, or whatever—if the pot is opened faster than the wheel is going, it will be off-center or torn.

Again in trimming; the tendency not to trim enough, or to trim too much, reflects how you are.

We try to create conditions where the pot will stay as alive to us as possible. For example, one apprentice recently had the task to shape a bowl in three pulls. It called her to drop her self-involvement and concentrate on the material.

January 26, 1973

At 4:00 a.m. I could see the flames rising high over the big barn and my heart sank. Oh no! This barn, the animals, the hay, the woodshop connected to it, the print shop in it—so vital to our common existence.

In an instant, I asked myself what mistake had we made that we deserved this. I ran toward the fire hoping against all obvious facts, that there might be something I could do. Rounding the corner, I saw that the barn was not on fire at all, but that the kiln shed was, a building we had built ourselves only a year and a half before.

Apart from keeping the fire from spreading, there was nothing to do but accept the fact that the fire would consume all, and watch it burn. As the building burned, I felt my pride and ambition burn; and in front of my eyes were scenes of the construction of the building and the three-chambered wood kiln, and all the many moments when the work was not done from a right place; all this burned too. Step by step, as the building was built and filled, so it burned and emptied. What was left? How to start again? Fire is a great transforming element, when used correctly; out of control it is the great destroyer.

But the old part, the chicken coop attached to the kiln shed, did not burn. The chicken coop, where in 1967 we dug out three feet of manure and dead chickens, was where we made our pots and glazed them. Two inches of metal fire door kept the inferno from destroying that building too. The door itself was red hot, and flames streaked through the cracks in the door three to four feet into the chicken coop. We stood as close to the door as possible, throwing buckets of water on it. The chicken coop did not burn.

In the repetitive process you see how you repeat your mistakes. You see your habitual self. The laws are the same, whatever you do. You see how to bring about intention in yourself and carry it—and not just in pottery. The experience shows that something exists to strive for which is strong, and can be intentional.

What in me prefers some forms, rejects others? Sometimes a pot appears that is unlike any I have made before. That is a shock. Who made that?

I am amazed at how universal laws are immediately visible in the process of pottery. There is evolution right in front of you with every pot. Something is revealed, just through the basic process of the craft.

Who can be accepted in the pottery? Just anyone can't break in, unless they come on their knees and be guided by those in front of them.

I was amazed when S. got into porcelain. It came with a wave of what I would have to call inspiration. And when it was shown, the public felt this impulse. It sold before we had digested it. I was "flabbergasted" by this response. Will another such wave come? We don't know. There is no rest.

Whatever my state there must be attention and sensitivity or nothing can be done with the clay. With each pot I throw, there is a fresh opportunity to focus my attention, to find a way to be sensitive to the material. Each pot is a measure of that, and a very clear one. It can't be evaded.

All the old potters never made just one of this or one of that. There is a story of one woman who never did any but one form. One million in her lifetime. Her breath, her life, made one million. But there is variety, room for initiative, search, and melting one's own nonsense into respect for what was called law.

One thousand, or even 200 years ago, one man's or group's contribution to his craft might be, for example, that in one moment he recognized that a particular stone, when ground up, produced a particular result in a glaze. The whole contribution of his life was that one discovery. But it was a real contribution. He did see something. Today everything is handed to us. The pottery has been here for eight years, and six or seven before the farm. What can anyone do in eight years? Maybe in a lifetime a group of people working together could find a stone, contribute something to the craft. It is not just what we get from the craft, but our responsibility to pay that back.

There is also a magical point (in repetition): where the rhythm is established. The time for each pot gets shorter, the body forgets it's tired, the emotions become quiet: all that exists is the turning of the wheel, which never stops.

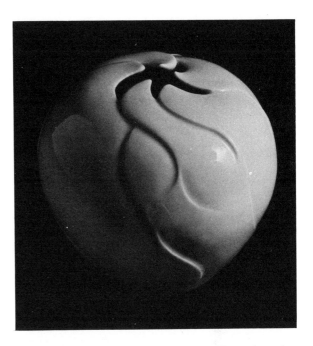

It's inexpressible. It doesn't happen often. You can't work up to it every day. It goes. You are not interfering. The best bowls come from these times.

We are six potters, all at various stages of understanding of the craft, including beginning apprentices. The pots we make are stoneware, salt-glaze ware, flameware, and porcelain. We have fired intensively with a variety of fuels and kilns including wood and gas-fired kilns, oil, multiple-chamber kilns, and have used various salt-glaze techniques. Primarily our ware has been high fired in the range of c/10 to 13.

All potters are assigned specific work to aid in developing a healthy respect for the outer and inner processes of the craft, not specializing in just one area.

In a very practical way, individuals are assigned responsibility for specific duties in the shop, for mixing the clay, for different production items, for preparing glazes, for keeping the business records, for shipping, and so on. These responsibilities are changed from time to time.

All sales of crafts go to the Guild, a nonprofit, tax-exempt organization. Individuals are responsible for their own living expenses.

CHIMNEY POTTERS COOPERATIVE STUDIO

by Mary Murchio

Chimney Potters is a 20-year-old pottery cooperative studio in Berkeley, California, with 10 members, four of whom have been with the group for 14 years. The common denominator for all of us over the years has been the need to share a high-fire kiln.

At present we own a 20 cubic foot Westcoast kiln (updraft gas fired) which is housed in a store location at 1609 Salono Avenue, Berkeley, CA. Four of the members work in the store studio and five work in satellite home studios where they bisque their ware and then bring it down to the studio for glaze firing. Aside from the kiln, the group owns only two kickwheels in common, and a glaze scale or two, otherwise all equipment belongs to each potter. The privately owned power wheels include: one Shimpo, one Wemco, one Omni, and three Skutts. The home studios have various collections of electric kilns, none over 12 cubic feet. We have no clay-making equipment or ball mills but buy clay from a variety of local manufacturers, or have our own formulas compounded by a local man.

The economics of our cooperative goes like this. We all buy a share in the kiln and pay monthly rent on a sliding scale of between $15 and $25 apiece, depending on the use of the studio. Our store rent is currently $145 up in five years from $85. Because in recent years costs have been escalating, we have added, in addition to rent, a firing charge of $15 on each glaze kiln. We feel this taxes us fairly according to use. In addition to this group cost, each potter, of course, has to buy materials. Often two or more members will buy large quantities of clay or glaze materials together to lower costs. The largest pool is the glaze pool which has its own separate bookkeeper.

Even though we are in a store location, because no one has wanted to be bothered with the process of running a business, each member is relatively autonomous as far as the economics of their pottery is concerned.

As a group we cover a wide range of ages with more women members than men. We like to take in members who have finished their school education and have advanced to a degree of independence which allows them to make full use of our flexible, self-reliant (though sharing) working environment. The Bay area is awash with educational institutions that teach pottery; from universities and state colleges to community colleges and recreational facilities, and most of us have come to pottery via their facilities. Our potters have worked with such people as Carleton Ball, Tony Prieto, Herbert Sanders, Franz and Marguerite Wildenhein, Peter Voulkos, and Ron Nagel. None of our members have come from Alfred University or an engineering technical background. I think it would be a valid generalization to say that most of us have found out for ourselves much of what we know now during our years in the Chimney Potters.

At this point I would like to say that while it is important in a sound cooperative group to be economically solvent, and it

helps to keep things simple, and to be a workable size, the most important factor is the character and serious commitment to pottery of the members. Choosing the right members therefore is of great importance. In spite of this we have never devised a standard procedure for this selection and yet on the whole we have done very well. Sometimes I think members really choose us.

Our group summer and Christmas sales just sort of grew out of the former private sales of several of our members. As the years went by we planted and cultivated a mailing list of customers who provide us with a known buying public. We have these sales away from the studio, outdoors if possible, since the pots are at their best in natural light. At these events the customers can really see the pots while enjoying themselves. These sales do not support us, but they do give each member a guarantee of covering his costs. As the years go by the sales are put on with less and less extra effort and a minimal amount of advertising or cost.

What characterizes all of us is financial independence and, therefore, the freedom to pursue our own personal artistic goals. None of us have to turn out hundreds of mugs and flowerpots; none of us have to hustle in the art gallery world for recognition; the atmosphere of Chimney Potters is basically mellow. We are not terribly uptight about trading glaze formulas and there is relatively little competition among us, even though all of us take our work very seriously and define ourselves as potters.

About our work—all of us work in a variety of styles, and spend a great deal of time doing decoration, handbuilt, and nonfunctional pieces. Also, somehow, many of us tend to animate our creations, giving them arms and legs, animal forms, and fantasy. Most of us work in stoneware and porcelain at c/9 to 10, but recently some have been involved with low-fire work decorated with lusters and enamels, and also with raku and firing pots at the beach in sand and seaweed, bonfire style.

A bit of history—about 1955 a group of potters who had worked together at Berkeley High Adult School decided to take over the lease of another pottery studio. This studio had a Charles Addams type setting in an old pottery factory which had manufactured dolls for many years prior to WW II. The place was filled with abandoned large-scale industrial equipment, the greatest ruin of all being two very large sagger-stacked beehive kilns, with their interesting looking stacks, hence the name Chimney Potters. The group bought an Alpine kiln from a North Carolina folk potter who had brought this piece of equipment to Pinole, CA and then ceased to be a potter. This was our first kiln. The people I know of who were in that first group were Bucky Clausen, Bruce and Marsha McDougal, Dale Hayes, and Paul Volkening, but there were others too. When for various reasons people left this studio, Bucky Clausen assumed their shares and in 1959, when that building was demolished, she moved the kiln into a store in the same building as Leslie Ceramics (the main supplier of ceramic materials in this area). This began a long-lasting symbiotic relationship of producer and supplier. The fact that the Tokis were potters and pottery collectors gave us a very empathetic climate where the supplier recognized and even anticipated the potters' interest in exploring new materials and having dependable sources of standard necessities. We owe them a lot.

For several years in this new location the studio departed from the coop pattern and was run as a one-owner operation by Mrs. Clausen. She chose the members, from 10 to 20, and did all the firing and divided the costs on a monthly basis among the members. When Bucky Clausen moved to Southern California in 1962 we became a cooperative once again, as nobody wished to assume as much responsibility as she had in the past. We decided to share and share alike and have each person self-reliant for the total process of producing his own ware. This did not happen as an instantaneous change but rather developed gradually during several transitional years.

About five years ago, because Leslie Ceramics outgrew their quarters and assumed ours, we moved again to another store. Because we had outgrown store-sized space, we decided to have five of our members work in satellite home studios. Before this we had always been opposed to members who did not work in the studio because we did not want, at that time, to become a mere firing service. Now we could do this, however, because of the cooperative structure we had devised. So far this has worked quite well and does give us flexibility. We decided to buy our present kiln

(and sold our much traveled Alpine to some people in Santa Cruz) and in order to do so, we threw a sale and accomplished that hurdle in one fell swoop. And that brings us right up to where we are now.

Perhaps one could liken the coop structure to a trellis up which many vines can grow freely, being supported by its presence, but not enclosed by it. The Chimney Potters have been in my life now for so long that I have come to take it for granted and in trying to describe it I feel as if I've merely gone around the edges and neglected the indescribable volume of the center. The center, the work, and the security of knowing we can continue doing it.

THE CAPE COD POTTERY COOPERATIVE

by Harry Holl

In the spring of 1972, I found myself suddenly becoming the old experienced potter on Cape Cod. Bearded and successfully potting on a beautiful wooded lakeside, I became a prime target for apprentices and beginning potters. Even though I love to talk and share any information I have, I soon found that too much time was taken away from my work. I decided I couldn't handle it alone, so I called together the most frequent visitors to my shop. We met at my home, about 10 of us: Ken D'Agastino, Gail Turner, Janet Burner, Tina Holl, Roger Harvey, Rob Huller, Susan Lord, Mike Garrison, and myself. I brought up the possibility of forming a group of self-help potters. We agreed that our needs were many but that the major ones were: dependable source of inexpensive materials on Cape Cod; a way to mix clay that could be shared by all; and a way to share resources and information. All of us felt that many established potters were too secretive. We decided that glaze formulas, clay recipes,

and any other information passed on for centuries should belong to all potters. It is, after all, what a potter does with this information that counts. In this way, we hoped to make better potters of ourselves, without fear of competition—for there will never be enough really good potters.

Our first step was to locate an inexpensive storage location. Luckily, we found a large barn locally which was in bad repair but was available for $25 a month if we did the needed work on it. We also found a dough mixer in excellent condition for $800. We borrowed $2,000 from a bank on the signatures of three of us who had credit. All of us pooled our orders and promised to buy all our materials and pay cash together as soon as the orders came through. We held work meetings to get the barn in shape, and to get a clay-mixing room in shape.

In looking back, I find those days were the most exciting. I especially remember sunny Sundays and a busy work crew dusting up a storm getting the barn cleaned up to move into. It was fantastic, the amount of work we did in one afternoon! These experiences working together formed lasting bonds between people who otherwise would never have met. Friendships developed which made it possible for us to survive rough times.

During the first year we were forced to spend a great deal of time doing the inevitable: discussing money. It took us two years to pay off our bank loan. Our suppliers were patient with us as long as we paid them something. Collecting money was also a problem especially with schools. Members had to pay cash as soon as they received the goods, as we found billing to invite too much paperwork with few results. (We have two types of members: working fee $10 a year, nonworking fee $50 a year.) We had to decide on prices with their appropriate markups: base price, coop member's prices, public prices, and school prices. We began by charging 10% above costs to members but had to raise it to 20%, as we found 10% insufficient to carry our overhead.

After two years, all the repairs were done and our rent went up. Our inventory was spreading to include tools, glaze materials, electric kilns, and almost everything else potters might need. In spite of our 20% markup, our prices were considerably lower than anywhere else. In addition, there was the convenience of no shipping charge. Our price per pound was the same whether you bought one pound or a bag. Here are just a few price comparisons:

	Co-op price	Other market price
Flint	6 cents/lb.	10 to 50 cents/lb.
Feldspar	12	18 to 60
Ball clay	8	10 to 53
EPK	10	14 to 60
C. H. bonding	6	8 to 35
Tin	$4.30 lb.	$8 to $10 lb.

We try to stock enough to avoid shortages, keeping a close check on inventory so that it is rare that we are out of anything even during the so-called shortage crises. We have people who are tracking down new sources of materials all the time. All of us contribute to this constant search. At first, we bought from retail dealers who gave us discounts on quantity sales. Then we found area distributers who just handled a few materials wholesale. Now we are buying some supplies direct from importers or mines; they usually sell one or two related materials. However, sometimes, while the price is low, the shipping costs, which are often high, make this sort of purchasing impossible.

Buying from large corporations can be very difficult. Frequently, because of the small size of our orders, we are referred to local distributors, rather than sources which do not want to be bothered dealing with us. Occasionally, a top-level person will take an interest in the lowly potter and therefore cut a lot of red tape. I've had this happen to me several times in my 25 years of meeting people in my shop. I've discovered many vice-presidents to be frustrated potters.

Meetings must not be attended out of responsibility alone. Our cooperative meetings have become exciting events. Everyone agrees that the work meetings are the best. It has been my job from the beginning to chair the meetings, except for special presentations. Currently we are working on a plan to pass responsibility to different people.

At first, all business was conducted at our regular meetings with all members present. This became impossible when our membership grew to 55, and over 30 people attended meetings. Now a small committee does most of the planning and makes day-to-day decisions. This committee is made up of the heads of the work committees, who are responsible for various maintenance tasks. There are usually 10 to 12 attending this meeting.

Here are the titles of the committees, so you can get a feel for what we do. Barn Cleanup, Barn Maintenance, Unloading, School Deliveries, Inventory, Pricing, Claymaking, Mailing Program, Membership, and others as we need them.

The planning committee decides what has to be done and who we are going to get to do it. It meets once every two months. Our regular meetings are once a month and anyone can attend. The work committee heads try to get together their various work crews for at least two hours work every month.

Our big monthly meetings usually have three parts. First, a short business meeting is held, usually to make announcements. Second, the main body of the meeting takes place: a workshop, movies, slides, or a discussion. Third, we have refreshments and general socializing. (We try to move our meetings around so that we can get to see the workshops of different potters.) Here is a small list of the programs we have had: Making Cane Handles for Teapots, Toolmaking Evening, Visit to a Sculptor's Studio—Fifty Years of Work, slides of potters apprenticing in England, three potters demonstrating different approaches to clay, Basic Brushwork, Glaze Calculations, Keeping Records and Paying Taxes, Kiln Building, and many others.

We have also spent many meetings trying to draw up by-laws and trying to become incorporated as a nonprofit organization. The main idea was to try to get some grant money so we could have our own center for potters on Cape Cod. We spent over a year on all this only to give it all up as a waste of time. It took too much time and energy away from our work and running the coop itself. We would have had to set up a phoney organization in order to sell supplies to ourselves and invent projects in order to get funding for them. Nothing we needed was in a category that was eligible for funding. What we needed was what we were doing for ourselves. It would be nice to have our own building and land but that would require a very generous and understanding benefactor, which we do not have.

It is difficult to advise other coops, as their needs will differ from that of ours. Generally, it takes a core group of hard workers to carry the coop through the first couple of years. Although everyone will agree that a cooperative is a necessity, not everyone sees his responsibility equally. It would almost appear that people must be educated in order to cooperate and initiate on their own. More than once, emergency meetings were called to either disband the coop, or to put it into a viable business form. After three years and countless reorganizations, we have worked out a plan whereby the work is distributed through committees, and they along with the general overseer are responsible for getting things done. It is advisable that any coop constantly assess the needs of its membership and evaluate methods of organization towards more efficient and responsible goals.

I remember once when we were ready to give up, some-one said, "If we can't make cooperation work, what hope is there?". Very often when people find they cannot make it alone, they turn to some cooperative effort. There are so much energy and untapped resources in people to be shared, we miss out on this when we go it alone. I've found that no matter how much I give, I've always gotten much more in return.

THE FINDHORN FOUNDATION

by Mimi Luft

The Findhorn Foundation in Northern Scotland is a community of 175 people (as of 1977, 250)—many from America and Great Britain, others from Australia, South Africa, and numerous points in between. It was started 13 years ago by Peter and Eileen Caddy who, with their family, settled in a trailer park and planted a garden. The garden was a source of vegetables for the Caddy kitchen, but also became the focus for a developing sensitivity to the forces of nature.

Cooperation with these forces was the key, and as the expression of cooperation expanded others joined with the Caddys to help create an environment where people could grow into a new realization of their identity with the energies found in themselves, in nature, and in all else.

"Beloved Pan and you other gods that haunt this place, give me beauty of the inward soul, and may the inner and outer man be as one. May we count the wise to be wealthy . . ."

First there were gardeners, then came a plumber, a carpenter, and now there are departments—publications, audio, photographic, office, maintenance, construction, grocery store, and craft studios.

Findhorn is a community where people can apply an interior spiritual vision of the wholeness of themselves and their world to everyday community life. One important aim of each department is that it be a vehicle for each of its participants to express in a tangible way his insights into the limitless regions of consciousness. So, in the studios, the crafts are not pursued for their own sake nor solely for financial return. Each artist creates freely, knowing that the creative impulse is of prime importance, and that if this is expressed, all needs will be met perfectly.

The pottery is one of four studios, including weaving, candles, and design, and was built by community members. The windows of its main room open onto a great expanse of soft-lit Scottish skies, barley fields, and Findhorn Bay (where cormorants and wild swans can be seen). There are three electric wheels and one kick wheel, and ample space for handbuilding.

Prepared stoneware clay is shipped from Stoke-on-Trent, the traditional center of the English ceramic industry. When reduced, it turns to nice chocolate.

The kiln, "Mother," so named for her abundant nature, was designed by David Ballantyne, a craftsman from the south of England. The interior is approximately 50 cubic feet. Mother is fired by a simple drip-feed system, using kerosene, sump oil (waste engine oil, obtained at no cost from a truck garage in a nearby town), and water. And lots of love, as she is very temperamental.

"The New Age is a release of new energy. It represents for the planet an unfoldment to the time in man's life when his soul takes a tighter grip over its lower vehicles and his body, emotions and mind, and all become oriented to the direction and life of the Higher Self."

The number of people working in the pottery varies as members of the community are continually changing.

Scot Goldberg, who is doing most of the throwing right now, has been at Findhorn for two-and-a-half years since coming from Pennsylvania, U.S.A.

"Sometimes I get the romantic notion that I am a potter; that I am devoted to mysterious clay, water, fire and air, Japan, China, Greece, past lifetimes; that my pots are my life this time. But always I am reminded that I am not that kind. When I am away from the wheel, when my hands are washed clean from clay, and the kiln has cooled from my face, then I am no longer a potter. I am a friend, or a bicycle-rider or a cloud-watcher. It's hard sometimes not having a pot's-life to cling to, but it's of that 'not clinging' that the pots are always telling me . . . broken pots, stuck lids, under/over fired . . . let it go and what are you living now? Where are your eyes, what are you touching, how are you experiencing every point up that spinning shining wall of earth?"

Mimi Luft, also from the U.S.A. (Cambridge, MA) is hand-building.

"I began as a painter with a strong interest in form. This involvement led me to begin handbuilding a few years before coming to Findhorn. When I came here it seemed unbe-

lievable good fortune to be able to spend almost all my time exploring form in clay. As I've lived and worked here, I've found my 'good fortune' consists ever more importantly of the experience of learning to blend energies and ideas with my friends in the synergistic operation of the studio. As I

find my own rhythms and discover how to relate them to larger rhythms, I find my creative energies seem to be flowing more freely."

Margie Elliot, from Australia, has also been handbuilding.

"Working with clay is one of many ways, many journeys.

"How beautiful to work with the earth, with all the elements. The pots describe our life, our thoughts, our awareness. Life dances through our fingers into the pots, and through the clay into us.

"I discovered the need to open to the clay as I would to a friend, seeing the reflection of myself, opening to its being, to its knowing, learning to respond each moment to what it tells me, letting go of preconceptions, flowing . . ."

Each day every department begins work with an attunement where all can focus, first as individuals, and when centered affirm the harmony and consciousness of the group. In this way attunements help us meet the challenge of creating an atmosphere conducive to creative work for the artist/craftsman who in the past may have, by choice or necessity, worked alone. For at Findhorn we believe that man's continuing existence depends on our acceptance of our deep interdependence.

"Not farewell
But fare forward, voyager."

ANALYZING ELECTRIC WHEELS

by Paul Soldner

When I was asked to write this article, my first reaction was to refuse. I thought that as a manufacturer of pottery equipment, I would probably have personal biases which could seem unfair to other manufacturers.

However, after considering the importance of such an article and recognizing my dual position as potter/teacher, as well as manufacturer, I decided to give it a try. I will be as objective as I possibly can. I will attempt to explain the advantages as well as the disadvantages of the different kinds of electric potter's wheels. But I prefer not to evaluate specific equipment. In the end, the buyers of any equipment must sift through all the information available in order to sort out their own preferences.

As background: my interest in building potter's wheels goes back to a college art class in the year 1941. Ceramic instruction was offered in slip casting and clay sculpture. At first I naively thought that the function of the one potter's wheel at our disposal was to function as a lathe, to turn solid clay into shapes which could then be cast in plaster to make slip molds! The wheel was a standup vertical-pump treadle wheel. It served to frustrate me enough to begin looking for a better solution. And so began a lifelong search for a better wheel.

Most of my early models had parts from junked cars. One which evolved used a Model A Ford crankshaft for the bearings, flywheel, and eccentric shaft. Another used part of a Model T Ford rear axle and wheel. Concrete was cast between the wooden spokes of the wheel to form my first flywheel.

When I turned my attention to making an electric wheel, it had a Willy's transmission for the speed reduction, so there were three forward speeds and a reverse! It worked fine; high gear for centering, second for raising the walls, and low for finishing.

Later, while I was working on a graduate degree, I learned about the advantages of throwing on an electric wheel which had a continuously variable speed. It was the old Denver Fire Clay wheel with a variable speed, a.c. motor. The motor was coupled directly to a reducing gearbox with the throwing head attached to the vertical output shaft. I and other wheel manufacturers soon used the same unit but increased the motor horse power to ½ h.p. Incidentally, a 12″ bronze head was standard equipment in those days! The only problem connected with those a.c. motors was the excessive noise and their eventual unavailability. After technological breakthroughs brought a.c. motors into a competitive price bracket, the old a.c. "growlers" were discontinued. Electric wheel manufacturers, including myself, were forced to change over or seek other solutions. It was from this forced research that I learned of other alternatives.

I now turn to the specific question of what to look for when purchasing a wheel. Generally speaking, there are three basic methods of powering a potter's wheel with an electric motor:

1. A variable speed from a constant-speed motor as a power-assist kickwheel

2. A variable speed produced by a mechanical device from a constant-speed motor

3. A variable speed, electronically controlled motor

All three drives have one problem in common: that is the necessity to slow down the high speed of the motor (about 1875 revolutions per minute) to a slow speed which can be used by a potter (around 200 rpm). This can be accomplished with a speed reduction ratio between the motor and the throwing head through gears, belts, or a flywheel. Following is an explanation of the three drives mentioned above:

1. A variable speed from a constant-speed motor as a power-assist kickwheel

This is sometimes also called a momentum or friction drive. Essentially, it is a method of powering a kickwheel with a constant speed motor. The motor is used instead of the foot to increase the speed. Undoubtedly, this is the most economical power alternative.

In theory, it combines the best of two wheels, the power of electricity, to help center large amounts of clay and the sensitivity of kicking the flywheel for refining the final shape.

A rubber drive wheel, mounted on a motor shaft, temporarily engages, by friction, the outside of the flywheel, whether on the rim, top, or bottom. This speeds up the flywheel to a maximum speed of about 200 rpm, depending on the particular flywheel/drive wheel ratio. Because of the momentum put into the spinning flywheel, it continues to revolve after the motor is disengaged. This allows the potter to throw a pot. However, it is almost impossible to complete a pot on one momentum cycle, so as the wheel slows down, the potter must either begin to kick the wheel or engage the motor drive again. A skilled potter can engage the motor smoothly, but it is difficult. What happens is that the wheel suddenly is going too fast. Because of this surging, even skillful potters have difficulty maintaining just the right speed when throwing a really large pot.

One other problem to be considered with power-assist wheels is the uneven wear of the small rubber drive wheel. If one habitually starts using the motor from 0 speed (instead of kicking it first), the rubber develops flat spots which then cause vibration. If it is not replaced, this vibration can be so intense that it will damage the motor bearings.

In spite of these problems, many potters prefer the power-assist wheel because they feel they get two wheels for the price of one, a kick and an electric.

2. Variable speed produced by a mechanical device from a constant-speed motor

Mechanical drives are related to the power-assist drives in that both of them employ friction (between a drive wheel and a flywheel) to transmit power from the motor to the head. One difference between them is that mechanical drives generally have a smaller flywheel. Of more importance is some kind of changeable drive wheel which provides for a continuously variable speed under full power. This feature overcomes the disadvantage of the fixed speed (on and off) of the power assist wheels.

There are five methods commonly used by which mechanical drives transmit power and vary the speed in one operation:

A. This first method will be mentioned only briefly because its performance is unsatisfactory. A belt tightening drive is used. This is supposed to speed up the wheel when the drive belts are tight, and then slow down the speed when the tension is removed, allowing the belt to slip a little. Aside from its lesser cost, the advantages are not great. The belt tensioner needs constant adjustment, and the loss of power due to belt slippage makes this device unsuitable.

B. Another belt drive sometimes suggested for a potter's wheel is the moveable pulley. By moving one side of a V-pulley, the belt is made to run higher or lower in the pulley to change the pulley ratio. Again, this can hardly be recommended because the speed reduction is too compressed. This results in speeds that vary little over a very short spectrum. As a result, the potter finds himself short at both ends of his speed needs.

C. One of the oldest variable speed devices was that employed by the Crosley wheel, among others. I call this a moveable drive wheel. A small drive wheel turns against a larger flywheel (as did the power assist wheel) but it moves from the middle of the flywheel for slow speed, to the outside for faster speeds. Although this wheel is seldom used any more in this country, I have seen it in schools and studios in England and Australia. I am told that Harry Davis of New Zealand prefers this type of wheel. Inasmuch as many production potters once used this type of wheel exclusively, it should probably be considered as suitable for today's needs as well. The only disadvantage I can think of is its large and unwieldly size and stiffness of operation compared to modern electric wheels. (See Illus. A.)

D and E. Similar to the moveable drive wheel just described, but more compact, are the cone drive and the hemisphere drive. In both, a variably shaped drive wheel (sometimes called a stepless pulley) is driven against the rim of a small flywheel. In the case of the cone, the speed increases as the cone is moved forward or backward against the flywheel from its smallest part (the point) to its widest outside diameter. (Illus. B.)

The hemisphere, on the other hand, increases its speed as the hemisphere drive is rotated against the flywheel from its center to its outside. (Illus. C.)

Advantages of both the cone and the hemisphere drive are similar. They can be compact. They can give a continuously variable speed control from 0 to 200 rpm and because they drive against the outside of the flywheel only, they deliver maximum power at slow speeds. Also, like the moveable drive wheel above, when disengaged at 0 speed, the head is free wheeling. This feature makes the wheel func-

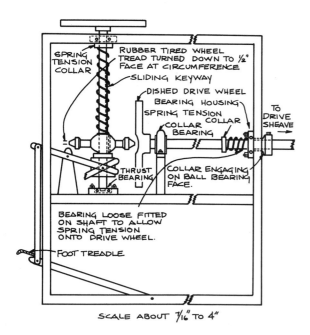

SPRING TENSION COLLAR

RUBBER TIRED WHEEL TREAD TURNED DOWN TO 1/2" FACE AT CIRCUMFERENCE

SLIDING KEYWAY

DISHED DRIVE WHEEL

BEARING HOUSING

SPRING TENSION COLLAR

COLLAR BEARING

TO DRIVE SHEAVE

THRUST BEARING

COLLAR ENGAGING ON BALL BEARING FACE

BEARING LOOSE FITTED ON SHAFT TO ALLOW SPRING TENSION ONTO DRIVE WHEEL.

FOOT TREADLE

SCALE ABOUT 7/16" TO 4"

tion rather like a large banding wheel. However, this last feature can also present a headache to potters if they forget to completely disengage the wheel after use. Unless it is disengaged, a flat area forms on the rubber flywheel belt. This can happen overnight and results in a bad thump every time the wheel revolves, somewhat like a scratch on a phonograph record. Also, a problem related to the last three wheels is that of sluggish and stiff speed control. This is because of the spring-loaded friction required to maintain transmitted power between the drive wheel and the flywheel. The stronger the spring, the more powerful the wheel, but also the more difficult it is to change speeds. It was probably this stiff pedal action that first led to the concept of throwing at a fixed speed. I understand that Japanese production potters routinely throw their small bowls and cups at one speed, which may help explain the origins of the fixed pedal.

Related to the spring loading is another difficulty pertaining to ease of operation. In all three wheels, the foot pedal must be fixed to the side of the frame. Therefore, the operator has no choice except to work at the wheel from one position.

Furthermore, because so much mechanical complexity is involved in the manufacture of these wheels, their selling price is often the same as the more flexible and powerful electronic wheels.

3. A variable speed, electronically controlled motor
Wheels which fall into this last category can be considered to be pure electric wheels. Whereas the aforementioned wheels also use electric motors, all the motors revolve at a fixed speed. Speed changing must then be achieved mechanically. Electric control means that motor speed itself is changed electronically.

Electronically controlled wheels use either a d.c. (direct current) motor or a cheaper, series-wound motor. The series-wound motor is similar to that used in electric hand-drills and sewing machines. It turns at high speeds, tending to be noisy, has poor brush life and low power output. It spite of the low cost, series-wound motors are seldom used to power potter's wheels. The exception are toy types.

The most popular variable speed motor in use today is the d.c. permanent magnet motor. Its speed can be accurately controlled from 0 rpm through an infinite range, to top speed. It is available in horsepowers sufficient to handle any potter's load requirement. It is quiet and relatively free from maintenance problems. The expected brush life is in excess of 5,000 hours. With good electronic voltage control, the torque (power under stress) can be fairly constant at all speeds.

One disadvantage of the variable speed d.c. motor is the cost factor. The motor, including controls, is four to five times more costly than a constant speed motor. However, this basic cost can be offset by savings in labor and parts. It is relatively easy to add a direct coupled gear box or a simple belt drive to achieve the necessary speed reduction. All that remains then, is to add the throwing head and frame.

As has been pointed out, the advantage of d.c. motors is their ability to change speeds under full power throughout the entire throwing range. In order to control this, two electric functions must take place: voltage regulation and alternating current rectification.

Most electronic controls are one of two types: either SCRs (Silicon Control Rectifier) using transistor circuitry for both voltage and rectification in one stage, or two stage controllers that regulate the a.c. voltage independently (with a variable transformer) and then rectify this voltage with diode circuitry. As one might suspect, there are pros and cons to both systems.

Without attempting to explain the complicated theory of both systems, let me simply compare them in terms of results. The SCR system is the most compact and cheapest to produce. Its disadvantages are an annoying and constant motor hum and transistors easily damaged by overload conditions. It produces radio and television interference, has poor slow speed control and a touchy foot pedal which tends to respond too quickly when changing speeds. This inability to change speeds smoothly is a real nuisance to the potter because it becomes most critical just when fine control is needed, that is, when the walls of a pot are thinned out and final finishing requires a sensitive touch.

The variable transformer control is very rugged, slow to burn out if overloaded, and has an extremely smooth speed change without erratic spurts. It does not produce radio or television interference, is equally powerful at low or high speeds, and produces a gentle wave form which results in a quiet motor performance. Its disadvantages are its higher cost to manufacture, larger size, and need to be shielded against water.

Both systems share the specific problem of operating the electronic controls with a foot pedal. Different manufacturers have solved the problem in a variety of ways, most of them satisfactory and getting better. There are two styles of pedals available, but not always on the same wheel. One is called the accelerator style, which operates like the gas pedal of an automobile. That is, it returns automatically to off when foot pressure is released. The other style is the fixed speed pedal, which must be pushed off as well as on.

There are proponents of both styles, one side saying the fixed speed control results in lazy throwing habits and an insensitivity to the correct wheel speeds, the other side maintaining that the accelerator style is too uncomfortable.

As a wheel manufacturer, I admit that the customer should probably be offered a choice, but as a teacher, I prefer the accelerator style simply because it does make for more correct speed awareness. In this connection, I have often speculated why potters want to throw at one speed when when they don't want that for their automobile or sewing machine!

Conclusion

To conclude this survey of types of electric wheels, there are several knotty issues which need to be raised. One is the question asked regarding horsepower. The problem is one of truth in advertising. Because there are no regulatory rules or even industrial guidelines for manufacturers of wheels to follow, each is free to make his own claim without comparison to any standards. Naturally, the result is one of confusion. How do you rate horsepower? At the motor? At the wheel head and after reduction? Under full-load starting conditions or at no-load running speeds? For industrial, continuous use or for hobby, intermittent use? Because it is common practice to remove the specification plate from the motor, there is no way of knowing how it was originally rated by the manufacturer in compliance with industrial standards.

Until uniform electric wheel standards are adopted, I can only recommend that the buyer ask the amperage draw for the motor. As a rule of thumb, the more amperes required, the stronger the motor. If the motor's horsepower is guaranteed to be given as "industrially rated for continuous use," then ⅓ h.p. will suffice for all throwing demands up to 50 pounds. A ½ h.p. motor, so rated, will handle any other loads above that amount.

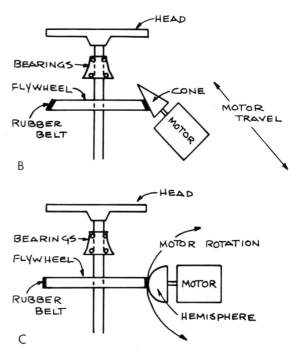

B

C

To reduce the high speeds of the motor, either worm gears or belt reductions are acceptable. At one time, gear reducers were thought to be the best solution. Coupled directly to the motor, they provided a strong, compact unit. But now, with increased costs, slow delivery, and lower manufacturing tolerances (resulting in increased noise and vibration), gear boxes are giving way to improved belt drives. If the belts are of good quality and installed properly, they will be quieter than gear boxes, and capable of delivering full power from the motor.

I have said nothing about frames, table tops, splash pans, or any options offered by the wheel industry. In most cases, the quality of these parts is obvious to the eye. Also, depending on one's ceramic education and tradition, the final choice will be made as a personal preference anyhow.

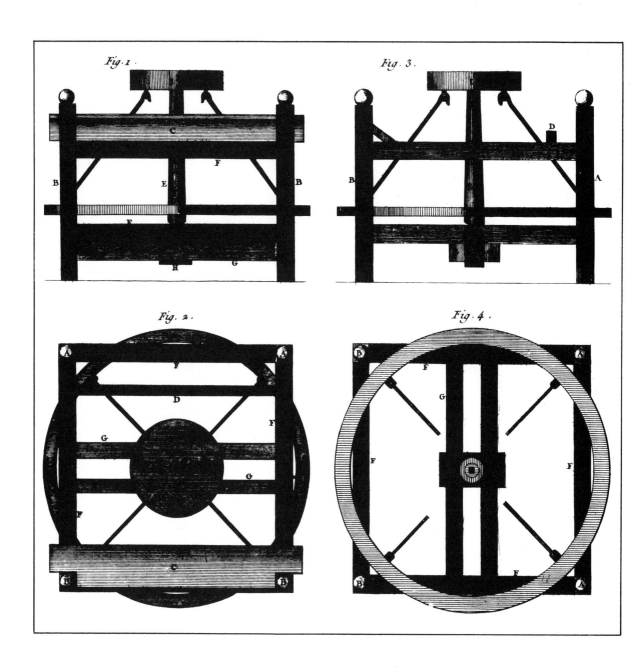

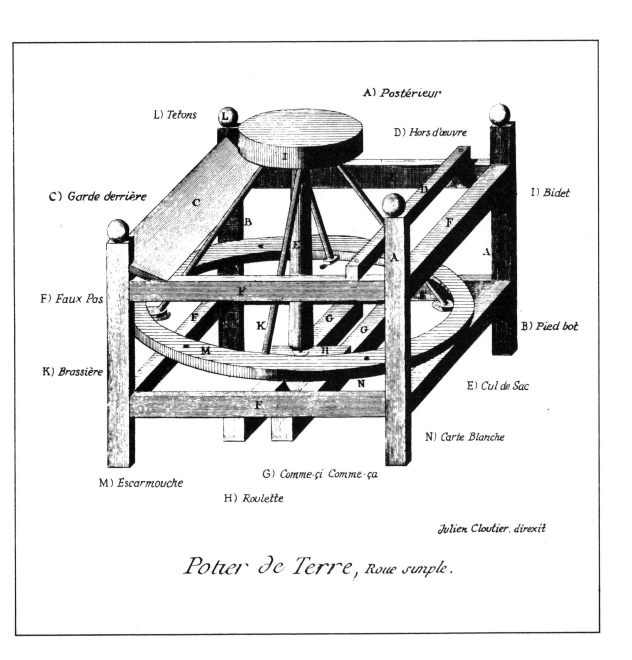

A) *Postérieur*

L) *Tetons*

D) *Hors d'œuvre*

C) *Garde derrière*

I) *Bidet*

F) *Faux Pas*

B) *Pied bot*

K) *Brassière*

E) *Cul de Sac*

N) *Carte Blanche*

M) *Escarmouche*

G) *Comme-çi Comme-ça*

H) *Roulette*

Julien Cloutier. direxit

Potier de Terre, Roue simple.

FUNKY TOOLS

by Michael Cohen

What are funky tools? Well, you won't find them in a supply catalog. They won't be all purpose. Probably they will do only one specific job. Funky tools are the kind that become so indispensable that work can't go on until they are found. They are made from wires, tubing, branches, nails, broom handles, pebbles, spoons, and pizza rollers. The need for a funky tool usually comes from the frustration of wasting time doing a repetitive job that could be done in no time if you only had the right tool. Production stops! The prototype is patched together in five minutes and used for months until it wears out. The refinements come when the replacement is made. The walnut handle instead of pine. The carefully coiled wire instead of string. Here are some tools found in my studio, and some from Ron Burke's and Dan and Maryanne Gehan's. Rip 'em off!

Holemakers

A lot of time has been wasted trying to make perfect holes in clay with a potter's knife. Such holes are uneven, torn up, and require much scraping and sanding. English potters have a holemaker, and I saw one at Byron Temple's studio five years ago. I've since made my own version, improving on the English one. (See Fig. 1) Take about 6'' of thin metal tubing (diameter depends on the use of the hole—I allow ⅜'' to ½'' for hanging planter rope and ¼'' for colanders—and hacksaw a beveled cut at a very oblique angle, about 20°. (Fig. 1 A) Sharpen by filing the point and cutting edge and mount on handle. (Fig. 1 B)

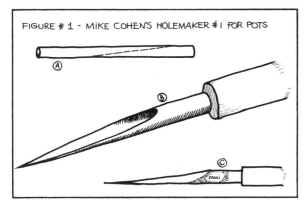

FIGURE # 1 - MIKE COHEN'S HOLEMAKER #1 FOR POTS

Smooth some epoxy into the opening of the tube. This refinement feeds the clay pellets off the tool. (Fig 1 C)

It was an easy transition to make a holemaker exclusively for use on flat tiles of clay. Take a short piece of the tubing and cut off a ¾'' piece at right angles to the tubing, cutting only half-way through the diameter of the tubing. (Fig. 2, A & B) Mount tubing on a handle and sharpen cutting edges. To use, push into tile and give a half turn, then lift out clean plug. (Fig. 2 C)

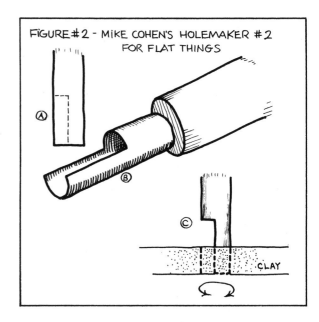

FIGURE #2 - MIKE COHEN'S HOLEMAKER #2 FOR FLAT THINGS

CLAY

FIGURE # 3 - MIKE COHEN'S BEVEL MAKER

Beveler

Another tool that seems to draw comments from visitors to my studio is my beveler. The backs of my large slab mirrors are beveled to make them easier to wax. I made a beveler for speed and uniformity. It's merely a thin, taut wire across a right angle. (Fig. 3 A) The tool rides on the edge of the slab. (Fig. 3 B) The wire draws off a perfect bevel. (Fig. 3 C)

Measuring Devices

Two interesting measuring devices are found in Dan and Maryanne Gehan's studio. They use a bent wire as a thickness gauge, with projection indicating the exact depth. Useful, now that more potters are switching from plaster bats to pressed wood. More clay must be left on the bottom because of the need to use a cut-off wire. (Fig. 4A) By binding a forked branch and a crossbar (Fig. 4B) together, the Gehans have made an automatic height and diameter gauge. They have a set of these corresponding to the outside of standard greenhouse pots. So in order to compensate for shrinkage, the gauges are about 20% bigger than the manufactured planter, so they end up with planters in which terracotta pots will fit. (Fig. 4C) Dan says he got the idea for this gauge from Bernard Leach's *A Potters Book.*

Scorers

For people who do a lot of slab work, scoring can be one of life's more monotonous chores. Ron Burke put a piece of coarse-tooth saw into a wood holder, then nailed the holder to the worktable. Stiff slabs are then drawn across the saw. This kind of fast scoring speeds production of slab boxes. (Fig. 5A) I made a good scorer by cutting the heads off good steel map pins, then, using needle-nosed pliers, pushed the pins into a piece of pine. To reinforce the wood I taped it all around. (Fig. 5B) The old five-tined fork scorer seems gross and clumsy after using this fine, precision-type scorer. It gives deep, fine score lines with very little pressure, so that one can achieve a clean, rectangular slab form or avoid denting the lid of a casserole or side of a pitcher where a handle is to be joined.

Waxing Device

Ron Burke also makes a lot of flat things which have been painstaking to wax. He finally came up with the ultimate waxing device. This is a hotplate with a paint roller and a time-proportioning temperature controller which automatically keeps the wax at 230° F. The piece is merely drawn across the roller. The hot wax coats the bottom and comes ⅛'' up the side. Ron uses a cheap cardboard paint roller

(plastic melts), low or high nap. The wax is microcrystalline brown sculptor's wax (Mobil Wax 2300). (Fig. 6)

For the past few years Harriet and I have used an electric frying pan to melt wax. You can set the temperature desired and not worry about wax fires. These thermostatically controlled electric pans are easily found in junk shops, cheap.

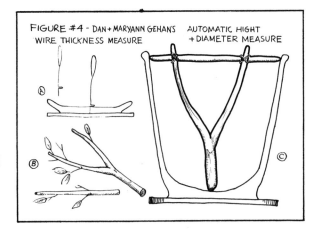

FIGURE #4 - DAN + MARYANN GEHAN'S AUTOMATIC HIGHT WIRE THICKNESS MEASURE + DIAMETER MEASURE

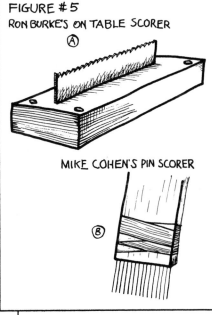

FIGURE #5
RON BURKE'S ON TABLE SCORER
Ⓐ

MIKE COHEN'S PIN SCORER
Ⓑ

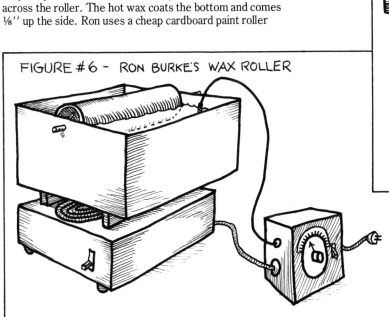

FIGURE #6 - RON BURKE'S WAX ROLLER

WELDING FOR THE COMPLEAT POTTER

By John Powell

Welding is the joining of any two pieces of similar material by fusion. Fusion welding properly uses no filler rod. A filler rod is the stick of metal used when doing torch welding (oxy-acetylene) or heli-arching, commercially referred to as TIG (Tungsten, Inert Gas) welding. Manual arc or arc welding uses a consumable electrode, or arc rod, as the filler metal. The arc "flame" serves the same function as the oxy-acetylene flame, consuming the electrode and depositing it on the work piece. The flux on the outside of the rod acts to produce a protective gas shield or atmosphere around the "puddle," to float impurities out of the weld, and to protect the weld from oxidation. Most manual rod characteristics are determined by this coating—whether the rod has a "fast freeze" or "fast fill' specification—and innumerable other characteristics required by different applications of the manual arc process.

For joining two pieces of ferrous (iron or steel) metal I prefer arc welding because it is cheap, fast, safe, and strong. Oxy-acetylene welding requires far more skill to be done properly, is expensive (high oxygen and acetylene consumption), and tends to overheat the work piece (the flame of an arc is about 9000°F, whereas the oxy-acetylene flame is 6000° F, requiring a longer "preheat" for the same weld). Arc welding can be as portable as oxy-acetylene, if you pay attention to line drop (length and size of extension) and make *sure* there is adequate amperage at your A.C. supply. Anywhere you can run an electric kiln you can run an A.C. arc welder.

In my opinion the best all-around maintenance welder is a 225 Lincoln A.C. machine. It sells for around $130.00. Essentially any transformer welder that will deliver 100 amps at least 60% duty cycle (6 out of 100 minutes of operation) will perform adequately.

Leads or Cables

Best ask your local dealer in any store specializing in commerical welding supplies—but not the salesman at Sears or the local body shop. Describe exactly what you will be welding, how often, and what thickness. Then get nonkinking cables in the size you want; that is, "soft" cables as opposed to "hard" or stiff ones.

Electrodes or Rods

The most widely used size is 3/32'' and 1/8'' diameter (of the metal core). If you buy them from Sears or the Wards catalog make sure the description of the rod's performance matches your application. If you go to a supply house, buy rods meeting American Welding Society (AWS) specification 6011 or 6013. Besides being common they are usually the least expensive rods available. The numbers indicate the tensile strength of the weld, whether an a.c. or d.c. rod, and the application for which the rod is intended: 6011 and 6013 are general purpose electrodes; 6013 is designed for sheet

metal and light tubing sections. This rod does not penetrate the metal as deeply as 6011; therefore, there is less chance of burn through on light material. The 6011 has much better penetrating characteristics, and is intended for heavier metal sections. Both these rods and their equivalents are meant to be used with an arc from 1/16'' to 1/8'' long. The distance from the end of the electrode to the puddle should be no more than 1/16'' to 1/8''.

Operator Protection

Wear leather gloves and a canvas or leather long-sleeved coat—also boots that go under your pant leg. Low quarters and any external boot will gather molten flux and weldment like a funnel, and you can never get the damn thing off before it stops burning! Also, no flammable liquids at hand, no matchbooks in pockets, and anything damaged by sparks like glass, glazed pottery, or porcelain enamel should be covered by something like a canvas tarp. As for your head, use a hood with a lens of your choice. I prefer a number 8 or 9. I used a 7 once, but it was too light and hurt my eyes. A 10 tends to be too dark—I can't get any idea of local surroundings. It's up to the individual: if it's approved by AWS for manual arc, it won't hurt you. Wear the hood that fits—not the super fancy one or the cheapest but the one that is most comfortable.

Arc Welding

Arc welding, as with most electrical phenomena, requires the completion of a circuit for work to be done. In other words, there has to be some way to ground the electrode back to the power source: therefore, the ground clamp. The most frequent cause of intermittent or broken circuit welding problems is an improperly placed ground, or a deteriorating connection somewhere in the ground circuit. The ground clamp should hold firmly to the work or to another piece of metal in good contact with the work. There should be no rust or paint between the ground and the work.

Now, with your electrode in place and work grounded, close your hood, hold the electrode holder with both hands, and bring it slowly into contact with the work piece. If it sticks, break contact by bending down and pulling up. Then try again until you can maintain an arc of the proper length.

Sticking is a matter of heat (or amperage) and skill. If you are inexperienced it is hard to strike an arc the first few times. If your amperage is high there's a lot of splattering and sparks—too low and the rod sticks. In between and you will have a controlled arc. The length of the arc can determine to a limited extent the heat at the puddle—also the size of the puddle. Generally, you want to maintain a short arc (less than 1/8'') and a continuous puddle, so you are feeding the rod to the arc to the puddle (as in gas welding you are feeding the filler rod to the puddle).

Use both hands to hold the electrode holder. Feed the rod

into the puddle as you make your weld. Try this on some ¼'' plate scraps or pieces of ungalvanized 2'' pipe. When it's done right your weld should look like a stack of dimes falling over.

The illustrations demonstrate how the rod angle relates to work and feed rate. There is also an amperage chart, as well as a rod chart for special applications. These would be my choices in these circumstances, which leaves the whole thing open to anybody else's speculation.

I've spent an inordinate amount of time here with arc welding because I feel it is often misunderstood. It is not dangerous, and not hard to do right, but it is easy to make a mess of things and burn holes. So take your time and think the job through.

Oxy-acetylene Torch

The oxy-acetylene torch, to me, is most useful cutting steel. Now that I'm rich (relatively speaking) I have a metal cutting band saw, and prefer that to the torch. But as a basic tool for fabrication, a good torch, set of tips, and a right angle grinder have probably put together more smashed equipment than all the machine shops in Detroit.

A torch does two things to steel. It heats it to kindling temperature (the preheat), then it burns or cuts the metal with the oxygen lance (the center hole). The critical factors are the size of the tip, the gas pressures, and the thickness of the metal being cut. Skill and steadiness are "givens" acquired through experience. The torch does not melt steel—it burns it to magnetite (a black iron oxide) through rapid combustion of the steel in the oxygen lance. The magnetite left on the edges of the cut will embrittle the weld and should be removed (with the right angle grinder) before welding the parts together.

The chart gives some general rules for cutting steel. These are my rules that I use with my equipment. They vary as to equipment and experience, so don't be afraid to experiment.

Hacksaw and File

The hacksaw and the file I believe are at least as misunderstood as the arc welder. A good ($7 to $10) hacksaw with good blades, at the proper tension (as tight as you can make the thumb screw by hand) will cut through 2x2x3/16'' angle in very little time at all, and for a lot less investment than an oxy-acetylene outfit. A mill bastard file at least 12'' long and 1¼'' wide will do wonders for amateur acetylene cuts, as well as beveling prefabricated pieces before welding. (If you use the file or hacksaw on soft firebrick it will not work on steel as the brick acts like a grindstone and removes all the points or cutting edges from the tool.) Don't bear down as hard as you can—try to let the weight of your arm and the saw be the determining factor. Excessive weight simply bends the blade and breaks teeth. It cuts no faster. Light cutting oil helps as well.

Safety

1. Absolutely *no one* around without *protective eye covering* when arc welding or flame-cutting steel.

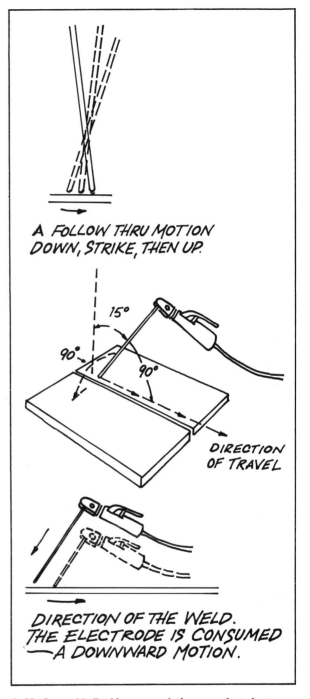

A FOLLOW THRU MOTION DOWN, STRIKE, THEN UP.

DIRECTION OF TRAVEL

DIRECTION OF THE WELD. THE ELECTRODE IS CONSUMED —A DOWNWARD MOTION.

2. No flammable liquids, paper, cloth, or sawdust about.
3. Always disconnect machine when not in use for any length of time.
4. Always turn off gas supply and bleed lines when finished.
5. *Never* use *oil* on any oxygen equipment or fittings.
6. Any high-pressure gas equipment must be repaired by an authorized shop. Home repairs are out!

PREHEAT

CUTTING LANCE

Oxy lbs. 1/8 3/16 1/4 1/2 PIPE (WALL THICKNESS TO .250)

Oxy lbs	1/8	3/16	1/4	1/2	PIPE
12-15	1/8				
15-18		3/16			
15-20			1/4		
25-30				1/2	
15-18					PIPE

ACETYLANE OR FUEL GAS NO MORE THAN 5 lb.

FOR SECTIONS OVER 1/4"
BEVEL EDGES TO AID
IN WELD PENETRATION

ALWAYS LEAVE GAP IN BUTT ENDS

AMP	1/8	1/4	5/16	TUBING (.065)	PIPE (.125-250)
45				3/32 ROD	1/8 ROD (.125)
30-40	3/32				
85-90					1/8 ROD (.250)
80-100		1/8			
100-120			1/8		

FOR BEST CUT, METAL SHOULD BE CLEAN & FREE OF RUST

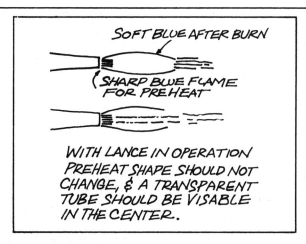

SOFT BLUE AFTER BURN

SHARP BLUE FLAME
FOR PREHEAT

WITH LANCE IN OPERATION
PREHEAT SHAPE SHOULD NOT
CHANGE, & A TRANSPARENT
TUBE SHOULD BE VISABLE
IN THE CENTER.

APPENDIX

SUPPLIERS

Ceramic Chemicals and Clays

A&A Potter's Warehouse
2100 Wilmot Rd.
Tuscon, AZ 85712

American Art Clay Co.
4717 W. 16th St.
Indianapolis, IN 46222

A.P. Green Co.
1018 E. Breckenridge St.
Mexico, MO 65265

Arch T. Flower Co., Potter's Supplies
Queen St. & Ivy Hill Rd.
Philadelphia, PA 19118

Baldwin Pottery
540 Laguardia Place
New York, NY 10012

Bennett Pottery Supply, Inc.
707 Nicolet Ave.
Winter Park, FL 32789

Bog Town Clay
75-J Mendel Ave. SW
Atlanta, GA 30336

Boston Mountain Pottery Supply
Box 32
Winslow, AK 72959

Byrne Ceramic Supply Co., Inc.
95 Bartley Rd.
Flanders, NJ 07836

Castle Clay Products
1055 Fox St.
Denver, CO 80223

Cedar Heights Clay Co.
50 Portsmouth Rd.
Oak Hill, OH 45656

Ceramics Hawaii Ltd.
543 South St.
Honolulu, HI 96813

The Ceramic Store, Inc.
706 Richmond
Houston, TX 77006

Clay Art Center
40 Beech St.
Port Chester, NY 10573
and
342 Western Ave.
Brighton, MA 02135

Clay Gallery
1001 S. 4th St. W.
Missoula, MT 59801

Clay Suppliers
115 N. Montclair
Dallas, TX 75208

Cole Ceramics Labs
Northeastern Office, Box 242
Sharon, CT 06069

Creative Ceramics
2556-A Albatross Way
Sacramento, CA 95815

Creek Turn Pottery Supply
Route 38
Hainesport, NJ 08036

Debcor
557 W. Taft Dr.
South Holland, IL 60473

Eagle Ceramics
1226-A Wilkins Ave.
Rockville, MD 20852
and
1300 W. 9th St.
Cleveland, OH 44113

The Earthen Vessel
7116 Miami Rd.
Cincinnati, OH 45243

Earthworks
1667 Penfield Rd.
Rochester, NY 14625

Georgia Kaolin Co.
433 N. Broad St.
Elizabeth, NJ 07207

Good Earth Clays Inc.
501 Atlantic
Kansas City, MO 64116

Hammill & Gillespie, Inc.
225 Broadway
New York, NY 10007

Industrial Minerals Co.
987 Commercial St.
San Carlos, CA 94070

J. Clay Co.
886 Gable Way
El Cajon, CA 92020

Kickwheel Pottery & Supply
802 Miami Circle, NE
Atlanta, GA 30324

Leslie Ceramics Supply Co.
1212 San Pablo Ave.
Berkeley, CA 94706

L & R Specialties
Box 309
Nixa, MO 65714

Marjon Ceramics Inc.
3434 Earl Dr.
Phoenix, AZ 85017

Miami Clay Co.
18954 N.E. 4 Ct.
Miami, FL 33179

Minnesota Clay Co.
8001 Grand Ave. So.
Bloomington, MN 55420

Newton Potters Supply, Inc.
96 Rumford Ave.
Newton, MA 02165

North Florida Pottery Supply
567 Industrial Dr.
Tallahassee, FL 32304

Owl Creek Pottery
11416 Shelbyville Rd.
Louisville, KY 40243

Paramount Ceramics, Inc.
220 No. State
Fairmount, MN 56031

Robbins Clay Co.

1021 W. Lill St.
Chicago, IL 60614

Roven Ceramics
6912 Schaefer Rd.
Dearborn, MI 48216

Runyan Pottery Supply
Box 287
Flint, MI 48501

The Salem Craftsmen's Guild
3 Alvin Pl.
Upper Montclair, NJ 07043

Sculpture House
38 E. 30th St.
New York, NY 10016

Seattle Pottery Supply Inc.
400 E. Pine
Seattle, WA 98122

Spencer Pottery Inc.
5021 S. 144th St.
Seattle, WA 98168

Spokane Ceramic Supply
W, 38 Third Ave.
Spokane, WA 99204

Standard Ceramic Supply Co.
Box 1435
Pittsburgh, PA 15205

Stewart Clay Co.
133 Mulberry St.
New York, NY 10013

Studio Supply
1215 Shop Rd.
Columbia, SC 29202

Trinity Ceramic Supply Co.
9016 Diplomacy Row
Dallas, TX 75235

Van Howe Co.
1185 S. Cherokee Ave.
Denver, CO 80223
and
2602 Durango Dr.
Colorado Springs, CO 80239
and
3825 Commercial NE
Albuquerque, NM 87107

Westby Ceramic Supply & Mfg. Co.
620 N. 85th St.
Seattle, WA 98103

Western Ceramic Supply
1601 Howard St.
San Francisco, CA 94103

Westwood Ceramic Supply Co.
14400 Lomitas Ave.
City of Industry, CA 91744

Jack D. Wolf Co.
724 Meeker Ave.
Brooklyn, NY 11222

Burners and Parts

Flynn Burner Corp.
425 Fifth Ave.
New Rochelle, NY 10802

Johnson Gas Appliance Co.
Cedar Rapids, IO 52405

Maxon Corp.
201 E. 18th St.
Muncie, IN 47302

Mine and Smelter Industries
Box 16607
Denver, CO 80216

Pyronics Inc.
17700 Miles Ave.
Cleveland, OH 44128

Ransome Gas Industries, Inc.
2050 Farallon Dr.
San Leandro, CA 94577

Refractory Suppliers

Babcock & Wilcox Co.
Refractories Div.
161 E. 42 St.
New York NY 10017

Burns Brick Co.
Box 4787
Macon, GA 31208

A.P. Green Co.
1018 E. Breckenridge St.
Mexico, MO 65265

Carborundum Co.
Refractories and Electronic Div.
Box 337
Niagara Falls, NY 14302

Denver Fire Clay Co.
2401 E. 40th Ave.

Box 5507
Denver, CO 80217

Grefko, Inc.
299 Park Ave.
New York, NY 10017

Johns-Manville Co.
Greenwood Plaza
Denver, CO 80217

Metropolitan Refractories
Tidewater Terminal
So. Kearny, NJ 07032

New Castle Refractories
Box 471
New Castle, PA 16103

Norton Co.
Industrial Ceramics Div.
Worcester, MA 01606

Pryo Engineering Corp.
200 S. Palm Ave.
Alhambra, CA 91801

UK

Deancraft Ceramic Supplies
15-21 Westmill St.
Hanley, Stoke-on-Trent,
ST1 3EN, England

E.J. Arnold & Sons Ltd.
Butterley St.
Leeds 10, England

Ferro Ltd.
Wombourne
Wolverhampton, Staffordshire, England

Fraser Ltd., Keramos
Parkside, Trentham
Stoke-on-Trent, Staffordshire, England

The Fulham Pottery Ltd.
210 New Kings Rd.
London SW6 4NY, England

Harrison/Mayer Ltd.
Meir, Stoke-on-Trent
ST3 7PX, England

Instrument Services Newport
24 Church Rd.
Newport, Gwent, South Wales

Labert Supplies and Maintenance Ltd.
18 Main St.
Sterlingshire, Scotland

Medcol Ltd.
Sun St.
Henley, Stoke-on-Trent, England

Moira Pottery Co., Ltd.
Burton on Trent
Staffordshire, DE12 6DF, England

Podmore & Sons Ltd.
Shelton
Stoke-on-Trent, Staffordshire, England

Potclays Ltd.
Warf St.
Stoke-on-Trent, Staffordshire, England

Ratcliffe
Shelton New Rd.
Stoke-on-Trent, ST4 6DJ, England

South Wales Art and Craft Supplies
108 Bute St.
Cardiff, Wales

Watts, Blake, Bearne & Co., Ltd.
Park House, Newton Abbot
Devon TQ12 4PS, England

Wengers Ltd.
Etruria
Stoke-on-Trent ST4 7BQ, England

TABLE OF TEMPERATURE CONVERSION

°C.	°F.	°C.	°F.	°C.	°F.	°C.	°F.
100	212	500	932	900	1652	1300	2372
110	230	510	950	910	1670	1320	2408
120	248	520	968	920	1688	1340	2444
130	266	530	986	930	1706	1360	2480
140	284	540	1004	940	1724	1380	2516
150	302	550	1022	950	1742	1400	2552
160	320	560	1044	960	1760	1420	2588
170	338	570	1058	970	1788	1440	2624
180	356	580	1076	980	1796	1460	2660
190	374	590	1094	990	1814	1480	2696
200	392	600	1112	1000	1832	1500	2732
210	410	610	1130	1010	1850	1520	2768
220	428	620	1148	1020	1868	1540	2804
230	446	630	1166	1030	1886	1560	2840
240	464	640	1184	1040	1904	1580	2876
250	482	650	1202	1050	1922	1600	2912
260	500	660	1220	1060	1940	1620	2948
270	518	670	1238	1070	1958	1640	2984
280	536	680	1256	1080	1976	1660	3020
290	554	690	1274	1090	1994	1680	3056
300	572	700	1292	1100	2012	1700	3092
310	590	710	1310	1110	2030	1720	3128
320	608	720	1328	1120	2048	1740	3164
330	626	730	1346	1130	2066	1760	3200
340	644	740	1364	1140	2084	1780	3236
350	662	750	1382	1150	2102	1800	3272
360	680	760	1400	1160	2120	1820	3308
370	698	770	1418	1170	2138	1840	3344
380	716	780	1436	1180	2156	1860	3380
390	734	790	1454	1190	2174	1880	3416
400	752	800	1472	1200	2192	1900	3452
410	770	810	1490	1210	2210	1920	3488
420	788	820	1508	1220	2228	1940	3524
430	806	830	1526	1230	2246	1960	3560
440	824	840	1544	1240	2264	1980	3596
450	842	850	1562	1250	2282	2000	3632
460	860	860	1580	1260	2300	2100	3812
470	878	870	1598	1270	2318	2200	3992
480	896	880	1616	1280	2336	2300	4172
490	914	890	1634	1290	2354	2400	4352

To convert degrees Centigrade to degrees Fahrenheit: multiply by 9, divide by 5, add 32. To convert degrees Fahrenheit to degrees Centigrade: subtract 32, divide by 9, multiply by 5.

INDEX

CREDITS

April '76

Dear Mr & Mrs Cohen,

Saw your notice posted in a studio while visiting in Michigan, guy named Geick. Thought I would write and see what you thought of my chances of becoming an apprentice. I am a hard worker with a well developed work ethic — in fact, I overdo details and can't bear to do a job half-way. I have had six years of school training in ceramics with two years of studio assistantship work. So, I know a lot about running a ceramics workshop ... would that be helpful?

Regarding the details listed on your poster ... I certainly do have a good sense of humor. Here is a ceramics joke. A teacher told his students to bring in for class, an elephant ear sponge and an infant ear syringe. (Now, you have to picture this part in your mind to really get the funny part) The student arrived in class next day carrying a 20 gallon syringe and a 1"x1" size sponge and when the teacher said "What on earth is going on?", the student said "But, I thought you said to bring in an elephant ear syringe and an infant ear sponge!" And, this is just one of my ceramics studio stories — I have dozens of em! ... and I usually like to tell them, all day. Also, I wouldn't want anyone else around while I am working, it sort of bothers me, you know, can't concentrate. So you would probably have to arrange your working schedule accordingly. I prefer the daytime, personally.

Would there be someone on hand to help me with the heavy work and clean up after my work sessions? I really get fed up with sloppy studios and I am usually too tired to do all that boring stuff myself.

Also, I assume you are looking for someone who is a good artist and I can assure you that I am one of them! I was twice awarded the Malcome E. Witherspoon award for outstanding artistry in our schools' annual student exhibition (twice!) Probably this little skill would come in handy when I design work for you and the like.

Also, what type of room would be provided for me? I prefer a private bath and my own kitchen facilities — of course. Does the $50⁰⁰ a week include, in addition, a generous food allowance ... I eat a lot!

Let's see — I guess that about covers it, except — I don't allow anyone to smoke around me, no loud noises while I am being creative, no undue pressure and — clean, clean, clean! Well, I hope I have given you enough facts about my qualifications so there is little question left as to just how I would work out. I would be willing to give you a trial, to see how things would work out. If this seems agreeable to you, forward my plane fair as soon as possible.

Expectantly, confidently

Georg Niloak

P.S. (You may have seen some of the work I did for Studio Potter magazine which I help out now and then .... gives em a boost!)

304